Svalbard
(Spitsbergen)
with Franz Josef Land & Jan Mayen

the Bradt Travel Guide

D1313367

Andreas Umbreit

Updated by
Roger Norum

edition
5

www.bradtguides.com

Bradt Travel Guides Ltd, UK
The Globe Pequot Press Inc, USA

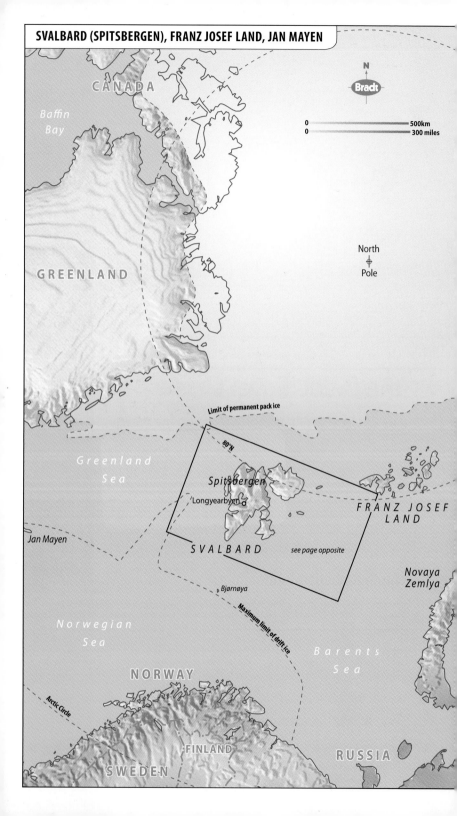

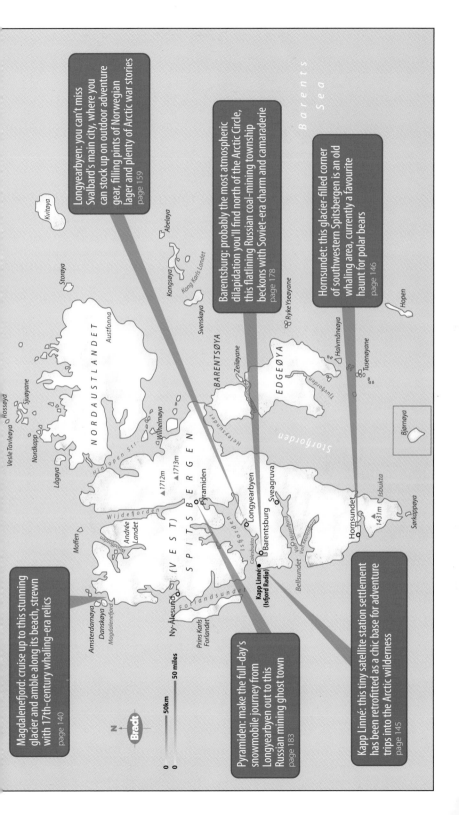

Magdalenefjord: cruise up to this stunning glacier and amble along its beach, strewn with 17th-century whaling-era relics
page 140

Longyearbyen: you can't miss Svalbard's main city, where you can stock up on outdoor adventure gear, filling pints of Norwegian lager and plenty of Arctic war stories
page 159

Barentsburg: probably the most atmospheric dilapidation you'll find north of the Arctic Circle, this flatlining Russian coal-mining township beckons with Soviet-era charm and camaraderie
page 178

Hornsundet: this glacier-filled corner of southwestern Spitsbergen is an old whaling area, currently a favourite haunt for polar bears
page 146

Pyramiden: make the full-day's snowmobile journey from Longyearbyen out to this Russian mining ghost town
page 183

Kapp Linné: this tiny satellite station settlement has been retrofitted as a chic base for adventure trips into the Arctic wilderness
page 145

Svalbard
Don't
miss...

Spectacular wildlife

The flora and fauna of the archipelago are a highlight of any trip to Svalbard. Polar bear usually top the list of must-see animals, but the islands abound with reindeer, arctic fox, walrus and extensive seabird breeding colonies

(VM/S) page 47

Franz Josef Land

More northerly than Svalbard, the Russian archipelago of Franz Josef Land is one of the most inaccessible islands on the planet and plays host to an important breeding colony of seabirds — Rubini Rock on Hooker island, home to 40 species.

(VM/S) page 191

Longyearbyen
Svalbard's capital and the oldest existing settlement in the archipelago, colourful Longyearbyen is impossible to miss
(SS) page 159

Cruising around the fjords
Whether you decide to ᴠenture into more remote areas on an expedition ᴄruise such as this Zodiac Ⅿeerenburg glacier or ᴄhose a more traditional ᴉtinerary, you'll be sure to experience one of the most remarkable ᴉandscapes on the planet
(AVZ) page 133

Magdalenefjord
ᴛhe most-photographed ᴉandmark in Svalbard, ᴛhis stunning glacier is a common cruise stop — take a stroll along ᴛhe stretch of beach and ᴈeadland at Gravneset Peninsula to see the remnants of its 17th-ᴄentury whaling heyday
(AVZ) page 140

Svalbard
in colour

left   Explore the remains of Svalbard's rich whaling history at sites around the archipelago, such as this early 17th-century whaling station at Virgohamna on Danskøya (AVZ) page 139

below left   Filling the sky above Longyearbyen with its enigmatic light, the Aurora Borealis entrances in the Svalbard polar night (I/KL/FLPA) page 65

below right   Snowmobile day-long excursions from Longyearbyen take visitors to see the neighbouring fjords (RN) page 78

above   **Researchers weigh an adult bearded seal** (FN/MP/FLPA) page 33

left   **The Global Seed Vault outside Longyearbyen holds seeds from several hundred thousand crop varieties from around the world** (SS) page 172

below   **Research has long been an integral part of the Svalbard archipelago, with settlements such as Isfjord Radio at Kapp Linné serving as important communications bases for the scientific community** (RN) page 145

AUTHOR

Andreas Umbreit is an acknowledged local expert and resident in Svalbard. A tour operator specialising in the Arctic and Antarctica, he runs logistics for film and research expeditions and works as expedition leader and lecturer on some polar expedition cruises.

UPDATER

Roger Edward Gregory Norum has suffered from a life-long addiction to maps, languages and the power of cold places to illuminate the various meanings of life. Born in New York, Roger studied literature and linguistics at the University of Tromsø, Norway, and graduated from Cornell University in Near Eastern Studies, after which he was awarded a scholarship to study Bengali at the American Institute of Indian Studies in Calcutta. He later took his doctorate in social anthropology from Oxford University, where his thesis focused on transient and itinerant communities of mobile professionals. He has worked for a variety of international organisations, including UNICEF, Mercy Corps and the BBC World Service, and has written and photographed for publications such as the *Sunday Times Travel Magazine* and *Wanderlust*, and is currently based in Oxford. He tweets @oxroger and some of his academic and journalistic work can be found at www.rogernorum.com.

FEEDBACK REQUEST

At Bradt Travel Guides we're aware that guidebooks start to go out of date on the day they're published – and that you, our readers, are out there in the field doing research of your own. You'll find out before us when a fine new family-run hotel opens or a favourite restaurant changes hands and goes downhill. So why not write to us and tell us about your experiences? Contact us on ☏ 01753 893444 or e info@bradtguides.com. We will forward emails to the author who may post 'one-off updates' on the Bradt website at www.bradtupdates.com/svalbard. You can also visit this website for updates to information in this guide. Alternatively you can add a review of the book to www.bradtguides.com or Amazon.

PUBLISHER'S FOREWORD *Hilary Bradt*

The first edition of Spitsbergen was published in 1991 – one of the first of our 'extreme' titles. The decision to publish followed a meeting at Frankfurt Book Fair when it became clear that Andreas Umbreit knew more about Svalbard than anyone else on earth. Once I'd been shown where it was, and been filled in on its somewhat complicated political history, I became equally enthused. Up until then Bradt guides had only covered eastern Europe and 'The Third World'. In contrast here was a snowy wilderness, a place as near to the North Pole as you can easily reach, and a land of polar bears and walruses. It sounded wonderful! Svalbard seems virtually unchanged in the last 22 years, and how many countries can make that claim? Welcome to this fifth edition; welcome to a true wilderness.

Reprinted September 2015
Fifth edition published May 2013
First published in German by Conrad Stein Verlag
First published in English 1991

Bradt Travel Guides Ltd
IDC House, The Vale, Chalfont St Peter, Bucks SL9 9RZ, England
www.bradtguides.com
Print edition published in the USA by The Globe Pequot Press Inc,
PO Box 480, Guilford, Connecticut 06437-0480

ISBN: 978 1 84162 459 4 (print)
e-ISBN: 978 1 84162 764 9 (e-pub)
e-ISBN: 978 1 84162 666 6 (mobi)

British Library Cataloguing in Publication Data
A catalogue record for this book is available from the British Library

Photographs Andreas Umbreit (AU); Ariadne Van Zandbergen (AVZ); Corbis: Keenpress/National Geographic Society (K/NGS/C); FLPA: Dickie Duckett (DD/FLPA), Flip Nicklin/Minden Pictures (FN/MP/FLPA), Imagebroker (I/FLPA), Imagebroker/Kerstin Langenberger (I/KL/FLPA), Jasper Doest/Minden Pictures (JD/MP/FLPA), Kevin Schafer/Minden Pictures (KS/MP/FLPA); jomilo75 (j); Paul Goldstein (PG); Roger Norum (RN); Shutterstock: Alex Justas (AJ/S), Bjorn Stefanson (BS/S), Gail Johnson (GJ/S), mevert (m/S), P. Fabian (PF/S), Tyler Olson (TO/S), Vladimir Melnik (VM/S), Wild Arctic Pictures (WAP/S); SuperStock (SS)
Front cover A polar bear leaps between pack ice while hunting (SS)
Back cover Colourful houses in the capital of Longyearbyen (TO/S); Sea kayakers near the Monaco glacier, Woodfjorden (AVZ)
Title page Arctic tern (*Sterna paradisaea*) on Danskøya (AVZ); Cape Flora vegetation covers the tundra with bright blooms during spring (AU); Sunset colours the altocumulus clouds above the main island of Spitsbergen (BS/S)

Maps David McCutcheon FBCart.S

Acknowledgements

This book has developed and expanded from edition to edition, incorporating countless detailed contributions. There are too many people to mention by name, but I would like to thank them all for their help.

A special thanks is due to all who contributed to the first edition. The range of nationalities involved reflects the internationality of Svalbard and these people laid the foundation of this guidebook together with my own experiences:

At the Sysselmann's office, former Sysselmannen Leif Eldring during his second term (1987–91), former Sysselmannen Odd Blomdal (1991–95), Assistant Sysselmannen Bernt Moe (until 1990), Assistant Sysselmannen Torodd Veiding (1991–93), Overbetjent Harald Petersen (1986–91), Overbetjent Halvard Tømta (1990–93), Informasjonssekretær Mette Bleken, Naturvernkonsulent Ian Gjertz (helpful later also during his period at Norsk Polarinstitutt), Naturvernkonsulent Endre Persen, Kulturvernkonsulent Lisen Roll, Kjell Huseby, interpreters Bård Olsen and Anne Berteig, Kulturminnekonsulent Kristin Elisabebeth Prestvold.

Scientists Kand Sissel Aarvik (N), Dr Dag Avango (S), Susan Barr (GB/N), Prof Dieter Blümel (D), Dr Pete J Capelotti (USA), Dr Ian Gjertz (N), Prof Louwrens Haquebord (NL), Dr Ulrich Glaser (D), Dr Ko de Korte (NL), Prof Patrick Martin (USA), Dr Bulat R Mavlyudov (RUS), Dr Karsten Piepjohn (D), Dr Kuno Priesnitz (D), Mag Per Kyrre Reymert (N), Prof Heinz Slupetzky (A), Prof Vadim F Starkov (RUS), Dr Alexander M Tebenkov (RUS), Dr Nick Tyler (GB/N), Prof Jan Marçin Weslavsky (PL), Prof Urban Wråkberg (S), Dr Evgeniy Zinger (RUS).

And furthermore Geir Åsebøstøl (N), Birger Amundsen (N), Thor Bendixen (N), Evgeniy Bouzney (RUS), Dag Ivar Brekke (N), Atle and Birgit Brekken (N), Kjellrun Eggenfellner (N), Alan Hall (GB), Gustav Halsvik (N), Halvard Holm (N), Norman Holm (N), Freia Hutschenreuter (N/D), Dr Lothar Knoch (D), Rinie van Meurs (NL), Kjell Mork (N), Thorgeir Mørk (N), Gunnar and Rebekka Nordtømme (N), Kjell Onarheim (N), Finn Pedersen (N), Bolette Petri-Sutermeister (CH/DK), Anne Raastad-Mæland (N), Anne Lise Sandvik (N), Inger Sletten (N), Rolf Stange (D), Conrad Stein (D), Magnus Storhaug (N), Turid Telebond (N), Marlis Tolkmit (D), Berit and Karl Våtvik (N).

Privately, the extensive work on this almost completely rewritten edition has been supported enormously by the patience and understanding of my life partner Martina Kötting.

Thank you all!

ACKNOWLEDGEMENTS FOR THE NEW EDITION Great thanks go to Adrian Phillips for inadvertently and unwittingly asking me to work on this book in the first place, and for regularly dispensing wisdom and life advice. Much appreciation, too, I give to my editors Kelly Randell and Anna Moores for being such easy, communicative and understanding colleagues to work with, and to the cartography team at Bradt for producing such crackerjack maps. The book would definitely not have been possible without the encouragement and support of Hanne Knudsen, ex-Innovation Norway, as well as the tireless assistance, hospitality and fact checking of Kjersti Norås at Svalbard Tourism in Longyearbyen. I'm grateful too for the logistical assistance of Brita Knutson and Sigurður Jónsson. Thanks, in some small way, must also be communicated to Duncan Craig, Chris Leadbeater and Nick Boulos, for shared billiard games, beers and lost (and yet unpaid) bets in Longyearbyen hotel parlours. I am grateful for the love and moral support of my parents and grandparents, for indulging in (and, if I remember correctly, funding) my early interest in cold places, and to my sister Tracy and brother-in-law Angelo, and their charge Houdini, for not questioning my seemingly irrational decisions. Finally, plenty of emoticonned shout-outs are due to SKM, who, in spite of her distaste for the cold, may one day see the light and journey with me to the Far North.

Contents

FOLLOW BRADT

For the latest news, special offers and competitions, subscribe to the Bradt
newsletter via the website www.bradtguides.com and follow Bradt on:

🅕 www.facebook.com/BradtTravelGuides
🐦 @BradtGuides
📷 @bradtguides
📌 www.pinterest.com/bradtguides

NOTE ABOUT MAPS

The map of the capital, Longyearbyen (page 160) uses grid lines to allow easy
location of sites. Map grid references are listed in square brackets after listings
in the text, with the page number followed by grid number, eg: [160 B3].

LIST OF MAPS

Introduction

This book deals with three groups of islands high up in the European Arctic: from Jan Mayen on the Mid-Atlantic Ridge, the tectonic western border of the continent, via Svalbard, the main place of interest in this book, to the northernmost land area of Europe – the Russian-owned Franz Josef Land.

Svalbard, Spitsbergen, Spitzbergen, Spetsbergen, Spitsberg – this High Arctic archipelago is an unusual place of interest. It is the largest area of wilderness in Europe, holding few human traces and even fewer settlements today. This is, in fact, the reason for the primary difference between this guidebook and most others: whereas guidebooks for more developed parts of the world would have route descriptions, urban infrastructure, restaurant and hotel recommendations, these features remain almost entirely absent in this book, given that the area is virtually free of these amenities. On the other hand, the archipelago offers maybe the widest variety of Arctic nature – extremely varied landscapes, low to High Arctic, different ecosystems – within its relatively limited area, especially when compared to the vast stretches of Greenland, northern Siberia or the American Arctic. And in terms of history, too – again in spite of the limited size – Svalbard is one of the most fascinating, truly Arctic regions: its surprisingly easy accessibility (despite an extreme northern position) allows human migration from a wide range of countries at considerably less cost than to other islands at similarly high northern latitudes around the Pole (eg: northern Greenland, the Russian Arctic archipelagos, the Canadian High Arctic). This variety of immigrants from several nations is also reflected in the many names on the map of the archipelago and even in the different names for the archipelago itself – as this diversity illustrates, Svalbard is a very international place.

Being easier to access than all other equally northern Arctic regions creates a challenge on Svalbard regarding conservation of the fragile Arctic nature and the scarce traces of polar history. Many traditional human activities – whaling, hunting, mining and fishing – have already depleted, or are about to destroy, their own resources on and around the archipelago, with occasionally serious side effects. Recently, growing activities such as adventure tourism and even scientific research have increased their impact on Mother Nature, and the visible effect is multiplied several-fold somewhere in this remote region. Norway has taken on the ambitious goal of making Svalbard one of the best-managed wilderness areas of the world, with high emphasis on environmental issues. The aim is two-fold: that the archipelago be so well protected that the traces of human impact become negligible, and that the lands can serve as reference points for a true, unchanged Arctic nature. On land, strict regulations (especially regarding tourist activities and behaviour) have been put in place as one important step to secure this aim. Yet the main elements of Arctic nature – the marine environments – which also have a strong influence on the much more sparse life on land, are still surprisingly poorly protected due to the strong fishing lobby and, in the long term, perhaps the Norwegian oil industry too.

Penning a guidebook about Svalbard is something of a challenge due to the wide range of user interests. For most other guidebooks, independent travellers and sightseers comprise the majority of readers, but this may not be the case for most readers of this book. With very few concise and comprehensive sources of information available about the archipelago, this book serves as an introduction not only for tourists, but also for scientists, journalists, politicians and other visitors with a professional interest in the archipelago, as well as a large number of polar enthusiasts who enjoy reading about such areas without necessarily travelling there. Among the buyers of this book, tourists might make up less than 50%, and among these, independent travellers may only comprise a few percent, because tourism in the High Arctic primarily takes place as part of organised tours. Nevertheless, this small group of independent travellers expects more practical advice from a guidebook than most other readers. It has, therefore, been necessary to include sections covering safety equipment and the required procedures for the registration and permission of expeditions – even when such sections may take up more page space than the low number of independent travellers might justify. This is also based on the hope that reliable, comprehensive information in advance reduces the number of accidents and rescue operations, which tend to cast Svalbard tourism in a bad light. Unfortunately, the very small number of independent travellers are responsible for almost all of these incidents – mostly due to a lack of familiarity with (and experience in) the Arctic, insufficient equipment and an overestimation of their own abilities.

I am in love with this archipelago. Travelling these islands since 1986 and being registered as a resident since 1991, running my tourism business there, doing logistics for scientific and media projects and writing books, managing the campsite in Longyearbyen, lecturing on cruises along the coasts of Svalbard and the neighbouring Jan Mayen and Franz Josef Land, I have many roots in the islands and love the special way of life. This also facilitates an excellent knowledge of the region – something that is hopefully of benefit to readers. Occasionally, as the author of an independent guide to Svalbard, my involvement in organised tourism has been criticised, but without it, such a detailed book that is of benefit to all people interested in these remote Arctic regions – and not solely the customers of my companies – would probably not exist.

This book is written for all with an interest in Svalbard, Franz Josef Land and Jan Mayen, be it just general, or for preparation for travelling to these destinations – organised or independent – as part of your work or purely out of private interest. If this book helps you to deepen your knowledge and to facilitate your preparations, to increase the quality of your voyage and not least to reduce negative impacts on the regions described in this book, it was worth the effort put into it.

SPITSBERGEN, SPITZBERGEN OR SVALBARD?

From the days of its official discovery in 1596 by the Dutch expedition under Willem Barents, the archipelago was long known worldwide as 'Spitsbergen' – a highly descriptive name taken from Dutch that means 'pointed peaks'. Originally, the traditional name 'Spitsbergen' referred to the whole group of islands including the main one, then known as 'West Spitsbergen', and the other major islands – 'Northeast Land', 'Edge Island', 'Barents Island', etc – plus the various smaller islands and skerries around them. Not considered as part of Spitsbergen were 'Beeren Eylandt' (Bear Island), halfway between northern Norway and Spitsbergen and also discovered by the Barents expedition in 1596, and the remotest eastern parts of the archipelago such as Kong Karls Land and White Island (Kvitøya) that were discovered much later. Spitsbergen quickly became a highly international destination for sailors, hunters and others from various European countries and, later on, also North America, which led to the parallel use of translations and adaptions of the names in the various languages. Therefore, depending on the origin of the maps, the archipelago may have been addressed as Spitsbergen (Dutch, English, Danish, Norwegian), Spitzbergen (German, also partly English), Spetsbergen (Swedish) or Spitsberg (French). Up until the 20th century, the term 'Spitsbergen' was used to connote the archipelago as a whole. Of this Spitsbergen archipelago, the main island (the largest) had the Norwegian name 'Vest Spitsbergen' ('West Spitsbergen' in English).

As with many European countries, the Scandinavian nations were swept up in a wave of ardent nationalism during the 20th century, particularly Norway, which became independent from Sweden only in 1905, having been the inferior half of a union under the Swedish king (and earlier, the Danish one) for many centuries. This inferior role led to a strong need for national self-esteem. One suitable tool was the recent spectacular achievements by Norwegian polar heroes like Nansen, Amundsen and Sverdrup, fostering the self-image of being a polar nation. Another approach was digging in the past for myths of national greatness, particularly the Icelandic Viking sagas. In the Icelandic annals, an ambiguous passage can be found in the entry for the year 1194, stating:

Svalbardʒ fundinn (Svalbard found), followed by a fairly vague sailing description. As the Old Norse (or Old Icelandic) term *svalbard* can be translated both as 'cold coast' or 'cold rim' (*svalr* 'cool' or 'cold' and *bard* 'edge' or 'rim', thus 'coast') and the specific sailing description mentioned in the annals is somewhat unclear, this mysterious *Svalbard* could be referring to anything from Jan Mayen and northeast Greenland to Spitsbergen itself – or even simply the beginning of the solid ice border in the north. Technically, the Vikings were undoubtedly able to reach Svalbard, but there is no archaeological proof that they ever got there, nor is there any certainty that the Old Icelandic *svalbard* refers to any part of modern-day Svalbard.

For the nationalistic Norway of the early 20th century, though, the idea of continuity from those bold 'Norwegians' who ventured that far north during the Viking period, and their descendants who were now taking possession of the archipelago again through the international Spitsbergen Treaty of 1920, was obviously highly tempting. Based on such nationalistic dreams, and though the archipelago was known only as Spitsbergen in common Norwegian thinking and 'Spitsbergen' was the term used in the treaty by which the islands became Norwegian, Norway decided to rename the entire new territory 'Svalbard' after 1920. (In similar manner, *Kristiania, capital of Norway, was re-renamed Oslo in 1924* – though this was a return to the original name, which had been replaced only in 1624 by the Danish King Christian IV during his absolutist reign.)

In the case of Spitsbergen/Svalbard, this act of nationalism led to confusion, even within Norway: now, there was the term 'Svalbard' for the whole area of the Spitsbergen Treaty (Svalbard including also Bear Island (Bjørnøya), Kvitøya and Kong Karls Land), 'Spitsbergen' was the traditional name for almost the same area, and 'Vest Spitsbergen' for the main island. Therefore, it was decided as late as after World War II that 'Spitsbergen' should be used as the official name for the main island only, thus doing away with the former name 'Vest Spitsbergen' and reducing the usage of 'Spitsbergen' from referring to the entire archipelago to just one island. It would have been more in line with the history books to extend the well-established archipelago name 'Spitsbergen' to also include Bear Island (Bjørnøya), Kvitøya and Kong Karls Land. But, as these same history books have shown us, nationalism and reason do not necessarily go hand in hand. Although previous updates of this book used the title 'Spitsbergen', the term 'Svalbard' has now made its way fully into English usage to refer to the entire archipelago – hence the reason for changing the book's title to 'Svalbard' (note that other languages, such as German and Swedish, continue to use 'Spitsbergen' to refer to what English and Norwegian now call 'Svalbard'). For other place names, even though historic adaptions for various languages exist in many cases, usually just direct translations (Beeren Eylandt – Bear Island – Bjørnøya – Bäreninsel) and in most cases known only to specialists, we largely stick to the Norwegian versions, which helps with orientation on maps. To facilitate understanding of the names, you should be aware that the definite article (in English: 'the') is added to Norwegian words as a suffix at the end of the word, being an '-a' for female nouns, an '-et' for neuter nouns and an '-en' for masculine nouns. In geographic names, usually these definite forms are used. Here are some frequent geographic words that appear as parts of names:

øya	the island (eg: *Bjørnøya*, 'the Bear Island')
elva	the river (eg: *Adventelva*, 'the Advent River')
fonna	the ice cap (eg: *Austfonna*, 'the Eastern Icecap')
sundet	the sound (sea passage, eg: *Forlandsundet*, 'the Forland Sound')
fjellet	the mountain (eg: *Nordenskiöldfjellet*)
byen	the settlement (eg: *Longyearbyen*, 'Longyear's City', as its name originally was)
toppen	the mountain top (eg: *Newtontoppen*)
breen	the glacier (eg: *Larsbreen*, 'the Lars glacier')

A WORD ABOUT PRICES

The research for this edition was done between June and November 2012, and consequently the prices are for the 2012 season except where noted in the text. The currency used throughout is the Norwegian kroner (NOK) unless otherwise stated.

ATTENTION WILDLIFE ENTHUSIASTS

For more on wildlife in Svalbard, Franz Josef Land and Jan Mayen, why not check out Bradt's *The Arctic: A Guide to Coastal Wildlife*? Go to www.bradtguides.com and key in SVALWILD40 at the checkout for your 40% discount.

Part One

GENERAL INFORMATION

Location North Atlantic (Greenland Sea), Barents Sea and Northern Polar Ocean

Neighbouring countries Greenland, Norway, Russia, USA (Alaska), Canada

Size/area Svalbard 62,500km^2, Franz Josef Land 16,100km^2, Jan Mayen 380km^2

Climate Low Arctic to High Arctic

Status Svalbard: part of Norway with special international status due to the Spitsbergen (Svalbard) Treaty; Franz Josef Land: part of Russia by annexation in the 1920–30s; Jan Mayen: part of Norway, but some special legislation

Capital Svalbard: Longyearbyen (pop 2,080). Only stations in the other two territories.

Other settlements Svalbard: Barentsburg (pop 350), Ny-Ålesund (pop 50), Hornsund (pop 9)

Economy Svalbard: coal mining, tourism, scientific research and education, small enterprises

Languages/official language Svalbard: Norwegian (official language), Russian; Franz Josef Land: Russian; Jan Mayen: Norwegian

Religion Svalbard: mostly Church of Norway (Protestant), with some Russian Orthodox and Roman Catholics

Currency Svalbard and Jan Mayen: Norsk Kroner NKR (international: NOK)

Exchange rate £1 = about NOK8.6, US$1 = about NOK5.5, €1 = about NOK7.4 (February 2013)

National airline/airport Svalbard: Longyearbyen Airport (LYR)/ Scandinavian Airlines (SAS). No civil airports and regular flights in the other two territories.

International telephone code Svalbard and Jan Mayen: +47. No regular telephones in Franz Josef Land.

Time Svalbard and Jan Mayen: Central European time (GMT+1, also in summer); Franz Josef Land: Moscow time (GMT+3)

Electrical voltage 220–50V AC/DC in all three territories

Weights and measures Metric (SI standard) in all three territories

Flag Svalbard and Jan Mayen: Norwegian; Franz Josef Land: Russian

National anthem Svalbard and Jan Mayen: Norwegian; Franz Josef Land: Russian

National flower Svalbard: polar poppy (*Papaver dahliamum*)

Sports Svalbard: Nordic skiing, snowboarding, jogging, soccer, badminton, surfing, golf

Public holidays Svalbard and Jan Mayen: 25–26 December (Christmas), 1 January (New Year), 1 May (Labour Day), 17 May (Constitution Day), Easter, Ascension of Christ, Whitsun

1

Background Information

GEOGRAPHY

POSITION From Bjørnøya in the south at 74°N to Rossøya at almost 81°N in the north, the Svalbard archipelago extends northwards over roughly 700km, leaving about 1,000km of packed drift ice to the North Pole. From Rossøya southwards, it is another 1,000km to North Cape, 'way down south' in mainland Norway. The total area of the archipelago is about 62,500km² – approximately equal to Holland and Belgium combined, or the Republic of Ireland, though this varies, as glacier fronts form several hundreds of kilometres of ice along the coastlines, which move back and forth over time, thus changing the total area. Roughly 60% of the land area is glaciated, 30% is barren ground (rock, scree, moraines, fluvial sediments, etc) and only the remaining 10% is covered by vegetation – the last especially in the sheltered wider inland valleys of central Spitsbergen.

Svalbard forms the northwest corner of the Eurasian continental plate, which is submerged under the relatively shallow Barents Sea that lies between the archipelago and northern Norway with typical depths of just 200–300m, and a maximum depth of 550m. North of the islands, the continental slope leads down into the depths of the Arctic Ocean, with more than 4,000m depth around the North Pole. To the west, there is the deep Greenland Sea, the northernmost part of the Atlantic. The Arctic and Atlantic oceans meet between Svalbard and Greenland in the Fram Strait, the most important connection between the almost-locked-off Arctic Ocean and the other oceans of the world.

Svalbard is one of the northernmost landmasses on the planet. To the east, only the Russian archipelagos of Franz Josef Land and Severnaya Zemlya (Northern Land), and to the west, only northern Greenland and the islands of northernmost Canada, reach as far or further north. Contrary to all of these, which are mostly locked away in heavy drift ice, Svalbard is favoured by a branch of the Gulf Stream, which keeps much of the west coast free of ice for most of the year. This means that getting supplies to Svalbard is easier, and thus the maintenance of fairly normal settlements is possible here, further north than almost anywhere else in the world. This again is the reason for Svalbard being the most visited High Arctic region – all other comparable places are much more difficult and expensive to reach.

With regard to land, Svalbard is by far the largest area of wilderness in Europe – a fact that is particularly hard to fathom, it would seem, for those few visitors who set out on ambitious hiking expeditions without previous Arctic wilderness experience. As long as there is no fog or white-out, the general orientation is easier in this tundral landscape where no trees obstruct the view. Experience is needed mainly for finding a suitable route through this pathless terrain with its Arctic peculiarities, often related to the special conditions created by the permafrost which affects everything, from the surprisingly deep mud areas to the peculiarities of streams and rivers which have to be crossed (without bridges or marked fords, of course). A lack of previous practical experience with Arctic terrain inevitably will lead to, at the very least, a loss of time due to much trial and error. After the geological section, this guide deals with some of the typical features of this landscape, including practical aspects for the few who intend to get around on foot in this wilderness. However, no book can replace your own experience of this terrain (or the experience of those travelling with you).

GEOLOGY AND GEOMORPHOLOGY A detailed discussion of Svalbard's geology lies outside the scope of this guide. Nevertheless, it is useful for visitors to have a basic overview, particularly as even the name 'Spitsbergen' is of geomorphological origin.

Svalbard is, as the name 'Spitsbergen' (pointed peaks) indicates, composed of mountainous areas, with the highest points being Newtontoppen (1,713m) and Perriertoppen (1,712m). The eastern islands are not quite as high. Even the layperson will be struck by the almost horizontal stratification of most of the archipelago, to which one can attribute its unusual topography: table mountains with steep scree-covered flanks and brittle rock faces, forms that are further worked over by glaciation. The alpine scenery with its pointed peaks that gave the island its name is mainly limited to the west coast on account of tertiary folding.

Svalbard is of great interest to geologists for its insights into our planet's geological history. Furthermore, the limited (if any) topsoil of the ice-free areas and the lack of much vegetation cover make research logistically relatively easy.

The last thousand million years of the Earth's history are represented, almost without pause, in Svalbard's rocks. Research in the northeast has uncovered minerals up to 3,200 million years old embedded in younger rocks.

NORTHERNMOST

In connection with the polar areas such as those described in this book, there appears frequently the question of 'northernmost' records. Positions are usually given in degrees (°) of northern latitude, starting with 0° at the equator, to 90° northern latitude at the North Pole, a degree being subdivided into 60 minutes (') as the next smaller unit. From one latitude degree to the next, the distance on the Earth's surface (assuming this to be without elevations and depressions) is 111km.

NORTHERNMOST LANDPOINTS The northernmost landpoint of all is a tiny gravel island just north of the northern coast of Greenland at almost 84° northern latitude. For Europe and even Eurasia, the northernmost landpoint is Cape Fligely on Rudolf Island in Franz Josef Land at 81°52'N. The northernmost landpoint of Norway is tiny Rossøya at the north tip of Spitsbergen at 80°50'N.

NORTHERNMOST BASES The northernmost permanently manned bases of the world are scientific/touristic stations, mostly Russian, on the Arctic drift ice close to the North Pole. On land, the northernmost bases are Alert on Ellesmere Island and Station Nord in Peary Land/Greenland (only seasonally manned). On land in Europe and Eurasia, the northernmost manned base is the decaying Russian airforce base Nagurskoe on Alexander Island in Franz Josef Land with its small guard force (before this, until 1995, the northernmost manned base was the now-abandoned station on Rudolf Island).

For most of the Earth's geological history, Svalbard was completely submerged under water. On the sea bottom, materials and the remains of lifeforms lay relatively undisturbed, while newer layers increased the pressure, thus forming sedimentary rocks. Periodically, the land would rise above sea level, by slight tilt movements of the continental plate for example, leading to periods of erosion and to terrestrial deposits rather than marine ones; this can be seen clearly in the layers. Most prominent among the terrestrial sediments are the coal seams dating back to the Devonian/Carboniferous and Tertiary ages (for further reading, see *Appendix*, page 231).

The process of sedimentation was interrupted several times by the upfolding of mountain ranges and the subsequent erosion. The biggest of these events was the formation of the Caledonides 400–500 million years ago, which affected a huge area – a fact suggested by the name, which refers to the Latin name (*Caledonia*) that the Romans gave to the land of what is now Scotland. The older layers were folded and morphed into other rock forms due to the heat and pressure. Liquid magma was forced nearer to the surface where it solidified as granite. These Caledonian rocks – metamorphites and magmatites – are called 'Hecla Hoek' in Svalbard geology.

After the Caledonian age, a long period followed, during which the Caledonides eroded, leading, together with marine sediments, to new layers of mostly horizontal sediments. The Devonian period is rich in fossils – sea creatures and plants – often in typical red sediments, along with economically important coal seams. These remains indicate that Svalbard had a much more favourable climate in the past than it does today. The only explanation of this is the continental drift theory, which states that the Earth's surface consists of solid tectonic plates floating on a liquid core and changing their positions over millions of years. During the Devonian period, Svalbard lay south of the equator and has been drifting northwards ever since with the continental plate on an erratic course.

NORTHERNMOST SETTLEMENTS The northernmost settlement of the world, with normal family life year round and a wide range of facilities, is Longyearbyen on Spitsbergen with about 2,080 inhabitants, which lies at 78°15'N. Accordingly, Svalbard can also claim the northernmost hotel, newspaper, post office, swimming pool, regular civilian airport, full-service campsite, locomotive, cable car, kebab shop and so on. Quanaaq and Siorapaluk in Greenland, which like to claim to be the northernmost settlements, are both below 78°N – to say nothing of certain spots in Alaska which often lay claim to such records, despite being at only 71°N or even lower.

And Nordkapp (North Cape) in northern Norway? Here, it is easier to define what it is not: it is certainly not the northernmost landpoint of Europe, nor of Norway, nor of the Norwegian mainland (being situated on an island); Rossøya on Svalbard is almost 1,000km further north. The uncontested record of Nordkapp is that, since the opening of the road tunnel, it is the northernmost point of Europe that can be reached without interruption by car; it is the northernmost rock of the world that has an entrance fee; and it is the northernmost mass tourism attraction which has been visited by more than 200,000 paying visitors within half a year. In view of this, the masses of visitors are, first and foremost, a tribute to a brilliant marketing campaign. So by visiting Svalbard or Franz Josef Land instead of Nordkapp, you get not only the more authentic, but also the much less-crowded, attractions of northern Scandinavia.

Above sea level, the Devonian and Carboniferous periods featured lush swamp vegetation, providing the biomass which, covered by residues from the huge Caledonides, formed the coal deposits mined in the settlement of Pyramiden today (and previously on Bjørnøya). During the Permian period, Svalbard reached the latitude of the Bahamas and the Persian Gulf and large areas were again below sea level due to the progressive erosion of the mountains; fossil crustaceans from warmer coastal waters bore witness to this.

At the beginning of the Mesozoic period, 250 million years ago, Svalbard had reached the latitude of present-day Spain. Large areas lay just below sea level, with fossil remains indicating extensive tidal zones. This was the great age of the dinosaurs, who found suitable habitat in the coastal marshes. Fossil remains include bone and footprints; a footprint cast from an iguanodon can be seen in the Svalbard Museum.

Important in the formation of today's landscape were igneous intrusions, penetrating often horizontally between rock layers to the east and in the centre (Diabasodden, Sassendalen) at times of tectonic faulting. Igneous rock is far more resistant to erosion than sedimentary layers, giving rise to a distinctive pattern of irregular, vertical rock bands. In many places the former upper sediments which once covered the hard igneous rocks have eroded away.

The change from the Cretaceous to the Tertiary age brought about a fracturing of the continental plate which led to the opening of the North Atlantic, with Eurasia on one side and Greenland and northern Canada drifting apart on the other. Originally, northern Greenland, Ellesmere Island and Svalbard belonged to the same plate and when looking on a map which shows the continental rims and the bathymetry, one can still see the position where the Svalbard corner of the Eurasian continent fitted in between northern Greenland and Ellesmere Island.

During the Tertiary period (starting around 60 million years ago), Svalbard had reached the latitude of today's southern Norway and consisted mainly of low-lying flatland with extensive swamps. Over the millennia, these formed deep layers of peat, which were later covered by further sedimentation and formed new coal deposits. This Tertiary coal is mined at Longyearbyen, Barentsburg and Sveagruva (and also formerly in Ny-Ålesund). Excellent plant fossils remain from this time, including deciduous and coniferous trees, and may be found in several places in the centre of Nordenskiöldlandet.

Also during the Tertiary period came the second great disruption of the sedimentary layers, when folding of the east and (particularly) the west coasts brought pre-Devonian rocks to the surface and formed the jagged alpine mountain range that gives Sveagruva its name. Central areas were unaffected, the flat tableland now sitting inside a bowl-like rim. In addition, the land rose considerably and some volcanic activity occurred (Woodfjorden, on the west side of Wijdefjorden); thermal springs (to 25°C) in remote Bockfjorden are the remnants of this. Compared with Iceland, which owes its relatively short geological life to the liveliness of the Mid-Atlantic Ridge, volcanic activity in Svalbard plays only a modest role.

The current geological period, the Quaternary, began some two million years ago and is characterised by its ice ages. The centre of Svalbard then was most likely a high plateau with a range of differently sized valleys. Today's great fjords and wide valleys were primarily caused by erosion from huge ice-age glaciers followed by frost, water and wind in the warmer intervening periods. During the most intensive periods of ice cover, the whole of the area, with the possible exception of the mountaintops, was cloaked with an impenetrable layer of solid ice. Displaced boulders and signs of their movement can be seen near mountain summits. The ice joined Svalbard to Scandinavia and filled the shallow Barents Sea repeatedly, last occurring as recently as 16,000 years ago. The more precise course of the various ice sheets and their exact extent and thickness are still a subject for intensive ongoing studies, which lead to a gradually more detailed and surprisingly varied picture of the ice ages. It seems for instance that lower parts of the west and north coasts have been free of glaciers for 60,000 years. The centre of the ice masses seems to have been somewhere between the east of Svalbard and Franz Josef Land.

The enormous pressure caused by ice sheets of up to more than a kilometre thick led Svalbard to subside somewhat, flooding some of the lower land as the ice thawed. At the same time, those sections that were freed from the ice rose slowly again; evidence of this process can be seen in old shorelines behind and above today's coast. The oldest of these shorelines have yielded organic remains dating back 40,000 years. To the east, shorelines indicate a more rapid and extensive rise of the land over the last 10,000 years – up to 130m on Kong Karls Landet – though there was also more severe subsidence. This was no doubt due to thicker and more prolonged ice cover, compared with that on the west coast. The rising of the landmass explains the presence of shells, driftwood and whalebone high above today's shorelines; they could not have been brought here by man. The presence of some of the shells also indicates a warmer climate at some stage since the last ice age. Whether or not Svalbard is still moving or rising is unclear. There are theories that the landmass is tipping, with the east rising as the west sinks.

In any case, it would be wrong to presume that Svalbard's ice conditions of today arise directly from the ice ages; several warm periods lasting several millennia brought about the extensive thawing of glaciers and one can imagine the islands with less ice cover than today. The lower levels of land were then flooded by sea water, leaving the higher ground as islands, which gradually accumulated the surrounding lowlands as the land rose from the sea. A warmer period is well documented for about 6,800BC with considerably milder conditions than today, including species living here which became extinct only with the climatic cooling. There are indications that Svalbard may have been almost free of ice as late as about 1,500 years ago. These mild conditions also support speculations about a possible earlier Stone-Age population, though no proof has yet been found.

The cooler climate of the past 1,500 years, together with the lifting landmass which has raised the majority of Svalbard above the snowline and thus created conditions for glacial growth, has brought about – with some milder interruptions – an increase of ice cover again with a maximum up to the middle of the 19th century, when the glaciers advanced further than ever before since the end of the ice age. Since about 1860, we have found ourselves in a warming period again with both glaciers and Arctic sea ice in retreat, but still colder and with more ice cover than for instance during the period of the Roman Empire. It is difficult to say whether or not this present warming is mainly a result of natural climatic cycles or if it has been in part caused by man's influence on the environment; there is as yet insufficient data to support either view.

For those interested in reading more about this subject, I would recommend the outstanding and readable *The Geological History of Svalbard*, as well as *The Geology of Svalbard* and its companion *The Geography of Svalbard* (see *Appendix*, pages 243, 240 and 241 respectively, for details of these three titles), plus explanatory notes on various geological maps.

Glaciers Around 60% of Svalbard today is covered by ice. Thus, the greatest obstacles are glaciers, especially those that reach the sea and cannot be walked around. You need local knowledge and experience as well as familiarity with the correct safety procedures. Even the smaller glaciers (eg: Longyearbreen and Larsbreen) have crevasses, and caution is well advised. Areas with relatively little glaciation are primarily in central Spitsbergen. There are only a few other limited areas in the northwest (Ny-Ålesund, Mitrahalvøya, the north coast) that are glacier-free and this sets limits on longer treks.

Experienced alpinists who wish to ski over the glaciers should visit from April to mid-June, when most crevasses are still full of snow and the melts have not yet fully started. In high summer there are other dangers in addition to crevasses: basins of slack water, rapid streams cutting into the ice surface and smooth, slippery ice. Special care must be taken when glaciers break off into neighbouring water. The birth of icebergs can unleash substantial waves, mixed with ice fragments. It is also advisable to keep any equipment on shore high above the likely reach of such waves as well as high tide. Boats should keep a respectful distance from glaciers. Occasionally, young icebergs can be formed underwater so that huge blocks of ice suddenly shoot up from below the surface near a glacier front.

Around glaciers the hiker is almost certainly going to come across young moraines. While the vast moraine landscapes of central Europe were left behind by glaciers well over 10,000 years ago, Svalbard's moraines have existed only for a few centuries as the glaciers still go through periods of advance and retreat.

The last main period of glacial growth occurred until the second part of the 19th century. Since then, most glaciers have been in retreat, for example Paulabreen (Van Mijenfjorden) and Nathorstbreen (Van Keulenfjorden), each of which have receded by some 15km. There are of course exceptions. A significant surge of the Negribreen was recorded in 1936–37, its 12km-wide front moving 15km into Storfjorden, though it's now breaking up. More recent surges have affected Bakaninbreen, Osbornebreen (1989), Fridtjovbreen (1994–95) at the entrance to Van Mijenfjord (which hadn't moved since its spectacular surge in 1860–61) and others.

These irregular, rapid advances of glaciers are called surges and happen independently of climatic change, with an individual rhythm for each glacier demonstrating this surging behaviour. During a growth period, the glacier accumulates more ice in its upper part than what is transported away by the flow of the ice stream, which can be retarded by special underground conditions or by insufficient lubrication due to the lack of a water film between the underlying rock and ice. In this period, the glacier is retreating quickly in its lower part due to a lack of sufficient new ice from above. Meltwater streams create channel systems in the ice which again increase the melting process and the retreat. At the same time, accumulation in the upper part leads to growing ice pressure further up, until meltwater develops at the border between ice and rock, which acts like a lubricant and reduces friction considerably, thus leading to the sudden advance of the entire glacier by sometimes many kilometres within one year, as well as a massive loss of thickness in the upper part. Then the whole process starts again: accumulation in the upper part, quick retreat in the front, until the next surge some 50 to 200 years later. As this surging is a fairly common phenomenon among glaciers in Svalbard, it is obvious that maps cannot be highly accurate in glacier and moraine areas.

How drastically glaciers can affect the landscape may be illustrated by the following three diagrams.

The first diagram (opposite, top) is based on an aerial survey by the Norsk Polarinstitutt in 1936–38. Glacier *M* has retreated considerably. Moraine banks on the eastern side indicate a preceding surge within the last 100 years. Glacier *E* and

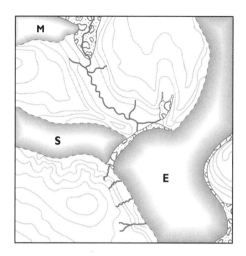

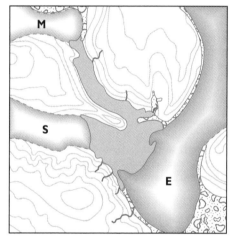

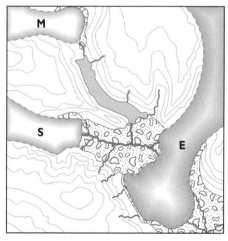

its adjoining glacier, S, seem to have advanced considerably in the previous century. Large areas of the southern valley floor are covered in ice. Sir Martin Conway first described this area in 1896. Glacier E must have surged in the few years before his visit and closed off the whole valley with an ice wall of over 100m.

Diagram 2 (middle, left), based on Norsk Polarinstitutt map D9, shows the area in 1970, when it had changed significantly. While glaciers E and S have thawed, leaving boggy moraine fields, glacier M has moved forward in the late 1960s and blocks the valley to the north with its ice wall, causing meltwater from the three glaciers to form a new lake.

I have based Diagram 3 (below left) on my own observations in 1988. Further significant changes have taken place. Glacier M's surge has come to a halt and E and S have melted still further. The lake's outflow has changed; water is now being discharged through an enormous ice tunnel under glacier E instead of northwards towards Isfjorden. It is possible that the outflow is using an old bed or ravine. The lake has all but disappeared, leaving behind a bed of mud. Previous water levels can be seen on the surrounding slopes.

This process of surge and retreat continues to change the landscape, as it has done since the last ice age. These changes make it impossible for cartographers to keep maps up to date. Hikers relying on maps must be prepared for quite big surprises.

As mentioned already in the *Geology* section, glaciers are, on the whole, currently retreating in Svalbard, though their present extension is still much greater than it was some 1,500 years ago, when the climate was also milder in Svalbard than it is today. In order to understand these fluctuations, temperature is not the only key factor, in spite of the one-sided focus on 'global warming' in the current climate discussion. Equally important are precipitation – both snowfall in winter as a supply for new ice and rainfall as a factor for increased melting – and also, taking a longer perspective, changes in elevation: a rise of the land can lift larger parts of the glacier above the snowline, leading to a greater accumulation of snow. With the low precipitation and therefore also low snowfall quantities of the Arctic today, the wind and the orientation of the mountain ridges are key factors too. Studies in Svalbard have shown that many of the glaciers there cannot survive with the small quantity of snow falling directly on them, but survive only because of the considerable transport of additional snow from surrounding areas by wind, which then drops its snow load on the leeside of ridges where it accumulates as a precondition for sufficient development of new glacier ice. A lasting change of the main wintry wind directions may have more serious consequences on the ice cover than a slight change in temperatures.

Moraines Younger end or side moraines – sections of unconsolidated glacial debris – are integral to glaciers and are made up of a mix of ice and other materials which have been scraped or fallen onto the glacier and form very dirty ice layers. The ice eventually melts and the remaining solid material forms an insulating layer from a thickness of a few centimetres upwards, slowing down further thawing. Accordingly, more ice melts on the less-insulated inner part of the glacier than at its extremities and the moraines are left as walls, separated (in the most extreme contexts, at least) from the glacier itself. The ice in the moraine holds back any water and the walls frequently work as a dam as the glacier melts. There are often two to four debris-covered moraines in front of the visible part of the glacier. These have cores of 'dead' ice which may be very long lived – over 100 years – and often end up kilometres away from the (retreating) visible glacier. In and between the moraines, the melting ice can create ice tunnels, crevasses and subterranean streams. The moraine walker often first realises that he or she is on top of an iceberg when he or she comes across a recent crack and gets a view of the moraine's internal workings.

In the summer young moraines undergo a period of transformation as the ice core slowly melts: surfaces become stubborn, flowing sludge. In other places the cold ground refreezes this material or the meltwater turns into sheets of ice camouflaged by partly frozen chunks of material. In this way the moraine becomes difficult or impossible to traverse, a problem often encountered in Svalbard.

Eventually, after many years, the moraine reaches the point where its water content is the same as that of the surrounding permafrost, particularly at its periphery. The coat of debris is now relatively thick and the rate of thaw very slow, so the moraine takes on the appearance of an ordinary hill, complete with vegetation. Still, melting may continue, though at a much slower pace, and occasionally by sublimation, a process by which ice becomes vapour without becoming water first, evaporating slowly and leaving cavities which occasionally collapse to form depressions or clefts. Large collapsing hollows of this kind, in Siberia for instance, have captured mammoths, which are then preserved in the frozen ground.

Outside of these problems described, glaciers and moraines as experienced in Svalbard can show us how many of our own landforms have been created; when we get home we can look at many features with new eyes. A number of moraines can be rewarding for the amateur fossil-hunter as there are many newly broken rocks to search through.

Permafrost phenomena Permafrost and its associated phenomena are particularly remarkable. In permafrost areas, the summer days with temperatures above freezing are not sufficient for compensating the many days of the rest of the year when temperatures are well below zero. Therefore, deep down in the ground a frost layer stays over the summer and develops more and more every winter until a balance level is reached where geothermic warmth from the inner Earth withstands the cold from above. Permafrost is not exclusively an Arctic phenomenon – in fact, the strongest permafrost is found outside the Arctic, under the boreal forests of the Siberian taiga, where the permafrost zone can reach down more than 1,000m under the surface. Almost everywhere in Svalbard, the ground is frozen throughout the year to a depth of 100–150m in the valleys and up to 400m in the mountains. Only the topmost layers thaw in summer, allowing for plant growth. Worth mentioning are the old mine shafts which close up with ice (condensation of air humidity, freezing on the tunnel sides which are below zero) as soon as draining and ventilation cease.

The following are some permafrost-based phenomena, many of them related to the fact that the deeper ground is permanently frozen and thereby waterproof, while the upper ground layer can be attacked intensively by frost from both above and beyond, making the water in the upper ground layer expand when freezing and shrink again when melting, leading to movements:

Ice wedges More or less flat ground with fewer large stones can manifest a wide network of crevices, from small cracks to bigger ditches (up to 2m wide by 1m deep), sometimes further widened and deepened by meltwater streams running through them. Often visible only from mountaintops or from aircraft are larger 'net' formations with ice-filled cracks. Here, bigger blocks of ground shrink when freezing, creating a wide net of cracks, which eventually fill with drifting snow and water. The water expands when freezing, thus widening the crack, leading to more ice, expanding further when freezing again, and so on and so forth. Eventually, the upper part of the crack will remain free of ice and water, while the ice in the lower section may be covered by a thin camouflaging layer of material which has been falling into the crack from the sides, thus creating from above the impression of a normal ditch, which in reality extends very deep as an ice structure.

Cryoturbation and solifluction Cryoturbation is, effectively, movement of soil particles by frost. This process is often dependent upon different sizes of particles in the ground, which are then alternately caught and moved at different stages depending on their size and thereby contact to the changing frozen or thawed zones. Notable examples to be found in many Arctic flatlands are polygonal rings of stone encircling finer materials, graded by ice pressure and resulting movement. Also, with the formation of such ice wedges, cryoturbation is involved. Solifluction (frost creep) is the slow (1–10cm a year) downhill movement of soil saturated with meltwater. This can straighten the polygonal rings into a downhill direction. When there is an obstacle in its way (small enough still to be overrun), the slow-motion flood builds up behind it and creates a structure that looks like a frozen wave breaking over the obstacle.

Pingos Particularly noticeable due to their size – up to 50m high – these mounds or hillocks are formed when nearly freezing ground water under the permafrost or in newly frozen parts of the ground (such as a frost-free former riverbed) is under pressure and finds an upward escape route through a locally weakened part of the surface layer. By forcing its way up and thereby reducing pressure, the water cools down and freezes in the soil, creating a growing ice core, which lifts up the soil above to form a hill, the ice inside normally camouflaged by the external cover of uplifted solid material. As relatively transitory phenomena, pingos often arch up, perhaps over many years, but can eventually melt over several centuries.

Ice lenses Smaller than pingos and frequently much shorter lived (from one to five years), there are lenses of ice that form in the soil. The most obvious ones are the ice lenses close to the surface that grow to maturity within a few years, then lift vegetation by 1–2m before thawing again through cracks in the mounds that are sufficiently wide both to allow warmer air to enter and to look inside. They are mostly found in wet flatlands.

Block glaciers These are formed on some bigger scree slopes under rock faces when meltwater seeps into the spaces between scree and builds up a growing mass of ice deep inside the slope. They are practically an underground glacier, growing from percolating water inside instead of from snowfall on the surface. This cambers out the slope, often forming a gently tilted platform on top. Just as with 'normal' glaciers, the block glacier can flow; it loses mass from its outer end as material melts away and builds up more internal ice covered with new scree falling down from the rock wall at its inward end.

Bogs, marshes and fens In summer the permafrost is covered in places by impassable morass or bog, especially in flat areas. When snow on the surface and the upper soil layer melts or is hit with rain, vertical drainage is prevented by the waterproof permafrost layer slightly deeper, leading to a top soil layer soaked with water. In the case of a soil with little vegetation cover, this will lead to sometimes deep and sticky morass, often trickily camouflaged by small stones, kept on top of the morass by cryoturbation. In areas with stronger flat vegetation, the dead organic matter will decay extremely slowly under the conserving Arctic conditions, leading to a slow development of peat and swamp over morass – again, the water cannot drain away vertically. Beginning from minute differences in the surface, a differentiation of vegetation sets in and a combination of willow and others will initiate the development of soft peat mounds which insulate the ground – and eventually also their inner parts – causing the permafrost to move up under the mounds. This again leads to further damming of the water in and on the ground between the mounds. Such terrain can be extremely tiresome to cross, with either bog between the mounds or the extremely soft mounds themselves to step on.

There is an advantage in having cooler summers: as bog and morass will not thaw as deeply, it is easier to get across. But hanging moors are different. Often found on very steep flanks under bird colonies, their peat layer can be up to 2m thick; guano and moisture from fog and rain combine to encourage rich growth and the cold discourages bacterial decomposition, while the permafrost moves up inside the growing and insulating peat layer, thus stabilising it even in very steep slopes, where a moor would be geologically highly unlikely without the permafrost as stabiliser.

Rocks and cliffs In combination with water seepage, frost is responsible for the poor condition of many cliffs and since frost in permafrost areas can attack from both directions, its effects are much stronger. Cliffs which may look easy to climb are so split by frost damage that they no longer offer reliable footholds. Solid cliffs for climbing are to be found in the northwest and northeast of the archipelago where there is granite and gneiss, as well as remnants of a volcano and thermal springs. These areas are, however, very remote.

Scree slopes One needs to be much more careful when walking in scree (as compared with the Alps, for instance), and solid footwear with very good traction is essential. Owing to frost erosion and movement inside the scree, these slopes are usually much more unstable and given to slippage when stepping into it. One larger piece stuck into your heel through a rubber boot or light trekking shoe can bring a hike to a speedy end.

Lack of drainage Permafrost seals deep ground against vertical drainage – all melt- and rainwater which cannot run off on the surface or evaporate will stay in the ground. Especially in flatter terrain with finer material, this leads to extended swampy areas or sticky, deep mud, in spite of low annual precipitation. Footwear should be adapted to these frequently wet conditions.

RIVERS AND STREAMS Rivers and streams in Svalbard are mostly seasonal, flowing from two to six months in summer only and freezing or drying up during the rest of the year. However, in some places, groundwater springs or more often all-year meltwater outlets of nearby glaciers may supply unfrozen water, sometimes accumulating in the deep snow blown into river canyons and transforming it into dangerous slush which is uncomfortable or even dangerous for skiers, hikers and sledges. Given these variations, it can be difficult to determine 'normal' water levels. During the Arctic spring and summer (May–August), one should be prepared for high water levels among the larger valleys (Sassendalen, Reindalen, Adventdalen, Agardhdalen, Kjellstrømdalen, Colesdalen, Dunderdalen, etc) and in streams from the larger inland glaciers, depending on the state of the snowmelt and recent daily temperatures. With only the upper soil layers thawing, water has nowhere else to drain away and therefore runs quickly into the streambeds, turning them into torrents. Also during summer and autumn, stronger rainfall can quickly result in surprising changes of water levels in streams and rivers.

The worst problems occur at the first extensive snowmelt, usually at the end of May. Watercourses surge and water attacks the ice from above and below until it cracks. Flooding can occur even on very warm days in July or August, in some years temporarily turning large valleys into wide riverbeds. In side valleys where glacial streams have cut into the valley floor, narrow channels carry water with great force, often pushing along large boulders, to the point you are unable to stand in them. In these circumstances a long detour is the only option.

Crossing streams and rivers The kind of extreme flooding outlined above is uncommon. Nevertheless, from May to the end of August, be prepared to cross thigh-high water levels; and even if the water isn't very deep, strong currents may cause you to get pretty wet. Large, loose stones – largely camoflauged while they are being swept along by brownish glacier meltwater at temperatures just above freezing – make it foolhardy to try to cross barefoot or in sandals, etc. Rubber boots that are at least knee high (even better with a light extension) provide the most versatile solution.

Snafus can be avoided by choosing a sensible crossing point. This requires experience that can only be acquired gradually, including close observation of one's guide. This advice cannot be overemphasised. By way of example, a participant on one of my tours rushed ahead and waded across a stream without waiting for the guide and the rest of the group. He slipped, took an involuntary body bath and paid for the experience with his camera. Also, despite the advice he had been given, he had not packed any spare clothing; his involuntary bath resulted in the inflammation of his lower back for the rest of his stay in Svalbard.

River navigation Barely a few kilometres of Svalbard's larger rivers (Sassenelva and Reindalselva) are normally navigable by flat-bottomed boats, and then only downstream due to the strength of the current. Streams are heavily forked and consequently often shallow; one frequently gets stuck, which requires dragging the boat over mud to the next navigable section. Svalbard is not well suited to river trips as there is either too much or too little water. Even the possibility of navigating rivulets at times of high water does not mean guaranteed success. I was frustrated once in July by a stream that rushed through a gorge but was still covered by a two-metre layer of ice, despite the surrounding countryside being snow free.

River mouths in fjord shallows are loaded with alluvium and, depending on the tide, canoeists can find themselves in the unpleasant position of being run aground 100m offshore. Much of the water is so cloudy that only eventual breakers can tell you where the flats are.

CLIMATE

The climate of Svalbard is determined by three main factors: its northerly position (causing the extremely cyclical annual supply of light and warmth from the sun); the strong influence of the surrounding ocean currents; and the winds.

OCEAN CURRENTS, DRIFT ICE AND DRIFTWOOD The furthest reaches of the Gulf Stream culminate in the Spitsbergen Current, bringing a milder climate than in other places at the same latitude. Northern Greenland and the northernmost islands of Canada and Russia are largely cut off by pack ice, whereas the west of Spitsbergen (and sometimes some of the other islands, too) can be reached in most summers without any contact with ice at all. The warmer water coming up from the south divides itself just before Bjørnøya into east-, north- and westward-headed branches.

In comparison, eastern Spitsbergen is influenced by a cold current moving towards the southeast which brings lower air temperatures and also masses of drift ice from the polar basin. In the polar basin, sea ice develops – in the outer parts annually, in the centre over many years with according thicknesses, moved around in circular currents over the Arctic Ocean, until it ends up in one of the currents leaving the basin – in our case between Franz Josef Land and Svalbard. On its way, the cold current also gets a grip on some of the icebergs which calved off the long glacial fronts of Franz Josef Land and moves them towards Svalbard. This cold water and drift ice meet the branches of the warmer Spitsbergen Current in the area between Bjørnøya and southern Spitsbergen and mix with them. This mixture creates ideal growth conditions for algae in the water and attached to the underlying side of the drift ice – with nutrients brought along in the cold current, slightly warmer water and the permanent light from April onwards as the source of energy. These algae are the basis of the rich food chain of the Barents Sea and

Greenland Sea, including the potentially huge masses of fish (if there wasn't permanent overfishing, endangering these stocks) and an abundance of seals at the top of the chain (if this place is not taken by hunters or polar bears).

Also the drift ice from the east is redirected after mixing with the warmer current and pushed by it northwards along the west coast of Spitsbergen, while slowly melting in the more temperate water. Westerly winds may blow it into the fjords. This movement of the drift ice from the south leads to the seemingly strange situation that the most southerly fjords – especially the Hornsund – are more often blocked by dense drift ice than the more northerly ones, where the ice has usually melted away in the warmer water already on its way north. The Isfjord, which holds most of the archipelago's settlements, and the Kongsfjord have therefore rarely been affected by this drift ice during the last decades. This has not been the case in the past: in cruise reports from the early 20th century, it can be frequently read that it was impossible to enter Isfjord due to dense drift ice even in July and August (Isfjord ('Icefjord') didn't acquire its name coincidentally). But, since about 1860, the ice cover of the polar basin has been shrinking, and accordingly, the drift ice arriving at the west coast of Spitsbergen has reduced considerably – the same applies also to the locally developing wintry ice cover of the fjords. Today, it is extremely rare that drift ice blocks any of the main western fjords after the end of June – in Isfjord, this might happen once every five years, and only for a few days. Only Hornsund down south is more regularly blocked by drift ice entering from outside.

A formerly important side effect of the cold current from the polar basin and its mixture with the Spitsbergen Current was the supply with wood to otherwise-woodless Svalbard. In particular, the big Siberian rivers wash a good number of trees and logs into the Arctic Ocean, where this driftwood becomes trapped in the ice and the circular currents, floating around for several years, until some of it is then pushed towards and around Svalbard, eventually being blown by the winds to the beaches. Stranded driftwood is a familiar feature of most beaches in Svalbard, pushed further up by wintry ice pressures and often lasting for centuries in the conserving climate. In the old days, this driftwood was a highly welcome construction material and fuel for hunters, among others.

CLIMATE TABLES The tables overleaf are based on information from Det Norske Meterologiske Institutt over the years 1961–93. The values shown come from different meteorological stations and show how great variations can be: from year to year and from place to place (even the 5km between Longyearbyen and the airport can show a 10°C difference!)

PRECIPITATION AND SNOW COVER There is a popular misconception that the Arctic is an area abundant with snow. This is plainly untrue. In fact, the highest Arctic is most often a cold desert, with Peary Land in northernmost Greenland as a good example. Even on a physical map of the whole Arctic, it is clear that Peary Land is mostly free of ice, in contrast to the huge ice cap further south. Though on a smaller scale, this similarly applies to Svalbard: here, too, there are only a few glaciers along the north coast which manage to reach the sea, and central Svalbard, too, more sheltered against wet clouds from the west, is only modestly glaciated. The reason for this is not too warm a climate but because of the fairly low quantities of precipitation, and thereby also snow.

Apart from the damper west coast, Svalbard has a dry, steppe-like climate, sometimes with less than 200mm precipitation per year (including snow) in central areas. In lower latitudes, this small amount of water supply would be insufficient for most types of agriculture without additional irrigation. Accordingly, the wintry snow cover is thin, accumulating gradually from October and reaching its maximum usually in April – but even then, larger stones peek through the thin white layer in many places, and especially on slopes. Furthermore, a large part of the snowfall is redistributed by wind. Some open coastal plains or plateaux, and also exposed slopes and inland valleys which channel katabatic winds rushing down from glaciers, can be blown almost free of snow. Some of the snow is blown out on the sea, but much accumulates on the leeside of ridges, filling up deep riverbeds and many glacier crevasses. Therefore, you may find a coast almost free of snow, and half a kilometre behind you can almost drown in deep soft snow in a sheltered valley.

TEMPERATURES (°C)

Month		Longyearbyen	Sveagruva	Ny-Ålesund
	Highest	+4.7	+4.1	+3.7
January	Mean	−15.3	−16.1	−14.1
	Lowest	−38.8	−44.1	−36.6
	Highest	+5.9	+4.6	+4.7
February	Mean	−16.3	−17.0	−15.2
	Lowest	−43.7	−44.8	−41.1
	Highest	+6.3	+5.4	+5.0
March	Mean	−15.8	−16.2	−14.6
	Lowest	−46.3	−43.7	−42.2
	Highest	+5.5	+4.6	+5.5
April	Mean	−12.4	−12.7	−11.3
	Lowest	−39.1	−33.0	−34.0
	Highest	+10.6	+6.9	+8.0
May	Mean	−4.4	−4.7	−4.2
	Lowest	−21.7	−23.7	−19.1
	Highest	+14.3	+13.3	+11.2
June	Mean	+1.8	+1.9	+1.4
	Lowest	−8.4	−8.0	− 8.5
	Highest	+21.3	+16.1	+17.0
July	Mean	+5.8	+5.8	+4.7
	Lowest	+0.2	0.0	−0.5
	Highest	+16.5	+15.3	+13.6
August	Mean	+4.8	+4.9	+3.9
	Lowest	−2.5	−2.0	−5.5
	Highest	+15.2	+13.5	+12.3
September	Mean	+0.4	+0.6	−0.1
	Lowest	−12.6	−11.3	−15.0
	Highest	+8.9	+7.5	+7.5
October	Mean	−5.5	−5.7	−5.6
	Lowest	−20.4	−26.7	−20.6
	Highest	+7.5	+6.3	+7.4
November	Mean	−10.3	−11.5	−9.6
	Lowest	−29.5	−32.5	−26.6
	Highest	+6.7	+6.5	+5.5
December	Mean	−13.3	−14.6	−12.6
	Lowest	−35.6	−38.7	−34.3

Even in deepest winter, thaw periods or even rainfall are possible, too. As the ground is frozen, these milder periods will inevitably result in extensive slippery ice layers, especially on surfaces with little or no snow cover, partially hardening the snow surfaces.

Statistically, April and May are the driest months of the year.

From the second part of May onwards, precipitation is more likely to be rain than snow, even though wet snowfall is possible even in July and August (though it normally melts again within hours, at least in the lower regions).

In summer, precipitation is low, too – which is good for outdoor activities. This does not necessarily mean blue sky and no rain, but heavy rainfall lasting more

PRECIPITATION PER MONTH (MM)

Month		Longyearbyen	Sveagruva	Ny-Ålesund
	Highest	30	66	65
January	Mean	12	29	27
	Lowest	6	15	5
	Highest	56	13	114
February	Mean	19	35	36
	Lowest	4	6	1
	Highest	56	66	143
March	Mean	20	31	38
	Lowest	4	10	3
	Highest	32	64	105
April	Mean	10	24	22
	Lowest	1	6	9
	Highest	23	56	34
May	Mean	7	15	17
	Lowest	2	1	3
	Highest	33	28	58
June	Mean	11	9	19
	Lowest	1	0	1
	Highest	26	18	54
July	Mean	18	11	29
	Lowest	2	1	7
	Highest	69	40	131
August	Mean	23	19	40
	Lowest	8	6	8
	Highest	37	35	154
September	Mean	20	19	46
	Lowest	4	6	10
	Highest	26	47	62
October	Mean	13	20	37
	Lowest	4	2	8
	Highest	63	78	272
November	Mean	13	22	32
	Lowest	5	5	6
	Highest	40	74	74
December	Mean	14	26	27
	Lowest	2	3	1

than a day is the exception rather than the rule. More typical are some drizzle or shorter showers, and wet fog.

To the surprise of many – we get a lot of requests for dog-sledging or snowmobile riding in July and August – the lower parts of the country at least become free of snow over the summer, permitting a limited and fascinating tundra vegetation period. The thaw period usually starts in May, though there are wide variations.

WHAT IS THE DEFINITION OF ARCTIC?

The truth is that there is no indisputable, official definition, but rather a number of competing ones:

POLAR CIRCLE The simplest definition (but the least useful) is that all areas north of the northern polar circle ('the Arctic Circle') are Arctic. Polar circles are found in both the northern and southern hemispheres and are defined as the lines around the globe, north (or south in the case of the southern hemisphere) at which the sun does not set for at least one night of the year. Currently, this is the case north of 66.5° northern latitude (respectively south of 66.5° southern latitude), but this varies in the course of natural history, as the tilt of the Earth's axis changes slowly. The closer one comes to the Poles (90°) from the polar circles, the more nights in summer the sun will stay above the horizon – about half of the year at the Poles themselves. This phenomenon of sunlight all around the clock is called midnight sun or the polar day. In the same areas, we find also the phenomenon of polar night – ie: the sun never comes above the horizon even at midday. From a mathematical point of view, polar day and polar night should be equally long at the same position above the polar circle. In reality, however, the polar night is somewhat shorter than the polar day, because the atmosphere of the Earth bends the sunlight so that it reaches slightly above the horizon. It is for this reason that the sun is still visible even when it has just sunk under the horizon. In central Svalbard, the polar day lasts about four months without any sunset, whereas the polar night lasts only about three months and 20 days. During the polar night, it is truly dark all around the clock only at very high latitudes, for instance around Christmas in Longyearbyen. This gives excellent opportunities for watching the relatively weak northern lights at any time of the day (provided the sky is clear). This is possible only in places as far north as Svalbard. At the beginning and end of the polar-night period, or in areas only just above the polar circle (for instance northern Norway), there is a 'dawn' during daytime, with the sun being only slightly under the horizon at midday. As for the natural world, it makes very little difference whether the sun sets for one night or not. For instance, in Sweden the polar circle runs through huge boreal forests, with nothing much 'Arctic' on either side. Therefore, the polar circle is not a useful definition for 'Arctic' when it comes to describing a certain type of nature. Instead, this definition is more popular as a boast, and the oft-romanticised attribute 'Arctic' is used a lot in northern Scandinavian tourism marketing, and for claiming subsidies from the European Union for northern Sweden and Finland for 'Arctic' agriculture. Canadians, on the other hand, would be rather less pleased with the polar circle as the border demarcating the Arctic, since both a typical Arctic landscape and polar bears reach much further south.

TREELINE This is the most easily recognisable definition of Arctic – though only on land. Here, the Arctic is everything north of the treeline – ie: everywhere where

During some years, most of the valleys are already free of snow by the end of May, while in other years the snow may last long into June, depending both on the previously accumulated quantity of snow and the weather in this period. On the glaciers, there may still be good skiing conditions sometimes into late June almost down to sea level. Higher up in the terrain, predictions about the development of the snow conditions become even more difficult and the situation will differ

there are no high-growing trees or bushes even under favourable conditions. This vegetation type without high-growing plants is called tundra. Isolated patches of tundra exist outside the Arctic and Antarctic, for instance in high mountain areas. Botanically, there are still trees (polar willows, dwarf birches) and bushes (dryas, etc) in the tundra, as botanists define trees as plants with wood, but these plants reach maximum heights of only about 15cm in Svalbard. The advantage of this treeline definition is that the lack of high-growing plants is a clearly discernible landscape feature. The disadvantage: the definition applies only on land.

10°C JULY ISOTHERMAL LINE This is a more theoretical definition, but can be applied on land and on sea. According to this definition, the Arctic is where the long-term mean temperature of the warmest month – normally July – is less than 10°C. This looks like a random value but if this line is drawn on a map of the northern hemisphere, it matches the treeline on land. Usable solar energy is insufficient north of this 10°C July isothermal line for the development of high-growing plants during the productive season of the vegetation. Before July, the white winter snow still covers too much of the land and reflects back much of the solar energy. With monthly mean temperatures of 4–6°C in July, Svalbard is well within both this climatological definition area of the Arctic and the botanical treeline definition, and the same applies for both Jan Mayen and Franz Josef Land.

In natural sciences, a combination of the botanical treeline definition and the 10°C July isothermal line makes most sense when describing a boundary for the Arctic. This would then include Svalbard, Franz Josef Land and Jan Mayen, most of Greenland (except the southern end), all of the northern Russian islands plus a wide zone of northernmost mainland Russia from Kola to the Bering Strait, the north of Alaska, all of the northern Canadian islands, and the north of the Yukon, the Northwest Territories, Quebec and even northernmost Manitoba. In the area of Hudson Bay, the Arctic even reaches south of the polar circle according to this definition, whereas in Scandinavia only a minor region around Vadsø would be regarded as Arctic whereas the Magerøy Island and the mass tourism of North Cape is actually still south of the treeline. Most of Iceland is also non-Arctic according to this line of definition.

Based on this, one can describe the Arctic geographically as the Arctic Ocean around the North Pole, encircled by and including the northernmost parts of the neighbouring continents and archipelagos. At the North Pole, the Arctic Ocean is about 4,200m deep, covered by drifting ice on the water surface. This is almost the opposite of the Antarctic in the south, which is basically a continent around the South Pole, surrounded by oceans and some included nearby islands. At the South Pole, the surface of the ice cap is more than 4,000m above sea level.

enormously from year to year. The summer snowline may move up to somewhere between 500m and 1,200m above sea level by late August. A pass at 400m above sea level can be free of snow, soaking wet with old snow, or covered with a thin layer of fresh snow.

Both snowmelt and rainfall have a fairly quick and direct effect on the water level in rivers and streams. As permafrost limits the water-storage capacity of the soil to the thin, thawed top layer and prevents any sub-surface drainage, much of the rainfall runs into the net of streams and lets them rise fast – within a few hours – into often impressively violent torrents; those travelling out in the wilderness will require a lot of experience and skill to tackle these.

The mountainous west coast, exposed to the summertime western winds loaded with humidity from the open sea, is considerably wetter than central Spitsbergen around the inner Isfjord and Wijdefjord.

CLOUD COVER AND VISIBILITY

Low levels of precipitation do not necessarily mean sunny weather; more often than not skies are overcast. Rain and snow do not normally last long and do not amount to much. It is worth noting, though, that the cloud cover is often very low, and on many slopes and passes it is easy to lose your bearings in the grey conditions. In a wintry white landscape, low clouds or thin fog quickly lead to white-out conditions where you feel as though you are floating in a pale grey cosmos without any contrasts, unable to recognise terrain features even from a short distance. This is not necessarily because of poor visibility but because of a complete loss of any distinguishing topographical features so that it is impossible to determine whether the terrain in front of you is flat or steep. Under such circumstances, you may be forced to halt even if you have a rough idea of your orientation thanks to a GPS or compass and map, as these cannot tell you about minor obstacles which may be hidden in the white-out right in front of you.

It is striking how clear the air is during good weather: even from the shore you can sometimes see as far as 150km. This makes distances seem so much shorter and canoeists, in particular, should study their maps carefully or they may underestimate the distance to their destination. The clear air makes it possible for landscape photographers to use extremely powerful telephoto lenses.

However, fog can develop, frequently and very suddenly, especially in the mountains. This presents a real danger to the inexperienced traveller. Be certain that you know how to put up an emergency bivouac and familiarise yourself with your compass, maps and the territory. It is well worth building extra contingency days into your plan. One July we were trying to cross a 900m crest when the fog came down, temperatures dropped to –8°C and a severe snowstorm began. In these conditions, an emergency bivouac seemed just as risky as blindly carrying on or trying to backtrack along the steep path which had begun to freeze over. We needed to get down into the valley as quickly as possible. Luckily I knew about another route from a previous expedition. Even if hikers, or the group leaders at least, have orienteering ability, maps and compasses cannot replace sound local knowledge, particularly as maps cannot show every detail of the terrain.

In poor conditions it is more sensible to await improvements in the weather. This should be kept in mind when making preparations and arranging provisions.

WIND AND STORMS

The worst storms occur in the autumn, but some can also appear during the summer. I remember the case of two canoeists who lost their tent in a summer storm, but luckily managed to rig up a shelter from the canoe's sprayhood. Even those who intend to stay only at Longyearbyen Camping should use a high-grade, wind-resistant tent as the campsite is exposed to wind from three directions. Indeed, there is a Frenchman who once used the site as a tent-testing ground for stability against wind.

As with all weather in Svalbard, the wind is variable, both in strength and direction. This is enough of a problem for the hiker, but it can be very serious for the canoeist: journey times are difficult to calculate and crossing fjords, even in a motorboat, becomes very risky with sudden changes of wind speed or direction.

In summer the winds come mostly from the west to north quadrant, with deflections caused by the topography. Katabatic winds are caused by the cooling effect of glaciers. Southerly winds are more typical in winter.

Thunderstorms are practically unknown in the higher Arctic – in my 23 years in Svalbard, I have experienced not a single one.

LIGHT AND DARK With Svalbard being so close to the Pole, both polar day (midnight sun) and polar night are accordingly extreme and one of the defining experiences of travelling to these high latitudes in the right seasons.

The midnight sun begins in Longyearbyen around 20 April and stays until around 22 August. The sun sits amazingly high in a bright blue sky on midsummer nights, even at midnight, with no trace anywhere of the evening atmosphere typical of a Nordkapp view; only a lightmeter would tell you that the light is in fact weaker than during the day. As the archipelago extends over about 800km from north to south, there are local differences in lengths of polar day and polar night depending on the actual northern latitude of your position. Furthermore, all dates stated here or in tables are based on mathematical calculations under the assumption of a free horizon to the south or north, which often is not the case. With mountains in the direction of the horizon, the sun may hide for much longer.

Polar day Even for experienced travellers of Scandinavia, the midnight sun in Svalbard with its full daylight all around the clock in late June or the first part of July is a new experience.

In high summer, the 'nights' can be more alluring than the days. It is strange for a hiker to be active at these times, but the 'night' has its own charms – not least because the weather on average is better and the atmosphere quieter. Alpinists who have good reason to be early risers when in central Europe should change their habits here – they'd do well to have a lie-in in the morning, saving their energies for night-time hiking.

Virtually undiscovered by others, but the favourite season for most Norwegians, is April and early May, with the fascinating combination of still wintry conditions but already permanent light. The polar day starts around 20 April, but even in early April it is already fairly light all night through, allowing outdoor activities around the clock, often with fantastic nuances in light.

Polar night At times even more exotic and certainly just as memorable an experience is the polar night. This begins north of the polar circle in northern Scandinavia for a relatively short period in winter, but on the mainland there is always something of a light dawn around midday – far too bright for observing the faint northern lights. In Svalbard, as with the midnight sun, this is quite different a phenomenon.

The polar night is extant in Longyearbyen from about 28 October to 14 February. During this period, the sun never rises above the horizon. During the first and last parts of the polar night, however, there is a bright dawn at midday, which becomes exponentially shorter every day in November and exponentially longer and brighter every day from early January onwards. During the central period – from around 10 December to early January – it will be truly black night around the clock, with only a very faint dark blueish touch above the southern horizon around midday (presuming the weather is clear). And yet even in the dead middle of the polar night, visibility can be surprisingly good in bright weather – thanks to the clear Arctic air and the reflecting white snow on much of the terrain, which together facilitates shorter hiking excursions by starlight. If the moon is above the horizon, too, the air can be fascinatingly bright with the unique, mild moonlight. The round-the-clock dark sky is also perfect for catching the northern lights. A possibly even more exotic source of at times spectacular, if faint, light is the luminescent clouds in the high atmosphere, which are effectively restricted to high polar regions.

Mathematically speaking, the polar night should end in Longyearbyen in mid-February. But due to high mountains to the south of the town, the sun's rays do not reach much of the settlement before March. As a result, the return of the sun is celebrated here as one of the main annual festivities – Soldagen, or 'day of the sun' – taking place over a whole week around 8 March (by contrast, this same event happens in Tromsø on 21 January). This hearty welcome of the sun should not lead one to think that the locals do not like the dark period. The beginning, with shrinking dawn and very little snow, may be occasionally depressing, but the true permanent night around Christmas and New Year's Eve casts a fascinating spell, followed by the gradual return of the light with often touching faint colours. And then there's the northern lights too. Many locals prefer the polar night to the permanent light of the summer, maintaining that winter is the cosiest and most social period of the year.

The **transition periods** between these two extremes are seasons of fast change: as only about two months pass between the period where the sun never rises and the period when it never sets. During these liminal periods, the days become 20 minutes longer every day between mid-February and 20 April, and accordingly shorter between late August and the end of October.

TEMPERATURES

Winter Though not entirely correct mathematically, the period from late October to the end of April can be regarded in practice as the winter – a period of six months. The first part consists of the three-and-a-half months of the polar night, followed by the late winter with increasingly longer days. Until early January, the winter does not get extremely cold, as the climate table shows (page 16). Extremes may descend to –30°C, but this is rare and does not occur every winter, with temperatures at this time more commonly hovering around –10°C to –20°C. Furthermore, temperatures above freezing occur once or twice within this first part of winter almost every year, sometimes also with some rain.

The second half of winter is different: as the old trappers said, the true cold comes with the return of the light. Accordingly, the coldest period of the year is usually between mid-January and mid-March. Records from that time of the year have shown temperatures as low as –50°C, but these occurrences are from some decades ago – in practice, temperatures under –40°C do not occur every year, while –35°C is not that unusual. Typically, the coldest temperatures occur when there is clear weather and no wind for a longer period.

From late March onwards, the sun gains strength again and extreme cold becomes accordingly rare. In April, still with wintry conditions but already permanent light, typical temperatures fluctuate between –20°C and –5°C.

Spring When defining spring not by the calendar but as a transition season from winter to summer conditions, spring in Svalbard is roughly May to mid-June – basically the period of snowmelt. Temperatures above freezing can also occur in the middle of winter, and in some years, the serious melting of snow may have started by late April, while in others, a largely closed snowcover even in the low valleys may survive until late June – so it is difficult to set fixed dates for these seasons. If temperatures rise suddenly in spring and/or if there was much snow, the snowmelt can be dramatic, changing what was only just previously dry beds of streams and rivers into impassable torrents within half a day.

The start of the serious snowmelt varies considerably. Usually, the area around Longyearbyen is free of snow several weeks earlier than most other parts of the country, partly due to a covering of dust on the snow which leads to less reflection of sunlight and thereby more warming. Most of the dust is spread from the riverbed of the Adventelv, but some also by the local traffic, for instance on the gravel road to Mine 7 and the research installations. In the colder eastern and northern parts of the archipelago, the thaw starts later.

Summer True summer lasts for about two months in central Svalbard, from late June to late August. This is the period where most of the non-glaciated terrain is free of lasting snow and is also the flowering season of the plants. Frost is rare in summer around Isfjorden, particularly in July and the first half of August. At this time typical temperatures in Longyearbyen range from 3°C to 9°C, occasionally reaching highs of around 16°C. In calm conditions sheltered areas can be even warmer. I experienced a high of 23°C in summer 1987, a temperature that may not be welcome for hikers, but does offer the opportunity to sunbathe in the midnight sun. Especially after the end of the midnight-sun period, ie: from 20 August onwards, or before the end of June, you must also reckon on cold spells, perhaps as low as –7°C, accompanied by fresh snow which will settle for a day or two.

In June and July, temperature differences between day and 'night' are minute, due to the polar day.

Autumn For the flora and fauna, autumn begins with the end of the polar day in late August and the return of light frost. From late August to the end of September, frost becomes increasingly frequent, first only at night, then also in day time, but rarely under –10°C. While still not extremely cold, the low temperatures let most rivers and streams gradually dry out and also the slowly freezing terrain becomes easier to walk on in those parts which are boggy or muddy in summer. October, with quickly disappearing daylight, will include colder periods.

SEA ICE The fjord ice develops often only in late winter since the relatively deep water of the fjords needs many months to cool to a sufficiently low temperature. Occasional intrusions of warmer water into the western fjords, which then stays there, may slow this cooling even further. Whether a solid ice layer can develop depends a lot on the winds and currents. If it is windless over a longer period with cold weather, a quickly thickening ice cover, which has a mostly smooth surface, will begin to develop. If disturbed by stronger winds, the developing ice will then be broken up and often blown out of the fjord; or the ice flakes will be pressed above each other, leading to a very rough surface, especially along the coast, where masses of ice can be pushed far up the beach forming chaotic walls. Owing to the tides, the ice cover moves up and down relative to the land, which leads to additional cracks and ice movements along the coasts, making it sometimes difficult to get down on the ice from the land even where there is an otherwise thick and continuous ice cover on a fjord.

Usually, the largest extension of sea ice will be reached in the course of April. It will vary, however, from year to year. Over the last two decades, a year with minimal ice cover of Isfjord by April may include only the inner fjord branches (Tempelfjord, inner Billefjord, Dicksonfjord, Ekmanfjord, Ymerbukta, Trygghamna, inner Grønfjord), while in a year with maximum ice cover, like 1998, nearly the entire inner Isfjord may become covered with a reliable ice layer east of a line between Colesbukta and Erdmannflya in April, with safe ice extending near the coast all the way from Colesbukta to Barentsburg. Obviously, this vast variation of ice cover from year to year makes it difficult to calculate and plan tours long in advance which include passages over fjord ice.

In some fjords, the frequent development of sea ice followed by movement out of the fjord due to wind and currents, is very typical. A famous example among oceanographers is the Storfjord between the main island to the west and Barentsøya and Edgeøya to the east, as this fjord is an important source for the development of heavy deep-sea water, which flows southwards on the bottom of the Atlantic as the counter-current of the Gulf Stream. When sea water freezes, the salt gradually drips out of the developing ice through thin canals in the ice as a concentrated salt solution, travelling into the water underneath and, from there, down to the sea bottom due to its higher density. If a fjord is frequently emptied of fresh ice by wind and current, this process of creation of salt concentrates occurs on a massive scale in the course of a winter, like in Storfjord.

Even in a year with extensive ice cover, the ice in the fjords is not reliable everywhere. Even in the innermost fjord branches like the Tempelfjord, there are a few places which never completely freeze over and which have taken their toll on life. If thin ice is covered by some snow, these danger zones are impossible to spot, so the only safe way of travelling there is with a knowledgeable local guide. Typical locations for such dangerous zones of unreliable fjord ice are above shoals and around narrow fjord passages (also around islands), where tidal water movements cause stronger currents (eg: entrances of Billefjord and Dicksonfjord, or around Akseløya in Van Mijenfjord). While these locations can be sussed out largely by studying the maps, places subject to submarine up-wellings or springs, which weaken the ice, can be significantly more treacherous. In addition, the enormous force of wind on large ice sheets can cause unexpected gaps in an otherwise inviting ice cover. The weight of thicker snow layers on the fjord ice presses the ice underwater somewhat, so that sea water percolates through cracks in the ice into the snow above, creating a soaking wet slush layer above the ice, which is camouflaged by dry snow above. For sledges and skiers, these can be unpleasant areas.

Around the archipelago, the sea ice cover depends largely on the currents and on the wind. Typically, the northern part of the west coast is mostly free of ice on the open sea (except for some open drift ice or occasional ice fields), while the east and north are blocked by heavy drift ice. In extreme ice years like 2003, the drift ice may reach down to all around Bear Island even into summer. In extremely open years, it is possible on the other hand to circumnavigate the complete archipelago, sometimes even including Kvitøya and Kong Karls Land, without seeing virtually any drift ice at all.

The drift ice border may partly retreat in extreme years to 84°N, while in others it may stay as low as just above 80°N all summer.

Much of the ice situation also depends on the winds. As the polar ice cap floats on the Arctic Ocean, it is very susceptible to lasting winds from one direction.

Accordingly, northerly or easterly winds will push it towards the archipelago, sometimes at several knots per hour, while winds from south to southwest will push the ice away.

For more information regarding the importance of the sea currents on the ice distribution, see the discussion of *polynia*, page 193.

These, then, are the extremes. By mid-July, the north coast of the main island is usually free of sea ice and Hinlopen Strait often opens up completely in the second part of July – the critical area being the ice that blocks its southernmost part.

The formation of new sea ice may have started by late September in some sheltered bays and there may be a thicker ice cover in some inner fjord parts in a cold year. But usually the main ice development begins only in January and the maximum is usually reached only in March if not April – both on the fjords and on the open sea around the archipelago.

SEA TIDES Being almost on top of the globe, the gravitational attraction of the moon with its more equatorial orbit around the Earth does not affect the waters around Svalbard as much as in areas of lower latitudes. Typical tidal differences are around 1.2–1.5m, with the extremes extending down to 0.3m and up to 2m. The maximal tide in late spring causes much of the breaking up of the wintry fjord ice.

Although tides are not particularly impressive in figures, they still can create surprising tidal currents in some narrow passages. The most famous of these in Svalbard is in the Heley Sound in the east between the main island and Barentsøya, where the current can reach up to 11km/h and where some boats have been destroyed, especially when driven by the current into some ice stuck in the sound. The narrow passages on both sides of Akseløya, which blocks Van Mijenfjord almost completely at its entrance, can create problems for vessels on account of the strong tidal currents. Therefore, the large ships that ferry coal to and from Sveagruva are allowed to pass only at the breaking points of the current and when accompanied by a tug boat as an additional safety precaution.

PRACTICAL CONSEQUENCES OF THE GEOGRAPHIC CONDITIONS Specific advice for special activities will be given in *Chapter 2, Practical Information*, pages 75–88. Generally speaking, the climate (except for the coldest periods and the extreme seasonality of light) is not significantly different from the conditions above the treeline in many other cold, mountainous regions of the world.

However, exposure might be a more crucial aspect: Svalbard is basically all wilderness – once you leave the settlement (almost always Longyearbyen) or the ship, there is no other shelter except for your tent, and no place for warming up. It is therefore important to take a lot of care so that you don't waste body warmth – both by avoiding freezing and also by avoiding getting too warm, as sweat can freeze too. This requires the careful and repeated adaptation of clothing to the actual climatic conditions and the changing degree of physical activity.

As for clothing, special attention in all seasons should be given to the issue of wind protection – loss of warmth due to strong wind is much more relevant than the actual temperature. Wind protection includes not only a suitable anorak, but also protection for the legs, hands and head (including eyes and nose). Wind protection should be provided by a windproof thin outer layer (usually at the same time as protection against rain), which should be permeable to allow any humidity inside to escape. Wind-protective clothing should not be particularly warm to avoid sweating – instead, wear additional warm clothes underneath for low temperatures or low activity.

Another aspect with regard to clothing is whether it is easily adaptable to take into account the changing conditions – overalls can be impractical when it comes to going to the toilet or when wanting to quickly change some of the clothes being worn underneath them. In summer, the main answer to permafrost and its swampy or muddy areas, as well as the many streams, is rubber boots, the most versatile footwear, possibly supplemented by sturdy hiking boots. We will examine these issues in the *What to take* section on pages 105–18.

HISTORY

INDIGENOUS POPULATION In contrast to other similar regions, Svalbard has no indigenous population. There is still a big question mark regarding the possibility of pre-1596 human activity in the archipelago, as there is regarding the links between the exploration of the archipelago (and other Arctic regions) and climate change. Climatic research shows increasingly that the conditions in the High Arctic were considerably milder than today for most of the time since the last ice age (warmer, less ice), but cooled down markedly from around AD500, with the harshest conditions since the ice age taking place in the first half of the 19th century, leading to a corresponding increase of ice cover on both sea and land. Therefore, early visitors, possibly up until the 17th century, may have been less hindered by ice and found more comfortable conditions, facilitating early exploration and exploitation. In contrast, navigation was especially hindered by ice in the 19th and even early 20th centuries, thus contributing to the many failures and tragedies. Then again, the warming and retreat of the ice since the middle of the 19th century made remote Arctic areas gradually more accessible, which, together with technological advances, supported the modern exploration of these areas. Combining research on climate change with that of polar history will only lead to new understandings of both.

DISCOVERY Regarding the first humans to set foot on the archipelago, there are a number of possibilities:

Stone Age It is not known whether there were Stone-Age settlements similar to those on the Scandinavian mainland. Owing to the considerably milder climate with an accordingly richer fauna and flora in the period from about 6500BC to AD500, a Stone-Age population would not be inconceivable, but it is possible that the remote archipelago simply went undiscovered by the seafarers of that time. A thorough examination around the year 2000 of a number of obviously suitable sites for a Stone-Age population on Spitsbergen led to no positive findings.

The next possible candidates for an early discovery of Svalbard are the Vikings and the Pomors.

Vikings In an entry from the Icelandic annals in 1194 (and in some later ones as well), there is a reference to *Svalbard fundinn* ('Svalbard found' in Old Icelandic; see page IX) giving a vague distance in (sailing) days. However, so far, there have been no archaeological findings whatsoever from Svalbard that can be related to a Viking presence. As late as 2001, the optimistic excavation of a structure that looked like a typical Viking burial mound led to no findings. As good navigators with reliable vessels, the Vikings were certainly capable of reaching the archipelago but any substantial empirical proof is lacking and today the area in the North Atlantic to which the Old Norse name *Svalbard* actually refers is unknown – though it might be the 'cold coast' of Greenland, four days' sailing northeast from Langanes in Iceland.

Nevertheless, this discovery by the Vikings, once eagerly maintained by Norwegian nationalistic circles as being definitively Svalbard, is still suggested in many Norwegian (and international) publications to be 'fact' instead of mere possibility.

Pomors Russian archaeologists maintain that sailors from the White Sea, the so-called 'Pomors' (Sea People), reached Svalbard by the 16th century at the very latest, and perhaps even before any possible Viking arrival, making use of the land for commercial hunting. There are a number of vague passages in several written sources which may be interpreted this way. More importantly, though, there are archaeological findings from old Russian settlements in Svalbard, which appear to date from the 16th century. A number of them can be seen in the interesting Pomor Museum in Barentsburg. Non-Russian historians remain sceptical: in the oldest Western reports from Svalbard voyages, some of which are very detailed, there is no mention of any Russian settlements there, while from roughly the late 17th century onwards, there are numerous Western quotations regarding Russian activity in Svalbard. One thing is for certain, however: the Pomors were the first regular winterers on the islands, even if the date of their first arrival is still a mystery.

The Dutch With no definitive evidence of either the Vikings or the Pomors ever having landed on the islands, the honour of the official discovery of the archipelago has been given to the third Dutch expedition sent out to sail around the north of Eurasia in search of a shorter way (than the route around Africa) to the important markets of east Asia. All the way into the 19th century there was a strong belief that the area around the North Pole was ice free, surrounded only by a massive ice belt, the challenge therefore being to find a passage through this hindrance. Seen against the background of our modern knowledge, these ambitions were bound to fail, and duly did: for instance the previous two Dutch expeditions, which met the ice borders already in the Barents Sea and Kara Sea. Had the various monarchs and heads of trade companies of that time known the real character of the Arctic Ocean, they would hardly have sponsored any of the early expeditions, which were effectively driven solely by economic and strategic interests – not benevolent or adventuresome ones.

The third Dutch expedition in 1596, again under Willem Barents, sailed north across the sea that later became named after him. On their way they discovered and drew the first maps of 'Beeren Eylandt' – Bear Island – which they named after an encounter with a polar bear there, then the west coast of Spitsbergen ('pointed peaks', as they named it for the dramatic mountain scenery they found) all the way up to the northwest corner. Stopped in his tracks by the ice, Barents turned east and his ship was crushed by the ice in the north of Novaya Zemlya, where they had to winter. Barents died there, but the surviving crew members and the results of their expedition were rescued the following year. Though this expedition was a failure regarding the original purpose of finding a new route to China, it brought information about seemingly inexhaustible stocks of whale, walrus and seals back to Europe. The following English exploratory expeditions to Svalbard, equipped by The Muscovy Company and led by Henry Hudson (1607), Stephen Bennet (1609) and Jonas Poole (1610), did much the same. Significantly, the Dutch with probably the best-documented proof about their discovery, never saw much reason to enter the Norwegian–Russian nationalistic quarrels about the first discovery.

THE PERIOD OF WHALING AND HUNTING The first human activities in the archipelago were directed at making use of the biological resources, especially the various sea and land mammals. This period had its peak in the 17th century with international whaling in summer as well as land-based hunting and trapping – practices that continue (albeit on a very limited scale) to this day.

Whaling The discovery of this seemingly unlimited supply of marine mammals coincided with the rise in demand in mainland Europe for whale and walrus products. These products comprise oil from the processed fat (which has a wide range of uses from soap production to fuel for lamps and the waterproofing of clothes, known as 'oilskins'), tusk ivory, the thick leather skin of the walrus and the huge bones of whales, with the leather and bones used as enduring construction materials. Furthermore, from the late 17th century various uses for the elastic baleen were found. Already from 1603 onwards, annual English hunting expeditions had started under Bennet to Bear Island (then also called Cherry Island after Sir Cherry), with mass slaughters of more than 600 animals per expedition not uncommon.

The necessary skills for hunting the much bigger whales were at that time known only to the Basques. They therefore played a key role as experts in expeditions in and around Svalbard from 1611 onwards by The Muscovy Company, soon followed by fleets from Holland (sent out from 1614 onwards by the joint trading company Noordsche Compagnie which consisted of merchants from several Dutch cities), France, Denmark, Germany and others. Quarrels and fighting, including even sea battles, were a natural consequence because of the limited hunting grounds and harbours in Svalbard. But they were also highly damaging to this profitable trade, so that the involved parties preferred compromise to conflict, dividing up the suitable bays and areas between them.

In the first decades, whaling took place largely in the fjords and coastal seas, facilitated by the incredible abundance of the slow and easy-to-hunt Greenland whale (which was thus also simply called 'right whale').

Once sighted, the whale would be tracked and harpooned by rowing boat. There were many human casualties. Dead whales were towed ashore, a task which became more difficult as their coastal numbers diminished. Shore processing stations carved up the whale and reduced the fat to blubber by boiling it in big ovens (a Greenland right whale could produce up to 100 tonnes).

Access to the west coast was easier and it was here where most stations were located. Names like Amsterdamøya, Danskøya, Hamburgbukta and Engelskbukta indicate which countries had stations here. The Dutch station of Smeerenburg ('Blubber Town') is probably the best known and biggest, founded at Amsterdamøya in 1619. As is the case with many lost cities, fables tell of 10,000 men, women and children plus a church, a bordello and a bar. Archaeological excavations have uncovered that the town was abandoned already at the end of the 17th century, after less than 100 years of existence. Well-preserved remains indicate a maximum of seven blubber boilers and a settlement of 16 or 17 houses, enough for several hundred men and quite large for Svalbard even in today's terms. Danish–Norwegian excavations on neighbouring Danskøya are also compelling anthropologically, remaining well preserved thanks to the Arctic climate and giving a fascinating insight into the everyday life of the time. In particular, clothes have been found that are practically the only extant 17th-century mariners' working garments in Europe. However, the stations were merely in use in summer and deserted when the ships returned south at the end of the season. From the entire period of whaling in the 17th century, only two winterings are reported. One was an unintentional but successful wintering in 1630 by seven English whalers who were left behind from an expedition, while the second wintering was by a group originally sent to guard against the possible plundering of a base and ended in the death by scurvy of all participants.

The supposed inexhaustibility of the whale stocks turned out to be a myth. First the fjords were depleted, forcing the ships further and further out onto the ocean. Eventually it made no sense anymore to tow the killed whales over longer and longer distances to the processing stations on land and the processing was done on board instead, which was highly dangerous in view of the big blubber ovens needed on a wooden ship. This meant the end of the land stations by the end of the 17th century. Nevertheless, the traditional landing sites were later used by whalers who still continued their business out on the open sea, but who came ashore to fill up their water reserves, bury their dead (in some places on Spitsbergen there are more than 100 whaler graves in one site) and to supplement their provisions with some fresh meat from reindeer and birds. Occasionally they also collected coal from the long-known open coal seams of Svalbard to fire the pantry stoves on the ships.

To date, the stocks of the big whale species have not recovered from the over-exploitation of the 17th century and, to a somewhat lesser extent, the hunting out on the open sea which continued into the second half of the 20th century. Renewed attempts at a whaling industry around Svalbard (Grønfjord and Trygghamna) at the beginning of the 20th century failed after a few years due to lack of sufficient stocks. The present limited Norwegian whale hunt near Svalbard by vessels from the Norwegian mainland focuses on a small quota of minke whales (out of a national quota of 400–600 annually). This much smaller species is nevertheless the one at the centre of the current international whaling debate. The Greenland right whale is almost extinct; sightings in the North Atlantic are rare, though a small population seems to have survived near Franz Josef Land. The near-extinction of the big whale species has resulted in ecological changes. With the disappearance of these huge consumers of plankton, other animals took over their position, namely auk species, which during the 17th century lived in the area in much smaller numbers due to food competition by the whales.

Traces of the 400-year-old slaughter – both whales and walrus – are to be found on just about every coast in Svalbard, with vertebrae and ribs lying on the shore, although some of these deaths were, of course, from natural causes.

Barents believed Svalbard to be part of Greenland, which was why Denmark asserted its sovereignty over the new territory. But within a few decades of Barents' discovery the whalers had charted the waters of most of the archipelago with astonishing accuracy, as evidenced by a map from 1625. This is even more remarkable as they depended not only on fragile sailing vessels in contrast to the powerful ice-strengthened ships available for exploration today, but also faced ice conditions that on average were more severe than today. A great deal of the whalers' knowledge was lost forever when whaling ceased, since many captains kept their knowledge to themselves instead of contributing to better maps, which would have been an invitation to competitors.

The hunters and trappers Just as the first recorded period of Svalbard's history was characterised by ship-based seasonal whaling, the next was typified by land-based wintering hunters. Their activities – apart from that of early Pomor hunters – had begun during the height of the whaling period and have not completely come to an end; there are two trappers who still manage to eke out an existence in Svalbard. Since walrus, polar bear and reindeer have become widely protected, this tough profession has become even more difficult.

The first known non-Russian overwintering in Svalbard arrived in 1630 when an English party was surprised by the ice and unable to sail south. The log is an impressive record of unwilling pioneering. Generally, the main problem was a lack of vitamins, from which many lost their lives. (The causes of scurvy had not yet been recognised.)

The arrival of the Russians in Svalbard remains a largely unsolved mystery. Dendrochronological datings from several excavated early Russian hunting bases led to a felling date of the trees used in their construction somewhere in the mid 16th century, a period confirmed by some inscriptions – though this still leaves the possibility that all these items were brought to Svalbard later. Some written sources about Russian activity in the north seem to refer to Svalbard, too, although with some uncertainty. The first definitive date of a Russian visit dates from 1697, but the records are written in such a way that they suggest that this was not the first visit.

If Russia participated in whaling at all, its share was marginal. Rather, Russians continued their long tradition of terrestrial hunting in Svalbard, focusing on the fur hunt, which required winterings. Usually, the expeditions were outfitted and sent by Russian monasteries and trade companies, often from the White Sea area. The population there, called Pomors (see page 27) maintained an ancient tradition of Arctic seafaring with sturdy vessels. Typically, the group based themselves in a main station with several smaller satellites nearby. The leader would frequently have been a representative of the monastery or the trading company and the hunters were (ideally) recruited from northern Siberia where they would already have had experience of polar winters. As well as hunting for their own food and furs, prey often consisted largely of polar fox and polar bear for pelts; reindeer were also taken and eider down collected. When the opportunity arose, they also took walrus and seals.

According to contemporary illustrations, landmark crosses, which marked graveyards and served as nautical orientation marks, were characteristic of such stations. It seems that the stations were used for a couple of years and then left empty, presumably due to overhunting in the immediate vicinity, before the hunters returned to the same area some decades later after the stocks had recovered. Remains of these stations are found all over the archipelago, even in the northeast.

The Russians abandoned Svalbard in the 1820s, moving instead further east within their own homeland as Siberia was gradually opened up. The last Russian monk in Svalbard, Starostin, died in 1826, having spent 39 winters there. For at least one – possibly even two – centuries, Russians were the only people who lived in Svalbard permanently, all year round.

Norwegian hunters first attemped to winter in 1778. Later, in 1823, during another well-known early attempt by the Norwegians, Hammerfesthuset on Bear Island (Bjørnøya), was established and remains the oldest extant building on the archipelago. In the 19th century, most Norwegian hunting carried out in the area was ship-based, with an emphasis on walrus, polar bears and seals, and was therefore restricted solely to the summer. Only from 1892 onwards did Norwegian winterings become customary, and occasionally entire families would stay.

The tradition of hunting and trapping as both the foundation for an economy and a way of life ended in the 1970s with the total ban of polar bear hunting and the installation of huge national parks and nature reserves, covering what was then 60% of the land area of the archipelago. By that time, however, hunting was already on the wane with many trappers forced into taking on an additional job, for instance in the mines, during the summer months. Nevertheless, for the traditional trapper in Svalbard hunting was a way of earning a very modest living, which, though meagre, was better than the dire poverty they faced back home in northern Norway, where other work was often difficult to find.

Hunting and trapping are to some extent protected by the Spitsbergen Treaty, which prevents a complete ban on these activities, as means of utilising the natural resources of the archipelago. The few trappers left today choose to do so mostly not on economic grounds, but as a lifestyle choice; a break for a year or two before they do their usual jobs. The sole trapper still earning most of his income by using the resources of nature has specialised in collecting and cleaning down. Generally, trapper life today is radically different from the lives of their predecessors, who depended entirely on income from such work.

POLAR EXPLORATION AND RESEARCH Svalbard is a classic area of polar research with a long tradition (at least since Barents arrived in 1596) and a broad spectrum: reasons for visits range from practical undertakings (formerly hunting, now oil) to pure science, through to flag-waving exploration and tourism. All these have contributed to our knowledge of the islands, and continue to do so.

The beginning of scientific work in the archipelago is usually seen in the published observations of ship doctor Martens from Hamburg in 1671, followed by two Russian expeditions in 1764 and 1766 (aimed at investigating the possibilities of a colony), and then of course the early British expeditions of Phipps (1773, young Nelson almost being killed by a polar bear), Scoresby (1806), Franklin (1818), Sabine (1823) and Parry (1827), who tried to reach the North Pole as part of the continuing interest in finding a northern sea route and who also explored, on their way, parts of the northern shores. Norwegians frequently mark the beginning of their exploration activities with the private expedition of the German Barto von Löwenigh, who invited the Norwegian scientist Keilhau on his tour to Svalbard.

From the 1860s onwards, Swedes dominated exploration and research in and around Svalbard for two or three decades, their most important names still being found as place names on the maps: names such as De Geer, Heer, Nathorst, Nordenskiöld, Torell and others.

In 1873, the first year-long scientific expedition, led by Swedish-Finnish Nordenskiöld, drove sleds across Nordaustlandet and explored many parts of the coast, having their well-equipped wintering base in Sorgfjord. From 1882 the Swedes De Geer and Nathorst investigated the geology of large parts of the archipelago. Important knowledge was gained by the joint Russian–Swedish expedition of 1898–1901 which surveyed the main island from Sorgbukta in the north to Hornsundet in the south as an important part of figuring out the true shape of the Earth by measuring as exactly as possible an Arctic part of a meridian. This undertaking, and the first crossing of central Spitsbergen by Conway in 1896 (later the author of the Svalbard classic *No Man's Land* and other related publications), were the first to discover that the interior was not fully ice-covered, but rather divided into mountain ranges. They also found the two highest peaks (1,713m and 1,712m) and, more importantly, laid many survey points as a future reference grid. Winter months were used for the collection of weather data.

In the northwest the seas were studied by Prince Albert of Monaco on his yacht *Alice*, while the land was researched by the Norwegian Isachsen. Bruce, from Scotland, went to Prins Karls Forlandet and various areas around Isfjorden and southern Spitsbergen.

A great many of these explorers also left their mark in geographical place names, giving maps of the area a characteristically international flavour.

A peculiarity of Svalbard is its important role as a springboard for attempts towards the North Pole. Until long into the 19th century, there was a mythical strong belief in an ice-free inner Arctic Ocean, which of course would have been highly attractive as an easy sea route from Europe to the Pacific. While this myth lost its believers the more and further man got north without finding anything but ever-thicker ice, reaching the Pole in itself also gained attractiveness as a feat in a period of increasing nationalistic competition, even though the scientific value of reaching it was marginal. Favoured by the Gulf Stream, Svalbard in the far north was an ideal starting point for such endeavours. While until 1894 (Wellman's RAGNVALD expedition) these attempts from Spitsbergen were by ship and partly sledges in addition, the new means of transport for the quest to the Pole from 1896 onwards was aircraft. This was the period of the well-known public polar heroes, their tragic or triumphant stories so often told that I mention them here only in keywords:

- **Andrée** (Sweden) and his crew 1896–97 by balloon from Virgohamna on Danskøya, crashing on the ice and finally dying on Kvitøya. It took until 2000 for a balloon to successfully fly from Spitsbergen to the Pole and back (David Hempleman-Adams).
- **Wellman** (USA) 1906, 1907, 1909 by airships from Virgohamna on Danskøya, failed due to various technical problems encountered either before or soon after departing.
- **Amundsen** (Norway and others) 1925 by sea planes from Ny-Ålesund, technical failure at 88 degrees northern latitude, but managed to return.
- **Byrd** (USA) 1926 by plane from Ny-Ålesund towards the Pole (today it is doubted that he actually flew over the Pole) and safely back.
- **Amundsen/Nobile/Ellsworth** (Norway/Italy/USA) 1926 – successful flight in airship *Norge* over the Pole and crash landing in Alaska.
- **Wilkins/Eielson** (USA) 1928 – Vega plane flight from Barrow/Alaska to Svalbard, masterly snowstorm landing on the north side of Isfjord entrance, finally flying on to nearby Grønfjord.
- **Nobile** (Italy) 1928 – successful flight in airship *Italia* to the Pole and survey of huge new areas of the Arctic Ocean as planned, but tragic crash on the ice on the way back, causing an enormous international rescue operation including the death of Amundsen and his pilot.

When adding further early aircraft expeditions within Svalbard (1923 Junkers aircraft were used for the first extensive aerial photography of the archipelago; 1924 air reconnaissance and photography by an Oxford expedition), it is obvious that the archipelago had an unchallenged key role in the development of early High Arctic aviation as a means of exploration.

These pioneer flights were the start of Ny-Ålesund's importance as a centre for polar research. Its accessibility from the sea is unrivalled by any other place at the same northern latitude.

A considerable part of our knowledge about Svalbard is not based on the results of pure science, but as a side effect of economic interests. This begins with the first exploration and cartography of most of the coasts by the old whalers. A second boom of industrial exploration started in the 19th century, often alongside national interests as adventurers and companies (including large state-funded expeditions) examined practically all coastal areas at least of the main island and Bear Island (Bjørnøya) endeavouring to find valuable mineral resources, and at the same time significantly improving geological knowledge. The state-funded expeditions could possibly lead to the establishment of mining activities by companies of the sponsoring country, which in turn would improve the influence of that country in the archipelago. One of many examples is 'Svenskehuset' (the Swedish House) on

Kapp Thordsen in Isfjord, the oldest extant building on the main island, erected by a Swedish company in 1872 to exploit the phosphate deposits discovered and claimed there by countryman Nordenskiöld in 1864. This fruitful interaction between scientific research and economic and political interests continues today.

As a result of success in sovereignty negotiations over Svalbard, Norway set up a permanent research institution in 1928, then called Norges Svalbard og Ishavsundersøkelser (Norwegian Svalbard and Polar Sea Survey), later renamed to its more convenient present moniker, Norsk Polarinstitutt. This was without doubt of far more importance to the Arctic than spectacular stunts. The institute, originally based in Oslo but now in Tromsø, was given a central role for co-ordinating research in Svalbard.

Following the period of 'heroic' exploration, from the 1930s onwards Svalbard itself and the surrounding waters came into focus again with a shift towards scientific research. Apart from the Norwegian research activities, this period included some major British expeditions (especially by the universities of Cambridge and Oxford), for instance to the inner parts of scarcely known Nordaustlandet (Northeast Land), the second-biggest island.

World War II caused a virtual cessation of scientific work, though some of the military parties, for instance at the weather stations (often manned with scientists in military service), did some research work that exceeded pure meteorological observations.

Research today Though the adventurous days of polar exploration are gone, Svalbard today is probably the most important area of Arctic research, thanks at least in part to its easy accessibility. Fully independent permanent research bases are run today by Norway (Ny-Ålesund, Longyearbyen and, for meteorology, Hopen, Bear Island and Sveagruva), Russia (currently only in Barentsburg) and Poland (Hornsund), which are described in more detail in *Chapter 6, Svalbard's Settlements and Stations*. In these 'settlements and stations' a number of other countries also maintain a presence with their own permanent facilities including China, Korea, France, Germany, Great Britain, Italy, Japan and the USA. Classic research topics like cartography, geology, botany, zoology, meteorology and archaeology are undertaken up here, but have been surpassed in importance by atmosphere and climate research as an interdisciplinary focus with contributions by geophysicists, oceanographists, glaciologists, geomorphologists and others, supported by and depending on advanced mathematical modelling and amazing high-tech equipment. Despite being at the edge of civilisation, much of modern polar research happens in sophisticated computerised laboratories in Svalbard. Since the 1990s, a fascinating array of large-scale technical research facilities has been installed, including the precision geodetic radiotelescope and laser and radar atmospheric research installations in Ny-Ålesund, the huge international atmospheric research radar telescopes of EISCAT near Longyearbyen, and the English and German transmitters and 'antenna forests' used for atmospheric research. Furthermore, our knowledge of marine biology will increase further with the marine biological laboratory in Ny-Ålesund (opened in June 2005). These pure research activities are supplemented by UNIS in Longyearbyen, the joint educational and research facility of four Norwegian universities with a present capacity of about 100 students of Arctic sciences. The Norsk Polarinstitutt is also present with its own facilities both in Longyearbyen and in Ny-Ålesund and has a co-ordination function for the various international research activities in Svalbard.

Also related to research is SVALSAT with their huge, antennae-studded 'golf balls' on the plateau above Longyearbyen. Data from satellites which circle the Earth on polar orbits can be read down here from each of the 12–13 circuits each satellite performs every day as they fly over the North Pole area, whereas those stations that lie closer to the Equator receive information only two or three times per day. Accordingly, data read down in Svalbard is available more regularly and thereby on average quicker (important for 'real-time' modelling such as those models used in weather forecasts). This has been the incentive for the big players in this business like NASA, NOAA or ESA to invest heavily in this ground station. A bottleneck had been caused when the information from the station was sent to users worldwide, because re-transmission of this rapidly growing mass of data involved beaming everything up to communication satellites above the Equator for redistribution. The limited capacity of this satellite link limited the further growth of SVALSAT. Therefore, the main users financed two parallel telecommunications glass-fibre cables between Svalbard and the Norwegian mainland with a capacity of 20 gigabytes per second each, which were put in use in early 2004. This has revolutionised the data facilities of Longyearbyen with more than enough capacity for the foreseeable future and at the same time with no more disturbances from cosmic radiation, which was a frequent problem of the satellite line. It is likely this cable will cause a further boom of new scientific activities that depend on safe and generous data links, and also for the establishment of new other activities in Longyearbyen (see the *Longyearbyen* section in *Svalbard's Settlements and Stations*, pages 159–72).

In spite of all this technology, classic fieldwork still exists, particularly in the fields of climate change reconstruction, the modelling of the current local climate, glaciers, erosion, development and change of ecosystems and much else besides. All of these subjects depend on lots of data and probes to be collected out in the wilderness.

As with the classic period, much of modern research in Svalbard is not pure science but closely related to economic and political interests. The search for exploitable mineral resources continues right to the present day, with oil, gas, coal and even gold recently discovered north of Kongsfjord. Deep drilling, especially for oil, started in the 1960s in Svalbard and even though some of the results were withheld due to competition between the companies, these expensive drilling programmes, like later seismic shootings, contributed a lot to the knowledge about the geological structures deep under the surface. From a broader perspective, even much of the seemingly 'pure' science of today is economically and politically motivated – countries often will sponsor expensive polar research in order that they can be present in these regions and thereby increase their influence. Even the subjects that nations choose to study are highly political – presently, climate-related research is extremely popular since global warming and other slogans sell well. It is easier to acquire funds for scientific projects if they are in line with this trend, and politicians can boast more easily with support for such issues, while other fields of research are less popular for the moment. Currently, research has become a field of international competition in Svalbard, as was the case with the previous jostling for mineral resources. Connected with the increase in research activity is the growing conflict between research and protection of the environment or between research and mining or tourism. Research has become one of the major local impact factors on land. Since the 1990s, several times as much terrain has been destroyed for research facilities and access roads, partly in plant reserves, than by tourism in more than 100 years. Research is a major customer of the coal-fired power plants in Longyearbyen and Barentsburg and – together with the Norwegian administration – the biggest user of helicopters, also in the protected areas. Along with fishing, tourism and administration, research vessels account for much of the ship traffic in the remotest and most sensitive parts of the archipelago. Compared with tourism, environmental regulations and restrictions for research are marginal, not least due to the traditional dogma of the freedom of science. For nature, however, this dogma helps little when it comes to real-world impacts.

ECONOMIC DEVELOPMENT AND SOVEREIGNTY FROM 1900 Until the end of the 19th century, Svalbard's economic importance was based exclusively on hunting commodities such as blubber, ivory, fox pelts, polar bear furs, seal products, down and eggs, among other products. Territorial disputes had been resolved by dividing the area first between the competing whaling countries and companies, and later for the hunting and trapping on land, by the gradual development of a generally accepted system of defined hunting grounds. From the time of discovery onwards, Denmark had a vague claim to Svalbard on the grounds that it was considered to be a part of Greenland, ostensibly connected by some supposed land bridge far up in the north. However, since quarrels could be settled mostly between the parties involved and as the area was huge in relation to the few hunters, there was no apparent need to change the status of the remote archipelago from being a de facto no-man's-land – even if the riches to be gained there were, in theory at least, unlimited.

This changed in the middle of the 19th century, when the industrialisation of Europe increased the need for mineral resources and the subsequent introduction of steam engines and later steel-hulled ships vastly improved the possibilities of navigation, even in partly iced-over waters. The deposits of coal and some other minerals in Svalbard thus became more attractive, sparking Sweden and other countries to increase their research activities in the archipelago.

The commercial exploitation of natural resource deposits began in the 1890s with coal. The year 1899 is regarded as the beginning of coal mining in Svalbard, when the first shipload of coal from a Norwegian pit on Bohemanflya was sent to Norway. Naturally, this new interest in mineral resources of the largely unexplored archipelago – only the coastlines had really been mapped at this point – invited a wide range of pioneers from Germany, Great Britain, Norway, Russia, Sweden and the USA, from individual adventurers to financially better-equipped companies. As in other pioneer countries, claims were marked with signs where any riches were found, often generously encompassing vast areas around them as well, and soon after reported to the appropriate institutions of the home country. Not surprisingly, this activity soon led to quarrels due to competing or overlapping claims to the same areas, and with no central 'claims' register to speak of, many optimistic entrepreneurs soon found out that it takes more than just a few claim poles to become rich. In some cases, company wars over disputed claims were avoidable by seeking help through the diplomatic channels of the home countries. In the long run, however, this situation was unacceptable and called for the installation of a legal framework, most naturally by extending the sovereignty of a suitable country to the archipelago. However, at first no country was particularly interested due to the expected costs of administering such a territory, while at the same time care was taken to secure exploitation rights. It took until 1920 to solve the Svalbard question, delayed to no small effect by World War I and the Russian Revolution.

In the meantime, a few major players appeared in Svalbard, established and enforced their claims and bought up others. Most important and successful among them was the Boston-based John Munro Longyear who, having founded the Arctic Coal Company together with his partner Ayer, established the mining settlement of Longyear City in 1906, which grew to become the main settlement of the archipelago. Other bigger companies established themselves in Grumant (1913–20,

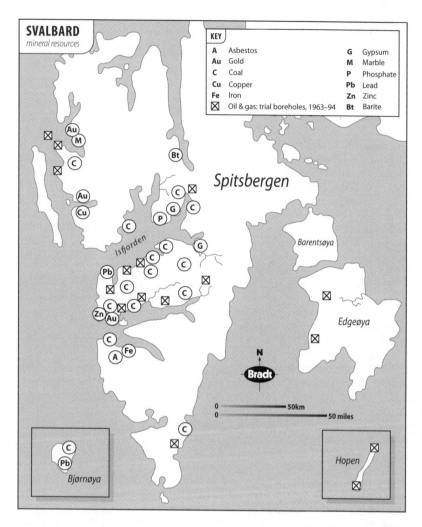

SVALBARD
mineral resources

KEY

A	Asbestos	G	Gypsum
Au	Gold	M	Marble
C	Coal	P	Phosphate
Cu	Copper	Pb	Lead
Fe	Iron	Zn	Zinc
⊠	Oil & gas: trial boreholes, 1963–94	Bt	Barite

Spitsbergen

Isfjorden

Barentsøya

Edgeøya

N

Bradt

0 ⸺ 50km
0 ⸺ 50 miles

Bjørnøya

Hopen

British–Russian), Ny-Ålesund (1916, Norwegian), Tunheim (1916, Norwegian), Sveagruva (1917, Swedish), Hiorthamn (1917, Norwegian), Barentsburg (1920, Dutch). In most cases, the involved companies were backed diplomatically (and in many cases financially as well) by their home governments.

Apart from coal, mining was also undertaken to try to extract asbestos, copper, gold, gypsum, iron, lead, marble and zinc. But not all mining ventures were successful. Maybe the largest gap between expectations and results was 'achieved' by the Northern Exploration Company (NEC) with Ernest Mansfield from Essex as the main actor. Between 1905 and 1926, the company embarked upon exploratory mining activities and claimed a large number of land areas. In 1927, approval was obtained for 16, with a combined total area of 655.3km², the biggest private land property of the archipelago. However, none of the pits, quarries and shafts got much further than the initial exploratory stage for various reasons, the most famous being the marble quarry of NEC on Blomstrand Island in Kongsfjord with its tiny settlement ambitiously named 'New London'. In 1929, NEC was practically bankrupt and in 1932, its huge land properties, 58 buildings and 34 mining claims spread over Svalbard were bought by the Norwegian state for NOK100,000.

During World War I, Svalbard gained strategic importance thanks to its coal deposits, as Norway could no longer rely on coal supplies from central Europe and Britain. This increased the interest of formerly wary Norway in the archipelago and led to the purchase of Longyear City from the Americans in 1916. In connection with the peace treaty of Versailles, negotiations on Svalbard were taken up again. With the USA having been bought out, Germany defeated, Russia seen as a pariah due to its new revolutionary regime and the Western Allies grateful for the support from the Norwegian merchant fleet, Norway was in a strong position. They could also point to some heavy involvement in the archipelago at that time with regular coal mining in Longyearbyen, Ny-Ålesund and Tunheim (Bear Island), the operation of the only telegraph station, Svalbard Radio, plus postal steamer services. In 1920, 'The Treaty concerning the Archipelago of Spitsbergen' was signed and came into force in 1925. Signed today by 52 countries, this treaty has so far proved remarkably enduring and has led to a unique legal status for the (now-named) Svalbard Archipelago due to its main principles:

Demilitarised zone Permanent military installations are blanketly forbidden across Svalbard. Occasionally, Norwegian navy vessels show the flag, though they are not based there, and the Norwegian Air Force supports the administration with some supply flights plus assistance for the rescue service. Military crafts of other nations are usually denied access, except for a few exceptions which cover research vessels or planes. So far, this demilitarised status has been violated openly only during World War II (by both the Allied/Norwegian and the German forces) and secretly during the Cold War, when the Soviet Union maintained some camouflaged special forces based in Barentsburg.

Non-discrimination Norway must treat all citizens of all treaty nations equally in Svalbard. Norway may set up laws applicable for Svalbard, but only if these do not lead to the discrimination of citizens of certain treaty nations. This rule has had some important consequences, for instance the Russian presence in Svalbard, which is part of a NATO country, during the Cold War. Until the 1980s, very few laws were introduced for Svalbard and, despite the adoption of many Norwegian laws by the archipelago, any attempts by Norway to actively promote the 'Norwegianisation' of the islands is generally frowned upon by the other nations present.

Low taxation Norway may not claim more taxes than what is duly required for the necessary administration of the archipelago, and no taxation income may be transferred away from the archipelago. In practice, this leads to a very low taxation as well as the quick development of an excellent infrastructure (eg: the new telecommunications sea cable). The Spitsbergen Treaty provides the framework for the archipelago's unique international status, as well as Norway's sovereignty. All land claims – often competing – were sorted out during the signing of the treaty, with those areas not claimed by anybody falling by default to the Norwegian state. In addition, the Spitsbergen Treaty was supplemented by the Code of Mining, which regulates matters around mining in the area.

Following the official incorporation of Svalbard into the Kingdom of Norway in 1925, the permanent presence of other nations gradually declined. Norway adopted a policy of gradually buying up foreign properties in Svalbard, when favourable opportunities arose, such as when companies ended up in dire economic straits.

At that time, not yet being one of the richer nations of Europe, Norway was not initially willing to invest much into such purchases. This attitude changed when the Soviet Union bought Barentsburg from the Dutch mining company NeSpiCo, which got into economic difficulty in the late 1920s, and Pyramiden from a Swedish company. Within a few short years the Russian properties in Svalbard had increased from one (Grumant/Colesbukta) to four (including Barentsburg, Pyramiden and Erdmanflya). This convinced the Norwegian government to buy up the Swedish-owned settlement of Sveagruva so as to avoid any further increase in the Soviets' presence on the archipelago, as well as the properties of the British NEC.

Despite various short-lived attempts with other minerals, coal turned out to be the only viable mining industry. All settlements of today – Longyearbyen, Barentsburg, Ny-Ålesund and currently evacuated Pyramiden, as well as Grumant/Colesbukta were founded as coal-mining towns. Their individual histories will be dealt with in *Chapter 6, Svalbard's Settlements and Stations*. From the 1930s onwards, only Norway and Soviet Russia were running their own settlements and mines on the archipelago – all other properties held by individuals or companies from other countries having been bought up by then. With just three different landowners over the entire territory (the Norwegian state, the Russian state-owned mining company Trust Arcticugol and, the only private landowner, one Norwegian family who owned a huge area on the east side of Adventfjord), nobody was willing to sell land and accordingly, no properties could be bought.

On the Norwegian side at least, coal mining in Svalbard proved to be profitable for the first few decades owing to the energy demand of northern Norway. For Russia, too, it was easier to bring coal from Svalbard to Murmansk and Archangel than all the way from their own coalfields in the Donez area. Whether this justified the extent of the Russian presence in the archipelago is another matter.

WORLD WAR II With Germany's attack on Poland and the invasion of Norway in 1940, Svalbard's development reached a sudden turning point. While Norway became occupied, Svalbard was spared, and while Norwegian and Soviet mines continued to operate, there was a great deal of anxiety.

The situation changed in 1941 with the German attack on the Soviet Union. Svalbard acquired strategic significance for convoys running south of the archipelago through the Barents Sea to Murmansk. It was possible that fighting would reach the area and the Norwegian government-in-exile agreed to the evacuation of Svalbard by the Royal Navy. Russian settlers were evacuated to Archangel. Despite Norwegian protests, the British burnt all coal stocks and rendered mining facilities useless – in Barentsburg, the fire set to the coal stocks spread and also destroyed major parts of the settlement itself. But the following war years saw only minor skirmishes in Svalbard as a lasting occupation would have blocked too many resources, for which there was a greater need elsewhere.

A small troop of Norwegian exile forces in Scotland was sent to Svalbard, based in evacuated Longyearbyen and Barentsburg, to capture German weather stations repeatedly set up to provide information to the northern fleet. As a result a force led by the battleship *Tirpitz* and the cruiser *Scharnhorst* was sent to the islands in 1943. Hopelessly outnumbered, the Norwegians nevertheless put up a fight and were forced to retreat into the mountains as the Germans razed the settlements. A mine near Longyearbyen that was set on fire continued to burn until well into the 1960s. Nonetheless the German occupation never arrived. Neither side had full control of the archipelago as neither could spare the manpower and equipment necessary. One of the German weather station crews stayed on Nordaustlandet for a while after the war's end, iced in. They broadcast their weather reports openly from May 1945 onwards, until a Norwegian fishing boat, transformed into an auxiliary navy vessel, managed to make it through in September 1945 for the surrender of this last German unit.

Norway found herself in a complicated situation: there were still Soviet troops in Finnmark, Norway's northernmost province, and the Soviet Foreign Minister Molotov was pressuring for a revision of the Spitsbergen Treaty. The Soviets proposed that either the USSR took possession of Bjørnøya (which they reckoned had been theirs before 1920), or that the whole of Svalbard become a Soviet–Norwegian condominium with a joint defensive army. A large majority in the Norwegian parliament rejected the proposals in 1947.

POST-WAR MINING The rebuilding of Svalbard's mines began immediately after the end of the war. Those at Longyearbyen, Ny-Ålesund and Sveagruva (closed two decades earlier) were swiftly put back into operating condition. As Norway's only economic area of coal deposits, Svalbard was of enormous importance, particularly for northern Norway, and especially as worldwide coal prices had risen steeply. Production quickly surpassed pre-war levels, reaching almost 500,000 tonnes by 1948. Several explosions in Ny-Ålesund forced the closure of the mine there in 1963. Sveagruva was subsequently closed again, then reopened and modernised in the 1980s, though it shut yet again in 1988 due to tumbling markets for resources.

By 1948 it was clear that Longyearbyen would be the main centre for the Norwegian coal industry. The mines on the slopes of the Longyear Valley were exhausted in 1970. Today only Mine 7 is still exploited on a low scale (50,000 tonnes per year) for supplying the power station in Longyearbyen and a few international customers who need specifically that type of coal – a German firm that casts church bells, for example.

Today, the bulk of Norwegian mining takes place in Sveagruva, which itself is a remarkable economic success story. In the 1990s, after the end of the Cold War, Norway decided it was no longer willing to subsidise the low-scale mining around Longyearbyen with limitless pots of money. It insisted the mining company operate under free market conditions, leading to high uncertainty for a time in Longyearbyen about the future of the settlement. However, the mining company accepted the challenge and, thanks to excellent coal deposits discovered in the 1980s near Sveagruva, production has risen to an unprecedented level of three million tonnes per year. In 2001, the mine first reported a modest profit; three years later the profit had soared to around NOK200 million – probably a unique case in modern European coal mining. Owing to increased exploitation, however, these deposits will be more quickly depleted, meaning a possible end to Norwegian coal mining in ten to 25 years – unless of course further deposits in the Svea area can be successfully exploited.

Reconstruction of the Russian settlements first began in 1946, with coal production resuming in 1948 – Pyramiden being the most important place of the first few years. Grumant, now a ghost town, was at that time second only to Pyramiden in size and during the winter of 1951–52 had more inhabitants than Barentsburg: 1,106 full timers. This figure included the population of Colesbukta which served as the mine's port and was linked to it via a narrow-gauge railway running through a tunnel in the cliffs now closed up by ice. Today, the Arcticugol company is in production only at Barentsburg; Grumant was closed in 1962 and Pyramiden in 1998. Barentsburg is the main settlement and even has a consular office, but because its stocks are so depleted and the last mine still in operation there has such geological difficulties, the Russians have been looking into a new mine in Colesbukta, where exploration until 1988 indicated promising coal deposits. Initial work has started in Colesbukta – but at a slow pace.

At Pyramiden, there are still considerable deposits, but its difficult geology – up to six months of ice cover on the inner Billefjord – make transport much more difficult. In 1994–95, while drilling for new coal deposits, Trust Arcticugol struck oil and gas in Ebbadalen near Pyramiden. According to most geologists, the deposit is likely to be rather limited due to the general geological structure of the area. The Norwegian administration, meanwhile, is worried about the implications of a possible oil spill. It is quite possible that the Russians' interest in exploring and possibly exploiting this deposit is more political posturing – in ensuring they are seen by Norway to have continuous interest and activity in the area – than a sign of any real expectation of truly profitable oil or gas production. The Russian companies involved promote the project in the hope, not so much of bountiful oil and gas, but of attractive state subsidies.

TOURISM (See also pages 150–1.) Svalbard tourism had some early pioneers in the European upper class, who organised their private pleasure and hunting cruises into Arctic waters, especially Svalbard, from the 1820s onwards, some of them later publishing books about these journeys. Classics among them are the diary of the German Barto von Löwenigh, the Marquess of Dufferin's *Letters from High Latitudes* and James Lamont's *Yachting in the Arctic Seas*. The Englishman Arnold Pike built himself a nice house for wintering in Virgohamna in 1888–89. The tradition of such pleasure cruises in yachts or chartered Norwegian hunting vessels has continued in principle to this day, except that one of the prime earlier pleasures – shooting polar bears and walruses with weapons for trophies – has changed to shooting them with expensive camera equipment.

In 1892 Captain Wilhelm Bade of Wismar (northern Germany) chartered the steamer *Admiral* and ran the first touristic package cruise tour to Svalbard. From 1896, Hurtigruten, the Norwegian coastal steamer service, offered a weekly scheduled tour. These years were the birth of commercial package tourism in Svalbard. Apart from trapping and research, tourism is thereby the oldest still-existing commercial activity in the archipelago, older than even mining or administration.

Cruise tourism led to the establishment of the first summer post offices (Adventfjord 1897, Bellsund 1907, Grønfjord 1907) and developed continuously with the only exception of the two world wars, even though the Hurtigruten scheduled service between Tromsø and Svalbard was abandoned in 1982 as a consequence of the reduction of ships and competition by Longyearbyen's new airport. Today, cruises are by far the most popular way of seeing Svalbard – or at least a part of Spitsbergen's west coast.

Land travel in Svalbard played only a minor role and was restricted mostly to private explorations, at least until 1989. A major drawback of land travel is the very limited transport infrastructure in a colossal, wild territory and the expense of transport, which restricts tourist expeditions either to the small easily accessible areas around Longyearbyen or to expensive private expeditions that include own/ chartered transport by boat or snowmobiles.

Owing to an almost complete lack of a tourist infrastructure outside the settlements, Svalbard tourism was, and still is, the domain of commercial tour operators. They do, however, provide a wide range of options from small wilderness expeditions to big cruise ships, as these companies can split the high basic costs across a larger number of customers.

The opening of Longyearbyen Airport at least made Svalbard accessible all year round and reduced the time needed in getting there and back. However, land-based tourism only really started in 1989, and even the internal travel agency of the mining company SNSK was restricted to taking care of solely the travel needs of employees and official guests. Accordingly, the only place to stay in Longyearbyen for normal tourists was the campsite at the airport (which until 1985 was nothing more than a tundra strip with a toilet cabin). There was only one restaurant in Longyearbyen and almost no shopping possibilities, as the local population was supplied through the mining company, from which they could order most of what they needed. The first tourism company was registered for Svalbard only in 1987 (Spitsbergen Tours) and only since 1989 has tourism been officially recognised and welcomed as an industry in Svalbard by the Norwegian state.

Since 1989, land-based tourism has certainly developed dramatically in Svalbard, with about 800 tourist beds and 87,000 overnight stays per year in Longyearbyen today. However, it is rather easy to experience sharp growth rates when starting from almost zero, and during the last few years this growth has tended to flatten out. Svalbard is an expensive travel destination and its main attractions – nature and history – combined with the strict environmental limitations do not always appeal to everyone. The clear majority of the land-based tourists are still Norwegians, for whom Svalbard has a special attraction as the mythical northernmost part of their country. Especially in the peak season, April and early May, about 90% of the visitors are Norwegians and other Scandinavians. Few other nationalities even know about the beauty of that special period and its unique mix of winter conditions and permanent light.

In spite of these seemingly high numbers, it should not be forgotten that most tourism is concentrated on Longyearbyen. Walk more than just a day from Longyearbyen in summer and it's more than likely that you will not see a single other soul. Accordingly, by far the biggest part of the archipelago is minimally affected by tourism, a situation that is unlikely to change anytime soon.

Tourism has become a major pillar of the local economy in Longyearbyen, providing not only a source of income but also the basis for a much-improved infrastructure. Without tourism, there would not be such a surprisingly wide choice of shops, restaurants and bars, of which much of the local population takes full advantage. At the same time, tourism is one of the least damaging industries in Svalbard: the impact on Mother Nature by fishing, mining, research and even administration are in many aspects considerably more detrimental.

ADMINISTRATION, DEMOCRACY, LEGALISATION AND TAXATION Stately administration is one of the newest activities in the archipelago, dating back to only 1925 with the official beginning of Norwegian sovereignty over the islands. Owing to its special status, Svalbard is not integrated within the normal Norwegian local government system, being neither a province nor a commune. Instead it is governed directly from Oslo with the Sysselmann (governor) as the regional representative, who is appointed by the Norwegian government (formally by the king) for a period of three years. The primary other Norwegian top official in Svalbard is the Inspector of Mining (Bergmesteren), who is responsible for all the things his or her title suggests. There is no locally elected representative in charge of the archipelago as a whole.

Politically, the people's voice isn't heard that much; only in Longyearbyen is there a locally elected body: Longyearbyen Lokalstyre. Whether such a body makes sense is still highly disputed, especially given the problems with finding suitable and willing candidates who are likely to remain long enough to make a difference. Initially, the population feared that the creation of Longyearbyen Lokalstyre would allow the government to increase taxes or place more costly burdens on the community, which before were covered by the state. The Spitsbergen Treaty restricted taxation to a level needed for the administration of the islands, so Norway wasn't, and still isn't, allowed to profit from taxation in the archipelago. Hence the remarkably low taxation (currently 8% on employee incomes, 10% on company profits, a minimal tax on capital, no VAT, no customs and no luxury taxes) as an incentive for companies and people to establish themselves here. But while the taxes are indeed low, Norway is not obliged to subsidise the comfortable infrastructure of Longyearbyen further.

In Oslo there are several different ministries with responsibilities for Svalbard, but most decisions are taken or prepared by the Polar Department of the Ministry of Justice. Other government ministries and institutions with relevance for Svalbard include those for the Environment, Industry, Fishing, Transport, Church, Education, Health, Conservation and the tax office.

The Spitsbergen Treaty states that only the Norwegian civil law and penal law are automatically valid for Svalbard, while all other laws have to be made explicitly valid for the archipelago as well as follow the principle of being non-discriminative against the citizens and companies of the other treaty nations. Because of the non-discrimination rule, the introduction of new laws and regulations is not always easy.

In the other settlements, especially the Russian ones, there are no local democratically elected bodies and the intentional lack of a democratically elected council for all of Svalbard does not give the Russians additional local influence on the politics in the archipelago, either. The taxation of the Russian settlements takes place in practice through a completely different model – a fixed (and rather small and symbolic) tax amount per person is multiplied by the number of inhabitants reported by the Russian mining company. Obviously, this is a rather simplistic and arbitrary way of raising taxes and quite contrary to the official tax law for the whole archipelago, reflecting the problems for the Norwegian authorities to gain proper information on the income of the inhabitants of the Russian settlements. With the ongoing normalisation in Svalbard, this preferential treatment of the Russians may well become a bigger bone of contention.

INTERNATIONAL RELATIONS Since the 17th century Svalbard has existed as something of a cosmopolitan area, first with the whalers and trappers from various countries, and later with the exploitation of its mineral resources. Increased and often competing activity – both from mining companies rivalling for promising claims and for the islands' growing strategic importance post-World War I – required an end to the archipelago's status as a no-man's-land, which as we have already seen led to the Treaty of Svalbard of 1920.

Renewed political attention to Svalbard was sparked by the Russian Revolution and the subsequent Soviet attempts to strengthen its position in the north due to the isolation and hostility it had experienced from the West during the Russian civil war. Aware of its maritime disadvantages, with Murmansk and Vladivostok being their only ice-free access ports to the open oceans, the Russians thus came to view Svalbard as increasingly vital strategically, not least because of its location on the northern side of the sea route leading from Murmansk into the open Atlantic. Furthermore, the development of the Kola and White Sea area depended on the country's coal supply, so the coal deposits of Svalbard became increasingly desirable for the Soviet Union too. Accordingly, the Soviets jumped upon the chance to purchase the mines of Barentsburg (Dutch) and Pyramiden (Swedish) to add to its existing mine in Grumant. The sudden and increasing presence of the Soviet Union in the archipelago concerned the Norwegians, particularly once Russians annexed the neighbouring archipelago of Franz Josef Land.

The events of World War II demonstrated clearly the strategic military importance of Svalbard, even though no-one had the resources for an outright occupation. The appearance of nuclear weapons, strategic bombers and nuclear submarines patrolling under the polar ice cap, combined with the upgrading of the Soviet Northern Fleet in the Murmansk area, served only to heighten interest in the archipelago. While both sides were probably better off maintaining the islands' demilitarised status, both also worked behind the scenes to ensure they maintained a strong grip on their Svalbard territories. Recently published documents prove that the former Soviet Union had even prepared an invasion of Longyearbyen and its airport by special forces in the event of war. Mostly, however, the war was fought with civilians, with the Soviets building up their presence in Svalbard so that they outnumbered the Norwegian population two to one. Whether the Soviets' goal was to see a dismantling of Norwegian sovereignty and an assertion of Soviet rights, is a moot point. Until 1975 the Sysselmann's office only maintained four permanent staff, a boat (for summer use) and a single sled team to cover an area the size of Ireland. By contrast, the Russians had at the end of the 1950s two large helicopters and frequent use of icebreakers from the mainland. Thus in practice, the Soviets were largely free to do what they wanted as well as keep a critical eye on the Norwegian activities.

One possible source of contention was the construction of Longyearbyen Airport, against which the Soviet Union protested vigorously on the grounds that the Norwegians could use it as a military installation. To placate them, Norway replied by continuing to allow a permanent Aeroflot office with half-a-dozen (officially military) staff at the airport, even though the only Aeroflot flight was a connection to Murmansk once a fortnight. A helicopter crash at Hornsundet in 1977 and the crash of a military reconnaissance plane in the following year were both covered up by the Soviets, who removed most traces before the Norwegian police could reach the scene. This led directly to an improvement in local resources for the Norwegians and a modification of political approach. Thanks to the new airport, specialists could be rushed to the island at any time of the year. Two helicopters were placed at the Sysselmann's disposal in 1978, with regular replacements and updating of equipment thereafter.

Although Norway has sovereignty, there were no Norwegian police stationed in Russian settlements and Russians were allowed to regulate their own affairs to a large extent. On the surface, both sides tried to minimise tension, holding regular cultural and sports exchanges and working together on any major practical problems. All this, however, was limited to official contact – direct, unobserved private contact between Norwegians and Soviets were a rare exception and not always looked upon favourably– certainly not on the Soviet side. Most meetings would be carefully watched over by both Norwegian and Russian authorities. Recently released files of the Norwegian secret service documented an extensive observation activity on their own population in Longyearbyen.

The developments that have taken place in the former USSR since 1987 have also affected Svalbard. A Western television crew was allowed into Barentsburg for the first time in 1988, and in that year the Russians gave up protesting against regular visits by a Norwegian frigate. (They'd always claimed this broke the demilitarisation rule, to which the Norwegians replied that the Aeroflot staff at the airport were technically military officers and thus represented a permanent military presence where none was allowed.)

In short, relations between the Norwegians and Russians became much more relaxed towards the end of the last century. In addition to the continuing official cultural and sports exchanges, private contact increased and a barter trade under the motto 'Western nylons for Russian vodka and ham' began, soon followed by use of Western currencies. The kroner has since become the whole area's principal currency.

The dwindling of state subsidies has resulted in the decline of both the Russian presence and its mining. Once at the same level as the Longyearbyen mines, with about 500,000 tonnes per year, the closure of the mine in Pyramiden caused a major reduction. Barentsburg, the last remaining mine, is also facing serious problems such as dilapidated equipment, insufficient supplies and deadly accidents. The worst, a coal dust explosion in 1997 which destroyed most of the mine and killed 23 people, was in part caused by a lack of proper equipment to maintain safety. This does not mean that Russia will give up its interest in Svalbard but a reduction in its activities is plainly evident in the reduction of population (from 2,000 to 350) and in the cutting down of its social structure (including the closing of newspapers, a reduction in the number and size of schools and kindergartens and the emergence of bottlenecks in hospitals). The regular Murmansk flights have gone, too, with Russian planes now a rare sight at Longyearbyen Airport: Russians now take Norwegian flights, and employees are primarily exchanged by ship. Norway made good use of this Russian weakness by gradually increasing its control over the Russians' activities, introducing more and more regulations and enforcing them, at least partly, within Russian settlements. Perhaps the most visible demonstration of this superiority is the emergence of Norwegian road signs in Barentsburg (with Norwegian text first and Russian second), a Norwegian post office (though it's manned by Russians) and the introduction of Norwegian fire regulations in Barentsburg. Even though fires in the Russian settlements are much rarer and easier to control due to the use of mainly bricks and concrete, in contrast to the widespread use of wood in the Norwegian settlements, Norway insisted on the application of its own standards for fire safety, threatening to close the Russian hotels. The introduction of more and more regulations by the Norwegian authorities could lead to conflicts with the non-discrimination rule of the Spitsbergen Treaty as it is obviously more difficult for companies and employees from other countries to adapt to specific Norwegian standards. These may not be better – just different – and may therefore require extra training for employees from other countries, for example. Thus, the special status of Svalbard may lead to problems where Norway tries to simply introduce Norwegian laws and standards to the archipelago instead of creating special non-discriminatory rules. With the Cold War now consigned to the history books, then, the normalisation of Svalbard brings about new international challenges.

On the official Russian side, Svalbard received growing attention from the late 1990s onwards, though with limited results. A secret 1997 decree by President Yeltsin declaring that tourism should be developed in the Russian settlements has had no visible effect 15 years later – tourism in the Russian settlements is still mostly day excursions from Longyearbyen, despite a large, functioning, affordable (and recently remodelled) hotel. More obvious is a strengthening of the Russian scientific research activities in Svalbard. The research complex in Barentsburg has been partly reactivated, housing several summer expeditions, with emphasis on glaciology, geology, archaeology and geophysics. Some research projects are run throughout the entire year. More turmoil was caused by the Russian decision to start a new mine in Colesbukta as a replacement for the inefficient Barentsburg mine. Norway gave in to considerable Russian political pressure and gave permission for this new mine with only a minimum of conditions but so far only very limited activity is visible in Colesbukta. Most of the intended activities are being hindered or delayed by repeated changes in the personnel of the ministries in Moscow, where political manoeuvring and in-fighting regarding access to and control of funds often takes precedence over everything else. Still, it is apparent that Russia has rediscovered its Svalbard outposts and is no longer willing to retreat in the face of Norwegian dominance.

Locally, the atmosphere among the Barentsburg population can be tense, with repeated massive criticism of the new management in charge since 1999. Supplies with acceptable food are unreliable, wages and other benefits have been cut and pressure and control by the leadership has increased. The resulting social tensions led to a sensational court case in early 2005. A Barentsburg worker convicted of killing a colleague was sentenced to just four years in prison, the Norwegian court having accepted that the current sharp social tensions in Barentsburg may have contributed considerably to the struggle that ended in the killing.

Looking towards the future, the primary political and economic concerns likely to afflict Svalbard in the years ahead will most likely be connected to the islands' surrounding seas, and their vulnerability. As technology advances, there will be more interest in the Barents Sea and, eventually, in the North Atlantic to the west and the Arctic Ocean to the north – areas which may bear yet-unknown deposits of oil, gas and minerals in addition to the already heavily exploited fish resources. Oil and gas production has already reached the southern part of the Barents Sea in both Norway and Russia, raising environmental concerns during recent years. New protected areas were introduced in Svalbard, including the southernmost islands Hopen and Bear Island (Bjørnøya), both of which are ecologically important as seabird colonies but also highly attractive as potential logistic bases for the oil and gas industries. Norway claims a 200-mile economic zone exclusively for itself, not only around the Norwegian mainland but also around Svalbard – the latter claim so far being accepted only by Finland and Canada. All other countries disagree with such an exclusive claim for Norway only, maintaining that in an economic zone around the archipelago, the rules of the Spitsbergen Treaty have to be applied, giving all other nations access on an equal footing with Norway. At the same time, most countries acknowledge, that for fishing at least, some control is desirable and they therefore tacitly accept the fishing zone proclaimed by Norway around Svalbard and in the Barents Sea, so long as Norway gives appropriate quotas to the other countries who traditionally fish there. Only Iceland regularly challenges this Norwegian regulation. Unfortunately, Norway is known for colluding with Russia on the annual quotas, setting them high above the quantities suggested by scientists, leading inevitably to the depletion of much of the fish stocks of the Barents Sea.

With oil and gas production gradually moving north, competition around the resources of the marine areas will only increase. Apart from the disputed economic zone around Svalbard, there is an additional conflict in the Barents Sea between Norway and Russia over defining the border of their economic zones. Norway favours the so-called mid-line principle, which is applied over most of the world, while Russia insists on the so-called sectoral principle, ie: drawing the line from the Norwegian–Russian border to the North Pole, which would be favourable for Russia. So far, both sides take pains to keep this dispute under wraps.

In addition to this boundary problem, there are other potential pitfalls, particularly as other states become active in the region as technology allows further exploration and the opening up of the Arctic for recovery of valuable resources, particularly oil and other minerals. The rules of this game have yet to be agreed.

For more on wildlife in Svalbard, Franz Josef Land and Jan Mayen, check out Bradt's
The Arctic: A Guide to Coastal Wildlife. *See page x for a special discount offer.*

FLORA Despite Svalbard's High Arctic latitude the flora is amazingly varied, with the strongest vegetation being on the west coast, in central Nordenskiöldlandet, around Isfjord and where affected by guano. Vegetation is sparser in the east. In addition to general problems posed by Arctic conditions (short growing season, low temperatures, harsh winds), vegetation, particularly in inland areas, also has to contend with low precipitation and the concomitant lack of water in the summer and poor snow cover (insulation) during the winter.

Regarding precipitation, Svalbard has a steppe-type climate. In lower latitudes, vegetation would be fairly sparse due to lack of water. In the Arctic, however, the dry climate helps vegetation obtain sufficient water: permafrost in the ground prevents a sub-surface drainage of rainfall and meltwater in summer, which leads to a muddy thawed top layer in flatter parts of the terrain. The little water that is available is therefore stored close to the surface and remains available, while evaporation is less of a factor due to the low temperatures. Nevertheless, lack of water is a crucial factor in many places and nowhere is this more evident than the brilliant green and red colours of the moss and grass near some streams and puddles in otherwise more brownish-green-grey surroundings. In other places, the cold is a problem for vegetation as it conserves the ice core in moraines, just like the permafrost under the thawed surface in places over the summer. This causes solifluction ('floating soil'), a very slow slide of the thawed part of the soil on the frozen layers underneath – a movement that is detrimental to the roots of most plant species. Vegetation here is typical of tundra: no tall plants. The tallest growth comes from a few grasses in late summer, their flowering stems reaching up to 30cm. Additionally, there are few endemic species.

In botanical terms, Svalbard is in fact very 'wooded'. There are five sorts of trees, particularly the four willows, including the polar willow (*Salix polaris*) and the occasional polar birch (*Betula nana*) that here grow horizontally with branches no more than 5cm above the ground. The polar willow covers large areas, its green foliage (or, in autumn, brownish-yellow) being the dominant colour of many valleys.

Even if vegetation doesn't rise much off the ground, it is nonetheless astounding in its variety, bringing additional splashes of colour to the landscape; this is apart from the main flowering season and the later grasses, some of which mark the position of marshes. Changes can also be seen in simple plants: in wetlands there are lush growths of green and red mosses and on cliffs and stones may be found abundant lichen in red, orange, black, grey, greenish-yellow and other colours. Some of these are very slow-growing, and the larger patches are perhaps already 10,000 years old and have lived through the end of the last ice age, being among the oldest life forms on the entire planet. As well as these, there are many large fungi, which especially the Russian locals are pleased to collect. If you see red snow, it is less likely to be pollution than a colony of tiny algae.

For the uninitiated, the most noticeable of the higher plants (165 known species) are flowering species, including a poppy, *Papaver dahlianum*, which seems to grow in the most barren of places. Saxifrage grows in these areas also, as well as between stones on the beach, sheltering from the almost constant wind. In flatlands you frequently come across cushions of stemless moss campion, *Silene acaulis*, also called compass plant as its light-red blooms grow first to the south side of the cushion and then continue to its north, and its tiny leaves change from a succu. green to a dark wine-red in August. The white flowering cassiope, *Cassiop. tetragona*, is abundant, particularly in tufted peat beds in valley floors.

The season is very short – growth, flowering and seed production all have to take place within a few weeks. Many plants do not rely solely on seed production but also reproduce through suckers and runners.

Studies in Ny-Ålesund, the location of the world's most northerly research greenhouse, show that some of Svalbard's plants respond to changes in infrared in sunlight. Light in the infrared spectrum increases in August, particularly at night, when the sun is lower on the horizon. This enables plants to set their calendars and some of them stop growing even before the end of the period of midnight sun. This is different from the process in Lapland, where flora reacts to the amount of daylight available. As a rule, Svalbard's plants shrivel up when taken away from their own habitat. In view of this, and the fact that flora is very widely protected by law (not only in national parks and conservation areas), removal of plants is senseless. On a positive note, this is an ideal place in which to live if you are given to asthma, allergies or hay fever; there is virtually no pollen.

Because there are no large trees, there is no local wood for fuel, but on the shores of most fjords you'll find driftwood. Cutting tools are a useful addition to your equipment if you don't want to forego the romance of the campfire, as long as your tour takes you along the coast. However, because of the almost constant wind it is necessary to protect your fire; flying sparks cannot be controlled and burn-holes in your tent, sleeping bag or other items of kit will soon spoil the romance. Oversized, jolly fires have enormous appetites as even the thickest trunks burn in an astonishingly short time; in any case, they are neither necessary nor sensible for ecological reasons. Only build fires where there is no vegetation – and on frost-free ground.

Conservation With the installation of new protected areas (national parks, nature reserves, geotop) since 2003, the earlier plant reserves – especially the area around Longyearbyen/Grumant/Colesbukta and the area around Pyramiden – have been abolished. At first glance, this also ends the irony of establishing plant reserves in some of the few regions of Svalbard with massive human impact. In practice, this irony continues, as today all vegetation is protected all over the archipelago by the new environmental law, while the generous exceptions for mining and research have not changed all that much. It is currently forbidden to pick flowers or to camp unnecessarily on vegetation all over the archipelago, yet the bulldozing of acres of land for road construction, mining and research facilities continues.

Purple rockcress, *Braya purpurascens*, is protected all over Svalbard, not because it is rare, but because it comes under mainland law.

Bringing in any plant species is forbidden.

For more detailed information, the standard works are *The Flora of Svalbard* and *Flowers of Svalbard* (see *Appendix*, pages 242 and 240). Otherwise, there is good specialist literature in English on the region's lichen and fungi.

FAUNA If Svalbard's animals seem rather less shy than we are used to in Europe, there is a reason beyond the notion that they live in an innocent paradise: full advantage must be taken of the short polar summer to build up reserves for the long winter. Running away uses valuable energy. However, the seemingly untroubled animals are nonetheless bothered by human intrusion, and stress may lead to a temporary, but important, reduction in their ability to find food.

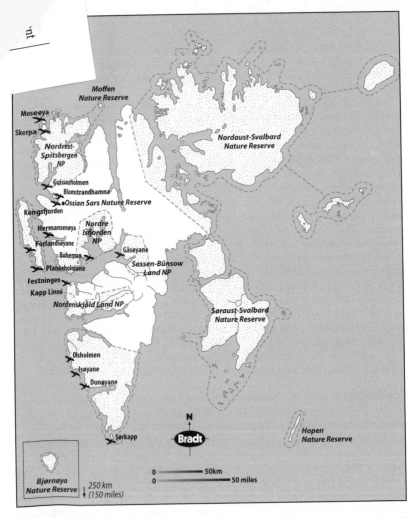

Even when the animal seems trusting, consider its predicament carefully and use longer lenses to avoid approaching too closely. Professional-looking wildlife photographs take much preparation, time and patience.

Mammals Svalbard has few species of mammals: the only terrestrial mammals to be seen are reindeer, polar fox and polar bear. Then there are the pinnipeds – walrus, seal and the like – and the whales. An experiment to introduce the snow hare has been as unsuccessful as that to introduce the Greenland musk ox, the last of which died in 1986. This was partly because of extremely hard winters and partly because the ox was competing for food with the reindeer, which has been returning to its full strength in terms of population in recent years.

Reindeer Definitely the easiest of the mammals to observe is the reindeer, a sub-species in Svalbard. Arriving here at the end of the last ice age, the reindeer has developed in Svalbard independently of its Eurasian cousins, although the possibility of some contact cannot be ruled out, particularly when Novaya Zem, Franz Josef Land and the winter ice pack are taken into consideration. Compared with its relatives in other parts of northern Europe, the Svalbard reindeer is plumper and has shorter legs.

Both sexes have antlers, shedding them every year and growing new ones. The bull has wider, shovel-like, forward tines. At the beginning of winter, the bulls lose their antlers first, making the females, many of them pregnant, superior in the hierarchy, and thereby also in access to the sparse food.

Since reindeer hunting was banned in 1925 the population has grown up to about 12,000 in good years, most of which live in Nordenskiöldlandet, which has large ice-free valleys with good vegetation. Other large groups are found on Barentsøya and Edgeøya, as well as on Reinsdyrflya on Spitsbergen's north coast. There is also a small herd in barren Nordaustlandet.

Unlike in Lapland or North America, where reindeer herds aren't rare, in Svalbard they are usually encountered singly or in small groups; the largest herd I have met so far numbered only 34. The reason may come from the sparseness of food available to support large numbers of animals in any one place. It would seem that after decades of protection the amount of food available has also set the limits on population growth. Evidence of this can be seen in the number of corpses of reindeer that seem to have died of weakness in the winter. This is particularly true of harder winters, or – even worse – when periods of intermittent thawing are followed by frosts which ice up vegetation; scraping for food becomes difficult and animals suffer bloody cuts to their mouths. Should the following summer be too short, these animals are then unable to build up sufficient fat deposits for the coming winter. Thus, the stock is subject to enormous natural fluctuations.

That Svalbard reindeer are fully wild, unlike Lapland's semi-domesticated animals, means they are the subject of detailed study, including the relationship between the reindeer and the Arctic environment. For instance, a long-term project was begun in 1978 when reindeer were reintroduced near to Ny-Ålesund. The effect grazing animals have on changes in vegetation is being studied. Some nearby areas are being fenced off to serve as controls (as in Nordenskiöldlandet). As part of another project, controlled hunting permits are granted to residents. One of the aims of these projects is to find out how long it takes herds to return to their optimal levels. The hunting season is short and only half or two-thirds of the quotas are used, depending on the weather. However, a number are also lost to poachers who travel on motorised sleds in the dark winter months.

Arctic fox Another land mammal that you are likely to see is the arctic, or polar, fox (*Vulpes lagopus*). The common winter coat is white, or sometimes dark grey, when it is referred to as the 'blue fox' and is a favourite prey of the few remaining trappers and resident hunters. Traps consist of a simple wooden frame loaded with some heavy stones on top and supported at one end by a thin, baited prop. As the fox takes the bait, the prop is dislodged and the frame falls, killing the fox without damaging the pelt (as buckshot or bullets would do). Despite trapping, fox population levels don't seem to be at risk. I have even seen arctic foxes, sometimes three at a time, at the Longyearbyen campsite, especially at the end of the season.

However, some precautions must be borne in mind because there is rabies in Svalbard, affecting reindeer, foxes and seals. Because of rabies, the import and export of live animals is strictly controlled. In the Bjørndalen-Grumant area, the fox population is also bearer of the dangerous tapeworm *Echinococcus multilocularis* (see *Health*, pages 98–9).

ecially hard for foxes as most birds have flown and there are no
y sources of food are ptarmigan or carrion, perhaps from a dead
vise, foxes like to follow polar bears to scavenge whatever the

⌐⌐ is also the subject of research: its populations are regularly
recorded, its dens studied and its movements monitored by electronic tagging.

As a general rule, arctic foxes should not be fed, even though this may be tempting for photos or simply because they are so 'sweet'. This reduces their minimal shyness even further, finally leading to trouble, for instance when forcing their way into tents, etc – not to mention infection risks. Feeding makes no sense in an intact ecosystem.

Pinnipeds The walrus (*Odobenus rosmarus*) is the largest of the pinnipeds but has become rare due to merciless slaughter over the centuries. From 1606 until 1953, these easily tracked animals were hunted for their blubber, oil and above all their ivory (teeth). The once huge numbers on Bjørnøya and Svalbard's coasts were all but wiped out, the last colony surviving on Nordaustlandet during World War II. Since they have become protected, numbers have increased (from 1970 onwards) on the northern and eastern coasts (Kvitøya, Nordaustlandet, Tusenøyane, Moffen) and it is believed that there are now around 500 in the summer months. Some come from Franz Josef Land, as generally mostly bulls dive off the Svalbard coast – not a recipe for an independent population. Only since the 1990s have females and calves appeared in increasing numbers again. It is now possible to study this suspected relationship with Franz Josef Land by satellite observations of animal movements: direction finders are attached to the teeth of many animals but unfortunately some do not survive the necessary anaesthesia. These studies show that the distances between the island groups present no problem for these animals; one swam from Svalbard to Franz Josef Land, rested for an hour, and then set off again for the return journey.

The total population is thought to be around 2,000, concentrated mostly in Franz Josef Land. How they spend their winters is not yet known.

Occasional observations are possible all over Svalbard; sometimes even in Adventfjorden, near Longyearbyen. Favourite resting places seem again to include Sarstangen (Forlandsundet) and Sorgfjorden to the north of Frieslandet, with the most numerous places in the east of the archipelago on the coasts of Nordaustlandet and Kvitøya as well as in the south of Edgeøya and on Tusenøyane. The flat, circular island of Moffen has been declared a protection zone. Boats and planes are not allowed to go within 300m of the island. Contrary to its reputation, Moffen is therefore not a good place for seeing these animals from a closer distance.

Walruses are carnivores with a varied diet, the major portion of which is taken from the seabed – they can dive down to 80m. Their great tusks, much stronger in the bulls than the cows, are used to open shellfish as well as for weapons. Mature animals can also take the occasional seal. Even the polar bear shows respect for a massive bull; it is not just the need for defence against his strength, his tusks or his two-tonne bulk, but also because of his thick skin and the blubber layer underneath there is no really effective way to hold them. Their strongest competition for food in the 1970s and 1980s came from mussel fishermen, including those illegally fishing off Moffen, but this had petered out by 1987. Those fishing for crustaceans pose a second threat, but this is not as drastic as they tend to work at lower depths, around 120m.

Walruses are nimble and attractive in the water – small boats should allow them plenty of room – and can also move fairly quickly on land. Even Zodiacs (motorised inflatable boats) are not impervious: I have seen at least one severely punctured Zodiac returning full of water from such an encounter.

Walrus are the largest animals on land in polar regions. They reach puberty at about six years old, bulls starting their harem-building battles a few years later (and a few hundred kilogrammes heavier).

The second-largest pinniped is the bearded seal (*Erignathus barbatus*), which winters in the Barents Sea but is usually met singly in the summer in the north and east. There they hunt in the pack ice for cod and on the seabed for animals. Usually one only tends to come across adult seals. As they tend not to congregate in groups, commercial hunting has never played much of a role and in the last ten years has more or less ceased altogether.

The most common seal is the ringed seal (*Phoca hispida*), which remains all year round and can be seen in all coastal areas. In summer, ringed seals stay near drift ice, where they find the most favourable conditions for hunting cod and crab. The young are born in spring in snow caves dug by their mothers to give protection against the cold, polar bears and polar foxes. The ringed seal is the only seal capable of keeping a breathing hole open in the fjord ice throughout the winter and is thus able to rest on the ice between dives or even deep inside inner fjords completely covered by stable ice.

As a rule, harp seal (*Phoca groenlandica*), hooded seal (*Cystophora cristata*) and harbour seals (*Phoca vitulina*) are summer visitors. There is one small harbour seal colony (approximately 500 animals) on Prins Karls Forlandet.

Even though seals prefer to stay around the drift ice, you can meet individuals almost anywhere on the coast, even near the Longyearbyen campsite.

The widespread death of seals on North Sea coasts in 1988 did not occur in Svalbard. However, it seems that some seals moved out of polar regions due to lack of food (mostly caused by overfishing) and headed toward northern Norwegian waters, where many starved.

Polar bear The most exciting of Svalbard's mammals is the polar bear (*Ursus maritimus*). Protected since 1973, there are now an estimated 3,000 of them in the area of Svalbard and Franz Josef Land, which together share the same polar bear sub-population.

Large males can rival Kodiak bears as today's largest land-based predators. They can grow to more than 700kg (world record: 1,008kg, in Russia; Svalbard record: 850kg). Females can reach 500kg or more. Despite their size, they are very agile and can sprint at up to 60km/h over short distances. They can also cover long distances, usually at a trot. At a slower pace they can also swim vast distances tirelessly – up to 400km has been recorded.

Widespread throughout northern polar regions, they tend to stay close to drift ice and pack ice but can roam into inner areas towards the North Pole. This nomadic existence brings various populations into contact with each other, but groups normally keep to their own areas. One such area contains Svalbard and Franz Josef Land, probably with Novaya Zemlya, and some intermingling with groups from Greenland's east coast. To the south and west, the area is defined by the extent of sea ice, thereby including only Bjørnøya in winter. Bears rarely go further north than 82°N. Research into their migration patterns is still in its infancy although the search for oil on Spitsbergen's east coast has led to thorough investigations, particularly to the south. Some animals have been tagged electronically in the area of the 'polar bear carousel', where, hunting seals, they travel on drift ice from the east coast to Hornsundet via the south cape and return across the peninsula. Since March/April 1988, dozens of females have been fitted with satellite transponders (tags don't stay on males; due to the muscularity of their necks they slip off over the head). It has been established that they can wander to Novaya Zemlya, to Bjørnøya and up to 88°N, but most animals stay in smaller areas or return to their original hunting grounds.

Polar bears are generally solitary but can gather during the breeding season, or when smelling something as tempting as a rotting stranded whale. This answers the rhetorical question of what to do when attacked by a pack of bears: it doesn't happen as they don't hunt in groups.

Seals are the bears' principal prey, most easily stalked when resting on the shore or on ice floes. The bear approaches the seal from the sea and cuts off the escape route as seals are far quicker than bears in the water. But seals are not the only food, alternatives being carrion, rubbish, even grass and seaweed. If need be, the bear can go for several weeks without food. Reindeer do not appear to be part of their diet. Observations have been made of bears passing grazing reindeer without either taking any notice. Perhaps young bears quickly discover that reindeer can run quickly and with stamina. Very hungry bears learn that it is not worth embarking upon a hunt that will consume precious energy and yield very little reward.

Of particular importance for individual populations are their breeding grounds. Females reach sexual maturity at three to four years and mate at three-yearly intervals. After mating in April, the embryo stops development for the summer, resuming in late autumn, when the mother has dug a snow den. One or two, rarely three, of the rat-sized, naked young, weighing about a pound, are born in January. During the first few months, they rely on their mother's warmth and milk, first leaving the cave at about three months when they have grown a downy pelt. By this time the mother will have spent several months in the cave suckling her young

A PLEA TO TRAVELLERS

Unfortunately there are still irresponsible cruise leaders who pursue fleeing bears in the water or on ice with the ship as a tourist attraction. Just as deplorable are photographers who pursue 'Arctic adventure' footage. Bears who accidentally come into contact with ships in this way are fed to stimulate photo-opportunities. This is nonsense; anyone in the know will immediately recognise the artificiality of the pose, typically photographed from above, stretching up on its hind legs. There have also been cases where cubs were separated from their mother by careless snowmobile drivers.

It may be that it is helpful to our disturbed ecologies at home to occasionally feed wild animals, but in such undisturbed spaces as the Arctic our interference cannot be justified. With polar bears, such cheap thrills risk the lives of bears and people. Bears habituated to the presence of people, and their food, can climb aboard small ships, bringing about a situation requiring drastic self-defence. Alternatively they will remember that the presence of people means good eating, becoming a danger for people they meet later in other situations. Passengers who allow or encourage tour leaders to act in this way are morally jointly responsible for any consequences. Are a couple of unnatural photos worth the death of a bear or a person? In the realm of the bear there is always some residual risk; it is irresponsible to increase these risks artificially. Show your awareness: protest strongly! Make sure when booking your tour that no wild animals will be fed.

Disturbing and feeding bears is in any event forbidden by law and can result in seriously high fines.

and foregoing any chance of hunting for her own food; often, she will have lost half her bodyweight. It is therefore important that she can find food in the immediate neighbourhood, as neither the weakened mother nor the small young have the strength for a long trek or swim. Cubs stay with their mother for another two-and-a-half years before they become independent.

In view of the high mortality rate during the first two years, successful breeding is central to the maintenance of a population group. Only a few areas provide the required conditions. In Svalbard, these are principally Kong Karls Landet, Nordaustlandet's north coast and perhaps Edgeøya, Barentsøya and the east coast of Spitsbergen. These islands border the drift ice area in summer and in most years provide sufficient food. Because of its importance to polar bears, Kong Karls Landet was declared a special protection area in 1939; since 1985 all vehicles, boats and planes have been prohibited from going closer than 500m. Nordaustlandet, Edgeøya and Barentsøya are all parts of nature reserves.

The polar bear has been desirable quarry since earliest times and plays a significant part in Arctic mythology. For the Greenland Inuit, pelts were essential for survival, but there was no threat to the species until the advent of modern weapons some 400 years ago. Since then, the polar bear has been persecuted. Until the middle of the 20th century, professional hunters on ice-strengthened vessels came mainly for seals, but took bears as well. In the 1950s the number of bears taken increased due to the number of trappers and residents hunting in Svalbard and especially the invention of self-shooting devices. Commercially organised 'safaris' with many customers became important. Around 300 bears were killed each year, with a high of 515 in 1969–70. It was estimated that there were no more than 2,000 animals in the late 1960s. With a population growth rate of 2–3%, Svalbard's polar bears were on the verge of going extinct. Following the Soviet Union's ban on bear hunting in 1956, Norway banned traps and hunting from vehicles in 1970. Finally, all Arctic states agreed on a total ban in 1973.

Dramatically, only five hibernating polar bears were counted during the 2012 winter here; in 1980 they counted 50 hibernates, while in 2009 there were 25. The jury is currently out as to what this suggests for the current state of polar bears in Svalbard, but it does not look like a good sign. In any event, be aware that you can meet a hungry polar bear almost anywhere and must reckon on it being extremely aggressive. See *Safety*, pages 99–104, and also the section on firearms in the *Practical Information* chapter, pages 112–16.

Whales Owing to ruthless hunting in the past, there are only a few large whales left in Svalbard's seas. Occasionally an individual can be spotted, particularly from a ship. There are 11 whale species in the area during the summer, but the winter pack ice makes it difficult for them to surface to breathe so they mostly move further south.

The most common is the white whale or beluga (*Delphinapterus leucas*), with schools frequently found in the fjords. These shy, white animals (the young are grey) can even be seen occasionally from Longyearbyen's campsite.

The former huge stock of Greenland whales (bowhead whales) is all but extinct due to merciless hunting. Today, whale sightings near the coasts of Svalbard are mostly the small minke whales and the much bigger fin whales such as baleen whales, killer whales and white-beaked dolphins in addition to the belugas.

Birds With around 130 observable species, birdlife in Svalbard is not as diverse as in more southern regions. Despite this, the archipelago is of great interest to ornithologists and birders, particularly if they enjoy travel by boat to different regions or are prepared to go long distances overland. There are few breeding grounds easily accessible from Longyearbyen – something of a blessing for the birds, perhaps. Although there are not too many species, the number of individuals of some species is high (there are over a million little auk), leading to a relatively inflexible and fragile ecosystem.

Typically for Svalbard, as with other Arctic lands, most birds are migratory, taking advantage of the rich sea feeding present by the round-the-clock daylight in the summertime. There are huge seabird colonies and birds rarely seen elsewhere, including the little auk (*Alle alle*), the smallest of the auks, which congregate in large groups and perform ritual formation flying around the rocks, accompanied by some bizarre-sounding cackling. Also relatively rare, breeding only in the northeast, is the ivory gull (*Pagophila eburnea*), easily recognised by its pure white plumage, and Sabine's gull (*Larus sabini*), which has also been seen breeding here. Ross's gull (*Rhodostethia rosea*) spends most of its time on the eastern pack ice, but only one breeding pair has ever been observed in Svalbard. These reclusive Arctic gulls are known to breed only here, in Greenland and in northeastern Siberia.

According to the standard work, H L Løvenskiold's *Avifauna Svalbardensis*, there are 23 breeding species in Svalbard, occurring in most of the archipelago: the little auk; Brünnich's guillemot (*Uria lomvia*); black guillemot (*Cepphus grylle*); puffin (*Fratercula arctica*); snow bunting (*Plectrophenax nivalis*), related to and in some ways similar to our own sparrows; red-throated diver (*Gavia stellata*); the dark phase fulmar (*Fulmarus glacialis*); long-tailed duck (*Clangula hyemalis*); eider duck (*Somatera mollissima*); king eider (*S. spectabilis*), more rare than the normal eider; pink-footed goose (*Anser brachyrhynchus*); Brent goose (*Branta bernicla*); barnacle goose (*B. leucopsis*); ptarmigan (*Lagopus mutus*); turnstone (*Arenaria interpres*); purple sandpiper (*Calidris maritima*); grey phalarope (*Phalaropus fulicarius*); arctic skua (*Stercorarius parasiticus*); long-tailed skua (*S. longicaudus*); glaucous gull (*Larus hyperboreus*); ivory gull; kittiwake (*Rissa tridactyla*); and arctic tern (*Sterna paradisaea*).

Snow bunting and sandpipers are commonly encountered inland. The sandpiper commonly tries to protect its eggs (usually four) by sitting very still until approached. Then the bird jumps up, mewling and appearing to flutter and limp. This is intended to draw attention away from its nest and seems to work with foxes. You, too, should move away.

Less frequently seen are ptarmigan, the only species regularly overwintering in Svalbard. Plover, phalarope and geese are also not that common, geese becoming more noticeable in August as their excited chatter speaks of preparations for southerly migration.

The beautiful and elegant arctic tern travels the furthest of all migrants, more than a few of them spending the (north's) winter months in the Antarctic. They are thus the animals with the longest exposure to daylight relative to their life span, experiencing night only in the spring and autumnal passages of their flight halfway round the world and back. Terns are very aggressive, both towards outsiders and within their groups, defending their eggs laid in shallow depressions on the bare earth. Every year some of them breed (or at least try to) by the lagoon near the Longyearbyen campsite. There they are regularly disturbed by the occasional thoughtless tourist overreacting to their defensive swoops or just spending too much time taking photographs. If you must pass a group of breeding terns, just walk by calmly and briskly, holding a stick over your head. If you must take a picture, do so from a distance, preferably with a telephoto lens. It can be appalling to read travel brochure statements such as: '... should you wish, you can go fossil-hunting, or climb rocks and ice walls looking for gulls' nests…' The presence of inconsiderate photographers (and others) can disturb the birds to the extent that the eggs and young may be abandoned to the cold and the hungry skua.

It might seem surprising that Svalbard, in the High Arctic, can support such huge colonies of seabirds, but the coastal waters provide rich nourishment. Even the drift ice plays a part, smoothing the sea's surface, providing resting places for tiring birds and accommodating a unique ecosystem, starting with the fast growth of algae as an often thick carpet, even on the ice underneath the floes which are sufficiently penetrated by sunlight. As food is available mostly in summer, depending on the sunlight, birdlife in the Svalbard area is extremely seasonal. Most species have to migrate over long distances southward after the summer, returning the following spring when food becomes available again.

This environment is, however, very sensitive to change. Overfishing in the Barents Sea is the likely cause of mass movement of seals to the south and of a severe drop in guillemot populations (90% of breeding pairs were lost in 1986–87 on Bjørnøya, the birds' most important breeding ground).

Fish Svalbard does not offer particularly good climes for freshwater fish. Depending on the season, most waterways are practically dried out, frozen solid or suffer from surging floodwater or sludge from glacier melt. None of these conditions makes them suitable for fish or for the larvae on which they feed. The only species, the arctic char, sometimes known as the Spitsbergen salmon, is to be found in just five to ten streams that are known only by local anglers. Taking your rods is, therefore, not worth the effort.

The sea, however, is full of fish, along with shrimp and mussels off the coast. Larger fish are also found here, although fewer are found in the fjords. In previous decades, shark fishing was good business (Greenland shark grow to 4m long), although there is not much commercial demand nowadays, which means local anglers largely ignore them.

Stocks from the Barents Sea allow commercial fishing further off the coast and is controlled by the coastguard (*Kystvakt*), who, among other things, checks net sizes and quotas for younger fish. Trawlers frequently land in Longyearbyen or Ny-Ålesund to refuel, take on provisions and make use of the post office. Fishing generally takes place on the high seas; shrimp catchers operate near the coasts, but mussel fishing has declined since 1987, following the almost complete depletion of stocks by overfishing.

Svalbard itself is ice-bound for parts of the year and if boats were based there, they would be laid up for too much time. So instead, boats come from Norway, as well as from other countries making up their quotas: Iceland, Russia, the Faroes and Spain are the most common. In the last few years the atmosphere has grown tense. As a result of lobbying from its fishing and oil industries, as well as in an attempt to reduce overfishing, Norway has declared a 200-mile economic zone around Svalbard. Only Finland and Canada so far have recognised this, which puts Norway in something of a difficult position. The coastguard has become ever more rigorous, but Norway is not interested in provoking international conflict; rather it would like to see an international ruling on (reduced) catch quotas for other countries to be regulated by Norway. Naturally, fishermen from these countries aren't in full agreement, including Norwegians – and fishery is sacrosanct in Norway. Accordingly, the Norwegian and Russian governments jointly grant higher fishing quotas in the Barents Sea than suggested by the expert commissions – with the repeated result of collapses in stocks and thereby less fish in following years. Within the Svalbard area, fishing is probably the biggest environmental problem, especially shrimp fishing, which scrapes most of the seabed destroying *en passant* much of life down there. Unfortunately, this is all out of sight out of mind for us 'land mammals'.

Insects and spiders Svalbard is also home to smaller creatures such as flies and a small round spider that always seems to end up in your tent. Mosquitoes also exist, despite rumours to the contrary. Thankfully, they become an annoyance only occasionally and never reach even a fraction of the numbers found in Lapland. Nor are they as cunning as their mainland Scandinavian brethren. The small population is not only due to the climate, but also to the shortage of the clear waters that are essential for breeding.

Because there are no bees, flowers have only flies as their pollinators. Many plants therefore ensure propagation by self-pollination, wind pollination or by use of shoots or rhizomes.

ENVIRONMENTAL ISSUES The threatened Arctic environment is a regular theme taken up by the media. There is some justification for this, but there's also a good element of sensationalism. Even in those features purporting to be serious, the principle of 'the worse it is, the more papers it sells' seems to guide the journalism. What is noticeable in prejudiced discussions are the crass distortions and weight given to the consequences of tourism in Svalbard – a media favourite – when almost nothing is heard of the effects of fishing, mining, scientific research or even the administration itself.

Compared with heavily populated central Europe and mainland Scandinavia, Svalbard's environment remains relatively unscathed. But here are some of the main problems.

External human-related impacts on the environment Svalbard is affected by worldwide environmental pollution, a great deal of it coming from Europe. As in other Arctic lands, it is no wonder that residents have little patience for the frequent European criticism about a bit of seal or whale hunting or the use of motorsleds. The Arctic point of view finds it incredible that such moral objections can be made by Europeans who don't display at least as much vehemence about the dangers emanating from their own lands. The arguments run that whoever calls for a boycott on Norwegian goods in protest against seal hunting should also boycott European goods because animals there are not only slaughtered horribly, but are also raised and transported in dreadful conditions. In any event, seals hunted in Svalbard are shot (and only in small numbers), not clubbed *en masse* as elsewhere. And locals do *not* take part in whale hunts.

Included in the effects of external pollution are those on the atmosphere and on the sea, with consequences for the climate and the food chain. Tourism has thus far played a minimal part in this.

Air pollution The view that Svalbard's northerly position protects it from worldwide air pollution is false. For nearly six decades observations from aircraft have shown a vapour layer over the whole polar area, especially in winter and at heights of 2,000–4,000m. Researchers have been charting seasonal sulphurous oxide levels since the 1980s. In summer there is a boundary between cold polar air and warmer continental air, which forms a barrier to pollution; but not in winter. In the winter, the cold air reaches further south, allowing exhaust gases from northern Russian industries to affect the Arctic. In Ny-Ålesund, sulphurous oxide levels are four to five times higher in winter than in summer, and, at the same time, much higher than around Trondheim, which is, along with Iceland, the cleanest part of Europe. In this respect Svalbard is still relatively clean, but by no means unaffected.

Climatic changes Based on a new scientific model, climatologists calculate an increase in Svalbard's mean temperature of 1–2°C in the next decade. This could result in higher precipitation, perhaps bringing an increase in glaciation (or in other models a decrease), and increased spread of some vegetation, including birches and willows. A retreat of the permafrost boundary is also possible, caused by warmer summers and fewer exceptionally cold winters but a greater spread of ground-insulating snow cover. An additional cause could be the release of carbon dioxide that is currently held fast in layers of frozen peat.

Increased warming would also, according to some models, bring about changes to ocean currents, particularly to the Gulf Stream. Should north-flowing warmer currents succumb to colder, south-flowing currents, Svalbard's 'heating' would disappear. Mainland Europe's own climate would suffer from this change in circulation: there would be no chance for growth of large trees north of Denmark and agriculture in central Europe would become more difficult.

Climatic research shows that there have been similar variations of climate during the last thousands of years – with the so-called 'little ice age' and its peak about 200 years ago as one of the most extreme swings into the cold direction since the last real ice age. Today's glaciation, on the retreat since then, would still have to shrink a fair amount to reach the minimum seen before the 'little ice age'.

Marine pollution Marine pollution is most noticeable in the rubbish left lying on the beaches. But the worst pollutants are invisible.

High PCB (polychlorinated biphenyl) concentrations led scientists to ring the alarm for polar bears at the beginning of the 1990s. Anaesthetised female bears were found to have 60 times the concentration of PCBs in their milk as was found in Norwegian women. These chemicals effect sterility, especially in males. Should such toxic releases continue, the threat to the polar bear that was removed with the hunting ban would be replaced by PCBs in the food chain. Concentrations go up the food chain step by step, from algae to fish to seals, and end up in the bear – or, sometimes, in humans.

Radiation Little is known about the effects or extent of radioactivity around Svalbard. A few years could bring radioactivity into the food chain from the corrosion and break-up of the Russian atomic submarine *Komsomolets*, sunk off Bjørnøya. Measurements taken at that site from the German research vessel *Gauss* in 1995 showed relatively low levels of radiation, with the data obtained similar to that of other sources in Europe (ie: Sellafield). There's little radioactivity originating from the Chernobyl disaster – far less than in Lapland, for instance.

The intensity of and dangers from ultra-violet light up around Svalbard are also unclear. The research station at Ny-Ålesund discovered a hole in the Arctic ozone layer, with record low temperatures in the stratosphere (–94°C at the beginning of 1996). This ozone hole is a natural process, which has been accelerated by manmade chemicals that pollute the atmosphere globally. It is usually greatest in spring, but has shown a general decrease over the last few years, which may be related to the reduction of ozone-layer-damaging manmade chemicals during the last decades.

My very practical experience is that I've never been sunburned during Svalbard summers despite treks lasting weeks – and I'm light blond (and so hardly resistant in very sunny climes). Nevertheless, caution and skin protection can't hurt, especially when on glacier tours in summer or skiing in spring.

Local factors affecting the environment
Counted among local factors are the mining and fishing industries, rubbish, exhaust, water pollution and other threats. It can be established that these things have a minimal effect when compared to influences from outside.

Fishing Possibly in first place comes the fishing industry, particularly the practices of overfishing and use of equipment damaging to the seabed. Overfishing also displaces bird populations, as can be seen on Bjørnøya – a result of dwindling fish counts in the Barents Sea.

Shrimp fishing is especially devastating to all life on the sea bottom as it scrapes them by the square mile again and again without any regard to the species who make the sea's floor their home. As is generally known, the sea is the most important component of the Arctic ecosystem and even though its regeneration ability is higher than that of life on land, permanent disturbance must have an effect – through the food chain – on land. In view of the strict regulations on land, this blindness suffered by the Norwegian maritime authorities is striking, and is due to a large extent to the strong fishing lobby in Norway. While on land, all damage to any animal, including invertebrates, is forbidden, there are no such limitations placed upon fishing. A high percentage of the catch from shrimp trawling is made up of economically useless species, which are thrown overboard again, dying or dead. As long as the equipment used conforms to the prescribed standards, the environmental standards are met. However, by allowing these massive impacts, Norway can hardly live up to its self-imposed goal of making Svalbard one of the best-managed wilderness areas of the world and a reference area for untouched Arctic wilderness.

Furthermore, so far the only vessels to have sunk in the last decades around Svalbard are fishing vessels. Every time a vessel sinks there is the potential risk of an oil spill. Very little can be done in the middle of a stormy polar night to prevent fuel seeping out of a sinking vessel's tanks between the ice floes somewhere along the coasts of the national parks and nature reserves of northern Svalbard.

Mining In taking into account the areas of vegetation cover destroyed, the amount of rubbish produced and deposited, exhaust gases and liquid outflows, the mining industry is responsible for most terrain destruction in Svalbard. The Norwegian SNSK built a 12km road (partly on glacier, though) in the 1990s, while the Russians got permission for an even longer road between Barentsburg and Colesbukta. Coal mining is hard to imagine without surface traces, but at least a gradual improvement in attitude can be seen, especially in the Norwegian SNSK. Mining is also responsible for much of the helicopter use, including for instance the flying of exploration teams to their drilling rigs and back every day.

Research Third place goes to research projects. Smaller examples of interferences in the name of science include: shooting down over 100 chicks to study the effects of parasites on ptarmigan; fitting transponders to walruses and polar bears even though some do not survive the effects of tagging; and leaving marker crosses and other equipment all over the place even though experiments (eg: aerial photography in the late 1980s) have been completed.

These are perhaps relatively small things, but there are larger intrusions, too. Large installations like the EISCAT radar has been built over Mine 7, as well as access roads. In 1996 a further road was blasted and bulldozed up Platåberget for an access road to the SVALSAT satellite ground station. These projects have gone ahead without discussion or much media attention, sacrificing an expanse of plant protection area and destroying more terrain just around Longyearbyen than tourism has managed in over a century all over Svalbard.

Furthermore, research is one of the biggest users of small aircraft and helicopters within the archipelago, both of which produce both CO_2 emissions and noise pollution (a helicopter on average tends to emit roughly three times as much harmful exhaust than an average road transport vehicle). Even though flight permissions have become somewhat more limited, scientists are still a long way from being forced to prove that their project is impossible without helicopter use.

Administration At fourth place in our league table we can place Svalbard's administration: local government, the Sysselmann (governor), coastguard, mining authorities, the military and so on; principally through the construction of administrative buildings (even in protection areas) and the near-excessive use of helicopters.

Tourist use of helicopters is effectively banned but flights supported by the Norwegian state seem to have the freedom to venture anywhere. In view of the masses of tasks and limited staff, the Sysselmann hardly has any other choice but massive helicopter use. However, if the Norwegian state puts environmental issues so high on the agenda, shouldn't it then take care that its own representative can fulfil necessary tasks with minimal helicopter use if only to set a positive example? A good chance of promoting environmental thinking was also wasted in 1995 during a royal visit by the Norwegian king. He was flown by helicopter into a national park for sightseeing – while the royal yacht, a means of transport more in line with the propagated standards, was standing idly by in Spitsbergen.

Tourism There are in Svalbard a number of shorter tracks, traces of camping places (damaged vegetation, rubbish), animal disturbances (eg: to breeding birds or by over-enthusiastic photography) to be found, which must be added to the extra effect tourism has on emissions and so on, in addition to that which would normally originate from the locals.

Up until now there has been very little extra building to support the tourist industry outside Longyearbyen.

Most seriously taken are the potential risks of ever-increasing ship tourism around the archipelago. Especially worrying is the trend towards bigger and bigger ships. During the last few years, the biggest cruise ships visiting the archipelago have a capacity of 2,000 passengers. These stick primarily to the west coast. Expedition cruises are also growing – both in numbers and in the sizes of the ships they use – and these visit more and more landing sites with ever-increasing frequency. Not only does this increase the risk of erosion and disturbance of wildlife along more and more coasts, but the use of bigger ships and more traffic also increases the risk of a catastrophe at sea. This includes the possibility of a major rescue operation, which could not be handled with the limited local resources, and an eventual major oil spill from a damaged vessel. These are risks indeed, even though tourism is only operating in Svalbard waters in summer, as opposed to fishing that takes place all year round. Currently, new regulations for cruises are under preparation. A lot can be achieved already by raising the technical standard requirements for ships (ice class, double hull, no heavy oil) and by the employment of qualified lecturers and staff who can promote the codes of environmental conduct to the travellers. On the whole, these travellers are very co-operative and understand the need for environmental protection – they just have to be informed.

Generally, tourism is today probably the most strictly regulated human activity in Svalbard – touristic helicopter use for instance is completely forbidden for environmental reasons, even though it made up for only about 2–5% of all helicopter use by 1995, when the ban was introduced, while the main helicopter users – administration, research and mining – have even increased their helicopter activities since then.

Miscellaneous Space taken up by settlements and their demands on air and water also have an effect. In the construction of the new centre of Longyearbyen, some of the most productive vegetation areas of the valley were sacrificed and even between the houses, large areas were filled up, to be recultivated with artificially sown grass – something that will never have the original multitude of species. Svalbard has no sewage plants. This might seem strange to Europeans, but with so few people, so much space, and considering the sea's ability to break down organic waste, biological risks are few.

But Svalbard has all of Norway's (and one of Russia's) coal mines – which currently total three. Only Longyearbyen's power station (built in 1983) is relatively efficient and modern, using about 20,000 tonnes a year of local, relatively sulphur-free coal. The Russian mine and power station at Barentsburg are hardly efficient, utilising some 80,000 tonnes in total and wasting a good amount of the energy generated.

ENVIRONMENTALLY FRIENDLY TRAVEL

Getting there and back Unfortunately, apart from cruise ships, it is not easy to get to Svalbard without flying – hardly an environmentally friendly form of travel. Luxury cruise ships use slightly more fuel to Svalbard and back per passenger than the plane, but ship exhausts do not affect the vulnerable higher atmosphere as much as plane exhausts.

For more information on the practicalities of getting to Svalbard, see pages 93–8. For more information on cruising, see *Chapter 4*.

When travelling in Svalbard There is no legal way to tour Svalbard that is particularly damaging to the environment; the problem is more to do with how many people travel together at a time and how they behave while doing so. A few snowmobiles, despite the noise and exhaust fumes, can do less damage than a few hundred hikers tramping a summer path. In any case, where 12,000 reindeer can wander about, a couple of hikers aren't going to make a very significant difference.

By ship The majority of visitors go by ship, doing only minimal damage, especially if they go ashore only at regular stops (eg: Magdalenefjord), are well informed about environmental issues and have been issued with a code of conduct.

Ski tours Done properly, ski tours can be one of the most environmentally friendly ways of travelling. In winter, on frozen ground with few animals around, there is little likelihood of damage and disturbance. Compared with cruising, though, there aren't very many people who are prepared to put up with the discomfort. This also applies to kayak paddlers, except that in the summer there are more animals to disturb.

Snowmobiles and dogs Both forms of transport push the limits of ecological acceptability in their own way, the former much more so than the latter. Snowmobiles have an impact because of the usual arguments against petrol-powered combustion engines. Husky driving has its critics, who take issue with the activity's reliance on large quantities of meat as fuel – meat which almost certainly has to be hunted in parts.

Hiking Even hiking brings its problems, in particular the involuntary disturbance of breeding birds and perhaps also of reindeer and, of course, erosion. Here, unfortunately, there are no quantitative research results. My guess is that 200 people per summer tramping on the same narrow route on a typical dry, even, vegetated tundra ground will eventually form a visible and partly eroding track over the years. However, such a concentration of hikers on a narrow track happens only in those places where nature channels them all on the same route. This is not very often the case – normally, each group tends to take slightly different routes, which spreads them and thereby reduces the erosive force per square metre. Thus, erosion through usage first becomes a problem when paths are dedicated and controlled. Much more endangered by hikers are wet tundra areas, where damage occurs much more quickly – a problem especially with landings of cruise ships or hiking groups very early in the season on ground that is still soaked from the snowmelt.

Staying local Staying in villages is similar to cruising, in that the open country is not affected. But the more visitors there are, the more luxury and comforts will be required, with all the attendant construction, rubbish collection, extra sewage and so on that this entails.

About half of Svalbard is protected as a national park or nature reserve. The Sysselmann's office can give details of regulations. Ask for *Environmental Regulations for Svalbard and Jan Mayen* and *Forskrift om Turisme og Annen Reisevirksomhet på Svalbard, 1991* (Regulations for Tourism and Travel in Svalbard).

The most important rules are:

- No motorised off-road traffic in thawed or snow-free terrain. Exceptions include snowmobiles on frozen and snow-covered ground within the areas opened for them (see map, page 91).
- No littering or burying of rubbish (burying is useless due to frost movements, bringing everything up again if it's not buried several metres deep).
- No landing helicopters outside designated landing places (especially for tourists).
- Compulsory registration of season-long camps one year in advance.
- No low aircraft flying in bird-breeding areas.
- No motorsleds in protected areas. There are exceptions for residents with special permits and the snowmobile-free areas (see map, page 91).
- No entering Svalbard's 15 bird sanctuaries and the Moffen Walrus Reserve during the summer period, 15 May to 15 August. These areas must also not be approached to proximity by ships or by air during these times.
- Absolutely no entering or approaching Kong Karls Landet, Svalbard's most important polar bear breeding area.
- Tents should not be set up on vegetation where other possibilities are within reach (sand, snow, etc).

It can be said that conservation is generally taken more seriously in Svalbard than in Europe, at least outside the mining areas, and only on land, not in the surrounding seas. This is no doubt due to the fragile nature of the environment: even vehicle tracks, for instance, can last for decades. Check the regulations in detail, especially when planning an independent tour, by either requesting them by letter to the governor's office or by checking the website www.sysselmannen.no.

Preservation of historic monuments Up-to-date regulations can be obtained from the Sysselmann on request by letter or by checking their website.

- All remains of human activity from 1945 and before are considered historic monuments, including a 100m zone around them. The most banal items are included, eg: rusty petrol barrels, nails from wartime weather stations, etc. Even some objects from after 1945 may count.
- All graves and their accoutrements (crosses, bones) are protected, regardless of their age or whether they have been removed from their original positions.
- Any object found must not be altered or taken away. Instead, positions should be marked and sketches made or photographs taken showing the items in relation to their surroundings; then they must be registered with the Kulturvernkonsulent in the Sysselmann's office. It is often difficult to do much with a piece once it is taken out of context. Traces of the past should be left in place.
- Breaking the rules can lead to a large fine or even imprisonment for up to a year. Svalbard is not heavily populated and solitary people can wander far without being watched; but that also means that there aren't many suspects when a misdeed is discovered, and not many possibilities of leaving Svalbard either. Not surprisingly, there have been arrests of such thieves at the airport.

Rubbish If your rubbish cannot be burned safely and completely, take it back with you. This applies also to plastics, etc, which may be burnable but release gases that are highly hazardous to the environment. You'll find special-purpose bins in the settlements and a free, multi-language information leaflet is available from the airport, the Sysselmann's office and the campsite. Burial of rubbish is not allowed; you can't dig deeply and frost movements will soon bring it back to the surface.

Until 1991 all rubbish went into one large dump area, but since then sorting and recycling has been introduced. This is good news as local residents create more rubbish per head than their cousins on the mainland, mostly because of the extra packaging required in just getting goods to the islands. Russian settlements have yet to follow suit.

In passing, I am constantly surprised by the contradiction posed by the nature-loving rhetoric of some hikers and guides on the one hand, and the quantities of rubbish they produce on the other, even if they do carry it around the wilderness until they find a suitable bin. Why do they need to bring portion-controlled, instant foods in rarely recyclable packaging (most commonly made of aluminium-coated plastics)? Far better to carry individual dried foods in re-usable containers: foods keep well and may be mixed creatively to give a varied menu.

2

Practical Information

Most people who visit Svalbard know that they are not the first to set foot in the archipelago, and that they will come across an airport, a coal mine, some restaurants and so on. They will also have read or heard about environmental problems (holes in the ozone layer, marine pollution or a sunken nuclear submarine). Yet there are still those who arrive expecting to find a completely untouched paradise. This it is not. Those who believe that Svalbard is made up of 62,500km² of untouched wilderness are going to be disillusioned when they see their first car park (after their arrival by comfortable plane), a land blackened with coal dust just next to the airport, and several construction work areas. Whoever has Christiane Ritter's *A Woman in the Polar Night* in his head, with its trappers and dog-sleds, is going to be surprised and maybe disappointed by the sight of videos, computers, kids on mopeds and other signs of civilisation; even in the countryside there are signs of man, his tracks and his rubbish. But the fascinating thing about Svalbard is that those tracks could be 50 years old and that tin can could be 70, both preserved in the Arctic atmosphere.

The bottom line is that Svalbard is neither Disneyland, trying to match the dreams of the visitors, nor an open-air museum. It is a modernised part of our modern world, despite its relative remoteness from it, and the inhabitants of Svalbard like to live a normal Western life. They are not exotic creatures there to be studied. And they appreciate good manners as much as the rest of us. They don't take too kindly to hikers using a pleasant restaurant as an old hut, leaving their muddy boots on or laying out their moist sleeping bags, putting dry smelly socks on radiators or lounging around in filthy clothes. Nor do they particularly care for tourists who find an open cabin and decide to move in for the night, using the equipment and fire material they find there without permission from the owner. Unfortunately, because of the archipelago's remote, untamed, 'frontier' reputation, some visitors bring with them to the Arctic the manners and attitude of the 'Wild West'.

But if you come to Svalbard with reasonable expectations, are properly prepared and have respect for both the fragile Arctic natural environment and the locals' way of life, you will be pleasantly surprised by the archipelago. And hopefully you will leave the place with very little sign that you have been there, except for the experience and memories that you will take away with you.

One of the most common questions I am asked in my capacity as a tour operator in Svalbard is 'When is the best time to travel?' Well, there is no general answer to this question – the best season depends primarily on your interests. Each season is different, with its own advantages and disadvantages, and all I can do is give a broad outline. It seems to depend also on national and cultural background: to the surprise of most non-Norwegians, the best-booked season is not summer but spring, the so-called fifth season when it's still wintry but already bright all around the clock, when Scandinavians have Svalbard almost to themselves. Also the polar night can be a special experience, and obviously the summer is a major travelling time.

In fact, it may be easier to name less favourable seasons, at least for those interested in outdoor activities: these are first of all late September to mid-December, mid-January to mid-March and mid-May to mid-June.

The following provides a quick tour of the year.

POLAR NIGHT Technically, the polar night begins in Longyearbyen in late October and lasts until the second part of February. However, the really special polar nights (ie: when it is true night all around the clock), that occur only this far north, can be experienced from mid-December to the beginning of January. This is quite a contrast to northern Scandinavia, where the sun admittedly does not rise for some days or even weeks, but there will always be some light still at midday, even around 21 December. For 24 hours of night, you have to travel as far north as Svalbard, when you may also be lucky enough to see the northern lights in the middle of the day, because it is sufficiently dark. With a clear sky, even the stars can provide enough light in this clean air for easy hikes over the snow-covered tundra – it is quite surprising what can be seen at night, once one's eyes have adapted to it. The moon, too, can be rather special – if it is close to full, it stays above the horizon most of the day and casts a magic and surprisingly strong white light on everything. But be prepared also for the opposite: a snowstorm can tie you just as well for a day or two to Longyearbyen. Moreover, the period from late October to early December can be partly stormy, often with very little snow but with rain which freezes on the ground, providing unpleasantly slippery ice.

As practically everything is closed over the Christmas holidays in Longyearbyen – including accommodation and the shops – the best period for experiencing true polar night is over New Year. Plan in good time and aim to spend at least a week, to experience the different climatic variations and to increase the chance of having periods of good weather. Temperature-wise, anything can be expected from below –25°C to above 0°C, with the most important factor affecting the temperature being the wind. Nevertheless, thus far tourism has not yet discovered the polar night fully, and the New Year is a pleasantly quiet time for experiencing this unique period. Independent travellers should have very good outdoor and winter experience for coming during the polar night, but there are also a few package offers for small groups. Be aware that there may be little snow and limited fjord ice at this time, so do not count on touring by ski or snowmobile.

Moving further into January, the light gradually comes back at midday with more and more intense dawns. This is also a fascinating period, sometimes with incredible light, but it requires a certain amount of luck to be in the right place at the right time.

MID-JANUARY TO MID-MARCH This is the time of the returning light. With clear skies and an open horizon to the south, the sun can already be seen by the second half of February. An old trapper saying has it that with the return of the light comes the cold. Certainly, February and March are the coldest months, with the thermometer falling in some years to –40°C or lower.

Outside activities are difficult at this time: the light returns, but slowly, and there are early storms. Snow cover on land and fjord ice are still building slowly, and sometimes it can be very slippery on land; as a result, one should not rely on the possibility of crossing even the inner fjords, yet.

END OF MARCH TO THE BEGINNING OF MAY The last few days of March and all of April are the best times for winter tours. Daylight returns more and more each day until the sun stays up permanently (from around 20 April). Already by the beginning of April there's a fairly good light all through the night. The temperature may still be as low as –30°C, especially with the wind chill, but it starts to become milder from mid-April on, although hard frosts are still possible until well into May. On the other hand, mild weather with temperatures just under or above freezing are possible, and if there is no wind and sunlight this can be a wonderful time for travelling the grand white wilderness. Statistically, April and May are the months of the year with the best weather.

During the course of April, or maybe even a little before, the first birds arrive, starting with fulmars and auks, soon followed by snow buntings. In some years, melt weather can become a problem come late April; in other years not before the second half of May, possibly making the terrain impassable and thus limiting the suitable season for longer tours. Unfortunately, the area around Longyearbyen is usually one of the first where the snow and ice turn into deep slush, puddles of meltwater and the beginning of meltwater streams.

The cold weather of late winter causes the inner fjords to be frozen over until the end of April, though with enormous variations from year to year. But even the ice on seemingly solidly frozen inner fjords should not be trusted. Even on Tempelfjord, one of the standard excursion areas for snowmobile tours, there are a few places which never freeze over fully, and which are often camouflaged by a light dusting of snow on top; unsurprisingly, these have caused some serious accidents in the past. Moreover, it is impossible to predict the levels of freezing. In some years only branches of Isfjord are frozen over, but in others the whole fjord is solid and you can reach the north coast from Longyearbyen by a much shorter route. Sometimes icebreakers may clear fjords that you would expect to be frozen sufficiently to ski across. If there should be a thick snow cover on fjord ice, the weight of the snow may press the ice underwater, leading to a water layer at the bottom of the snow above the actual fjord ice, which can be quite a problem both for skiers and sledges.

The occasional lack of snow on land can cause difficulty for skiers, particularly when the wind blows the land clean. Often there is not enough snow until April, and then it covers crevasses, causing further dangers. It is better to stick to proven routes and not to cross glaciers unless you know from summer observation that they're crevasse-free. In mountainous terrain, there is often a risk of avalanches.

Also, the expectation of good weather should not lead to insufficient preparation for the opposite – Easter 2004 was a clear warning, when several days of snowstorms caused no fewer than 11 independent groups out on tour to activate the beacons on their emergency signal equipment. Tours leading out of the settlements should always be seriously prepared for enduring some unexpected extra days under very harsh conditions.

Easter is so obviously an attractive date for visiting Svalbard that most of the facilities are full at that period. On the weekends before and after Easter, too, capacities may be short. That spring is the most popular period of the year for Svalbard tourism is reflected in the accommodation rates, which are higher than in most other parts of the year.

So far, winter activities like skiing, sledging, snowshoeing and even winter hiking (the snow is often thin and hard blown, allowing for easy hiking) are the only activities possible. There are plans, however, to install a small icebreaker, which may offer tours from April onwards.

MID-MAY TO MID-JUNE These are the most difficult months to predict for those venturing inland – for everyone except cruisers, that is. The snowmelt is not yet widespread and wonderful views of white bergs can be seen from the sea, while spring is already well underway in the valleys and lower regions, with lots of water and the first green in between. Sea ice is breaking up gradually, but may last in inner fjords in some years as late as July. For the seals, the drift ice is a favoured resting place. The midnight sun is at its highest on 21 June, blending day and night.

In the valleys snowmelt can occur with a vengeance. Meltwater shoots through riverbeds that were previously filled with dry snow, the ice becomes unsafe, and much of the surrounding land turns to deep mud.

A special risk caused by snowmelt, mostly in flat valleys or on gradual glaciers, is that of slush floods, which may reach up to 100km/h with accordingly devastating force. On steeper slopes, avalanches must be anticipated. In rock faces, thawing leads to rock fall especially in early summer, when frost that fixed loose stones disappears.

What is often overlooked is that there is very little chance for a tourist to make use of any type of vehicle in this transition period. Under unfavourable circumstances sleds can't be used because of the meltwater, boats are hindered by drift ice, while helicopters aren't allowed to be used for tourism purposes. Large parts of Svalbard are thus cut off.

From the second part of June onwards, the snowmelt is usually finished, at least in the lowlands, though the terrain may still be quite marshy and rivers and streams may be violent and high. Cruises begin, but often have to adjust to difficult ice conditions.

In theory, June should be an excellent month for birdwatchers to study nesting in the bird colonies. However, the difficulty comes in trying to get to these colonies.

JULY AND AUGUST It is not without reason that July and August are by far and away the most popular months for summer tourism in Svalbard. The midnight sun stays until 20 August at least, there is almost no frost or snow, and the snowmelt is usually over by the beginning of July in the lower areas so the terrain is accessible again.

Grey-brown vegetation quickly turns green, and flowers develop in only a few warm days, lasting for only a few weeks. Grasses come a little later but are fully grown by mid-August, when most of the flowering has already finished.

Birdlife is at its most intensive until about the third week of July, by which time most of the young have usually left their nests.

For hiking, the first part of July can be hard because of the difficulty of the terrain, but at the same time the midnight sun is spectacularly high and there can be a spring-like atmosphere, with nature full of life, that brightens up the senses. Also, the contrast between the still snow-covered mountains and the green of the lowlands is very pleasant. The other end of summer, August, allows increasingly lengthier and more demanding tours thanks to its drier terrain, but vegetation begins to prepare for autumn and winter and birdlife lessens. With the end of the midnight sun period after 20 August, light frosts at night should be expected and the evenings can have dramatic light effects.

July and August are also the main months for cruise activity. Those keen on successful circumnavigations of Svalbard (or at least of the main island) should book tours from the second half of July onwards, even though earlier departures are often advertised as 'circumnavigation attempts' – the chances for really getting round at the beginning of July are quite limited.

END OF AUGUST AND SEPTEMBER By the end of August the first migrants have already left and the first ground frosts at the end of the period of midnight sun turn willow leaves an autumnal yellowish brown. There are now sunsets and soft evening light. There is very little snowmelt now and waters in streams are retreating; on the other hand the first frosts are hardening the morass, making it easier to get around. There is still sufficient light round the clock to allow night-time travel so you can enjoy some of the advantages of a High-Arctic summer. Be careful where there is new snow as it can camouflage subsidence. Though one should be prepared for temperatures as low as −15°C by late September, this is probably the best period for relatively easy – if somewhat long-distance – trekking.

The last migrants, including wild geese, prepare noisily for their flights south at this time. Coastal boats head the same way, back to Norway, their season having ended even though most fjords are navigable for months to come.

OCTOBER TO THE YEAR'S END From the middle of September onwards the nights rapidly become colder and darker. Storms are frequent, especially from mid-October onwards, with fine autumn days in between. October to mid-December are uncomfortable months for travel. There is little snow yet. The polar night sets in, with its characteristic midday twilight at the beginning, which decreases towards December.

CULTURAL EVENTS
Polar Jazz Held over a long weekend at the end of January, this is a celebration of music featuring jazz, blues and bluegrass.

Solfestuka Celebrating the return of the sun on 8 March, this is a pot-pourri of events: exhibitions, concerts, scooter races, a revue and the 'Ta sjansen' competition.

Svalbard Ski Marathon As it says and held at the end of April. For more information, visit http://svalbardturn.no.

Spitsbergen Marathon Held at the beginning of June.

Dark Season Blues Held at the end of October as the polar night begins, this is a series of events and concerts of blues music.

KunstPause Svalbard (Arctic Art Time Break) Held during the second week in November, this is a series of artistic and cultural events based around nature.

TOUR OPERATORS AND INDEPENDENT TRAVEL

Whatever way you choose to travel, there is one important lesson to learn: less can be more. You will learn more – and truly experience more – if you don't try to do it all in a week or two. Once, when I was lecturing on a cruise, somebody asked me whether we had now 'seen it all', because we had been to several fjords. In response, I said that simply staying close for a few days to just one of the many glaciers he had seen from the boat, watching the different light, feeling the wind, seeing the birds, then cuddling up at the end of the day in a good sleeping bag with the sounds of waves outside the tent, can often provide a deeper and more memorable experience of Svalbard than a cruise around the entire archipelago. This is not an argument against cruises – the desire to see and compare the different landscapes or getting to see the big mammals can be just as good a reason for travelling to Svalbard.

But make sure you are clear as to why you want to come to Svalbard and what you really want out of your trip, without cheating yourself and without listening too much to the colourful commercial prose of the brochures which promise it all.

When travelling with realistic expectations, Svalbard can be a fantastic place and it offers – in spite of the occasional clear signs of human presence – opportunities to experience almost untouched large-scale wilderness to a degree impossible anywhere else in Europe. There is also a wealth of options for special interests like polar history, birdwatching, geology, botany, glaciology, etc.

INDEPENDENT TRAVEL OR ORGANISED TOUR? A fundamental question for visitors to Svalbard is whether to set out independently or travel on an organised tour or cruise. This is as important for the tourist as it is for scientists, journalists and others.

Around 90% of travellers to Svalbard rely on some form of specialist support, whether from tour operators, logistics companies or local research institutions. Of the remaining 10%, few make it far out of Longyearbyen.

About half of all tourists visit the archipelago on one of the large cruise ships, going ashore only for a few hours in total, and spending most of their time enjoying the passing scenery from the lounge window or deck chair. Of the other tourists, most stay for at least part of their trip in Longyearbyen, combining cruises with a hiking tour, sledge tour or ski tour organised by one of the tour companies. Those who travel the archipelago independently on longer expeditions on foot, or by ski or kayak, are very much in the minority.

The Sysselmann's office recommends that visitors should make arrangements with one of the specialised companies, and with good reason. Though independent travellers are a tiny minority, they are responsible for practically all emergency rescue operations as well as for violating many of the local laws and regulations, including damaging the natural environment or cultural heritage, and illegally using cabins, etc.

The reasons why independent travellers cause so much trouble are numerous:

Lack of experience with vast Arctic wilderness For most travellers, the sheer vastness of Svalbard is hard to imagine. While dreaming of a 'wilderness experience', the practicalities are easily underestimated. Compared with Svalbard, other 'tourist' areas of northern wilderness (Lapland, Iceland, west and southern Greenland) are relatively civilised, offering a more or less dense network of marked routes, paths and even roads, shelters and emergency phones, for example. Outside of the few settlements, however, nothing of this sort is found in Svalbard. Moreover, the Arctic wilderness is a special place, and prior practical experience of living in non-Arctic wilderness is of limited use. Lack of knowledge usually leads to delays which can lead to problems with finishing the tour in time.

Lack of transport In most other wilderness areas, transport for independent expeditions can be organised even to the most remote points for a reasonable price. With motorised overland traffic and aircraft landings being forbidden for tourism (with the exception of limited use of snowmobiles in winter/spring) and very restricted for other purposes, and with boat transport being both very expensive and often impossible, large parts of the archipelago are very difficult (or impossible) for independent travellers to reach. As an independent traveller, the possibility of using transport organised by tour operators or scientific expeditions for their groups is very limited, as these professionals have to take care of their own groups first of all – accepting extra obligations like dropping and especially picking up others can lead to very unpleasant complications.

Equipment problems

Setting out into Arctic wilderness requires appropriate and high-quality equipment, which may seem very costly for just one expedition. Good safety equipment (including emergency communication and firearms) and the right high-quality camping equipment have their price – and, accordingly, high is the temptation to chose lower quality or do without, which in some cases then leads to problems. What's more, a number of rescue operations are caused by expensive equipment, which nevertheless turns out to be inappropriate for the actual conditions.

Lack of reserves

If stuck in dense fog or a snowstorm a few days away from the nearest settlement, it will not help you to know exactly where you are thanks to your GPS, nor will anybody be able to help you despite your satellite emergency calls. Instead, you'll just have to sit it out and wait for the weather to improve. So you will need to have sufficient reserves (especially food and fuel) for such situations, and equipment of a quality that allows you to survive such delays.

Nevertheless, every year there are some serious and successful independent expeditions around the archipelago. For some, it is part of the challenge to do all the preparation themselves, in spite of the higher costs and extra time required to organise such an expedition. For some projects, it is also not possible to find a suitable specialist as a provider. So the above-listed critical points are no general statement against independent travel – just plan and do it realistically, with sufficient respect for the Arctic.

The current strict regulations on tourism in Svalbard have been caused not least by bad experiences of the past. The compulsory insurance coverage has been introduced due to a growing number of rescue operations. All of us who love the archipelago and want to maintain the freedom of experiencing it in the future, should therefore do our best to minimise problems for the environment and for the rescue service. In fact, this should be self-evident even without the threat of further restrictions.

INDEPENDENT TRAVEL

See also *Tourist Access* map, page 91.

Essential rules for independent travellers:

- **Equipment** Only the best quality is to be used in the Arctic. This especially goes for equipment for emergency conditions.
- **Practical experience** Be absolutely sure that you know how to use your equipment. You must be able to put up your tent in a sleet storm without breaking anything; without realistic training your gun is just more ballast; at least one of your party should have Arctic experience, even if you don't plan on crossing any glaciers.
- **Travelling companions** Don't go it alone. Set up your team and establish its effectiveness by travelling together elsewhere, and for many days at a time, as a test before setting off to Svalbard.
- **Fitness** Make sure that you are very physically fit. Not only will you have to carry everything but, in small groups, the weight will be divided between very few shoulders.

- **Planning** Ensure that there is plenty of contingency time allowed for in your plan. There may be bad weather to contend with that will cause delays; it is easy to lose your way and you shouldn't underestimate how much a heavy pack can slow you down.
- **Permits** Register your journey with the Sysselmann many months in advance. Be aware that there may be high insurance (search and rescue) charges to pay.
- **Transport** Plan to use motorised transport as little as possible. If you're going to be collected from a certain point, make sure that you can get there in plenty of time, but be prepared for the transport itself to be several days late. Position your collection point where it may be seen from many different directions and make yourself highly visible. When negotiating to be dropped off or picked up somewhere by a vessel chartered for organised programmes, do not expect to get substantial reductions on the complete tour price, if any at all. Lower prices for passages are more likely on very short notice – if there is any space left then. Tour operators are especially reluctant to pick up expeditions at a remote spot, because this can easily lead to unpleasant and costly surprises if the ship for some reason (ice, weather, etc) is then not able to fulfil the arrangement. The less transport you include in your plans, and the less you depend on being picked up in a remote position, the easier and less costly will be the logistics of your project – but this may of course reduce the ambition of your project accordingly.
- **Emergency reserves** Don't base your plans on the use of cabins – there are only a very few, they are not for tourists and most remain locked. Some maps show huts that no longer exist. Instead, be certain that your fitness, equipment, supplies and allotted time are more than sufficient, and that you are prepared if something in your plans does not work out as expected.
- **Protection of nature and cultural monuments** Make sure you know the general regulations of protection and where the protection areas are and if there are any special conditions or prohibitions anywhere near your probable routes. Take care to disturb the environment as little as possible. Take your rubbish with you; do not disturb birds and other animals; do not damage vegetation in any way. People belong to the environment, too; respect others and follow the rules and conventions of your hosts and their country.

It is difficult to make general statements about independent travel as there is such a wide range of variables, including one's experience, fitness, suitable equipment and ambitions. Accordingly, there are ambitious expeditions that fail due to a lack of competence and overestimation of one's own abilities and margins, while others with realistic aims, good experience and equipment, sufficient reserves and the right respectful attitude may do very well.

ORGANISED TRAVEL These days, when any tour company with a half-decent web designer can appear professional on the web – regardless of their actual competence – it is vital to choose one's tour company carefully. The following should help.

Possible criteria for choosing a tour company
The following criteria are those that, in my experience as both a traveller and a tour operator, should be considered when choosing. Ask the questions before you book. Don't be shy; your holiday – and maybe even your life – could depend on these points!

- **Facilities** What does the operator offer that would otherwise be difficult to arrange (for example: pre-arranged shelters along the route)?

- **Competence** For how long has the operator been working in Svalbard? Is it a specialist in Svalbard, or at least in the Arctic region? Can the operator guarantee that staff have prior practical experience and training or is it one of these companies where guides arrive with the participants without ever having been to Svalbard before?
- **Safety** How seriously do they take safety? Are there at least two guides for bigger groups, giving more flexibility than just one? Are their weapons of heavy calibre and are their camps alarmed? Do they always carry flare guns or emergency satellite beacons? Have they travelled extensively in the area?
- **Information** Is the information about terrain, climate, etc, really detailed? Are restrictions and warnings described clearly or are they just 'small print'?
- **Clear requirements** Does it seem as if selling a tour is more important than getting together a group that fits? Are there a lot of offers to hire out gear, particularly items that you should try out before you travel? If so, you may be right to wonder whether the tour may take on a large number of unsuitable participants with little or no experience.
- **Support** Does the company have a supply depot or a manned base in Svalbard that can offer support? Possible situations where such a backup can be useful may include the following: if your rucksack doesn't arrive, the airline can't help and your kit cannot be replaced quickly in the local shops, your company should be able to supply you with substitutes from its base; if a skiing trip has not returned on time and your company has a base in Longyearbyen, it can send out a motorised sled to ensure that flights are not missed; if there's an emergency call to one of your tour party, it can sometimes be transmitted from the base to the camp; if a traveller needs to go to hospital, the organiser can look after things while the rest of the group continues its tour.
- **Advice** Is the provider capable of answering detailed relevant questions thanks to good relationships with the locals and experts, or does most of the information seem to come out of a book or seem a bit vague? From my experience, I can say that wrong information given by insufficiently knowledgeable sales staff is a major source of later problems.
- **Paperwork** How well are the paperwork requirements, including insurance, etc, explained?
- **Choice** Does the provider offer a wide range of options, or might you discover later that there are other tours that might better fit your interest? Are tour combinations possible?
- **Environmental protection** Is there information about environmental protection? Does this provider seem to care – in practice, not just with some vague global statement?

How you travel is well worth long and hard consideration. Perhaps your prejudices make you think cruises are just buffet orgies, or see trekking as pointless drudgery. Neither is true, of course, and to think in this way is restricting. Indeed, there is a case for trying more than one method of travelling, so that you can see more than one side to Svalbard.

Tour operators As mentioned before, most travel around Svalbard is done with the assistance of specialised companies. Here is an overview of some of the possibilities. Prices listed are per person and do not include flights to Svalbard. Most of these programmes can be booked either directly with the tour operator in Longyearbyen or, in the case of cruises, through specialised agencies in your home country which can then offer a complete package with flights, insurance, and so on. Be aware that sometimes these packages are more expensive than when booking only a tour and adding flights, etc, yourself (see pages 68–72).

While cruises to and in Svalbard have a history dating back 100 years, locally based tourism is young. The first tourism company based in Svalbard was officially registered in 1987, and only since 1989 has tourism been officially accepted by the Norwegian government as one of the economic pillars of Longyearbyen.

As you've probably gathered, there is a huge range of different activities that can be run, and a correspondingly huge range of prices, which makes listing them a little pointless. On the whole though, prices do not vary widely between the various operators.

Arctic Adventures Postboks 480, NO-9171 Longyearbyen; 79 02 16 24; m 47 80 59 90; e info@arctic-adventures.no; www. arctic-adventures.no. Flexible tour operator who organises customised short or long tours/ expeditions for individuals & groups. Based 12km outside of Longyearbyen with 30 Greenland huskies. Winter & spring: ski tour with dogs & pulks (transport sledges), dog-sledding, snowmobile trip & trip to glacier. Summer: ski tour with dogs & pulks, hike with pack-dogs, transport by boat & kayak & glacier crossing. Year-round: visit to the Greenland husky kennel.

Basecamp Spitsbergen Postboks 316, NO-9171 Longyearbyen; 79 02 46 00; e svalbard@basecampexplorer.com; www. basecampspitsbergen.com. Located in the town centre. A range of somewhat upmarket day trips & overnight stays including 'The boat in the ice', the trapper's station & kennel in Bolterdalen valley, hotel at Isfjord Radio at Kapp Linné & a cabin in the moraine at Nordenskiöld glacier. Dog sledding, ski ascent, snowmobiling. Tailor-made arrangements for groups & private cruise ships. Bicycle rental.

Henningsen Transport & Guiding Postboks 353, NO-9171 Longyearbyen; 79 02 13 11; m 91 85 37 56; e mail@htg.svalbard.no; www. htg.svalbard.no. Snowmobile rental. Guiding, by the hour or day by day. Custom-built tours on request. 2 small boats for cruises available for day trips, rental by the hour or day by day.

Jonathan Adventure Sailing Postboks 243, NO-9171 Longyearbyen; m 97 12 99 53; e info@jonathanadventuresailing.com; www. jonathanadventuresailing.com. The SY *Jonathon* is a yacht custom-built for sailing in Arctic waters, & can arrange expeditions & tours for small groups.

Polar Charter Postboks 330, NO-9254 Tromsø; 97 52 32 50; e pcharter@online.no; www.

polarcharter.no. They have a handful of boats available for sightseeing, fishing trips & 'skiing-by-boat' tours.

Poli Arctici Postboks 89, NO-9171 Longyearbyen; 79 02 17 05; m 91 38 34 67; e stefano@ poliarctici.com; www.poliarctici.com. Small, Italian-run tour operator arranges short & long trip/expedition for individuals & groups. Transport in field. Winter & spring: ski tour with dogs & pulks, snowmobile trip & ice caving. Summer: ski tour with dogs & pulks, hike with pack-dogs & Zodiac trip. Overnight tours & camping in field. Support/ logistics for film/TV.

Spitsbergen Experience Postboks 524, NO-9171 Longyearbyen; m 91 70 37 25; e priitta@spitsbergenexperience.com; www. spitsbergenexperience.com. Winter: full-day dog-sledding trip. Week trip to the east coast of Spitsbergen by dog-sledges, overnight in tents. Tailor-made multi-day trip. Summer: dog-sledding on wheels. Offers guide services in English, Finnish, German, French & Norwegian.

Spitsbergen Tours (Terra Polaris) Postboks 6, NO-9171 Longyearbyen; 79 02 10 68; m 97 74 46 96; e info@terrapolaris.com; www.terrapolaris.com. Owner of Longyearbyen Camping (& the author of this book), Andreas Umbreit has been operating in Svalbard since 1987, & can provide advice, guiding & support to tourists & media projects.

Spitsbergen Travel Postboks 548, NO-9171 Longyearbyen; 79 02 61 00; e info@ spitsbergentravel.no; www.spitsbergentravel.no. One of the longest-established tour operators in the archipelago, running cruises, 1-day & longer treks, kayaking & more or less all of the possible activities. They operate throughout the year, with both summer & winter programmes. You can also rent your own snowmobiles, clothing & gear including weapons.

Spitsbergen Outdoor Activities Postboks 182, NO-9171 Longyearbyen; m 91 77 65 95; e post@spitsbergenoutdooractivities.com; www. spitsbergenoutdooractivities.com. Horseback riding on Icelandic horses along Isfjorden towards Vestpynten. They also run kayaking, glacier hiking & ice-caving trips.

Svalbard Husky Postboks 1039, NO-9171 Longyearbyen; m 98 87 16 21; e info@ svalbardhusky.no; www.svalbardhusky.no. As the name suggests, dog-sledding, kayaking & other tours, including fossil hunting.

Svalbard Maxi Taxi Postboks 172, NO-9171 Longyearbyen; 79 02 13 05; e post@taxiguiden. no; www.taxiguiden.no. A taxi which offers 2hr-long minibus tours of Longyearbyen & its surroundings, both scheduled & bespoke.

Svalbard Nature 6-37 quai Arloing, 69009 Lyon, France; +33 478 92 30 88 (France); e info@ svalbard-nature.com; www.svalbardnature.com. A focus on hiking & kayaking tours.

Svalbard Snøscooterutleie Postboks 538, NO-9171 Longyearbyen; 79 02 46 41; e post@scooterutleie.net; www.scooterutleie. net. Located on the seafront, they rent out snowmobiles, snowmobile equipment & weapons. Also offer guided snowmobile trips, both day trips & several days.

Svalbard Villmarkssenter Postboks 396, NO-9171 Longyearbyen; 79 02 17 00; e info@svalbardvillmarkssenter.no; www. svalbardvillmarkssenter.no. Winter: short & long dog-sledding trip. Overnight trip to hut in the wilderness. 3-day trip with accommodation in tent. Summer: dog-sledding on wheels, day trip to mountains & glaciers with or without pack-dogs including lunch.

Svalbard Wildlife Expeditions Postboks 164, NO-9171 Longyearbyen; 79 02 22 22; e info@ wildlife.no; www.wildlife.no. Wilderness tours for individuals & groups. Overnight & day trips in the area of/around Longyearbyen. Winter & spring: snowmobile trip, dog-sledding, ice caving, trappers hike, ski expeditions. Summer: glacier walks, fossil expeditions, kayaking & boat trip. Wilderness camping, ski expeditions, 7-day hiking trip, cruises.

Svalbard4You Postboks 144, NO-9171 Longyearbyen; m 90 18 65 36; e post@ svalbard4you.no/pal.remen@gmail.com; www.svalbard4you.no. This tour operator is predominantly based around snowmobile operations & hiking journeys, but is also able to arrange other activities.

Many operators based outside Svalbard advertise tours there, but you should be aware that many of these will be relying on the Svalbard-based operators to provide the on-the-ground experience. The value added by these operators will be in smoothing your way to Svalbard, organising travel and overnight stays and so on. It's really for you to decide whether you want this service or are more willing to make the arrangements yourself – the latter will not necessarily be the cheaper option. In addition, some of the operators offer both cruises and land tours, so will appear both here and in the section on cruise operators:

Askja Reizen Van Lawick van Pabststraat 66, 6814 HK Arnhem, The Netherlands; +31 26 352 9390 (Netherlands); e info@askja.nl; www.askja.nl (website in Dutch)

Five Stars of Scandinavia 1804 Black Lake Bd, SW Suite 203, Olympia, WA 98512, USA; +800 722 4126 (USA); e info@5stars-scandinavia.com; www.5stars-scandinavia.com

High Places 63 Bower Rd, Sheffield S10 1ER, UK; +44 114 268 7760 (UK); e treks@highplaces. co.uk; www.highplaces.co.uk

International Wildlife Adventures PO Box 1410, Vashon, Washington 98070, USA; +1 206

463 1943 (USA); e info@wildlifeadventures.com; www.wildlifeadventures.com

Naturetrek Cheriton Mill, Cheriton, Alresford, Hants SO24 0NG, UK; +44 1962 733 051 (UK); e info@naturetrek.co.uk; www.naturetrek.co.uk

Quark Expeditions 93 Pilgrim Park, Suite 1, Waterbury, VT 05676, USA; +1 888 892 0334; e info@quarkexpeditions.com; www. quarkexpeditions.com

Specialised Tours 4 Copthorne Bank, Copthorne, Crawley, West Sussex RH10 3QX, UK; +44 1342 712 785 (UK); e info@specialisedtours.com; www. specialisedtours.com

The Great Canadian Travel Company 158 Fort St, Winnipeg, MB, R3C 1C9, Canada; ☏+1 800 661 3830 (Canada); www.topoftheworldtours.com
Wildlife Worldwide Long Barn South, Sutton Manor Farm, Bishops Sutton, Alresford SO24 0AA, UK; ☏+44 1962 302 086 (UK); e sales@ wildlifeworldwide.com; www.wildlifeworldwide. com
Wildwatch Tours Manor Barn, 3 Church View, Bilsthorpe, Newark, Notts NG22 8TB, UK; ☏+44 1623 411 215 (UK); e enquiries@wildwatchtours. co.uk; www.wildwatchtours.co.uk

POSSIBLE ACTIVITIES

As you might expect, land activities in Svalbard tend to be based around nature – tours, skiing, hiking, and the like. They also tend to be almost endlessly adjustable and the prices will vary accordingly. Many will also have a minimum number of participants. All these variations complicate pricing structures until they become effectively meaningless, so the best source of price information is the tour operators themselves, and the prices given below are indicative.

TRAVEL IN THE POLAR NIGHT Experiencing the polar night in Svalbard normally means staying in one of the settlements, with the option of spending some time in a cabin in combination (reached by dog-sledge). Seeing a new year in is to be recommended, when even at midday the sun stays below the horizon and it is darker than twilight, giving the unique experience of night around the clock. Christmas would be a hypothetical option, too, but at that time almost everything is closed in Longyearbyen. From December to January, not yet the coldest period, the little light that is available is properly magical. The stars alone are bright enough to reveal a white wilderness and the bright moon, which when about full is above the horizon almost permanently, sheds a mild light on the partly white landscape; while when it's less than half full it stays almost always under the horizon. And then of course there are the northern lights. As it is dark for 24 hours, you may catch sight of the northern lights with clear weather even at midday, which is hardly possible in more southerly regions, where for instance in northern Lapland there is at least some sort of clear dawn at midday. Daily programmes will have to be planned on a day-to-day basis depending on natural conditions – you may be locked in by a snowstorm or, if you're lucky, enjoy some wonderful tours under the night sky with your armed guide. Unfortunately, the circle of northern lights and polar-night fans is small, so there are not many tours offered. (*Price per person for four-day snowmobile tours in the winter: from around NOK14,000.*)

SKI TOURS To discover the late winter on skis is a real experience. Covered in white, the landscape is finer, quieter and more spectacular. The route possibilities are almost endless, many of them requiring fitness more than refined skiing techniques. Much more important is that the skier is prepared for an extreme range of severe weather possibilities and also very variable snow conditions.

Of equal importance is the equipment and clothing used. I don't favour programmes that include the option of renting personal gear. This encourages people with insufficient experience to join the tour, and there may also be problems caused by ill-fitting kit.

There are differences between late-winter tours and summer ski tours over glaciers and high ground. Mixed tours can also be arranged, where the organiser looks after the base camps and the transport, but the clients do the actual skiing part unaccompanied. Ski tours are probably good ways of travel with minimal negative impact – at least once one begins skiing.

Late-winter ski tours Ski tours in late winter can be fantastic but demanding. They exact a toll on your stamina, your will, your experience and your equipment. Putting up your tent quickly enough at –30°C in swirling snow to avoid freezing, and then getting your stove going, is no game. For many skiers, too, it's a surprise to find that large stretches of terrain have only minimal snow cover, mainly due to wind drift, especially near the coasts where a lot of stones may be visible, which can be both exhausting to travel over and ruinous for the skis. In many places, the ground is covered more by thin, slippery ice than snow. Further inland, however, there is usually enough snow from March onwards. Also, one should not rely on solid ice cover on the fjords – this changes a lot from year to year, and strong wind may break up ice covers that were stable on the way out, making them perilous on your return journey.

Easter 2004 was a bad time for skiers, when 11 expeditions, most of them on skis, and all of them independent travellers, required rescuing when trapped in a severe snowstorm for several days. Among them was an Austrian expedition with extensive experience of the Himalayas and other places, whose equipment nevertheless proved not to be suitable to these conditions, their tent being insufficiently sealed against the intruding, very fine Arctic snow.

May and even early June are occasionally good for skiing tours too, with less risk of extreme cold. It's important to get out of Longyearbyen (and back again) before the snowmelt begins in earnest, as the melt starts in and around Longyearbyen before anywhere else, making the surrounding terrain impassable.

Classic Nordic touring skis with metal edges are well suited to this environment. Fishscales (an often waxless ski base) or waxing is a matter of personal choice, but in late winter waxing plus skins would be a good choice; in summer, with slushy conditions in lower areas fishscales may prove easier. At all times skins with a mix of mohair and nylon offer good glide and are not as prone to balling up with snow as all-nylon skins. Skins with dimensions similar to that of the Fischer E109 are a good choice for this type of expedition.

Recent years have seen the development of lightweight plastic boots suitable for use on many classic touring skis. With early morning temperatures that can drop to –30°C in late winter and slushy conditions in summer, traditional leather boots cannot offer the same levels of warmth and waterproofing as plastic. Avoid buying specific telemark boots. These will have stiffer plastic shells, are higher cut and are generally not as comfortable for covering long distances. The same can be said about alpine touring equipment.

Bindings have also changed in recent years with the development of New Nordic Norm (NNN) systems. Although heavy-duty backcountry (BC) versions of these bindings are available, they are prone to icing up in extremely cold conditions and the metal bar on the underside of the boot can be damaged if walking around on rocky terrain. Cable bindings without pins are probably the most reliable for these conditions.

In view of the equipment necessary and the supplies required for a longer tour, *pulks* (pulled sledges) make more sense than carrying heavy backpacks. Two-man tunnel and especially geodetic tents are to be preferred for winter use as they are less likely to be grabbed by the wind.

If planning to start from Longyearbyen, the best time to go is April. The temperature is less likely to be too extreme by then, although you must expect occasional swings down to –30°C. The snowmelt doesn't start in earnest until May, and you can take full advantage of the conditions to ski almost anywhere. You may be disturbed by the ubiquitous skidoo, though, and many tour organisers arrange for motorised sleds to take you outside of the normal snowmobile range first, perhaps 30–50km away – this increases the tour price, but makes for a significantly better tour without constant snowmobile noise or even smell along the main routes near Longyearbyen.

For individual skiing expeditions, such a transfer can also be arranged. Be aware, however, that nobody can guarantee that you will be dropped off and picked up at a certain point on a certain date – nature inevitably has a say in such arrangements. Therefore, always build enough time into your itinerary to allow for delays and rearrangements. Transfers further out of Longyearbyen, especially those following difficult routes, can be quite costly.

A popular destination for skiing expeditions is Newtontoppen (1,713m), not because this is necessarily the best skiing tour, but simply because it is the highest peak of the archipelago. Technically, this is not an extremely difficult tour, but it does lead over wide glaciated areas, where weather and snow conditions play a major role; indeed, sometimes a tour doesn't get to Newtontoppen at all, even when the group has allowed two weeks for a distance that under good conditions can be covered in five to six days. (*Price per person for 12-day tours: around NOK23,500.*)

Summer ski tours Summer skiing tours (June to September) are more comfortable because of milder weather. Still, expect –10°C to +10°C. However, the valleys are free of snow by then, as indeed are often the lower parts of the glaciers, on which a zone of unpleasant slush may follow. In the course of the summer, good snow conditions may retreat gradually to areas in excess of 1,000m above sea level. Extensive areas so high are fairly remote in the archipelago, requiring costly transfers and often a lot of sweat and toil just to get through the snow-free lower terrain. However, if these hindrances are overcome and the weather is good (which it should be), skiing the high areas of Svalbard under permanent light can be a unique experience.

Skiing-wise, summer in Svalbard can be compared to other glaciated areas elsewhere in the world. As the thaws set in, the glaciers are more active, once-secure snow bridges may become unstable and new crevasses may form. Accordingly, safety equipment and techniques are even more important with summer tours. Again, tents must be stormproof and safety measures must be good enough – you will be a long way from civilisation.

Offers for organised summer skiing expeditions in Svalbard are rare as this is a very small market. Those tours that do exist are often run by alpine clubs or those tour operators who are closely affiliated with such clubs. As there are certain risks connected to these tours, too, and the typical areas for them are quite remote, the compulsory insurance against search and rescue costs is inevitably fairly expensive.

DOG-SLEDS Svalbard was never a place with a widespread tradition of using dog-sleds. There were no indigenous hunters and the mines were not particularly interested in the wide-ranging mobility in the winter months that dog-sleds provide. Indeed, dog-sleds first came to prominence only with the Norwegian trappers at the end of the 19th century, these hunters being the only people overwintering who needed to travel regularly. Dogs were also used by the Sysselmann until the 1960s. With the arrival of snowmobiles and helicopters, which require no feeding over the summer, sledge dogs almost disappeared, enjoying a renaissance only since the 1990s thanks to tourism.

The season runs from the end of February to well into May. Presently, most dog-sledge activities are day excursions for a few hours, just to get the feeling of it.

2

Tours of several days can be arranged on request, but this demand is unfortunately limited – probably a lot of customers want a little of the romance of dog-sleds, but not the complete package, which usually includes sleeping in tents with no shower, etc. And of course, dog-sledging is not a cheap activity, in view of the demands of keeping a pack of dogs year round, even when they are not working.

Some of the organised tour programmes include dog-sledging between cabins. Longer dog-sledge programmes are usually arranged by special request only – calculate on roughly NOK2,000 per day as a rough price indication; such arrangements should be made about half a year in advance. A good time for dog-sledging is from late March to early May and your party should consist of a minimum of two people or, better, four to six people.

Day excursions with dog-sledging are offered depending on snow conditions until mid-May but are sometimes continued throughout most of the summer on a mountain plateau as long as there is still sufficient snow. As these offers and their providers change, please check the weekly programme in the tourist information office for what is currently offered when you are in Longyearbyen.

SNOWSHOES AND LATE-WINTER HIKING
Contrary to common belief, the snow cover in truly Arctic areas off the higher glaciers is on average fairly limited and, moreover, varies enormously, primarily due to relocation by wind. In wide areas, the snow is hard pressed, and often so thin that stones peek through. Accordingly, winter hiking is often a surprisingly good alternative, especially when supplemented with snowshoes for stretches with deeper snow. Snowshoes should be of a type that are also good for the icy slopes in between. Such winter hiking can in fact be more pleasant than using skis in some areas with limited snow, and is a good possibility for those travelling unmotorised, as well as for people with few cross-country skiing skills, and it's far less costly than programmes with dog-sledges or snowmobiles.

SNOWMOBILES
For many residents the late winter (end of February to mid-May) is the time for departing Longyearbyen either on skidoo or on ski tours for Svalbard's white wilderness. At Easter, Longyearbyen is more full of visitors than in any other period of the year (hence especially high prices for much of the accommodation in spring). Many flights are fully booked. The best season for snowmobiles is usually April – before this time, it may be very cold more often and snow and ice cover may still be poor; while from early May onwards the risk of serious snowmelt increases considerably.

I personally am somewhat less than enthusiastic about snowmobile driving when it becomes a purpose in itself – I find it a pity when the grand landscape of Svalbard devolves to mere motor-sports arena. However, as a means of transport, snowmobiles are hard to match – with a dog-sled you may need two days for the distance you can cover by snowmobile in just an hour. At the same time, distance in itself is not necessarily a measure of enjoyment or the success of an expedition, and trying to cram as many places as possible into an itinerary by travelling fast does not necessarily lead to more lasting memories. Although there are programmes on the market that use snowmobiles as the main (or even sole) activity in Svalbard, I strongly recommend you use them only occasionally, to experience more of the Arctic nature, its peacefulness and beauty – which is hardly the same even when stopping occasionally on a snowmobile ride.

Motor-sled drives are a relatively new activity for the late winter. Only with Gunnar Paulsen's introduction of series-production vehicles in 1961 did the new era begin.

There are about 4,000 *snøscooters* in Svalbard, most of them in Longyearbyen, so nearly all inhabitants, particularly the young, have access to (at least) one. The obvious advantages over dog-sledging are their speed and the fact that you don't need to feed them all year round. Accordingly, the locals use skidoos almost exclusively, for day trips or to go to their huts for the night.

Motorised entry into national parks and nature reserves (more than half of Svalbard) is forbidden to tourists by law; local residents may obtain restricted permission on some routes. In addition, two snowmobile-free zones have been introduced in central Svalbard to offer skiers and dog-sledge travellers at least a bit of space near to Longyearbyen where one can exist without the frequent noise of snowmobiles.

Snowmobile driving has become the main part of spring tourism, which is still very much dominated by Norwegians, while visitors during that season from other countries seem more likely to prefer seeking out the silence of the archipelago. The government has reacted to the growth of snowmobiling by introducing more restrictions – tourists can drive snowmobiles now only in a minor part of the archipelago (see map, page 91). With a guide this area is somewhat bigger, then including also a stretch of the east coast. A positive aspect is the new introduction of four-stroke engines, which reduce both the noise and the exhaust fumes drastically.

Generally, snowmobiling has become an expensive pleasure, either when booking an organised tour or when renting your own snowmobile.

Rental Skidoos can be hired from one of the snowmobile rental outfits in Longyearbyen. Several tour operators will also hire out snowmobiles. On weekends in April and early May, all snowmobiles are usually booked out long in advance and, accordingly, there's a lot of traffic on standard routes such as Barentsburg and Tempelfjord – if possible, choose a weekday when it's slightly quieter. Costs depend on engine type (two-stroke/four-stroke and strength), which can exceed 1,000cc motors that produce up to 150hp. For longer trips, where storage space is needed for kit and emergency equipment and a sledge trailer is therefore needed behind the snowmobile, choose a machine of at least 60hp. As a minimum, you should go out with two skidoos, at least one of which should have two seats. Even civilised snowmobile driving means high wear and tear in the rough terrain of Svalbard and accordingly, it is not unheard of that one of the vehicles breaks down somewhere far out in the wintry wilderness. In such a case, it is nevertheless up to you to bring the vehicle back to the rental company yourself or pay quite a lot to have someone recover it for you. Moreover, in case of a breakdown, it is very nice to have spare seats on the other snowmobiles of your group to get back home.

In addition, you may need a sledge, cans (fuel, emergency equipment) and liability insurance; the renting of special snowmobile clothes is also highly recommended. I also recommend the use of four-stroke engines both out of consideration for the environment and, on longer tours, for their more economical fuel consumption. Just the rental prices for all this add up to around NOK2,000 per day, with fuel and oil (for two-stroke engines) not included. A two-stroke snowmobile may spend 25 litres of petrol per 100km, plus oil; a four-stroke engine may need only 60% of that fuel and no oil. There is also a great need for specialist clothing, because of the wind-chill factor inherent in sitting for hours on an open machine travelling at 60km/h. (Rental prices per day will start around NOK1,000 for a basic two-stroke and increase depending on the extras you choose. If you are interested in renting a snowmobile, bear in mind that, just as with renting a car, there will be some extra costs that you should take into account. Paraffin is in the region of NOK10 per litre at time of writing, and oil for the snowmobile will be around NOK50. Insurance against damage or loss of the snowmobile will start around NOK150. Most companies will rent you suitable clothing if you don't have your own – starting around NOK350.)

Guided snowmobile excursions

It certainly makes no sense economically to rent a snowmobile in comparison to joining one of the guided snowmobile day excursions offered by the same companies to Barentsburg or to the glacier front in Tempelfjord (the two standard routes). Such tours are offered almost daily in the high season. Again, I strongly recommend avoiding weekends, due to the size and number of groups at this time; with all the exhaust, it is not exactly pure pleasure to drive at the back of the pack. The preconditions for driving your own snowmobile are that you have a valid (car) driving licence and are over 18 years of age.

There are also a few programmes offered that tour central Svalbard for several days on snowmobiles, sleeping either in the few settlements on the way (Longyearbyen, Barentsburg) or in tents. (*Participating in a guided snowmobile day excursion costs around NOK2,000 per person if you have a snowmobile for yourself (which is strongly recommended in terms of driving comfort), while a passenger on the back seat pays around NOK1,500 for the tour.*)

Licences and traffic regulations

A motorsled licence can be obtained at the age of 16. A normal car licence also suffices. Currently, use of a helmet is compulsory.

Traffic regulations apply also to skidoos, even in the open country. Speed limits are 20km/h on the streets and 50km/h off-road on the central track in the streambed in Longyearbyen. Outside of town the Norwegian limit of 80km/h applies, although you will see some racers accelerate to over 120km/h. (The unofficial Svalbard record is 212km/h.) Skidoo speeds, too, are checked occasionally by radar controls, and drivers may be breathalysed for drunk driving (limit: just 0.2mg alcohol per millilitres of blood!).

Handling tips

The basics of driving snowmobiles are relatively easy. They have step-less automatic transmission, rarely with reverse, so all you have to do is start the machine, then operate the throttle lever and steer.

Snowmobiles should be equipped with a toolkit, a spare V-belt, spare spark plugs, a can and a funnel for refilling from cans (check before you start!). Make sure you understand how to look after these technical details before you go. Be careful when changing V-belts and use gloves as some of the components can get quite hot. Make sure your reserve canister is full before you set out; filling stations use magnetic cards, something few tourists will have.

- Throttle control, braking and emergency stops should all be practised before setting off to make sure that none of them is iced.
- Use the smallest amount of choke possible when starting a two-stroke engine.
- If the skidoo has been standing for a while in frost conditions, lift the back end after starting the engine to make sure that the belt is not frozen to the ground. Should the drive chain have been frozen to the ground, you could damage the engine if you don't take this precaution.
- All skidoos have an emergency stop; either a button or a key that's attached by a string to your wrist: the engine stops if the key is pulled out of its lock or the button pressed.

- Snowmobiles are not constructed to carry very much extra weight (5–10kg) in addition to the driver and passenger, especially not on the small baggage carrier behind the seat – and certainly this has not been constructed with a heavy and bumping fuel can in mind.
- Trailers should be loaded so as not to overload the coupling, so the weight should be balanced out. If a trailer has been standing for a while, check that it is not frozen to the ground.
- With very careful use of the accelerator, a sled can be made to move very slowly, so that you can steer it while walking and possibly pushing to the side of it. This is important over difficult terrain. It is a matter of feel, as is rapid acceleration or driving more quickly.
- On slippery ice or in deep snow you may have to move your body from one side to the other to get the balance and traction right. Getting stuck in a drift will demonstrate the usefulness of having a travelling partner – and shovel and ropes.
- Long trips on snow-free ice (or roads) can overheat the engine (snow flurries are designed to be part of the cooling system) and can harm the drive chains or steering.
- Do not park in an obstructing way (especially for snowploughs when parking in town overnight) and keep the prescribed minimum of 8m distance from any houses.
- Do not disturb wild animals. (Three drivers disturbing a bear, temporarily separating her from her young, were fined NOK8,000 each.) The most common encounters are those with reindeer, which, should they feel threatened, can react quite inappropriately, for instance by fleeing into your driving direction instead of to the side. It is your duty to minimise disturbance by reducing your speed drastically or by changing your course and evading them in a wide swing.

Terrain problems There are open areas of unsafe ice over fjords even in winter. Inland there may be slushy sections, especially near glaciers. Salt water may be flowing through fissures under a thin layer of dry snow on sea ice, causing a slushy foundation; once you stop you may not be able to get going again. Mostly, smaller crevasses on glaciers are full of snow and cause no problems. But in some cases there is a danger (eg: if driving in the direction of the rift). Stay on known routes, and remember that just following an old track made by somebody else can be risky, as conditions may have changed in the meantime, especially on glaciers and sea ice.

Loose snow is difficult for the drive system to grip; up to three men may be needed to get out of a drift. Icy patches are also difficult; you can hardly steer.

Snowdrifts can lead to unexpected jumps. Wide streambeds, full of snow, are favourite routes, but even here the wind can form shapes, leaving mischievous gaps where you least expect them.

'White-outs' happen with disorientating consequences. These occur when mist and the snow-laden sky conspire to make everything the same colour so that you have no idea of contours only a few metres away.

The ease and speed of transport on a skidoo means that you can cover a stretch in half an hour that may take you all day on foot, and then only if you're an experienced hiker. This means that you can very quickly get out of the range of help should something go wrong; it is not as if you can count on seeing any passers-by. There are regular stories of tourists who have not considered this and have therefore gone out with inadequate preparation. Even the possession of a GPS (Global Positioning

System) helps only if you're competent at orienteering (and have sufficient battery capacity). At best your map will be to a scale of 1:100,000 and your GPS might give you an accuracy of ±10m.

Safety rules

- Never set out alone on longer trips. Make sure that at least one of your machines has space for two people in case a snowmobile breaks down.
- When touring, make sure that you are fully equipped with tools, spares and all the necessary kit that you would take when hiking for an unexpected emergency bivouac or foot/ski tour back.
- Make sure that your clothing offers full protection against the elements.
- Make sure that you are fully conversant with the details of your planned route. Even local residents aren't aware of all the dangers outside the Isfjorden area. Select only routes that are known.
- Stay on your route wherever possible. The 1:200,000 map of Nordenskiöldlandet shows common routes, but this does not mean that it is possible to use them on the day that you travel. Furthermore, individual snowmobile tourists are not allowed to use some of these marked routes (eg: such as those on the east coast).
- Check machines out thoroughly and ensure that you have sufficient fuel and oil (two-stroke engines).
- Lodge details of your trip with the Sysselmann.

Two of the most important virtues when out in the wilderness are patience and the ability to keep cool. By being too hasty and impatient, unpleasant situations can easily be transformed into real problems. Remember: Mother Nature is much stronger than you, so there is no point in testing her.

DAY CRUISES IN ISFJORD From early June to September, day cruises are offered from Longyearbyen aboard smaller ships to destinations in the Isfjord area. Most of them head for the main Russian settlement of Barentsburg, though occasionally they also venture off in other directions, to Billefjord or Tempelfjord for example. Usually a minimum of eight to ten fully paying participants is required for these tours to actually take place, a stipulation that may be difficult to fulfil, especially in the early and late seasons and particularly on weekdays. Furthermore, these tours depend, of course, on natural conditions. Ice (especially in June to early July) in particular often poses limitations, and when there are very rough seas a tour may be cancelled altogether.

The various offers are published on the weekly programme in the tourist information office, which is updated from week to week.

SETTLEMENT-BASED STAYS WITH DAY ACTIVITIES Currently, Longyearbyen is the most popular base for day trips, although Barentsburg is also used. Longyearbyen, however, has the widest range of facilities. Settlement-based programmes can be adapted to various interests which differ depending on the time of year. While the settlement with its amenities serves as a base, day excursions lead out into the surrounding nature or to other attractions (museum, mine, shopping, etc). Excursions into nature are adapted according to the season and conditions, but can be conducted on foot, by boat, with a dog-sled or by snowmobile.

A settlement-based programme is a popular preface to one of the longer expedition cruises, allowing one to become acquainted with Svalbard before boarding a ship. The smaller groups of these programmes and the fact that you're on land all the time gives one a better chance of familiarising oneself with, and acclimatising to, Svalbard. A settlement-based stay can often be adapted to the client's needs regarding duration, the programme and the accommodation.

Two of the most exciting and engaging settlement-based stays are run by Basecamp Spitsbergen. In 2013, they opened a small wooden cabin just at the shoreline in Adolfbukta, one of the inner bays in Billefjorden. The wood-heated cabin has five bedrooms (with 11 beds), as well as a toilet and sauna, and views right out to the glacier. Stays at the cabin are bookable through Basecamp Spitsbergen (see page 73). Slightly more adventurous are stays aboard the *Noorderlicht*, a 120ft Dutch schooner that first sailed in 1911. Each winter, between February and May, the company sails the ship straight into the ice of inner Tempelfjord, some 60km northeast of Longyearbyen, where it serves as a base for explorations into Svalbard's hinterlands. With 20 beds, two lounges, a small library and a fully licensed bar, guests are well catered for aboard the world's only ice-bound hotel ship.

Hiking and trekking in summer
Longer tours on foot in the wilderness and sleeping in a tent offer a complete contrast to a hotel stay or a ship cruise: comfort is low, but the experience is accordingly intense, comprehensive and memorable. It is one thing to see Svalbard from a cruise ship; quite another to be in nature more or less all the time. Even from the comfort of your sleeping bag in a tent you can see the sunlight and shadows through the canvas, hear the wind and the waves or the deep thunder of the calving of a nearby glacier. The price for this closeness to nature is less comfort – but is comfort your main reason for coming to Svalbard? Yes, the washing water at the stream is cold – but when washing right after a day's hard walking, this can be truly invigorating. Yes, you will feel tired after walking in the pathless terrain, too, but you will also remember more of what you have done and what you have seen, because we are by nature made to discover the world on foot and at walking pace. Higher speed can be exciting, a thrill, but reduces our ability to truly memorising what we see. These lasting memories are the secret of why less can be more.

With this plea for hiking, I do not want to rule out other types of travelling; in fact, for many the ideal may be a cruise and walking holiday, to choose just one possible combination.

There are a number of areas in Svalbard that offer ample possibilities for extensive hiking, especially central Svalbard with the areas of Nordenskiöldland, Bünsow Land, Dickson Land, Andrée Land and parts of Heer Land, Sabine Land, Oskar II Land and James I Land, as well as Prins Karls Forland and smaller isolated areas around Ny-Ålesund, the Mitra Peninsula or in Albert I Land and Haakon VII Land up in the north. These areas are less glaciated and offer rich possibilities for guided hiking programmes or for the independent hiker who is fully conversant with the peculiarities of Arctic wilderness.

Because Svalbard is virtually a wilderness, hikers have to be more self-sufficient than in most other places. Even if they have a tour operator who has prepared camps or supply depots at various stages, more equipment has to be carried. On the other hand, lower levels of precipitation and the rarity of mosquitoes generally make for a more comfortable hike.

In contrast to the usual marketing language, where a short walk is still sometimes called a 'trek', the word is used here in its original sense: trekking means travelling on non-motorised transport on land from one camp to the next.

Tours based at stationary camps Organised hiking and trekking arrangements are offered for durations of a few days with one camp as a base, to trips of up to three weeks with as many as five tented camps (plus Longyearbyen) as bases, the longer tours especially providing the participant with a broad spectrum of landscapes and experiences. The advantage of these camp-based arrangements is that there is considerably less weight in your rucksack as tents, stoves, fuel and most of the food supplies do not have to be carried by you over long distances. Transfers between the camps are partly by boat and partly on foot – on these 'on-foot' trekking days, all personal gear has to be carried to the next camp, though in, say, a 22-day excursion the number of these 'on-foot' days never numbers more than three. Some arrangements do not include any trekking at all but only day excursions, where even some of the personal equipment stays in the camp.

Trekking tours without pre-arranged camps Considerably more demanding are long treks where expedition tents, cooking equipment, food and fuel are carried along in the rucksack. This gives more flexibility and freedom to adapt your route to take account of special interests, conditions and fitness. These physically more demanding long treks are a very limited market, and as the cache has to be brought out in spring, early booking is necessary.

For **independent travellers**, usually only this possibility – carrying their complete equipment and supplies – applies, as they have no access to the camps of the tour operators and usually no supply caches along the route either. As a result, independent treks are limited by the weight of the rucksack that one can sensibly carry. Of the few independent treks organised, most take place in the area between Longyearbyen, Barentsburg and Sveagruva, as this is the easiest to access and does not require special permission and insurance.

Guided hiking day excursions From Longyearbyen, a number of guided day excursions may be offered. Be aware that, while called 'day excursions', these tours may in reality last only a few hours – check what you are getting before putting your money down. You can also find themed tours that specialise in observing flora, for example, or searching for fossils. The offers on for each week are reported by tour operators to the tourist information office one week prior to departure, after which point they are published on the office's activity list for the actual week. (*Prices start around NOK500 for four or five hours and increase by roughly NOK100 for each additional hour of trekking.*)

CLIMBING A few mountaineering groups choose Svalbard as a destination for expeditions. Many parts of central and eastern Svalbard are unsafe for climbing, with weak and fragmented sedimentary rock, often with no handholds. Here, a 3m vertical step of crumbling rock can already be insurmountable. Areas of hard, crystalline rock that may be of interest to alpinists are as follows.

The northwest A classic destination for climbers, lying between Krossfjorden, Liefdefjorden and Smeerenburgfjorden. Every summer brings a few groups to this mountainous and glacial area after which the island of Spitsbergen originally got its name.

Southern Ny Frieslandet This is a seldom-visited region which includes Svalbard's highest peaks. There are innumerable routes, taking in imposing walls and glaciers.

Again and again there are those who set out on 'macho-projects' (climbing, canoeing, skiing, etc) with great ambition and little local knowledge. One example concerns four young climbers who, without any serious Svalbard experience and against all warnings, set out from Longyearbyen intending to cross to the north point of the main island and return in four to five weeks. Despite advice to the contrary, they had arrived with insufficient insurance cover, and consequently lost precious time while sorting things out. Finally, they set out, full of themselves and restricted by the Sysselmann's permission to attempt only half of their originally planned route. After a few days, the rigours of their daily schedule and the weights of their packs started to affect two of the party so much that they turned back. The remaining two managed to get to Newtontoppen and started to climb the peak. As one set off over the snow flank and reached the top, the other chose a route up an icy rock face without safety gear and didn't make it. The first took 11 days to search for him, get back to Longyearbyen and raise the alarm. The search and rescue operation itself put others at risk. And what were they left with? One dead, two slightly more sensible 'failures' and one rather miserable 'winner'. Proof – as if proof were needed – that a mixture of overconfidence, ambition, lack of local knowledge and a failure to heed advice invites catastrophe.

The southwest Between Recherchefjorden (Bellsundet) and south of Hornsundet is an area of hard rock and interesting possibilities, with the towering Hornsundtind (1,431m, rising from sea level) as the most obvious goal, but also very difficult to reach.

The remoteness of climbing regions means that rescue operations take longer than in the Alps. Self-sufficiency is the watchword here.

Owing to the risks involved, most tour operators don't include climbing in their portfolios, but they may help with base camps and other logistics.

Obviously, these regions are part of the areas of Svalbard for which both permission and insurance is required, which in the case of the latter is likely to be high for such expeditions (see *Red tape*, page 89).

PADDLING At first sight the heavily indented coast seems to invite paddlers. You can take in short trips along the southern shore of Isfjorden, or go on a 1,000km circumnavigation of the main island. But, as a rule, fewer than 20 independent paddlers a year visit Svalbard. Transporting your boat there can be expensive. In addition, climatic conditions mean that special equipment is needed and most trips make heavy demands on strength and stamina.

Quality craft are needed: either a good sea kayak or, if the possibility of dismantling is more important because of freight and a route that includes land portages, a top-quality foldable boat like the Klepper Aerius I Expedition. You will also need a stern rudder, compass, spare paddles, a spray hood, a rifle holder and a survival suit. Paddling in a sealed-off survival suit is not to everyone's taste.

Then there is the paramount need for plenty of experience and technical know-how.

For good reason, paddling is regarded as a high-risk activity by the authorities. Up to two-thirds of paddlers with more ambitious projects end up in rescue operations. Causes include being stranded due to the loss of a boat through polar bears,

2

exhaustion, or failing to get back in time for the rendezvous. There are also those who fail to secure their boats sufficiently and lose them during the night by storm or rising tide or waves caused by a glacier calving. In 2004, all three paddling expeditions trying to circle the north of Spitsbergen needed help. The unpleasant record is held so far probably by a German paddler, whose two failed attempts resulted in rescue operations both times. A search party was sent out the first time as she was late returning, due to errors in her estimation and bad weather. On the second occasion she was caught in bad weather and capsized twice. Wet through and suffering from hypothermia, she managed to get to a flat shore and set off her PLB to call for help (even though, before her tour, she had tried to convince the Sysselmann that she did not need insurance as she did not foresee the need for a rescue operation – an argument that, thankfully for her, was not accepted). Alongside such problem cases, there are a few impressive success stories, too, including successful circumnavigations of the main island by paddlers, which requires not only about six weeks, but – in addition to fitness and iron will – also some luck with weather and ice.

Special problems

Wind The wind makes it very difficult to estimate passage times. You can be struggling to get anywhere, or you could be rushing past possible landing sites with no chance of reaching them. Unsuitable wind is also the main reason why higher boats like canoes are not recommended, even when protected against waves by a cover – in the event of a strong wind from an inauspicious direction, you haven't got a chance.

Collision Shorelines are not charted very well, if at all. There is a real risk of grounding, especially in waves, and sometimes you can be stuck a few hundred metres from land. There are rocks just small enough not to cause waves to break and there are extensive shallows; take particular care when you are near river mouths or moraines. Also to be reckoned with are driftwood, rubbish and small, sharp pieces of ice.

Waves Just as weather can change quickly, so too can waves build up fast, sometimes within an hour. This can become very dangerous when trying to traverse wider fjords, for instance Isfjord, or when following glacier fronts or cliffs with no possibility of landing for kilometres. Glacier fronts often calve icebergs. Even several hundred metres off, the effects of a new iceberg can be the creation of substantial waves, which may break, particularly over shallows. Icebergs are also born underwater and can shoot up to the surface with surprising speed. When landing near glaciers, pull your kayak high up onto the beach, out of the reach of flood waves caused by calving.

Ice Drift ice and floating slush can trap your boat so that no amount of effort will free it. You can wreck your craft in this way – but even just being stuck in a drifting ice field is dangerous enough.

Polar bears A curious bear may damage your boat and take you prisoner when sitting on an island or another remote place which is hard to leave without a boat.

Walrus Awkward on land (but still surprisingly quick), the walrus is a different animal in the water. If you upset one in the water and it attacks your boat, your chances are minimal. Even a friendly, curious examination of you and your boat by one of these huge animals is enough. Therefore, paddlers should do everything possible to avoid getting close to walrus in the water, however tempting this may be.

With a tour operator Since the mid 1990s, two French tour operators have offered kayak arrangements in Svalbard. Seemingly, the attitude in France is different as complete novices are accepted among the participants. For safety reasons, one of the companies stays close to the shore, mostly, and in more sheltered fjord areas; the other company, in contrast, includes fjord crossings over many kilometres of open water, even with participants who had never sat in a kayak before this tour. It can only be hoped that they never get surprised by a sudden change of weather in the middle of the fjord.

Guided kayak day excursions At the innermost end of the small Adventfjorden, right from the beach of Longyearbyen, a seven-hour guided paddle is offered, depending on sufficient demand and good conditions. These tours are suitable for sporty beginners, as the bay is sheltered and small. (*Prices start around NOK900, but really depend on where you want to go.*)

Independent travel Most of the sporty challenges for kayakers have been done already by independent paddlers, including successful circumnavigations of the main island (which take five to six weeks). Not least due to the high risk, longer paddling tours are – apart from the two French companies mentioned – a typical case for independent travel. In most other countries, the majority of paddlers seem to prefer warmer destinations or consider their paddling skills as insufficient for Svalbard. There is a small elite of highly experienced sea kayakers, but they prefer to do their own expeditions when going to extreme destinations like Svalbard, instead of joining an organised group that also includes absolute novices.

FURTHER ORGANISED DAY ACTIVITIES Apart from hiking and paddling day excursions and day cruises in summer, and guided dog-sledge and snowmobile excursions in spring, there are a few other activities offered, which you will find advertised on the updated activity list in Longyearbyen's tourist office. Contrary to complete package arrangements, these separately booked activities usually last only a few hours of the day.

In addition, you may find on the weekly programme in the tourist information office some more activities, including for instance 'Grilling in Bjørndalen' (a short road and tundra walk, before sitting at a fire with the Isfjord scenery in the background, grilling food and listening to stories from the guide – surprisingly one of the best-selling programmes).

UNSUITABLE FORMS OF TRAVEL Having had many amazing requests and comments, I thought it worth listing a few impossible or unsuitable forms of travel.

Bus, car, camper or caravan Holidaying in Svalbard with any form of powered, wheeled vehicle makes little sense. There is a 70km network of roads in and around Longyearbyen (most of it being the streets within the settlement, with only two roads of 11km each leading out to mines) and no way of getting to any other community. Motorised travel overland damages the environment and is therefore forbidden.

Mountain biking Bicycles are a good way of getting around spread-out Longyearbyen. You can hire them. Otherwise, there is no point in having them, as they are of no use outside the settlement. Some visitors have tried mountain bikes, but they are not very effective due to the terrain and they aren't very eco-friendly (they damage the fragile tundra).

Open motorboats The use of open motorboats for long-distance travel was restricted by law in 1989.

Quick tour to all the highlights of the islands To whizz round Svalbard and see all the major sights in a short time is just not possible. Luckily, there are places in the world which cannot be just 'done' by the restless consumer in a weekend or even a week.

TRAVEL FOR NON-TOURISTS

SCIENTISTS AND RESEARCHERS There are so many disciplines and so many kinds of research that sweeping general statements cannot apply here. Classic fieldworkers will find most of what they need to know about travel, equipment, etc, elsewhere in this book.

Co-ordinating scientific exploration in Svalbard is the responsibility of the Norsk Polarinstitutt (*www.npolar.no*), which is based in Tromsø. It is well worth contacting the institute, not just for advice on when and how, but also to find out what else is going on in your field. Commercial local tour operators and others involved in logistics may also be able to help.

JOURNALISTS More and more reporters, photographers, film and television teams come to Svalbard every year.

The first point of call and the main contact point is the Sysselmann, who already has much to do in the summer months but is a good contact for information.

Even here, at the end of the world, flashing your press card or dropping the name of a large media company won't automatically result in offers for free flights, boat trips and so on at the expense of the Norwegian taxpayer. Be aware that you are not the first journalist to come here, and some colleagues have done their best to create doubts about their seriousness. There is an element of journo-fatigue, and only the best contacts or references are likely to open doors or get you support beyond information from the Sysselmann's office.

Working as a journalist is usually the same here as every other travel destination in terms of preparation and cost. In the end, when realising the difficulties of doing something new over a short space of time, this often leads to similar stories: some pictures of life in Longyearbyen, a visit to Barentsburg, an interview with some scientists and researchers working in Svalbard, a bit about the old train in Ny-Ålesund and a cruise up and down the northwest coast. Luckily, there have also been some projects in between with good time, preparation and new ideas.

RED TAPE

PASSPORTS AND VISAS For getting into Svalbard, neither passports nor visas are required for nationals of the countries that signed the original Spitsbergen Treaty. These countries include all EU and EFTA countries, as well as Japan, the USA, Canada, Australia, New Zealand and many others. However – important – a passport and maybe visas *are* needed for travelling through mainland Norway on the way up and down: Norway is a member of the Schengen Agreement, which regulates joint border procedures of the member states, which include most of the EU. Owing to its special status, Svalbard is excluded from that membership. Therefore, when landing in Norway on the way back from Svalbard, you cross the border of the Schengen Agreement, which automatically requires a valid passport, even from Norwegian citizens: just a valid identity card is not enough there. As for the need for a visa for transiting through mainland Norway, check with your Norwegian consulate or embassy; citizens of EU and EFTA countries and some other nations as well do not need a visa for Norway.

The Norwegian Directorate of Immigration have an excellent website at www.udi.no which gives clear information on visa requirements.

CUSTOMS AND VAT Svalbard is a free trade zone and as such is treated by Norway as a foreign country for these purposes. Goods bought in Svalbard may be subject to duty when arriving back in mainland Norway.

There is no VAT in Svalbard and therefore no VAT office; you can't claim back any VAT paid on goods in Norway. For more valuable items like laptops, cameras, etc, it can be a good idea to have a proof of ownership with you (receipt of purchase, etc) in case of problems with the customs.

Your weapons must be declared at each border crossing, complete with paperwork. Passport control officers are normally not customs officers: they are policemen. If you are travelling by rail you may be delayed sufficiently that you miss your train. There are further complications when trying to bring weapons across Sweden, which is very strict about the unofficial transport of firearms.

There are fewer problems when flying, though ammunition should be in its original packaging and has to be transported separately from the weapon.

TRAVEL PERMITS For tours in most parts of Svalbard, permission from the Sysselmann has to be obtained. Only the areas close to the settlements – Nordenskiöld Land, Bünsow Land, Dickson Land and a limited area around Ny-Ålesund – are exempted from this restriction (see map, page 91). Nevertheless, it may make sense to register voluntarily for tours in these areas, too, for your own safety. Applications for permission have to be sent to the Sysselmann's office, preferably several months in advance, as it may take quite a lot of time for permission to be granted. The application should include a detailed description of the planned tour, the equipment taken (including safety equipment like firearms, communication, etc) and the previous experience of the participants. Furthermore, the insurance against search and rescue costs is part of the requirements (see below).

INSURANCE The Sysselmann can demand that individual travellers have insurance cover against search and rescue (SAR) costs. This also applies to searches where there is no emergency. Since 1996 insurance has been compulsory for all tours outside of the settlements (except for Nordenskiöldlandet, Bünsowlandet and Dicksonlandet and a limited area around Ny-Ålesund) and can be demanded for some forms of travel (paddling, climbing, etc), even within the closer areas. Based on the intended tour project, the Sysselmann's office will demand a certain coverage sum and your insurance company will be asked to guarantee that it will cover any search and rescue costs up to that sum. The figures will be calculated for each person on the tour (so it is not possible simply to multiply a low coverage per person with the number of participants) and will also have to cover search operations which are not caused by a medical emergency but, for instance, by delay due to bad weather.

Two main aspects for the size of the required coverage are the maximum distance from Longyearbyen (the base of the rescue service) and the type of planned activity. Rowing and kayaking, the longer ski tours and climbing in remote areas are all regarded as especially risky, leading to correspondingly high coverage claims. Considering that the majority of long kayak expeditions get into some sort of trouble and tend to require assistance, this is not surprising.

Norwegian insurance companies Europeiske Reiseforsikring and Gjensidige Forsikring have developed special policies for Svalbard. Naturally, they are expensive (premiums can rise to over NOK4,000), with costs depending on specific conditions, the number of insured and so on. It makes sense to find out from the Sysselmann how much cover you need before talking to the insurers. It is easy to see how search costs can climb – the Super Puma helicopter alone costs NOK35,000 an hour to operate, and hours soon build up when there is a problem.

Tour operators offering programmes in Svalbard must have a company insurance covering eventual search and rescue costs, with the maximum coverage again fixed in each case by the Sysselmann's office. Nevertheless, tour operators usually require their participants to have some insurance to cover search and rescue costs, eg: NOK40,000, to cover the smaller rescue operations – long search operations are unlikely with the clearly defined programmes of most organised tours. Such limited coverage of search and rescue costs is included in many standard travel insurance packages.

An alternative for independent travellers, where the required insurance coverage and thus the premium to be paid for it is higher, is to arrange a guarantee with your bank to cover the amount required by the Sysselmann's office. This is usually cheaper if all goes well, but can leave you with a massive debt at the bank should a rescue operation be needed.

Health insurance policies must also be checked thoroughly: are costs incurred paid directly or must you wait until you get home? Is your insurance also valid for Svalbard? And does the policy also cover the cost of getting you home?

RESTRICTIONS ON TRAVEL Depending on the reason (tourism, research, etc), the season and the type of travel, there are clear restrictions that limit when and where you can go. Travellers are expected to obtain information about protected areas, cultural monuments and general restrictions for the areas they intend to visit. See also *Chapter 1, Environmentally friendly travel*, pages 60–3. Some major points, which should be kept in mind already when preparing a tour to Svalbard at home:

- A number of bird sanctuaries plus Moffen and Kong Karls Land are completely closed to any traffic, including a sanitary zone of 300–500m around and in the air for at least for part of the year, if not permanently.
- Any human traces from before 1946 are automatically protected as cultural monuments (including an automatic perimeter of 100m radius), no matter how trivial, damaged or difficult to discern they may seem. Within these areas, nothing may be changed and camping is forbidden. Some younger human traces, like graves or memorials, are similarly protected, and a few other objects, though dating from 1946 or later, have also been declared as cultural monuments.
- Ensure that you follow the minimum-impact code on vegetation and wildlife – so avoid camping on vegetation where not essential, pursuing birds and other animals for photos, picking flowers, and so on.

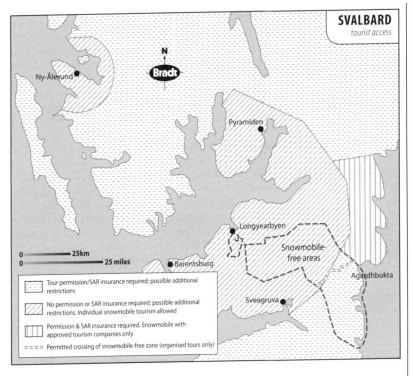

- Off the settlements, travellers have to be properly armed for self-defence in case of a polar bear attack. At the same time, everything possible has to be done to avoid disturbing, injuring or killing a polar bear.
- All cabins out in the terrain are off-limits to tourists, even if the doors are open and even if the guestbooks document the occasional abuse by tourists. It is a matter of trust that some locals still do not lock their doors, not least of all to make it easier for travellers in a real emergency to find shelter. The repeated abuse of such cabins by tourists without permission – for sleeping, making fire with fuel the owner has brought there for personal use, etc – has already led to the locking of many cabins. I doubt that these uninvited guests would be too happy to find complete strangers sleeping in their beds and cooking in their kitchen at home Goldilocks style – just because the door was open. Nobody is forced to go on tour in Svalbard – so do not expect the locals to provide you with their cabins without invitation. What is acceptable for safety reasons is a note in the guest book of the cabins which are open (without traces of having been opened with force – though, alas, this happens too), stating the date, names and planned route, etc.
- For tourist travel, a zoning of Svalbard has been introduced which is illustrated on the map above, showing the areas where you can travel without mandatory permission and insurance, and the area where use of snowmobiles is allowed both for independent travellers and for organised arrangements.
- For the nature reserves, national parks, plant reserves and the protected geotop, extra regulations apply which should be requested from the Sysselmann before travelling into these areas. Most regulations are also available on the internet at www.sysselmannen.no.

WORKING AND LIVING IN SVALBARD Owing to the Spitsbergen Treaty, there are practically no restrictions on living and working in Svalbard for citizens of the treaty nations. Specifically, no working permits, visa or immigration papers are needed for these citizens. As a result, the second-largest national group in Longyearbyen is the Thai, who enjoy exactly the same rights as other workers. The precondition for living in Svalbard is, however, that one must be physically, mentally and financially able to take care of oneself. Both seniors who need assistance and cannot finance this themselves, and persons without income or other financial resources, are not allowed to remain in the islands.

For officially published jobs in the Norwegian settlements there are usually many applications for Svalbard. For persons with no fluency in Norwegian and without special qualifications, the chances of finding employment are considerably lower, though possibilities can arise while you're there and trying to find a job directly. However, these are usually jobs with low qualification requirements and lower wages, for instance in cleaning. Another major problem with settling in Svalbard is the lack of available accommodation, as the population of Longyearbyen is growing faster than the construction rate of new houses; as a consequence, rental prices are fairly high. When staying longer than six months per year one can register as a resident, which gives certain rights, such as the possibility of buying a cabin. When living in Svalbard for more than a month, tax has to be paid on all income to the Svalbard ligningskontor. Jobs for shorter periods are also offered, for instance in tourism where companies like ours need seasonal guides. This is not necessarily a well-paid job, but does offer a chance to experience Svalbard for those with a wealth of outdoor experience, social competence and preferably a knowledge of languages (mainly English, German, French) as well as other relevant skills and qualifications (in natural sciences or medicine for example) – plus, of course, the time!

THE SYSSELMANN (GOVERNOR) The Sysselmann's office represents practically all state departments and is therefore responsible for the police, the church, registration, rescue services, low-level jurisprudence and all manner of other things, covering almost all aspects of state administration and execution.

The Sysselmann is in charge of granting permissions for tours – both for individual travel and for programmes for tour operators which need prior approval from the governor. Other non-tourist projects also need permission from his office, so it is wise to present your plan to the Sysselmann well in advance to check what rules and procedures have to be followed. Be prepared for some waiting time, and contact the office at least half a year in advance.

Staff, in common with most people in Longyearbyen who come into contact with foreigners, have a smattering of English. Some of them speak it very well. They serve in Svalbard for two to three years (as do most people from state organisations).

The current Sysselmann is Odd Olsen Ingerø, who has served between 2001 and 2005, and again from 2009. However, most applications, etc, are handled by his staff, so there is no need to address normal requests to the Sysselmann himself (Sysselmann is both the title of his position and the name of his whole office).

Sysselmannen på Svalbard Postboks 633, NO-9171 Longyearbyen; ☎ 79 02 43 00; e firmapost@ · sysselmannen.no; www.sysselmannen.no; ⏱ 08.30–15.30 Mon–Fri

The emergency number is 112. If you need to get in touch with the Sysselmann's office outside these hours, a policeman is on duty and can be contacted on ☎ 79 02 12 22 or m 41 40 31 65.

The Sysselmann's office is on the western side of Longyearbyen, above the harbour area and with an excellent view across Adventfjord and Longyearbyen. It's housed in a modern, zinc-plated (grey) and partly yellow-painted complex, which succeeded the former building on the same site which was destroyed by a fire in 1995.

PETS There is rabies in Svalbard, unlike on mainland Norway. The importing of living animals therefore requires permission by the Mattilsynet (Food Authority), which is represented locally in Svalbard by the Sysselmann, from where the necessary application form can be obtained. Ideally, the animal should have completed its rabies vaccinations. With an extra rabies vaccination for the tour to Svalbard, this should be done about a month in advance. A blood sample has to be taken in all cases by your vet, which has to be screened for sufficient antibodies in the blood and the test result must be added to the application. When not following these procedures, you risk having your pet put into quarantine and examined at your expense or possibly even put down on arrival. The importing of cats to Svalbard is forbidden. It is also forbidden to set free species other than those that exist in the archipelago naturally. Dogs have to be on a lead or chain at any time when outside to avoid any risk of chasing or harming other animals.

GETTING THERE AND AWAY

BY AIR The Scandinavian carrier SAS offers direct flights into Longyearbyen from Tromsø in northern Norway (or from Oslo in southern Norway with a short stopover in Tromsø), while the discount carrier Norwegian Air Shuttle flies direct from Oslo to Longyearbyen (*flight time 1hr 40mins from Tromsø; 3hrs (Norwegian) and 4hrs (SAS) from Oslo*). Flights are particularly frequent in the summer, although they should be booked in advance during peak periods (ie: Easter). Note that Norwegian only operates their route twice a week and only between March and October.

✈ **Norwegian** 0080 Oslo; booking ☎+47 81 52 18 15; +44 (0)208 099 7254 (UK); www.norwegian.com. Prices vary according to month (& direction) of travel, but one-way tickets from Oslo to Longyearbyen can be found on the website from NOK499.

✈ **SAS** 0080 Oslo; head office (based in Stockholm) ☎+46 87 97 00 00; booking m 91 50 54 00; www.flysas.com. Prices vary according to date & time of flight, but return tickets to Longyearbyen can be found for around NOK2,500 (Oslo) or NOK1,700 (Tromsø).

Norway is well connected with eight international airports around the country, the four biggest of which are amongst the busiest in Europe. As you might expect, Oslo Airport Gardermoen is the country's main airport. The SAS group has links worldwide; KLM, British Airways and Lufthansa all have routes into the country; and low fare operators with routes into Norway include Norwegian, Ryanair and Wideroe. United fly from the USA into Oslo. This is not an exhaustive list, so you might want to contact your local travel agent for the full range of options.

✈ **British Airways** www.britishairways.com
✈ **KLM** www.klm.com
✈ **Lufthansa** www.lufthansa.com
✈ **Norwegian Air Shuttle** As above
✈ **Ryanair** www.ryanair.com
✈ **SAS Group** As above
✈ **United** www.united.com
✈ **Wideroe** www.wideroe.no

Despite the frequency of connections, a number of flights are fully booked in summer and for Easter. Some package tours include the flights, others don't, which gives

Thanks to Prof Gericke for his support with this section

Each year private planes arrive at Longyearbyen, the world's most northerly public airport. Suitable take-off points for these flights are Tromsø, Alta and Banak. Be aware that in the event of bad weather keeping you out of Longyearbyen there is no alternative but to head back for Norway. There are two further private airstrips in Svalbard, but neither of them accepts visitor landings and they may be (as with Sveagruva) very difficult to negotiate. The tower at Longyearbyen is manned 24 hours a day; you can get weather reports from Bjørnøya Radio and should call them on approach to give you time to turn back if necessary.

The Arctic is open territory for fliers; only Bjørnøya and Isfjord Radio have beacons. GPS or Loran C is a must. We have used GPS north of Sjuøyane and near to Kvitøya. Any further out you definitely need resources such as survival suits, a life-raft, retractable undercarriage (for emergency landings on water) and everything necessary for an emergency bivouac.

Charts for this area include the ICAO sheets at 1:500,000 for Norway and at 1:1,000,000 for Svalbard. For flying by sight you need the four topographic maps at 1:500,000, with some charts at 1:200,000. These are good, except for glacier positions.

Obtainable are weekly season cards that cover landing charges for Norwegian airfields and are also good for Longyearbyen. Longyearbyen is the only place in Svalbard to get fuel, which must be booked three months in advance.

more options for tailoring your travel arrangements to suit your individual needs. Special tariffs may even allow cheaper travel than if you book your flights as part of a package. Your Svalbard specialist may be able to give you a few tips. A stopover in Tromsø is not necessarily a disadvantage: this bustling town, the largest in northern Norway, is not without reason called both the 'Gateway to the Arctic' and the 'Paris of the North', with a surprising vegetation and several attractions worth visiting. As a brief taster and introduction to the Arctic, especially the 'Polaria' (with a huge aquarium with species from the Barents Sea and well-presented information about Arctic nature) and the Polar Museum, it's hard to beat.

Watch your luggage doesn't exceed 20kg. This is normally enough for a guided tour where some of the heavier equipment is provided. You can of course send stuff by air freight (much pricier than by sea) but it is not necessarily going to travel in the same aircraft as you and could entail quite a wait. For longer stays, it may be an idea to send some items to yourself by post to Longyearbyen (up to 20kg) well in advance (about four weeks, to be sure), from where you can pick it up at the post office. The address: Your name, poste restante, N-9170 Longyearbyen, Norway/Svalbard.

The airport's main building contains a small waiting area and Duty Free shop.

BY SEA The Hurtigruten coastal steamer ceased its summer calls to Svalbard in 1982, presumably due to competition from the (then) recently opened airport at Longyearbyen. A limited-capacity service ran from Bergen up the Norwegian fjords to Longyearbyen for several years until 2012, when MS *Nordstjernen*, the oldest ship in the fleet, was sold off. As a result it's no longer possible to reach Svalbard from the Norwegian mainland by regularly scheduled ship.

If you are intending to travel in May then an option is to join one of the cruise ships. Typically these ships will have spent the November–March period down around the Antarctic peninsula and will then head up to the Arctic for April–September. The cruise market is complex, and you'll regularly find the same cabin on the same ship for the same cruise listed by several different agencies, sometimes at different prices. You should be aware that these cruises can book out over a year in advance, so planning ahead is strongly recommended. An in-depth discussion of the cruise industry is beyond the scope of this book (although

GETTING TO TROMSØ OVERLAND

While there are hardly any alternatives to the plane for the last part of the voyage for many travellers, it can be a good idea to travel to Tromsø overland (or sea!) – by train, bus or car, or by ship along the Norwegian coastline. Surface-based travel, in contrast with flying, gives a feeling of approaching the north as the landscape and nature changes.

Norwegian State Railways runs as far north as Bodø and from there you will have to use a combination of buses and ferries to get to Tromsø.

If you have some spare time and spare cash then you could consider a slight detour through the Lofoten Islands, the staggeringly beautiful archipelago north of the Arctic Circle.

If you do find yourself stuck, bear in mind that Hurtigruten have a regular schedule of coastal ferries, all of which will put into Tromsø at some point during their journey.

If you are travelling by car, Tromsø Airport has a long-stay car park. Long-stay in this context is up to three weeks, although you could stay longer if you arrange it in advance.

Tromsø itself is a pleasant, lively town, and you won't have any trouble filling in a few days there if you have to. There are several good museums, but of particular interest given your upcoming trip to Svalbard are Polaria, the Polar Museum and the Arctic-Alpine Botanical Garden. Information about all the museums, accommodation, routes to Tromsø, and indeed everything else you could need are on the superlative Tourist Information website.

NOR-WAY Bussekspress (the Norwegian bus network) Multi-lingual website: www.nor-way.no
NSB (Norwegian State Railways) www.nsb.no. *Standard prices: Olso International Airport to Bodø one-way NOK1500 (though if you book a week or more in advance this can be reduced to as little as NOK399).*
Hurtigruten For full details see *Getting there and away, By sea*, opposite; www.hurtigruten.no
Tromsø Tourist Information Office Visit Tromsø, Kirkegata 2, N-9253 Tromsø, Norway; ╲77 61 00 00; e info@visittromso.no; www.visittromso.no

If you are taking weapons it is easiest to avoid the time-wasting border formalities that take place on the railways and fly or take your own car; customs procedures when travelling by train may be both complicated and delaying.

you might like to raise it one evening in the ship's bar if you've run short of other topics of conversation), but the majority of ships are chartered out to third party travel companies and can be booked through those agencies. There are a couple of companies that own and operate their own ships and so may not appear on as many of these websites.

Cruise-ship operators and agencies

Aqua-Firma Square Sail Hse, Charlestown, Cornwall PL25 3NJ, UK; ☏+44 1428 620 012; e info@aqua-firma.co.uk; www.aqua-firma.co.uk. *Prices for 2013 start at £1,590 inc excursions.*

Blue Water Holidays Bridge Hse, Brook St, Skipton, North Yorks BD23 1PP, UK; ☏+44 1756 706 500; e advice@bluewaterholidays.com; www.bluewaterholidays.com. *Prices for 2013 start at £2,478, inc excursions.*

Cruise Norway 11 Broadway, Suite 330, New York, NY 10004, USA; ☏+1 212 480 4521; e info@ cruisenorway.com; www.cruisenorway.com. *Prices for 2013 start at US$4,360, inc excursions.*

Discover the World Arctic Hse, 8 Bolters Lane, Banstead, Surrey SM7 2AR, UK; ☏+44 1737 218 800; e travel@discover-the-world.co.uk; www.discover-the-world.co.uk. *Prices for 2013 start at £3,187 inc excursions.*

Exodus Travels Grange Mills, Weir Rd, London SW12 0NE, UK; ☏+44 20 3603 9368; e polar@exodus.co.uk; www.exodus.co.uk. *Prices for 2013 start at £2,500 inc excursions.*

Five Stars of Scandinavia 1804 Black Lake Bd SW, Suite 203, Olympia, WA 98512, USA; ☏+1 800 722 4126; e info@5stars-scandinavia.com; www.5stars-scandinavia.com. *Prices for 2013 start at US$2,135 inc excursions.*

Footprint Adventures 5 Malham Dr, Lincoln LN6 0XD, UK; ☏+ 44 1522 804 929; www.footprint-adventures.co.uk. *Prices for 2013 start at £1,075 inc excursions.*

G Adventures 19 Charlotte St, Toronto, Ontario M5V 2H5, Canada; ☏+1 416 260 0999; www.gadventures.com. *Prices for 2013 start at £2,299 inc excursions.*

The Great Canadian Travel Company Suite 370, 136 Market Av, Winnipeg, MB, R3B 0P4, Canada; ☏+1 800 661 3830; www.greatcanadiantravel.com. *Prices for 2013 start at US$3,390 inc excursions.*

Hurtigruten Bedford Hse, 69–79 Fulham High St, London, SW6 3JW; ☏+44 844 272 8961; e uk.sales@hurtigruten.com; www.hurtigruten.co.uk. Have a fleet of over 10 ships & have been plying the Norwegian coast for over 100 years. *Prices for 2013 start at £2,493 inc excursions.*

Journeys International 107 Aprill Dr, Suite 3, Ann Arbor, MI 48103, USA; ☏+1 800 255 8735; e info@journeys.travel; www.journeys.travel. *Prices for 2013 start at US$5,990 inc excursions.*

Mighty Fine Coastal Cruises 2 Sentinel Court, Wilkinson Way, Blackburn, Lancs BB1 2EH, UK; ☏+44 845 072 0090; e ask@mightyfinecompany.com; www.mightyfinecompany.com. *Prices for 2013 start at £1,062 inc excursions.*

One Ocean Expeditions ☏+1 604 390 4900; e voyages@oneoceanexpeditions.com; www.oneoceanexpeditions.com. *Prices for 2013 start at US$3,990 inc excursions.*

Polar Star Expeditions 55 Crane Lake Dr, Halifax, NS, B3S 1B5, Canada; ☏+1 902 423 7389; e info@polarstarexpeditions.com; www.polarstarexpeditions.com. *Prices for 2013 start at US$4,675 inc excursions.*

Quark Expeditions 93 Pilgrim Park, Suite 1, Waterbury, VT 05676, USA; ☏+1 888 892 0334; e info@quarkexpeditions.com; www.quarkexpeditions.com. *Prices for 2013 start at £3,170 inc excursions.*

The Travelling Naturalist PO Box 3141, Dorchester, Dorset DT1 2XD, UK; ☏+44 1305 267 994; e jamie@naturalist.co.uk; www.naturalist.co.uk. *Prices for 2013 start at £4,995 inc excursions.*

Travel Wild Expeditions PO Box 1637, Vashon Island, WA 98070, USA; ☏+1 206 463 5362; e info@travelwild.com; www.travelwild.com. *Prices for 2013 start at US$3,990 inc excursions.*

Victor Emanuel Nature Tours 2525 Wallingwood Dr, Suite 1003, Austin, TX 78746 (USA); ☏+1 512 328 5221; e info@ventbird.com; www.ventbird.com. *Prices for 2013 start at US$8,650 inc excursions.*

WildWings Davis Hse, Lodge Causeway, Bristol BS16 3JB, UK ; ☏+44 117 965 8333; e wildinfo@wildwings.co.uk; www.wildwings.co.uk. *Prices for 2013 start at £3,799 inc excursions.*

My thanks go to Mr Krämer, an experienced sailor in icy conditions, for a significant part of this section.

About 150 sailors on a total of 20 to 30 sailing boats visit Svalbard each year; motor yachts are seldom seen. A well-founded boat is a must, built of steel if possible, especially if you want to go to the pack-ice boundary or attempt a circumnavigation of Svalbard. Equipment must include depth sounder, radar, spares and tools so that all repairs can be made from the vessel's own resources. At the very least, sailors should have experience of passages near ice.

The first half of August, still with good 24-hour light and with the ice at its greatest retreat, is the best time; there are more storms at the end of the month. Boats approaching from the south are best advised to start their tour along the west coast, where there is virtually no ice at this time except perhaps in the south.

Longyearbyen is the best place to obtain water and diesel; possibilities in Barentsburg and Ny-Ålesund are more limited (check in advance before relying on these ports). Don't expect too much. Diesel costs around NOK5 a litre. All settlements have landing charges, sometimes at a fixed price and sometimes according to the length of the vessel and the number of passengers.

From the west coast you can move on toward the pack-ice limit; wait for light winds or those from the south. Rounding Spitsbergen is often not possible as the Hinlopen Strait may be iced up. Moffen is normally attainable, but don't go too close to this island reserve. Fines for approaching within the 300m limit are NOK5,000–10,000. There are also a number of bird sanctuaries along the coasts, where any landings in summer are forbidden. On your return journey, consider taking in Smeerenburgfjorden. From there you can move on to Magdalenefjorden and anchor in front of the glacier behind the graveyard island. With a tender, you can go ashore to collect glacier ice to put in your obligatory Svalbard whisky.

Svalbard is still not fully charted, and what charts exist are not always reliable. There are special problems associated with glaciers and their moraines; depths are variable and seabed contours inaccurate. Many glaciers have retreated by many kilometres since the last charting (and some have also advanced). You cannot guess the position of a submarine glacier front, and your chart will not show it in the correct position!

Echo sounders, lead lines and even calibrated poles must be used. Ice comes in all sizes, not always visible, and care must be taken not to damage propellers (including that of your tender's outboard) – also by driftwood.

As mentioned earlier, there are the potential problems of the calving of icebergs which can shoot up to the surface with surprising speed.

When you get to Svalbard waters, let the Sysselmann know. Lodging your passage plan is mandatory. By doing so you also receive as much local advice and information as possible. Find out where you are not allowed to go.

Don't forget polar bear risks. Your manifest should include at least two large-calibre rifles, with ammunition.

I recommend the 400-page book *Den norske Los/Arctic Pilot* (in Norwegian and English), with nautical and terrestrial information.

Practical Information   GETTING THERE AND AWAY

2

World Expeditions 81 Craven Gardens, Wimbledon, London SW19 8LU, UK; +44 20 8545 9030; e enquiries@worldexpeditions.co.uk; www.worldexpeditions.co.uk. *Prices for 2013 start at US$3,850 inc excursions.*

HEALTH *with Dr Felicity Nicholson*

RABIES AND OTHER DISEASES Svalbard, with its cool climate, is a tough area for many microbes – but it is not completely free of diseases. As mentioned before, there is rabies in Svalbard which has been observed especially in foxes, but also in reindeer and seals as well. This is another reason to abstain from attracting animals with food, which is a dubious practice anyway, in ecologically intact areas.

Rabies is passed on to humans through a bite, a scratch or a lick of an open wound. You must always assume that the foxes, reindeer and seals are rabid as there is no way of looking at them and knowing and medical help should be sought as soon as is practicably possible. In the interim, scrub the wound thoroughly with soap and running water for ten to 15 minutes, then pour on a strong iodine or alcohol solution. This can help to prevent the rabies virus from entering the body and will guard against wound infections, including tetanus. The decision whether or not to have the highly effective rabies vaccine will depend on the nature of your trip.

If you do decide to take the vaccine, ideally three pre-exposure doses should be taken over a minimum 21-day period. If you think you have been exposed to rabies, then treatment should be given as soon as possible. At least two post-bite rabies injections are needed, even for immunised people. Those who have not been immunised will need a full course of injections together with rabies immunoglobulin (RIG). This product may not always be available, but it is important to receive it if you have not had pre-exposure vaccine. Treatment should be given as soon as possible, but it is never too late to seek help as the incubation period for rabies can be very long. Remember if you contract rabies, mortality is 100%.

Since the 1990s, the presence of *Echinococcus multilocularis*, a potentially lethal tapeworm, has been found in the area between Bjørndalen and Grumant. Normally, this tapeworm switches in its two stages between fox and mouse, being fairly harmless for the fox but dangerous for mice. Unfortunately, man can replace the mouse in the development circle of the tapeworm, and dogs can take over the role of the fox. Incubation time of this disease, which is spread over wide parts of Europe, can be up to an amazing 15 years and, if discovered late, is very difficult to cure and is often lethal. As mice are not normally part of Svalbard nature, this disease should have little chance. But in the Grumant area, mice from Russia managed to survive and reproduce in the hanging moors, thereby closing the development circle of this parasite, which may therefore reach nearby Longyearbyen. Steps are already underway to prevent this, including stipulating the vaccination of all dogs. The infection is contracted by accidentally ingesting animal faeces. Do not handle fox or dog faeces without wearing gloves or better still avoid them altogether. It may also be spread by faecally soiled dog hair and harnesses. It is recommended not to drink the water in the Grumant–Bjørndalen area without previous boiling.

TRAVEL CLINICS AND HEALTH INFORMATION A full list of current travel clinic websites worldwide is available on www.istm.org. For other journey preparation information, consult www.nathnac.org/ds/map_world.aspx (UK) or http://wwwnc.cdc.gov/travel/(US). Information about various medications may be found on www.netdoctor.co.uk/travel. All advice found online should be used in conjunction with expert advice received prior to or during travel.

MEDICAL FACILITIES There is a hospital in the centre of Longyearbyen in the same building as the dentist and physiotherapist. Nearby is the medical centre and pharmacy, but not all medications and drugs are available, so try to bring what you might need with you. You should also have some sort of paperwork on you (including the international terminology) if you have specific problems such as allergies or diabetes, or are already using regular medication; this will help in the event of an emergency.

Hospital (*Sykehus*) ☏79 02 42 00; ⏰ 09.00–12.00 & 13.00–15.00 daily
Dentist (*Tannlege*) ☏79 02 42 30

Physiotherapist (*Fysioterapeut*) ☏91 75 26 86
Emergency ambulance service in Longyearbyen ☏113

There are basic hospital facilities in Barentsburg, a first-aid station at Ny-Ålesund and simple first-aid equipment at various weather and radio stations.

SAFETY

CRIME As far as crime goes, Svalbard is one of the safest places on Earth. Many residents regularly leave their car and house doors unlocked. Local crime statistics are modest and generally hinge around alcohol or driving without correct paperwork – and to a very minimal degree when compared with the rest of Europe.

POLAR BEAR RISKS Polar bears are a natural part of the Svalbard environment. Though the majority of them follow the ice border, some of them can also be met on land at any time of the year and are by no means restricted to ice-covered areas and marine environments only. One student group from UNIS was attacked by a polar bear far from the nearest ice border at an altitude of 1,100m above sea level. With the seasonal retreat of the ice border to the east and north in summer, the number of polar bears in central and western Spitsbergen becomes correspondingly lower – but, unfortunately, the few bears that remain have greater problems stalking the seals and grow more desperate as a result. In winter, when the western fjords are partly ice-covered and offer resting possibilities for seals on the ice, the number of polar bears increases too – even on the fjord ice just outside Longyearbyen, a polar bear trying to stalk a seal is not an uncommon sight. Contrary to grizzlies or Kodiak bears, which can reach similar sizes but are omnivores (living to a large extent on plants, insects and, in addition, fish and meat), the polar bear is a pure carnivore which cannot survive without a diet of mostly meat. What's more, polar bears have no natural enemies and are, like many polar animals, inquisitive in order to find new sources of food. Man is not part of the bear's natural environment, so the animals have no programmed behaviour when confronted by man. As a result, their response is unpredictable – from fleeing in panic to ignoring us altogether or, the worst-case scenario, a straight attack. When polar bears were first hunted, they quickly acquired a certain shyness with man. However, since the end of hunting in 1973, this acquired behaviour has vanished again, while their numbers have grown too, from a few hundred in Svalbard to 3,000, making an encounter much more likely than in the 1970s. Young bears which have recently been chased away by their mother after two years as cubs are perhaps the most unpredictable, particularly as, left to fend for themselves, they are often quite hungry and desperate. Even a small young bear of around 80kg is a potentially deadly opponent. Female bears with cubs are especially dangerous, too, particularly if surprised. Finally, elder bears, too slow for successful seal hunts, may also experiment with man as a source of food.

The possibility of a confrontation with a polar bear is all part of the Svalbard experience, but this should be met with reasonable behaviour and equipment, not with panic and fear; but neither should you underestimate the dangers. I like to compare this with motorised traffic: we all use cars in some capacity, even though they cost more than 10,000 lives per year in Europe alone. And as with driving, it's up to us to do what we can to minimise the chance of an accident, while at the same time accepting that there will always be a residual risk. The situation with polar bears is similar: when properly armed and trained (or at least when with somebody who is), one can enjoy a journey around Svalbard without unduly worrying about the bears. I myself feel much more unsafe on a bicycle in road traffic, than when properly armed out in the wilderness of Svalbard. Statistics support this: no properly armed person has been injured or killed by a polar bear in the last 50 years in Svalbard. There have been casualties, indeed, but all victims were unarmed or inadequately armed – here are some of these stories.

Harmful encounters
Magdalenefjorden, 1977 Unnoticed, a polar bear went into a camp set up by Austrian climbers, none of whom had weapons. At last one of the party spotted the bear and raised the alarm. The bear attacked a man who was creeping out of his tent, dragged him to the sea and onto an ice floe, ripping him apart in full view of the others. By the time the rescue helicopter had arrived, the bear and the corpse had disappeared.

Edgeøya, 1987 Two Dutch researchers were of the view that this was the polar bears' kingdom and using weapons against them was wrong. One day, they saw from their cabin window a three-year-old bear starting to mess with their rubber dinghy. One of the men rushed out and tried to chase him off with a flare, but the bear attacked the scientist instead. The second man succeeded in distracting the bear with a second flare and his severely wounded colleague was able to crawl into their hut. Meanwhile, the bear turned on his next victim, who, also badly hurt, eventually managed to join his friend in the hut. The bear besieged the hut for the next few days until the men managed to make radio contact with the small ship *Plancius*, which was on its way to collect them – luckily. The *Plancius* arranged for a helicopter to come from Longyearbyen to take the men to hospital, but in order to get to the injured men the police had to shoot the bear. By this, the scientists managed to keep their hands clean, leaving instead the nasty job of shooting the bear to others. The story has a sequel: one of the scientists returned a few years later to continue his research work, this time armed with a rifle – only to discover later that his ammunition was of a different calibre.

Longyearbyen, March 1995 Two Norwegian girls came to visit a friend studying at UNIS, only to find that she was out on an excursion. Having climbing experience, they decided on the first day to climb Platåberget, 400m above the town. Despite the very many warning posters around, neither had a weapon, following the widespread illusion that wild polar bears are unthinkable so close to a settlement. They saw a light-coloured animal in the distance and thought it was a reindeer; by the time they realised that it was a bear, it was too late to run. The bear turned against one of the girls, saw the other running and changed its mind. The first, uninjured, slid down a ravine straight into the town and raised the alarm. By the time the rescue operation was underway, the victim was beyond help. The bear refused to give up its quarry and even attacked the rescuers, and had to be shot. It was then discovered that it was a very young animal, weighing only about 80kg.

Kiepertøya, Hinlopen Strait, August 1995 The ship *Origo* was anchored offshore and a landing tourist party set off with a properly armed guide. Another five people of the crew set out separately with only a .22 pistol and a flare gun. After an hour's march, the second party were met by a bear, 75m away and openly aggressive. The bear was distracted neither by warning shot nor flare and attacked one of the party. As he did so, he was shot, from a range of only 15m and turned against the man who had fired at him. This man tossed the gun to the first, who shot again. The process was repeated, with first one man being attacked and then the other. By the time the pistol was emptied and a knife drawn, one man was dead and another badly injured. The survivors retreated to the ship.

A rescue helicopter was raised on the radio and the captain decided to try to chase the bear off his prey with a heavy-calibre rifle. The bear seemed completely uninjured, even though it had taken many close-range shots, but to put it out of its possible misery it was shot again. On examination, three shots to the head were discovered, none of them piercing the cranium.

The victim had three seasons' experience with the *Origo*, with many bear observations, and there were sufficient weapons on board to equip everybody. Light pistols have no effect unless a precise target is hit from very close range. This is not easy under moments of stress. The party of five had been irresponsible.

Hampus mountain, Von Postbreen glacier, August 2011 A group of British schoolboys, accompanied by two experienced, trained British adventure guides, had camped out roughly 25 miles from Longyearbyen for a five-week excursion. Early one morning, a 7ft, 39-stone bear rampaged into their tents, having made it past the traps that were intended to scare it off. By the time one of the leaders was able to fire the rifle and kill the bear, one boy had been mauled to death, while four of the 13 others present had sustained serious claw and bite injuries to their heads and arms while defending themselves. There is some evidence that the bear may have been suffering from a severe toothache in its canines and incisors, which can cause serious pain and change the behaviour of the bears. However, neither rifle nor the tripwire set up around the camp exhibited any signs of malfunction, leading some to suspect that the tripwire may have been incorrectly set up since it did not detonate when the bear entered the area where the tents had been pitched. Post-mortems and an investigation showed that more steps could have been taken to prevent the disaster, including using guard dogs, a polar bear watch throughout the night, and staying in cabins rather than tents. But legally speaking, every precaution that should have been taken, was.

Each of the examples concerns people without suitable weapons – there are no cases of victims with appropriate arms and sufficient training with these arms.

In connection with polar bears, the question of firearms has, inevitably, to be discussed. I want to make it very clear in advance that shooting a polar bear is the very last resort. Polar bears are protected and may be shot only in clear self-defence and where there is no other option that provides a good chance of preventing injury to people. Minor damage to material or other inconveniences, for example if trapped in a camp for a while by a besieging bear, are no reason for shooting it. It is also forbidden by law to chase polar bears, to feed them or to provoke an attack (for instance by approaching a bear for pictures, relying on the backup of somebody armed if the situation becomes dangerous). At the same time, a thorough preparation, including being properly armed and trained, is also in the interest of the bear – there have been several incidents where bears were shot in panic by insufficiently prepared travellers, who then lost their nerve.

What's more, the right type of weapon can actually save the life of the bear – we've had two cases already where the shooting of a bear was avoided only because we used pumpguns with a magazine capacity of seven to eight shots and a very easy and quick reloading possibility. In both cases, seven warning shots were needed to deter the bears, which finally ran away after approaching to within seven to ten metres. With less magazine capacity, for instance with a cheap rental rifle, one would have no option other than to shoot the bear after two or three warning shots, as there are then only two bullets left in the rifle. Proper arms are therefore important to avoid bear kills and I find it amazing that rifles with little magazine capacity and no fast reloading possibility are still allowed for self-defence purposes.

While weaponry is an important part of this topic, measures for avoiding confrontations should be taken equally seriously.

Not every bear you meet is aggressive – it may even run away just by seeing you or after you've shouted at it. What's more, not every group out in the terrain is likely to meet a bear. But appropriate preparation for such encounters is an important part of a tour to Svalbard.

How to minimise the polar bear risk

- **Be properly armed** Over the years, we have seen amazing examples of incompetence: youngsters boasting with a bowie-knife at the campsite before setting out on tour (later, they sought refuge in one of our camps after actually having seen a bear from some distance); a Portuguese family armed with a crossbow and arrows (I would like to see them fire warning shots!); a journalist who took lessons at a circus on how to handle bears unarmed (I guess the instructor avoided telling the traveller that he feeds his bears well before entering the cage); a man with a tranquilliser gun (the attacking bear will have a good sleep – after having mauled its prey); and then there's the hiker with the pepper spray (ask the bear to attack against wind direction, please, or serve yourself nicely peppered with the wind blowing in the same direction from which the bear attacks). I am grateful for all these 'alternatives' as good entertainment stories and some of these ideas may even be useful in addition to a firearm. But there really is no substitute for a big-bore firearm (see pages 112–16).

- **Be properly trained with the firearm you take with you** Some travellers bring along a firearm of a suitable calibre – but have hardly (or even not at all) trained with that weapon. The same applies to rental firearms with proper training impossible due to the lack of a licence for purchasing sufficient training ammunition. Nobody is a born marksman, and firing five rounds at a motionless target at a 100m distance while sitting on a bench is hardly adequate training. If you are involved in an emergency situation with a polar bear, it is speed and routine that counts. So don't just secure a weapon for yourself – get some proper training too.

- **Make sure that the firearm is ready for use at any time out in the wilderness** An amazing sight is hikers on tour with their rifle tied firmly to a rucksack or even partly stuffed into it. Sometimes I feel tempted to cry 'polar bear from behind' and then start counting the seconds … and seconds … and seconds … Then there are those who carry a big, heavy rifle for weeks out in the wilderness – and find out only after their return that its functions are totally blocked by dirt that's accumulated in the mechanisms during the course of the tour.

- **Supplement your firearm with further deterring devices** For instance a heavy signal pistol, flares, etc. The aim, if at all possible, should always be to try to deter a bear, not to shoot it. The rifle should be ready for action, but should be considered a last resort only.
- **Reduce the chance of confrontations** Keep an eye on your surroundings to increase your chances of spotting a bear from a distance, thus reducing your chances of a close encounter. Try to choose campsites which do not provoke a visit by bears: a French tour operator set up camp on the fjord ice, with many seals laying within sight on the ice, and ample polar bear tracks around – no wonder that they then had a curious bear entering the camp, which they eventually had to shoot. Especially on the east coast, where there are also more bears in summer, one should try to avoid camping right on the beach.
- **Take care of camp safety** The sleeping period is one of the most critical times of the day: a bear sees nobody but spots something new and strange (your camp), with interesting smells. It thus approaches to investigate, and may even enter the camp unnoticed. If somebody then leaves their tent, the bear may feel threatened and attack. Equally unpleasant is when a bear starts to tear apart the tent you're lying in, especially if it's a narrow tunnel tent and you have only a long and clumsy rifle inside. Therefore, all camps should have a proper tripwire alarm system around them (see *Camp alarm*, page 116) to avoid unwanted visits, even though the triggering of these devices is usually caused by sleepy hikers stumbling over the wire on their way to the toilet, or maybe a wandering reindeer; you thus need to take some replacements for the alarm system. To further decrease your chances of a visit, food should be stored in water- and smell-proof containers or bags outside of the alarm system, but within sight; the same applies to rubbish and other (mal)odorous things preferably. These, too, should be connected with something that makes a noise when touched (pots and pans, etc). In this way, an inquisitive bear is likely to be attracted by these things first, instead of the tents. To increase safety further, a group can set up a watch system. Certainly, this measure should be taken when fresh tracks or the sighting of a bear suggest a high probability of a bear visit. What's more, when you leave the camp unattended during the day, there is always the possibility that a bear will visit then too. Once again, therefore, food and all things that smell should be stored outside the camp, your alarm system can be put on as a deterrent and it may also be an idea to take down your tent, as a tent that's been laid down is less interesting and therefore less likely to be damaged by an inquisitive bear.
- **When you actually meet a bear** Keep your distance. Do not run away in panic – this may trigger the bear's hunting instinct. Instead, try to move on calmly. If a bear follows you and there is only a short distance between you and safety, it can help if you drop some pieces of equipment, which may temporarily attract the bear's interest. Never get between a mother bear and her cubs. Do not take the risk of provoking an incident, even if it may be tempting for pictures, by approaching a bear with an armed guide behind you. Follow the guide's orders for retreat immediately – if people hesitate in the expectation of getting some good pictures, this can cause unpleasant incidents. If a bear has to be shot because of a provoked emergency, this can lead to high fines or even prison for the person(s) who provoked the situation.
- **Do not feed the bears (or other animals)** The ecosystem of Svalbard is still largely intact, so feeding is therefore a disruption of the natural balance. Feeding bears or other animals will create a link in their mind between people

and food and will make them seek humans, break into camps, etc. Even if you yourself are safe, for instance on a ship, the fed bear may at a later date seek food by approaching other people, for instance on land, which can lead to dangerous situations. Moreover, pictures taken in connection with feeding rarely look natural.

Legal aspects Polar bears are fully protected. Shooting a bear is allowed only in self-defence, when there are no other possibilities left. Each kill of a polar bear has to be reported to the police and will be examined in detail. Unjustified kills can lead to high fines (NOK10,000 or more). It is forbidden to keep any parts of a killed bear as trophies. Legal aspects around firearms and ammunition are dealt with in *What to take*, pages 112–13.

Avoidable disturbance of animals is forbidden by the environmental law for Svalbard. This includes chasing polar bears (for example, to get better pictures): there have been high fines (around NOK10,000) for people caught chasing a bear by snow-scooter in order to get better photos; in addition, the camera equipment and film may be confiscated. Feeding is also forbidden and the regulations on camps require measures that reduce the risk of attracting a polar bear, as well as measures that ensure the safety of the camp and reduce the risk of a confrontation (eg: alarm system).

POLICE The Sysselmann's office incorporates a section of the Norwegian police, responsible for Svalbard in its entirety, including Russian areas. In order to service this huge area, extensive use is made of helicopters, the ice-going boat *Nordsyssel* (May to December), motorised sleds and Sno-cats.

To look after tourism, fishing and hunting in summer, teams of two (called field assistants) are stationed in huts along the main island's coasts. They are equipped with motorboats and radios and can be supported very rapidly by helicopter. In the settlements, police irregularly control traffic and are required to be present at the airport at flight times.

Emergencies ☏112
Non-emergencies ☏79 02 12 22

SEARCH AND RESCUE The Sysselmann is responsible for all search and rescue operations, working with the coastguard, the SNSK fire service in Longyearbyen, the hospital and the Red Cross.

EMERGENCY TELEPHONE NUMBERS
General emergencies ☏110
Police ☏112
Fire service in Longyearbyen ☏110

Emergency ambulance service in Longyearbyen ☏113

DISABLED TRAVEL

Svalbard is a difficult destination for the disabled. Firstly, whereas cruise ships themselves might be organised sufficiently well, gangways can be too narrow for wheelchair users to enter or leave the ship.

Secondly, the villages are not well equipped. Longyearbyen has only a few steep streets, but there is no pavement, only a few multi-storey buildings have a lift and older buildings may not be accessible without using steps. Only the most expensive hotel rooms can be used by wheelchair users without help. Barentsburg, which sits on a very steep slope, is the most difficult place for the physically handicapped.

Those with severe difficulties may find it hard to do much at all without a great deal of help.

WHAT TO TAKE

According to the laws of Svalbard, visitors are responsible for their own safety, which includes regulations regarding equipment. The Sysselmann's staff has the right to check a person's kit for suitability, and may restrict or even send back those travellers whom they feel are insufficiently prepared. Inadequate equipment is one of the main reasons why permission is withheld for a project.

Those on organised tours will have some items provided for them. Independent travellers need to do more and have to have the right Arctic outdoor experience if they are going to be adequately prepared – gaining that experience should not start with the first trip to Svalbard!

The Norwegian administration may inspect and control, but it does not provide a comprehensive list (and neither can this book); there are simply too many variables and factors. The responsibility lies with the individual. However, the following are officially required:

- Warm, wind-resistant summer and winter clothing, suitable for the chosen season
- Bivouac supplies with reserves for low temperatures
- First-aid kit
- Emergency signalling apparatus – at least a SARSAT PLB for travelling in areas where a tour permission is required
- Large-calibre weapon
- Camp-alarm system for tours that involve camping
- Survival suit (if going on the water)
- Sufficient provisions in addition for some extra days for unexpected situations.

TENTS The main criterion is stability in a strong wind. The tent should be easy to set up and be of rugged, high-quality construction. There should be a flysheet, preferably with storage space at the ends, but certainly reaching to the ground with a secure method of fixing it down. (An open flysheet can be lifted by the wind or can let in rain.)

Condensation problems make it important to have good ventilation, especially in summer. You must expect wind and snow at any time. A proper groundsheet is essential as the ground is often wet from thaws. Just as uncomfortable is drift snow blowing through cracks straight into your sleeping bag. Snow flaps are very useful.

For summer use On tours around Svalbard where tents have to be carried, the best choice is probably a tunnel tent as this offers good wind stability and has good storage space for luggage and sheltered cooking. Furthermore, ventilation is usually best with tunnels and it is easier to set them up in strong wind (if you start with the end against the wind), than with the standard cupola or geodetic tents with crossing arches, where one always has to fight with the wind at a certain point. Regarding stability, tunnels where you sleep in the direction of the tent are often better than those where you sleep across the main axis, with shorter and therefore more stable arches, and with all users having similar access to both apsides (spaces between the flysheet and the inner tent) from inside, both for access to luggage and for leaving the tent. What's more, snow slides down better from a tent with small arches. Note: it's important you have lots of fixing points for extra guy ropes to increase wind resistance, especially against lateral wind. High-quality tunnel tents are manufactured by the Scandinavian companies Hilleberg (Sweden) or Norrøna (Norway).

Cupola tents have their uses in summer, too, of course, and they have the advantage over tunnel tents if the wind changes direction, as tunnel tents struggle in lateral wind. However, ventilation is usually less good in cupolas, the apsides are smaller and many cupolas are more difficult than a tunnel tent to erect in a storm.

For winter use The cupola or so-called geodetic tents are often preferred, due to their stability in storms. With cold temperatures, condensation in or between the tent layers is less of a problem, as it will freeze anyway and can then be brushed off. What's more, some items of equipment, which in summer are stored in the apsides to stay dry, can be stored outside the tent when there is frost. Cupola tents need the least ground space and are the most efficient at holding in warmth. The North Face is perhaps the most renowned maker of geodetic cupola tents. However, winter tours are also possible with high-quality tunnel tents and today there are a number of cross-breeds between tunnel and cupola tents on the market. Especially in winter, an important aspect is that the inner tent should be as tight as possible against drift snow, which can be as fine as dust. If too much drift snow is blown right into your tent while a snowstorm rages for several days, everything in the tent is going to be moist, and with wet sleeping bags there is a serious risk of hypothermia.

Tents suitable for Svalbard are in the upper price bracket. But you get what you pay for: you will first notice the difference between a Svalbard-quality tent and a cheaper model, including second-class copies, when a storm blows up, perhaps with snow, in exposed, treeless terrain. (And remember: there are no real trees in the Arctic to find shelter under or between!)

V-shaped aluminium tent pegs are good. Bring them with you, along with some large T-shaped plastic pegs for soft ground. And bring some extra guy ropes. Alternatively, you should have wide sand pegs for use in snow and solid steel ones for frozen ground, plus a decent mallet and ways of increasing the tension of your guy ropes for extra stability. 'Spinnaker tape' is useful to patch tears. Setting up your tent must be as uncomplicated as possible as you'll be working in storms, in snowdrifts and in freezing conditions.

Of course, if you are setting up a base camp and won't be carrying your tent from place to place, a much larger model may be used. Make sure the material is tear-resistant. Even those who wish to stay 'only' at the site in Longyearbyen should take care as the wind can come from three sides. Every summer, many tents are lost – and not only the cheap ones.

For winter use, storm resistance is even more important; not only are storms more frequent, but it is also the time when the protection of a tent plays a particularly important role in survival.

RUCKSACKS Contrary to the general trend, I recommend backpacks with external frames for use in Svalbard for longer tours with heavy loads. For carrying a lot of equipment they make a better choice than those with inner frames – you can load them in many different ways and they are durable. Try models from Fjallräven or Haglöfs from Sweden, or Bergans and Norrøna from Norway.

External-frame models are also much better if you are carrying guns as it is easier to fix your rifle here to the frame in a way that allows you to grab it without losing any time.

High-volume rucksacks are desirable, particularly if you choose one with an inner frame but which can become extremely difficult to use when it has extras hung all over it. The inner-frame models do have advantages though, particularly when the contents are packed securely and don't exceed 20kg. When organising tours using stationary camps, I recommend a volume of 60 litres for treks of up to two weeks and 80 litres for longer hikes where camp equipment also has to be carried along. This is for people who don't have tents to carry or much in the way of food and provisions.

Make sure that you test the pack in realistic conditions well in advance. I know of one visitor to Svalbard who brought with him an expensive internal-frame rucksack. He had tested it on a full day's march, carrying 20kg. Then, in Svalbard, he set off on a longer tour carrying 40kg. The backpack became too unwieldy when hung with external packages and he was forced to give up his tour due to the resulting intolerable back problems.

It really isn't worth getting cheap models for these conditions. Expect to pay at least NOK1,000; most acceptable solutions will cost NOK1,500–4,000. Beware, though, as high prices are no automatic guarantee of suitability, and are certainly no guarantee that it will fit your back!

SLEEPING BAGS AND MATS Since days or even weeks are spent without sleeping in a warm shelter, the quality of your sleeping bag is also important.

For summer, bags filled with artificial fibres for insulation are usually best: they perform much better in damp conditions and dry out much more quickly than down. The disadvantage is their relative weight compared with dry down (wet down is very heavy). Du Pont's Quallofill-7 is a good filler, used by many manufacturers including Ajungilak (Norway).

Down is good for dry cold: in March and April, for instance, when temperatures of −20°C or considerably less are not uncommon. Suppliers include Ajungilak, Kugler and The North Face.

A problem when using your bag for a prolonged spell in winter with a strong frost can be condensation within the insulation layer, where it eventually freezes to ice, making not only the sleeping bag increasingly heavy, but also reducing its insulation qualities. No perfect solution seems to have been found so far for this problem, though one possibility is to put a damp-proof layer, for instance a foil sheet, inside the sleeping bag as a barrier, which keeps the humidity away from the insulation layer. The unpleasant side of this method is, of course, that all perspiration and condensation built up during the night will stay close to one's body inside this sheet, requiring an extra layer, such as an extra inlay, to absorb it all. But at least this way the warmth is kept in.

Irrespective of filler, bags should have good overlapping seams (no path for the cold), protected zips, tensioning neck collars and full-face hoods. Nylon inners are lighter and feel warmer, but can get sticky; cotton or cotton mixes feel more comfortable.

Unfortunately, there doesn't seem to be a reliable way of defining how warm a sleeping bag is; some catalogue claims can be quite adventurous and it is important to buy from a specialist. I've heard of skiers sleeping fully clothed and still shivering at −25°C even though their sleeping bags were supposedly good for −40°C. Consider, too, that temperatures can exceed +10°C in summer and a bag designed for a cold winter may be too warm.

Even the best sleeping bag is not all that efficient when the filler is compressed by bodyweight. An insulation mat is needed, not necessarily as a mattress, but for insulation against the cold. Closed-cell foam of at least 10mm is a minimum requirement, but it shouldn't be too heavy. Try Evazote (14mm, 180x55cm, 440g). Light air mattresses may be better for people with back problems, but they are more vulnerable to damage, are heavier and cost more.

STOVES After disappointments with two different gas stoves I have settled on a Trangia methylated spirit stove with a burner adapted for winter use. I prefer spirit stoves, even though they may not necessarily be the most efficient ones regarding fuel consumption, as they are simpler, more reliable and quite safe provided that you don't try to refill them while they are alight. They tend to use more fuel than other stoves, but I'm prepared to carry the extra weight in exchange for increased reliability.

Petrol or paraffin burners need more care, but are cheaper to run and maybe better for you during the winter. Take a cleaning kit and spare lighters/matches.

A good lighter is a must; one that can work in very cold temperatures without burning your fingers (stoves can take a few seconds to light).

Methylated spirit (in Norwegian: *rød sprit* – 'red spirit') is widely available in Longyearbyen in plastic bottles. Unleaded petrol can be bought at the petrol station, which also sells paraffin. However, a number of stove models are very specific regarding fuel. There was a Swiss winter expedition which had to be rescued because both of their petrol stoves stopped functioning after a while due to problems with the fuel bought in Longyearbyen which apparently did not meet the specifications required by the type of stove they had brought.

WATER CONTAINERS I have been pleased with a sturdy, bucket-shaped water bag which stands up by itself when filled.

There is enough water in Svalbard, but not always where you want it. The nearest stream may have safe water, but may also have unappetising silt, so be prepared to carry reasonably large quantities of water just in case.

Containers with taps are unsatisfactory. It is difficult to fill them from a stream and they have to be hung up in order to use the valve – not easy in a place with no trees.

It is not always necessary to carry a water container with you on summer trips; you will find potable water almost everywhere except, for instance, when climbing mountains. If you want a hot drink while underway, take a vacuum flask. Stainless-steel models are tougher than plastic and glass inners are too fragile. You should always take a high-quality Thermos during winter trips.

CLOTHING What you wear depends on what you are trying to do.

Good, fairly formal attire is in order for those on cruise liners or when visiting exclusive restaurants. Smart casual wear is suitable for almost everywhere indoors on land and on 'expedition cruises'. Take slippers or be prepared to walk around in stocking feet when visiting, even in hotels, as outdoor shoes are usually left at the front door.

For short stays with day trips around town or brief landings from a cruise ship you need weatherproof, hard-wearing hiking gear such as you might use in the Alps. A hood on a good anorak is useful, but umbrellas aren't (due to the wind). Knee-high rubber boots (see page 110) are highly useful in combination with sturdy hiking boots when it comes to crossing wild, ice-cold and often muddy glacier streams or extended swampy areas – and also on day trips when landing from a ship on a beach with some waves. For more extensive trips, more substantial gear is needed. Detailed advice should be obtained from your tour organiser well in advance.

The well-known layering principle applies: many thin layers work better than one thick one. Summer-season clothes should protect against wind-chill but should not impede sweat evaporation. Spare clothing should be carried, which you can change into after an involuntary bath in a stream.

It is important that the outermost layer be robust: preferably a hip-length anorak, impermeable to wind, with fastenings around the hips, wrists and hood, and sealed at the front fastening. This outermost layer should protect only against wind and rain, but have the least possible insulating effect: insulation should be confined to layers worn under the anorak, so that they can be taken off when it gets too warm – this is not possible with an anorak or jacket where insulation is inseparably integrated already. I prefer full-length two-way zips with press-stud cover flaps as they give better temperature control. High-quality anoraks in Gore-Tex or similar can obviate the need for extra rainwear. Consider products by Berghaus, The North Face, Sprayway or similar. If backpacking, ensure jackets have abrasion-resistant material on the shoulders. Military parkas tend to be too heavy, especially when wet, and they take an age to dry. Thick down-jackets are really useful only in summer in conditions where you are not going to sweat; otherwise, you will have to take your jacket off and get cold again, etc. Down can be comfortable to wear in camp when there is little activity. If backpacking, ensure jackets have abrasion-resistant material on the shoulders.

I often use army trousers as they are hardwearing and cheap, but they dry slowly. Rohan or similar trousers are fine. Skin-tight trousers are no good; there should be freedom of movement (and thereby automatically an air layer in the trouser that insulates a bit) even when wearing long underwear, and a layer of air between your skin and the fabric is necessary. Gore-Tex hiking trousers are sometimes used. These will protect against drops coming off a poncho and may even keep you dry when crossing small streams if you seal up the bottoms. (This also applies to any good rain trousers.)

Long underwear should also find its way into your luggage. Even in summer there are a few days cold enough to warrant this but it really comes into its own in camp or at night.

Fleece is a very practical material; it is sturdy, not sensitive to moisture content, extremely quick-drying, holds its warmth and is comfortable to wear for most people. You can get fleece socks and trousers as well as the fleece jackets that are seen everywhere nowadays. Canoeists will find it very practical to wear fleece under their waterproofs, but be careful when drying fleece as it doesn't like to get too hot.

High-quality hiking socks are a must, especially when wearing rubber boots; they absorb shock, keep out some of the wet and insulate your feet against the cold. All footwear, including socks, should be tried out at home well in advance. It is worth spending money on socks, so you need to be sure that you're buying something that suits you (some people are allergic to fleece next to the skin).

Clothing does not dry well in cold, damp weather. Under these conditions it is often better to let damp clothes dry on you, covering yourself up with a sleeping bag against the cold. The drying process can be accelerated by letting the moisture evaporate, ie: leave your sleeping bag open at the bottom. But it can still take several hours for items to dry.

Those using boats need particularly good protection against the water and the wind. Fingers are hard to protect without obstructing your paddling. On warmer, windless days you can find yourself sweating under your clothes. Wetsuits thick enough to offer protection are not comfortable and can chafe.

Winter tours are characterised by temperatures from –40°C to +5°C, with ranges of 20°C in a day not unknown. The warmest possible clothing is needed in preparation for extremes: down jackets with large hoods, balaclavas, thermal trousers, the warmest mittens with long sleeves and perhaps down shoes for use in camp. The layering principle applies here too so that you can adapt to changing conditions and activity levels.

Other important items include face masks, protective goggles, thermal underwear and gloves or mittens with thumbs and forefingers. Silk inner gloves are recommended as they fit under outer gloves and can also be used to grip frozen metal objects where there would otherwise be a risk of skin sticking. Many people still find woollen underwear and socks warmer than those made of high-tech materials.

Footwear

If you plan to stay around Longyearbyen in the summer only without heading off on any longer terrain excursions, you can get by with robust shoes or sports shoes. Most roads are now tarred. Hiking rubber boots are good enough for day trips or short boat landings, and trekking shoes suffice when it is dry. But who can tell in advance – bring both!

All footwear has to deal with two problems in Svalbard's summer: wetness and rock debris/scree. The terrain in Svalbard is damp with rivulets, marshes, bogs and wet snow. Shoes become terribly uncomfortable when they don't dry in the cold, moist conditions, however well you look after them. Physical demands on footwear are extreme. Soles should be able to cope with scree, streambeds and cliffs and should support your feet when walking, balancing or just getting a foothold. A shock-absorbing insole is very important, as is the general toughness of the outer material. Soles, toes and uppers should all be resistant to abrasion and piercing. I've known people completely ruin heavy plastic mountaineering boots in eight to ten weeks due to extreme wear from the terrain.

Perhaps the most practical footwear for country treks in summer are good-quality rubber hiking boots, such as you can buy from specialist hunting or hiking equipment shops. Anyone who is used to mountain boots finds it hard to believe that you can hike quite comfortably in rubber boots – I too had to be converted while on a trip to Lapland. Take care not to use fluffy integrated insulation inside, as the insides will never dry again on tour once wet – take additional warm socks instead. For more demanding treks, the boots should have a light extension that can be pulled up to the crotch for deeper water where needed.

Shoes or boots must, above all, be really comfortable and give good support to the foot. If necessary, try adding an insole. Good treads, providing good grip, are essential (most sailing boots, for instance, have treads that are too fine). Soles should be so thick that you can barely feel the sharpest of stones. I recommend taking two pairs: a pair of rubber boots and a pair of trekking shoes, when only a few hikes are planned.

Fairly new to the market are shoes with Gore-Tex water protection. Manufacturing quality is even more important with these, otherwise the whole point is lost. It is well worth undertaking extensive trials first. In my opinion, light trekking boots, with or without Gore-Tex, are not the most suitable for Svalbard. Either the sides of the shoe are not high enough or they are not rigid enough and the terrain is too much for them; they are really suitable only for short, relatively easy day trips.

Heavy plastic mountaineering boots are good for long treks, though not so good for wading through streams. Brands like Asolo, Koflach, Lowa and Raichle offer a wide choice. Again, you should look closely at the heavier models with separable inner shoes. The light inner shoes can be worn on their own in camp. The outers are good for scree, are firm on hard snow, can easily be fitted with crampons and, not least, they are waterproof too. For deeper streams you will need higher, rubber boots in addition. In desperation, though, you can remove the inners of your plastic boots and replace them at the other side of the stream (once you have emptied the outers!). I find plastic mountain boots so practical that I have occasionally made them mandatory for the more demanding of my tours. They have only two disadvantages as far as I can see: first, those who haven't tried them yet don't believe that they can be worn fairly comfortably for hiking as they are wrongly associated with skiing boots, and secondly they can get too warm – hardly a problem in Svalbard!

Popular with British visitors is a combination of plastic mountain boots and Berghaus 'Yeti' gaiters. These gaiters are waterproof and can be used in some cases where rubber boots might otherwise be needed. However, they reach up to the knee only and there is a temptation to keep them on for the whole tour, which reduces their lifetime considerably in the rough terrain. If you take both this combination and rubber boots, you can extend your hiking possibilities and protect your more expensive boots from accelerated wear.

Leather boots rarely have the opportunity of drying out properly and often end up with the soles parting from their uppers.

For winter use, thermo boots – like those, for example, manufactured by Sorel – are the right choice as long as no longer hiking or skiing activity is planned. They are excellent for snowmobiling or dog-sledging but also for a stroll around Longyearbyen when it is cold. For winter trekking or skiing tours, Sorels are usually too soft, offering too little stability for the foot.

In short, there are no shoes or boots that are ideal for all conditions that you will come across in Svalbard. Bring at least two kinds; three, if you want to be absolutely sure of dry feet. And whatever you bring should have been tested extensively at home first, not least of all so as to reduce the risk of blisters.

Rain and wind gear Since it seldom rains very hard or for very long in Svalbard and a rain suit (apart from Gore-Tex) can create a real sauna effect, I prefer to use a poncho as an inexpensive but practical form of protection although it does have its drawbacks in high winds, of course – fluttering and letting in rain from the side. The best ones are large enough to cover your backpack and have press-stud closures at the side. Very light models are available which can be folded up quite small.

Heavy military ponchos are also practical; if you buy secondhand, hold them up to the light to check for holes! They are durable and can double as groundsheets or an emergency bivouac.

However, even specialist mountaineering ponchos with gussets at the back fail to cover the largest rucksacks. Here, I prefer to use a plastic sheet as a separate cover. It is important to be thorough when tying it down, though; I have seen even specially fitted rucksack covers separating from the rucksack in high winds.

In lighter rain of shorter duration – the typical form of precipitation in summer – breathable suits of Gore-Tex, Sympatex, Texapor and others may be more comfortable; they will let out water vapour, but won't let in the rain. They don't need to be fully lined, expensive jackets with all the trimmings; on the contrary, every stitch is a potential failure point and such clothing can become too warm. Better to take something simple but large enough to fit more layers underneath as it gets cooler.

A protective anorak should reach below your crotch and should have a draw-string to give good wind protection. There should also be ways of sealing off the cuffs and tightening the hood until there's only an opening for your nose and eyes; they should be roomy enough for you to keep your cap on and not feel claustrophobic. Fashionable models with hoods folded into the collar or with separate hoods that need to be fastened with poppers rarely seal all that well.

On cold, windy days, when it rains, and when you may get spray, a pair of over-trousers will keep you more comfortable. Breathable trousers are a good choice. Select trousers with a high waist to protect your kidneys from cold, with braces to keep them up, and ways of sealing up the bottoms of the legs and also getting at the pockets of your inner trousers. Such a pair can also act as a spare for ordinary use.

FIREARMS Though the vast majority of Svalbard travellers will not have to bother with a weapon because they are on a tour with organisers who will take care of this issue, this section is included as a help for those who travel the archipelago independently – be it as tourists, scientists, or whatever. For these people, this issue can be of great importance.

Here I am speaking of firearms needed for self-defence against possible polar bear attacks – this section is not addressed to the very few who travel to Svalbard for hunting reasons, who probably know which firearms to take with them for their specific hunting purposes (for instance seals) anyway.

A firearm for self-defence purposes against polar bears has to meet different requirements from a hunting weapon. While both must be suitable to kill an animal efficiently, a self-defence weapon must also pay attention to the fact that polar bears are a protected species and thus a bear should be killed as the last resort only. This aim can be supported by the choice of the firearm. Surprisingly, this conservation aspect is mostly ignored when it comes to the issue of polar bears and firearms.

In my opinion, an ideal firearm for self-defence purposes should have the following qualities:

- Powerful and big calibre, which increases the chance of a quick kill if needed.
- Reliable even under rough terrain conditions (moist, dirt, snow, dust).
- Fast handling – self-defence against a polar bear requires a quick series of shots from a very short distance (if not from a short distance, it is not self-defence). For most hunting purposes, where you usually shoot at longer, safer distances, this is a secondary claim, which most hunting rifles do not meet.
- Ample capacity for cartridges in the magazine and/or the possibility for quick reloading of the magazine. The weapon should be ready for firing even while reloading the magazine: you should be able to fire many warning shots to give the bear every chance to back off and flee – and still have two or three rounds left if it doesn't. A typical hunting rifle has a capacity of one to five cartridges only and reloading a magazine makes a normal hunting rifle unusable for at least several seconds – unacceptable when there's a bear just a few metres away from you.
- Smooth shape and short: a hiker will not want to carry his firearm in his hands all day like a hunter stalking his prey, but wants to be sure that he can have it ready within two or three seconds even when carrying a big and clumsy rucksack or lying inside a narrow tent. A long hunting rifle, possibly even one with optics, can get caught up in rucksack straps, etc, when needed quickly, and is otherwise unpractical to carry due to its length.

So what is a suitable self-defence firearm for Svalbard?

This is a question of two components: ammunition and the firearm itself.

Ammunition A polar bear is one of the biggest land animals and killing an attacking polar bear fast enough and over a short distance requires high firepower in the hands of a trained shooter. The efficiency of a bullet is basically dependent on two aspects: its diameter – which causes an accordingly big injury, then its energy or velocity, which needs to be high enough to penetrate deep inside the polar bear. The potency of bullets can be increased by special design, which can cause them to expand or partly break up when entering a body. Basically, the calibre refers to the inner diameter of the barrel, which is about equal to the diameter of the bullet. Most commonly, the calibre name includes this diameter in a fraction of an inch (hence a dot followed by some figures: .308, .375, .444, etc) or in millimetres, then often followed by a cartridge length – also in millimetres: 9.3 x 62, for example. A small bullet with high energy (velocity) may fly through the body without doing much harm; a big bullet without much energy will not penetrate deep enough. The latter is a problem with almost all handguns. They are nice to carry and some big calibres also have suitable diameters, but due to the massive recoil that is caused by powerful ammunition in such relatively light weapons, almost all handgun calibres do not have the desirable energy and resulting penetration ability. Even a .44 Magnum, the biggest common revolver calibre, has less than half of the energy of a .308 or 30-06 rifle cartridge, which are considered the absolute minimum in rifle ammunition. A revolver with the potential to fell a polar bear might be a .454 Casull, which is not only very expensive but also has a massive recoil, requiring very strong hands and arms – and furthermore has a capacity of only five shots. Still, even this calibre does not have the same energy as most .308 cartridges. Revolvers or pistols are therefore not recommended as suitable self-defence weapons against polar bears, except for a few cases, for instance pilots or snowmobile drivers, where the risk of a dangerous polar bear encounter is very low.

So regarding calibre, for rifles the recommended calibres include: .375 H&H, 9.3mm x 62, .404 rimless, .444, .475. The absolute minimum is the widespread NATO calibre .308. A weapon of .308 or 7.62 calibre can produce energy in the range 3,200–4,400 joules, about the bottom of the range that most big-game hunters would select. To compare, 'proper' big-game calibre rifles range from 8 x 68 (5,600 joules) to a .458 Magnum (6,700 joules). The bigger firearms tend to kick back more, of course, especially in the heat of the moment when you have no opportunity to choose your stance. Alternatively, if you are going with a shotgun, cal 12 (or even cal 10) is the choice – and then with one big bullet, a so-called slug. Shotgun calibres are measured by a different and rather antiquated method: cal 12 means that for a shotgun barrel of this calibre, 12 spherical bullets could be formed from one English pound (lb) of lead. Therefore, the lower the number, the bigger the diameter. In calibre 12, the barrel and thus each of these bullets has a diameter of 18mm. Slugs are less accurate than rifle bullets and they lose energy quickly in their flight through the air due to their big diameter, but at close range these are not important aspects.

Type of firearm Pistols and revolvers have been discussed already as less than suitable – and moreover, the Norwegian authorities are not happy with tourists carrying handguns.

So a long arm is usually the right choice. Here, the main choice is between rifles (where the barrel gives the bullet a spin and thereby higher accuracy) and shotguns, which usually have a smooth barrel, mostly used for firing a lot of small pellets loaded within each cartridge.

Based on the above discussed criteria for a self-defence firearm, this should be rugged, have ample ammunition capacity and/or fast reloading possibility while

2

ready for firing, and relatively short. Self-defence is mostly undertaken at a short distance, so accuracy and long range are of little importance. These criteria are fulfilled by a number of firearm types:

Pumpguns At least in summer, I consider a pump-action gun to be possibly the most useful self-defence weapon in polar bear areas, especially if made from stainless steel and with a magazine capacity of seven or eight cartridges. It is extremely fast in handling (you can load a cartridge in the chamber while raising the weapon to your target line all in one movement, which is almost impossible with any other gun) and allows very quick refilling of the magazine. Should the seven or eight cartridges still not be sufficient (we've had two cases so far where bears turned round only after seven warning shots had been fired – with a normal repeater rifle, we would have been forced to kill these bears after two or three warning shots), it is possible to reload the magazine of a pumpgun while it is ready to fire. With extra training and strong hands, pumpguns can be refitted with a pistol grip, thus cutting their lengths down to a handy 80cm even with an eight-shot magazine. Apart from the recommended slug ammunition, a pumpgun can also be loaded with normal shot ammunition, police rubber bullets or even signal ammunition. So if there are two pumpguns in a group, one person can try to deter a bear with warning shots or a rubber bullet, while the other gun can function as a backup with slugs if the bear remains undeterred.

Under-lever action rifles Known as 'the Western rifle', these are also very fast in handling and their magazine can be refilled while a cartridge is ready for firing in the chamber. Originally, these rifles were built for common revolver-ammunition calibres only, which would be insufficient for defence against a polar bear. However, now models for stronger calibres are also available, for instance by Marlin in calibre .444. The magazine capacity is only five cartridges, but thanks to the very easy and quick refilling possibility, this is not normally a major problem. Being a rifle, the range of precision and stopping power is longer than with a pumpgun, which can be of interest when in charge of bigger and more spread-out groups, for instance on a land excursion with passengers of a cruise.

In my opinion, pumpguns and under-lever action rifles are the best choice for summer and especially if you're going to have only one firearm on tour. If several firearms are available, then other types of rifles can be considered:

Normal repeater rifles These are the standard hunting rifles and there are huge stocks of cheap old military rifles of this type – those with the 'Mauser' system, for instance – on the market. They are the easiest to get hold of, but are a bargain only up to calibres .308/30-06 or 8 x 57. Their disadvantage is often the length, for instance 1.10m (not very handy when in a small tent or carried on a big rucksack), their weight and their limited magazine capacity (usually four, sometimes five shots). With most of them, refilling the magazine has to be done through the opened repeater mechanism, which means that no cartridge will be ready for firing in the chamber at that moment. Some models have the possibility of exchanging the complete magazine for a full spare one, but even here this leaves only one cartridge in the chamber at that moment. So, when confronted with a bear at close hand with such a rifle, you are basically confined to the few shots you already have in the magazine. Many cheap, outworn rifles on the market are fine for decoration or for target shooting on the range, where a malfunction is less of a problem, but having an outworn rifle for self-defence on tour is not a good idea. Rental rifles are usually such normal repeater rifles, with all the aforementioned disadvantages, and are usually available only in calibres .308 or 30-06, which are at the lower limit of what is recommended. There is at least one type of use where a normal repeater rifle (though preferably of better quality and bigger calibre than the cheap rental ones or bargain offers) is the best choice: during longer outdoor activities in winter. Some of these rifles, with a smooth, closed mechanism are less vulnerable to fine drift snow, which tends to penetrate into the smallest openings, causing problems. Suitable rifles for this kind of use do not come inexpensively, however.

Semi-automatic rifles (and semi-automatic pumpguns) These are basically very efficient, if equipped with a suitably big magazine. Legal limitations on magazine capacity exist for hunting, but not for self-defence. As long as there are no malfunctions, a semi-automatic weapon is certainly optimal when considering firepower. Disadvantages? They are usually heavier and more prone to malfunctions due to a more complex firing system. I am a firm believer in Murphy's Law (what can go wrong, will eventually go wrong), so I am a bit reserved about the idea of semi-automatics during prolonged outdoor activities.

Fully automatic firearms are forbidden in Svalbard.

Training There are a few visitors to Svalbard who turn up with a firearm they have not yet tried, or have tried once or twice only in comfort on the range (including rental firearms). Perhaps they are happy that they learned enough in their national service – of course with a totally different type of weapon. I am very much in doubt about such approaches, which in my opinion are first of all self-deception, which hopefully will never be revealed in a real test. Also, just sterile firing practice on a range is not everything: I have seen some hikers out in the wilderness with their firearm well packed in a cover or firmly tied to (or even inside) the rucksack – do they want to throw it together with the backpack in case of an attack? Practice must include preparation – that is removing your gun from your backpack and loading it before firing at a target in a hurry. Two seconds may be all you have for the whole process. The better you get at this, the more self-confidence you will have and the less likely you will be to panic.

Make sure the safety catch works easily. You may also like to stick some tape over the barrel to stop grit and water getting in (the British Army use condoms for this).

Licences The licence issued in your own country for your firearm is likely to be recognised in Svalbard. This licence is also essential when transporting your firearm there and back.

Firearm rental In view of the possible inconveniences of purchasing a licence and a firearm and then taking it to Svalbard, the idea of renting a rifle may be tempting. In my opinion, this is an acceptable option only in very few cases, for instance for a sailing yacht travelling to Svalbard with minimal visits to land planned.

Usually, only normal repeater rifles are offered for rental – with all the aforementioned shortcomings: limited ammunition capacity, long and heavy, and usually fairly old.

Perhaps even more worrying: you may rent ten cartridges along with the rifle, but you are not allowed to buy further ammunition in sufficient quantities for training (this requires a licence). Therefore, this arrangement makes sense only if you have the possibility of realistic training on a range with the same model of rifle at home before setting out on your tour to Svalbard.

Maybe not surprisingly, those who are interested in gun rental are often those persons with the least shooting experience – more experienced shooters rarely consider relying completely on an unfamiliar weapon without good prior training. For lengthy independent tours out into Svalbard's wilderness without a tour operator, the best solution is your own suitable firearm that you are familiar with.

CAMP ALARM Sleeping in your tent, stuck in your sleeping bag, is potentially the most dangerous situation, particularly as the animal may be very close already. A bear, realising your presence at just a few metres' distance, may itself feel threatened which could provoke an attack. When camping in Svalbard (except in Longyearbyen Camping), therefore, the minimum safety measure is a tripwire alarm system around your tent, typically equipped with military alarm mines (which flash and bang when ignited). There have also been attempts with electronic tripwire alarms – the advantage being that their triggering is less expensive than an alarm mine (most alarms are not caused by bears but by four-legged reindeers and sleepy two-legged 'reindeers' on the way to the toilet). The disadvantage of electronic alarms is their greater potential for malfunction, accordingly only alarm mines are officially accepted. In any case, great attention should be paid to a proper installation of the tripwire. It should be about 50–60cm above the ground (there have been sightings of careful bears actually crawling under a wire that's been placed too high, while a lower wire is easy to step over). A bear approaching something as unfamiliar as a silent camp usually takes its time and is very attentive, sometimes avoiding contact with such strange things as wires. Support poles should be properly fixed so that they do not simply fall over when the wire is touched, which may prevent the necessary tension of the wire needed to trigger the alarm.

Be careful too: alarm mines can be harmful to humans (and animals) at close contact because of flying parts or the intense heat of the flare. Alarm mines are occasionally on offer in Longyearbyen in some of the outdoor shops, but often sold out.

If a bear (or evidence of a bear, at least) has been observed in the vicinity, the alarm system should be supplemented with a watch system. For further information see the *Safety* section on polar bears, pages 99–104.

DISTRESS ALARM Owing to the almost complete lack of crime, Svalbard can be a safer travel destination than most others, as long as one behaves professionally in the wilderness and nothing happens. However, if a serious accident or sickness should strike out there, organising help may be a problem. The option of getting quickly to a settlement is often unrealistic and normal cellular phones (of the GSM system) are of use only in fairly limited areas within range of Longyearbyen, Barentsburg and Sveagruva. VHF can be of use in parts of Isfjord, Kongsfjord, Magdalenefjord and Van Mijenfjord to get contact with a radio station or other vessels. The same applies to signal pistols and signal ammunition.

Signal ammunition Svalbard makes up a vast area. Firing a signal shot – and somebody else seeing it – requires some luck. Therefore, you should maximise your chances by using powerful pyrotechnic signals. Small signal starters as used by surfers or sailors near the coast are of limited use (the signal rises only 30–50m, and has a weaker light and a shorter burning time). A signal pistol of calibre 4 (28mm barrel diameter) is a useful solution, combined with long signal cartridges, which send a flare up to a height of 300m, with parachutes keeping them in the air for longer. The advantage of a signal pistol is that it can supplement your firearm by fending off a polar bear attack, first with a signal shot (firing it up in the air is less harmful). It's more impressive to fire it in front of the bear – then the flare might ricochet towards the bear. The risk is it might fly over the bear, maybe frightening the animal into running your way! You can even fire directly at the bear itself – which may be successful, but can also cause severe injuries; moreover, it is very difficult to fire precisely with a signal pistol. In order to frighten off polar bears, a signal ammunition type, where the projectile causes an impressive bang and flash after about one second, is recommended.

Important: Flare ammunition is potentially lethal for any person hit by it, and causes terrible wounds. Shooting red flares should be done only in real distress situations, as this is an official international distress signal. Unjustified use can lead to prosecution and a possible high bill for the resulting rescue operation. Therefore, have some other types of ammunition with you, too (green, white, flash/bang), and not only red.

SATELLITE TELEPHONES AND PERSONAL-LOCATOR BEACONS (PLBS) IRIDIUM
is the only satellite telephone system which works reliably so far up north. INMARSAT, Thuraya, etc, are not as suitable for such polar areas as their satellites are positioned in equatorial orbits and can therefore not 'see' so close to the Poles, while the IRIDIUM satellites circle Earth on polar orbits. An IRIDIUM telephone is about the size of the first clumsy GSM cellular phones, so is acceptably small. The big advantage in comparison to PLBs is the possibility of actual communication, and not just the transmission of a fixed signal. This allows you to announce a delayed return, for instance, or request help below the level of a full-scale rescue operation. The disadvantage: PLBs have a much longer duration regarding batteries and are less complex – therefore, the Sysselmann may require first of all a PLB as part of the equipment for emergency situations, with an IRIDIUM telephone only as a supplement. The leading manufacturer for IRIDIUM telephones is Motorola; price new around US$1,500 plus registration and traffic fees (a much more sensible option is to just rent one from your home country for the length of your stay).

Personal locator beacons are transmitters the size of a first-generation cellular GSM phone and emit a signal when started, which is then located by several of the COSPAS-SARSAT satellites. The calculated position of the PLB is then reported to the rescue service – which then knows only that there is a distress alarm from a certain position and possibly the owner of the PLB, if it has a registry code included in the signal. It is not possible to send any specified message with this system, so any time a PLB is triggered will probably cause a full-scale rescue operation. Therefore, it may be used only in situations where there is no other realistic way of preventing death or lasting damage to a person. Abuse, for instance because of blisters which would force a group to spend some days waiting and who therefore want a person picked up, or because of a delay which may result in missing a plane, can lead to prosecution and a huge bill for an unnecessary rescue operation.

Currently, PLBs are on the market for two frequencies: 121.5MHz and 406MHz. Those of frequency 121.5MHz are considerably less accurate (by several kilometres) and weaker, but are used by planes and rescue helicopters, mainly for homing in on the exact position of the PLB in the final part of a search (in addition to 406MHz equipment). Systems using 121.5MHz are becoming increasingly obsolete, although aircraft should continue to use them for some time. The alternative frequency, 406MHz, offers faster and more accurate satellite location – and soon, this will be the only frequency used for a satellite-based location. The newest generation of PLBs include a GPS, which encodes the exact sender position into the distress signal. With this method, the signal has to be picked up by just one satellite (instead of several) and the exact position of the PLB can then be forwarded to the rescue service immediately, ensuring that the party in distress is located quickly. Furthermore, all 406MHz PLBs are registered with an owner, which reduces the rate of false alarms considerably. These 406MHz PLBs with GPS function are available for about US$400 (markedly less without GPS). The disadvantage of all PLBs is that, so far, they do not allow the transmission of a more specific message. The advantage is their high durability and reliability. It seems highly likely that the Sysselmann would insist on 406MHz PLBs for any tour before permission is granted.

☞ **Attention:** Having a satellite telephone or PLB, even when functioning, is one thing, but it doesn't necessarily mean that a successful rescue operation can be launched. Bad weather may easily prevent this, even for days. So, despite the technology, all Svalbard expeditions should recognise that help from the outside world should not be taken for granted and therefore plan and act in a way that minimises dependency on external help.

CLIMBING AIDS Even those who have no plans to cross glaciers will find climbing accessories (first of all crampons, maybe also ice axes, ropes and ice screws, etc) useful in some places. Crossing small ice- or snow-fields in shoes without crampons or similar will be difficult. Crampons must be fastened with good bindings – the safest are still strap bindings. Step-in bindings may seem more comfortable, but are safe only on very stiff mountaineering boots designed for use with crampons – and then still preferably with a safety strap that prevents opening and loss. A protective cover is also necessary in order to stow these items safely.

GPS (GLOBAL POSITIONING SYSTEM) Use of GPS has become commonplace on Svalbard tours, especially in winter/spring when there's the additional risk of white-out conditions. A GPS leads to more exact results than a compass, is independent of local magnetic conditions and allows storage of positions and even routes. A major advantage is that it also provides a position and direction without any sight, where a compass often cannot be used anymore. These are clear advantages. The disadvantage is – apart from the increasing dependency on technology, which may fail – an exaggerated feeling of safety. A GPS can tell you only your position and course. It can tell you nothing about the dangers of the terrain right in front of you (crevasses, abysses, mud, insecure ice, etc) – so even with a GPS, common sense should make travellers stop when visibility gets very poor. Unfortunately, this is often ignored, leading to accidents due to a blind trust in the GPS; the same people with just a compass would not have moved on under such conditions. Sometimes a false sense of security is worse than no security at all.

ELECTRICITY

In both Norwegian and Russian areas, as well as most cruisers and other boats, the norm is 220V AC. The flat two-pinned standard European plugs will fit.

TIME

Svalbard, including the Russian settlements, runs on Central European Time, including summer time.

Part Two

SVALBARD

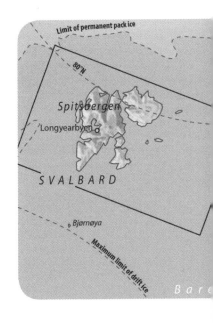

3

Svalbard's Regions

In a relatively small area, Svalbard offers an amazing range of different landscapes and forms, giving it a character all of its own.

The west coast, with the influence of the warmer Gulf Stream, has mid-Arctic flora and fauna, while only 100–200km to the east the true High Arctic may be found. Differences are also caused by varying levels of precipitation.

(VEST) SPITSBERGEN

Until a few decades ago, the island was still offcially named Vest Spitsbergen (West Spitsbergen), only to be renamed Spitsbergen by Norway, which had previously been the collective name for most of the archipelago. Covering 39,044km² out of Svalbard's total 62,670km², it is by far and away the largest island in the group. And, apart from the weather stations on Hopen and Bjørnøya, it is the only island with a permanent population. Even here, though, outside of a few settlements, the place is empty. Owing to the Gulf Stream influence, which means less trouble with ice, all the five settlements, plus the  Polish scientific station at Hornsund and most of today's trappers are situated along the west coast. For the same reason – favourable ice conditions – classic cruise tourism is also concentrated on the west and northwest coasts.

The island is very mountainous and split with fjords, so much so that it almost divides into more islands (from Wijdefjorden to Dicksonfjorden is a land bridge of only 20km or so). Folding along the west coast in the Tertiary period has led to a wild alpine mountainscape there, riven with fjords and featuring glaciers that tumble to the sea and 1,000m-high, pointed peaks that give Spitsbergen its name.

The beauty of the place and relative ease with which it may be approached by ship make Spitsbergen the archipelago's top attraction. It is also heavily attractive to birds, since the nutrient-rich sea and steep coastal rocks make this a place of huge seabird colonies.

The fjords are the dominant topographic features of the area. West to east, the folded mountain range is some 15–50km wide. Igneous and metamorphic rocks lie next to sedimentary strata, formed into bizarre shapes by weather erosion. In Bockfjorden are the last signs of volcanic activity – an extinct volcano and thermal springs.

Typical summer winds come out of the west to northwest and, accordingly, precipitation and low cloud are more frequent along the west coast – which is also the reason for the more extensive glaciation of this area, particularly so with the inland ice areas of Isachsenfonna and Holtedahlfonna in the northwest. In many places between the shore and the steep mountainsides you'll find flatland up to 15km in width, which has risen from the sea since the last ice age and continues under the water as shallows. Here you can see signs of previous water levels, telling the story of how the land has changed.

Much of the eastern sector of the main island, with fewer intrusions by fjords and weaker Tertiary folding, is an area of massive ice cover. This is especially true in the north, where the highest peaks of the whole archipelago can be found, namely Newtontoppen (1,713m) and Perriertoppen (1,712m) in the region called Ny Frieslandet. These and other high peaks rise out of a sea of glaciers and ice caps.

The thick ice of the east arises from the lack of Gulf Stream (ocean currents from the east are cold) and the snowfall brought in from the east by winter winds. Here is the most widespread glaciation, with long ice fronts falling to the sea; Negribreen in the northern Storfjorden is a good example. Glaciation from the east also enters the sea towards the west, in Wijdefjorden, Billefjorden or Tempelfjorden, for instance. These glaciers don't reach the size of those to the east, but have nevertheless carved great valleys with vertical walls through the massif. Included in these are Stubendorffbreen in the inner Wijdefjorden near Newtontoppen, Tunabreen at the end of Tempelfjorden and Nordenskiöldbreen, across from Pyramiden.

In the middle of the east side the hills are not so high and some shelter is given by Barentsøya and Edgeøya offshore; here the ice is not so thick or widespread. The terrain is formed by lower plateau-shaped mountains owing to a geology of almost horizontal sediment layers of alternating hard and soft rock. These, when eroded, together with the sparsity of vegetation, give a 'Wild West' feel – or rather, they would were there no ice. Similar terrain occurs on Edgeøya and Barentsøya and at Heleysundet to the northeast of the main island.

From Inglefieldbukta south, the glaciers become larger again, sandwiched between plateaux of sedimentary rock and meeting the western ice zone in an area of extensive glaciation on southern Spitsbergen. Isbukta is spectacular: three semicircular fronts of three crashing glaciers forming Sørkappfonna. In the background you can see the sharp peaks of the west coast range.

The central area, from the north coast between Woodfjorden and Wijdefjorden past the inner end of Isfjorden and on past Van Mijenfjorden to Van Keulenfjorden, is sheltered somewhat from rain and snow and is subsequently drier. There is less ice here, but there are still many glaciers in the valleys between the higher mountains, though very few reach the sea. The mountains themselves, rarely higher than 1,000m, are formed of horizontal strata, cut by glaciation, and with many scree slopes. Between them lie a few large, sheltered valleys (Sassendalen, Adventdalen, Reindalen, Colesdalen) and ice-age glacier beds. Together with small stretches of shore under bird colonies, these are the most fertile parts of Svalbard, feeding reindeer and geese.

The relatively ice-free parts of Spitsbergen (Nordenskiöldlandet, Dicksonlandet, Bünsow Landet) are the first choice for hiking as there is less traversing of glaciers to do. Even so, it is no easy option – this is the Arctic, after all.

Regarding tourism, the west and north coast between Isfjorden and Woodfjorden is the most-visited area for bigger cruise ships, due to its combination of spectacular scenery, historic sites and easier accessibility. In recent years, thanks to the friendlier ice conditions, the magnificent Hornsund in the south has also become popular. The other northern and eastern parts of the island are restricted more to expedition-type cruises on smaller vessels (24–100 passengers), usually with appropriately high ice classes. Land tourism – hiking and paddling in summer, and skiing, dog-sledges, snowmobiles, snowshoes or winter hiking in spring – are mostly restricted to the easier, more accessible central part of the island between Van Mijenfjord and Isfjord.

Various nature reserves, national parks, bird sanctuaries and a geological protected area (Festningen) cover the majority of the island.

NORDAUSTLANDET

At 14,710km², Nordaustlandet ('Northeast Land') is the second largest of Svalbard's islands and belongs to the Nordaust Svalbard Naturreservat, with its restrictions on travel and ban on landing aircraft.

With its north coast even further north than that of the main island, the climate is High Arctic: there is no Gulf Stream effect. The island is hemmed in by ice for very long winters and partly or, in less favourable years, even completely, in summer. Boats without reinforced hulls can often fail to circumnavigate the island even in summer; the greatest problems are with the Hinlopen Strait, stretches of which are often closed off. The north coast is regularly free from ice before the rest, due to wind and ocean currents.

The north and west of the island consist of many steep-sided fjords, with promontories leading to outlying islets. In the east and south, the ice cover keeps the topography hidden, its profile known only where radar measurements have been taken.

Off the north coast are the Sjuøyane ('Seven Islands'), a group of nearly vegetation-free, rocky islands containing, on Rossøya, Norway's northernmost point. This, at 80°49.6'N, is 1,000km more northerly than Nordkapp, just off the Norwegian mainland.

The ice-free area of northern Nordaustlandet is made of very old (1.2 billion years), hard-wearing rock. Here, at Platenhalvøya, the land itself (as opposed to land plus ice) reaches its highest point (607m). Smaller ice-free areas in the southwest are composed of sedimentary rocks from the Carboniferous, Permian and Triassic periods, and there are dolerite intrusions. Most of Nordaustlandet is covered by inland ice domes, the highest of which (Austfonna, 700m) reaches to the east and south with a 150km ice front to the sea, where it is 10–35m high. This is the longest glacier front in the Arctic. Here and there the retreating front uncovers land above the waterline, while surges may cause parts of the ice front to advance – like Bråsvelbreen, the westernmost part of the glacier, which was 36km wide in 1938 and has since pushed 9km further forward.

Vegetation, as would be expected in High-Arctic conditions, is sparse, but fauna is surprisingly varied. Alongside reindeer and arctic fox, there are marine animals: seabirds with breeding colonies as far as the north of the island, seals, walrus and numerous polar bears; even on the top of Austfonna at 700m an expedition surprised a bear.

The north coast was discovered by whalers by the beginning of the 18th century at the latest. The first circumnavigation (involuntarily) was in 1864. Tobiesen, Mathilas, Årström and their crew were hunting walrus and became trapped by the ice near the easternmost part of the north coast. They took to smaller boats and started to row south along the unending and (at that time) virtually unknown

3

glacier front, until they got to the Hinlopen Strait. At last they had reached the north coast of Spitsbergen, where they separated to try to get help. Tobiesen's boat rowed the furthest – 800km in 14 days – to Adventfjorden, before they met anyone else. The other boats had already found other ships by then. The north coast was also a starting point for several attempts at the North Pole, among them Parry's expedition of 1827 and Wellman's of 1894, in which he lost his ship.

The hinterland was first explored in 1873. The ill-fated Schröder-Stranz expedition set out in 1913 and the very successful Oxford University expedition followed in 1924. A Norwegian–Swedish expedition set out in 1931, and another group from Oxford wintered in several stations in 1935–36 and explored much of the northern half of the island. Also important in investigating the island were the aerial photography flights of 1938, the German wartime weather station Haudegen (1944–45) and the research station Kinnvika from the 1950s. There were also fur trappers until protected status was ordered.

Today, Nordaustlandet and its neighbouring islands are completely uninhabited. However, alongside the Sysselmann's fuel depots and the automatic weather station on Phippsøya there are other signs of human activity: remains of cabins (Franklinfjorden, Brennevinfjorden); graves (whalers and hunters); the ruins of the German weather station (Rijpfjorden) and the Swedish/Finnish/Swiss station of Kinnvika (Murchisonfjorden). There have been mutterings about reopening the station, but such a move won't be easy in a nature reserve.

Occasionally, groups from small coastal boats or individuals from yachts put ashore. There are also sporadic visits by canoeists. Helicopters and skidoos are prohibited.

EDGEØYA AND TUSENØYANE

Edgeøya is the third-largest island: 5,150km². As with Barentsøya, it is separated from the main island by Storfjorden. Barentsøya, Edgeøya and Tusenøyane ('Thousand Islands') together make up the Søraust Svalbard Naturreservat, with strict protective regulations and access restrictions.

The climate is High Arctic, the islands coming under the influence of ocean currents from the east, and the sea to the east of Edgeøya is often full of ice even in the summer.

Geologically, Edgeøya is principally horizontally layered sedimentary rock from the Triassic period with dolerite intrusions. The landscape is thus mainly a plateau, divided by glaciers, which have cut valleys with steep sides. Former ice-age glaciers have carved wide valleys in which there is now relatively thick groundcover supporting approximately 2,500 reindeer.

The west and north coasts are relatively free of ice, as opposed to the east, which has higher precipitation and is heavily iced. Inland are several minor ice domes. From the Edgeøyjøkulen two glaciers come to the sea: King Johans Breen and the much larger Stonebreen, which pushed forward in a surge as recently as 1971. The Deltabreen to the west no longer reaches the sea, having left behind a huge moraine which now forms a wall between Tjuvfjorden and Svalbard's largest lagoon.

Signs of land rise can be seen in the great valleys, particularly in the north, with post ice-age beach lines now up to 15km inland.

South of Edgeøya are many flat islets, the Tusenøyane and Halvmåneøya ('Half-Moon Island'). These, together with Edgeøya's south and west coasts, serve as breeding grounds for many geese, ducks, auks and seabirds of various kinds. The walrus, once numerous on these coasts, has returned, and there are many seals. Edgeøya is also, after Kong Karls Landet, the most important polar bear breeding ground of the archipelago.

The island is uninhabited, but has a few cabins for research and administrative purposes. Historically, Edgeøya was important for hunters, particularly Russians. There are many whale and walrus bones to be found on the beaches and more than a few places were known for their suitability in hunting polar bear. A case in point is the lonely and almost inaccessible island of Halvmåneøya, which nevertheless was home to trappers over many winters – their famous cabin 'Bjørneborg' ('Bear Castle') having been restored as a cultural monument in the 1990s.

Some parts of Edgeøya were charted in 1612, only 16 years after Barents discovered Spitsbergen's west coast, and were already known to whalers and walrus hunters. Its name is also derived from that period – Thomas Edge having been a key person in early English whaling. From the middle of the 17th century to the mid 19th, Edgeøya and Tusenøyane had many small settlements of Russian hunters, living extremely simply but sometimes in small hunting communities of up to 50 overwinterers. There are remnants of their huts and graveyards – Keilhau came here in 1827 and found a station capable of supporting 40 to 50 inhabitants. There are remnants of a Russian presence in quite a few places.

Other Russians went home for the winter, although some stayed involuntarily, including one group of men who lost contact with their ship on a hunting trip, which was intended to last a few days, but ended in fact only after two long, unplanned polar nights in the area. The first known case of Norwegians staying for the winter was in 1834–35; they, too, didn't do so through choice. The first who did so choose were an 11-strong party led by Martin Ekroll. Two huts were built, at Kvalpynten (Edgeøya) and on Anderssøyane, with a third station being their ship. The ship was driven by storms on to Kong Ludvigøyane (then known as Russøyane – 'Russian Island') and the four crew built a cabin out of the wreckage, living on reindeer venison and bear bacon.

In summer 1943, the German Luftwaffe built an automatic weather station which was collected in 1984 for the Forsvarmuseet (Defence Museum). In 1972 Fina, Caltex and Total attempted to find oil, drilling two bores down to 2,823m and 2,351m without success. The area was declared a nature reserve in 1973 and any outstanding mineral claims expired 20 years later. Oil exploration in the area is discussed in Jon Michelet's thriller *Orion's Belt*.

Since scientists first overwintered in 1968–69, there has been a regular expedition of Dutch researchers, mostly biologists who stayed at Kapp Lee, though these expeditions stopped in 1990. The Norwegians have also been coming here regularly as part of their investigations and documentation of historic monuments; in 2001 they began excavating an artificial-looking mound which bore a striking resemblance to a Viking grave – but no remains were ever found inside.

BARENTSØYA

Barentsøya lies east of Storfjorden and north of Edgeøya. Its 1,300km² of Triassic sedimentation is similar to its neighbour to the south. In the centre lies the great Barentsjøkulen, from which several glaciers extend in many different directions, four of them reaching the sea: to the west, the Duckwitzbreen has been retreating

3

since 1918 when it left a moraine wall in the fjord; in the north is the Besselbreen; and then there's Freemanbreen, which pushed its snow-white front southwards into the Freemansund, the channel between Barentsøya and Edgeøya. Finally, the minor Willybreen just about reaches the eastern coastline.

Barentsøya was thought to be a peninsula and part of the main island until 1858, when the narrow Heleysundet and the Ormholet ('Worm Hole') were discovered. The narrowness of these channels forces through strong currents of up to nine knots and is particularly dangerous in icy conditions. The volcanic landscape is reminiscent of Iceland, though it is of much older origin.

As with Svalbard's other eastern regions, Barentsøya is uninhabited. In contrast to its neighbouring islands, it had little part to play in the human history of the area. The Sysselmann maintains a few cabins there and the island is part of the Søraust Svalbard Naturreservat, with strict protective regulations and access limitations. Visitors are rare, arriving by expedition cruise, sailing yacht or kayak.

KVITØYA

Kvitøya (White Island), at 700km², is Svalbard's fifth-largest island. It is also the furthest east. Apart from three headlands (Andréeneset, Kræmerpynten and Hornodden), totalling perhaps 20km², the island is completely covered by an ice dome, sometimes as thick as 410m, gently falling towards the coasts, where it abruptly ends in long and mostly low glacier fronts. Geologically, the island is very old, but has yet to be explored in any detail. Most of today's knowledge has come from satellite pictures, including even its shape, which was thought to be

long and stretched until the 1970s, instead of its actual egg shape. The island is nearly always surrounded by pack or drift ice. To its east, on the same submarine ridge, is the Russian-annexed Victoria Island.

Despite the extreme conditions, there is life here, too: several flowering plants, ivory gulls, eider, various other birds, polar bear, seals and walrus.

Kvitøya was the last of Svalbard's larger islands to be discovered; spotted by the Dutchman Cornelis Giles, the place appeared on charts as 'Giles Land' for many years. Its next visitors were seal hunters from Tromsø. The Swedish balloonists Andrée, Frænkel and Strindberg, after a disastrous attempt on the Pole, ended up here and died in 1897, possibly from eating undercooked and trichinosis-infected bear meat. In the following year Nathorst visited the island, knowing nothing of Andrée, whose last camp was not discovered until the Franz Josef Land expedition of 1930.

There is an automatic weather station on the island but, not surprisingly, the place is uninhabited. There are visitors, though: sturdy icebreakers have been bringing tourists here from time to time almost every year since 1990. Aircraft are prohibited from landing.

PRINS KARLS FORLANDET

Prins Karls Forlandet lies off the west coast of the main island. Geologically part of the region's Tertiary folds, it is 11km wide and 86km long, with a total area of 650km². Most of the island is a mountain range, with wild alpine peaks rising to a maximum of 1,084m at Monacofjellet. There are many glaciers on the east side. The southern end appears from a distance to be a hilly island (rising to 430m), but it is connected to the north by a large flat area that rises to only 17m. Forlandsundet separates Prins Karls Forlandet from Spitsbergen,

part of it so shallow as to permit a maximum draft of only 4m. The island is a national park and an important breeding ground for seals (with the only known stable harbour seal population in the archipelago), as well as haul-out sites for walrus.

Prins Karls Forlandet is uninhabited, but has one cabin maintained by the Sysselmann. It is rarely visited and has very little trace of previous visits. Landing aircraft is prohibited, as is the use of motorsleds.

In 1967 the headlines were full of the crash of a French military aircraft on Methuenfjellet and subsequent search and rescue operation. Eleven men died in the crash.

The entire island is a national park.

KONG KARLS LANDET

Kong Karls Landet ('King Charles's Land') consists of three larger islands and several islets, totalling approximately 330km². Relatively low-lying (the highest points on each of the three are: Svenskøya 255m, Kongsøya 320m and Abeløya 20m) the islands are just about ice-free, but have several permanent snowfields. They mostly consist of low plateaux, wide flatlands and large bays. Characteristic formations of basalt going back to the Cretaceous period form Svalbard's only lava field. Apart from this volcanic material, the islands are mostly sedimentary rocks from the Triassic, Jurassic and Cretaceous periods.

Vegetation is sparse, but rich enough for a small reindeer herd which found its way here over the ice in the 1970s. Many seabirds breed here as well as the usual mammals – reindeer, arctic fox, seals and, above all, polar bear. This area, especially Kongsøya, is Svalbard's most important breeding and rearing ground for bears.

Kong Karls Landet was discovered by the Briton Thomas Edge in 1617, became known first as Wiches Land, and was then forgotten. The seal hunter Eriksen came here in 1859, and the area was charted by Nathorst in 1872 and 1898. The islands offer extraordinarily good conditions for the reproduction of polar bears. The female bear finds both suitable snowdrifts for digging her den and reliable drift ice around the islands with lots of seals in spring and summer – vital for when she leaves the den, when both she and her cubs are very weak and vulnerable and

3

dependent on favourable hunting conditions nearby. This concentration of polar bears made the archipelago an excellent hunting area, and they were nearly all wiped out; the record being the slaughter of 100 bears, during one overwintering Norwegian expedition. Hunting slowed down and then stopped with a ban on hunting in Kong Karls Landet, followed by a ban on all automatic weapons; then in 1973 came a total prohibition on bear hunting, and finally the whole area became protected as a reserve.

Boats may not come within 500m of the islands and so going ashore is prohibited, as is landing aircraft. The Sysselmann controls all approaches, allowing only some visitors for scientific purposes. This is probably Svalbard's most strongly protected area. Drift ice surrounds the islands and makes an approach very difficult anyway, even in summer.

Before the islands were given their protected status there were private hunting parties and landings from cruise ships, often without weapons. One of the ships, the *Lindbad Explorer*, set down its passengers without armed guards at a time when two men from the Norwegian polar institute had just counted 15 bears on the island, one of which had broken into their hut and had had to be shot. A passenger was lost in the fog, but luckily escaped unharmed, if not severely anxious.

BJØRNØYA (BEAR ISLAND)

Svalbard's most southerly island lies about halfway between the southernmost point of Svalbard and the Norwegian mainland. This triangular island, 178km² in size, rises vertically out of the Barents Sea with very few coves at the feet of the cliffs and very few ways of landing ashore. To the north, the island's gently rolling plateau lies 30–40m above sea level. Towards the south, the terrain rises slowly until a point is reached where the cliffs fall 400m down into the sea. Hills rise above the plateau in the south and southeast, with the highest point at Miseryfjellet (536m). Most of the plateau has small, round hills, and little lakes cover 10% of the area. There are no glaciers on Bjørnøya, but there is much permanent snow.

Geologically, the island is very old: to the south it is mostly Cambrian and Ordovician; to the north it is composed largely of sandstone and chalk from the Devonian and Carboniferous periods; the peak district around Miseryfjellet is sedimentary Triassic. There are also coal seams.

Constant erosion by the sea has led to fantastic formations in the cliffs, probably the best known being Perleporten, a 200m tunnel under Kapp Kolihoff in the south, a feature used by Alistair MacLean in his thriller *Bear Island* (which otherwise has little to do with the history of the island; the movie version was even filmed in a different location). Weathered rock pillars are also spectacular, particularly the stacks at Sørkapp (186m) and Sylen (80m).

Its southerly position means that the midnight sun doesn't last as long as in Longyearbyen (30 April to 13 August); nor does the polar night (7 November to 4 February). The climate is also milder. In winter storms, Bjørnøya offers the only ice-free coves north of the Norwegian mainland.

Warm air over the Gulf Stream and cold, eastern air masses meet to cause much fog (July's average is 21.5 days), and much low cloud cover. Precipitation is low but at an average of 359mm is still higher than many other parts of Svalbard. Snow is often driven from the plateau into the sea, but the land is nevertheless often impassable due to the length of time meltwater lies around. Bjørnøya is part of the permafrost zone, although its frost layer is only 60–70m thick.

Botanically, the plant list of Bjørnøya reflects its mid-lying position between mainland Norway and Svalbard, including some species which are typical here but rare or unknown in Svalbard, like the common and attractive *Sedum roseum*. The animal world is dominated by birds, and some of the steep cliffs here hold the largest colonies of the Arctic. There are huge numbers of Brünnich's and common guillemot, little auk, kittiwake, fulmar and many varieties of gull and other seabirds. These colonies, in the middle of fishing grounds, are under threat, particularly when certain fish species are overfished – guillemot numbers were reduced by 80–90% in the 1980s due to famine. The only indigenous land mammal is the polar fox, which is also endangered despite protection. The sea supports bearded and ringed seals. Walrus, which were once prolific, are now only occasional visitors. Polar bears, after which the island was named (one was shot during Barents's visit in 1596), normally come here only with the drift ice. Should there be any left during the summer they are usually crazed with hunger – a female bear with two cubs too weak for swimming long distances was trapped on the island in 2004. In 1971 one attacked Bjørn Tessen, a crew member of the weather station, only 50m from the buildings. In the winter, there may be 100 bears on and around the island if the dense drift ice encircles it; in other years when the ice stays further north, bears are a rare sight even in winter.

Barents discovered the island in 1596 and from Hudson's time, who came here 11 years later, Bjørnøya became an important base for whalers. The ruins of a relatively recent whaling station (1905–09) are still to be seen in Kvalrossbukta. English whalers came first, in 1604, seven years before the start of whaling anywhere else in Svalbard, and took large numbers of walrus for their blubber and ivory. A record slaughter of 600 in a day was registered. The organiser of this expedition, Sir Francis Cherry, gave his name to the island, at least on most English charts of the time. Naturally the hunts tailed off as the walrus disappeared and the English lost interest. In the 18th century the Russians came, overwintering occasionally, collecting eggs and down and catching walrus, seals and foxes. Now and again they would be able to take polar bear, too. Slowly the animals were overhunted. Russian presence is still evident in one or two place names and one of their hunters' cabins appeared on the first detailed chart made, resulting from surveys of 1922–31.

A nine-man group of Norwegians, sent by businessmen Akermand and Ågård, spent the winter of 1823–24 on the island, shipping skins and teeth from 750 walrus back to Hammerfest after the season was over. Most walrus hunts took place in the winter, mainly on the north coast where going ashore was easier and walrus and seabird colonies more plentiful. The expedition of 1823 lives on in the local name, Hammerfesthuset, which is the oldest intact house in Svalbard, extended by Sivert Tobiesen in 1865. It may be found next to the Bjørnøya Radio Station, for which it served as a pigsty in the war. It is now an official historic monument.

In 1827 the German botanist, Mayor of Burscheid, Barto von Löwenigh, invited the Norwegian geologist Keilhau to join him on a chartered ship going to Svalbard, visiting Bjørnøya on the way. For Norwegians this was the start of their scientific exploration of Svalbard.

Before the 1900s mineral treasures were the objective. That coal was present had been known since 1609, but it was not until the late 19th century that the German fishing fleet also became interested in attempting to extract it. Theodor Lerner privately set up a small concern and was tempted to claim the island for himself. This indirectly saved the island for the Norwegians. In 1899 the Russian gunboat *Svetlana* attempted to annex Bjørnøya for the tsar, only to meet Lerner's people on the march, armed and with the German flag raised. Rather than risk a conflict with the German Reich, the Russians backed down. A year later, Lerner had left the island.

In the years that followed, until World War I, Bjørnøya again became a whaling station. Remnants of a station from 1904 to 1908 are still evident. In 1916 a coal-mining settlement was set up in the northeast with 250 men in 25 houses; the settlement was called Tunheim. Seemingly successful, the concern grew to include a telegraph station and a post office, and reserves were estimated at 200 million tonnes. As prices stabilised during the war and coal, fish and whale products were in demand, Bjørnøya became a very attractive proposition. Thereafter, prices started to fall and technical problems hit the operation. One of the problems was the lack of a suitable harbour at the unsheltered steep coast. Coal loading could be done only in calm weather, directly down from the cliff (parts of the loading facilities are still visible). Up until 1925, 116,094 tonnes of coal were shipped out. Svalbard had also become Norwegian by this time. There were no longer any real political grounds for supporting the company, and mining ceased. There was also an attempt to extract galena (lead sulphide), which came to nothing. There is still an old steam locomotive rusting away, but railway enthusiasts have long since determined that it is way beyond restoration.

A radio station was set up after the mining ceased and was strengthened by the presence of Blakka. Blakka was a horse originally brought to the island in around 1918 to pull a freshwater tanker wagon, but became best known for eating meat. Transport intended to take him off the island was prevented from doing so by high winds so he stayed, augmenting his hay with seal or bear meat. He was eventually put down at the evacuation of 1941.

Owing to problems encountered in Tunheim, women had been banned from Bjørnøya, but an exception was made when a fellow who was due to replace a sick colleague as station leader refused to go without his girlfriend. Just before leaving to take up his post, they married. Their honeymoon during the winter made for a very long wedding night.

In 1941 the radio station was closed down by the Royal Navy. Then German U-boats came, their crew setting up an automatic weather station, as the Luftwaffe did with their own weather station. Over the following war years stations were damaged and replaced repeatedly. At the end of the war a temporary building housed the station, and in 1947 a new building was put up at Herwighamna on the north coast. This marked the beginning of Bjørnøya Radio, which remains a weather station as well, serving marine and air navigators.

Also in 1947, a young Norwegian national socialist decided to leave the mainland after the fall of the Quisling regime. He made his way to the island and started to extract coal in Tunheim, frequently rowing to Herwighamna to sell it to the station crew. One day, they discovered his boat on the shore, but no traces of him were ever found.

Between 1928 and 1937 laws were brought in to ban the collection of eggs and down. In 1952 walrus hunting was banned in Svalbard. Since 2003, Bjørnøya has been protected as a nature reserve – despite massive resistance from the oil and gas industry, which is interested in keeping an option on using the island as a base for future oil and gas activities further north in the Barents Sea.

Hopen, in the southeast corner of Svalbard, is 29km long by 2km wide, an island of plateaux and hills (total area 40km², maximum height 370m).

It is made up of mostly brittle sandstone and marl sedimentation from the Triassic and early Jurassic periods, with flint and some small coal deposits here and there. There are no glaciers but there is much evidence of earlier glaciation. Old lateral moraines are found along the hill flanks and marks of the old shoreline can be seen 67m above today's level; a piece of driftwood was found 51m above the sea and dated at around 9,500 years old.

The surrounding sea is shallow and the island may be approached only by smaller boats, with larger ships having to stand off or anchor at quite a distance. There are no bays, but fishing boats shelter here, waiting to transfer their catches to larger vessels. Hopen is surrounded by ice for most of the year, from December to the end of July at least.

Despite low precipitation (383mm annually), the weather tends to be damp and foggy and there are few cloudless days. The coldest month is March (average −13.9°C) and the warmest is August (average +2.3°C). Vegetation is sparse: moss, five kinds of lichen and 28 flowering plants. There are many birds, especially little auk, kittiwake (with a large colony on Krykkjefjellet), purple sandpiper, skua, Brünnich's guillemot (with a colony on Lyngefjellet, among others), common guillemot, puffin, snow bunting, eider, geese, glaucus and other gulls, foxes (the blue fox in particular), seals and walrus. Hopen is the only place in Svalbard with detailed statistics of polar bear, which show that, from 200 bears visiting annually in the late 1980s, there are now around 600. As everywhere else, the bears have been protected since 1973, before which time there were only about 1,500 of them left out of the whole subpopulation of Svalbard and Franz Josef Land together. Since then, the total number has doubled again and with the absence of hunting, the animals are less shy – which explains the dramatic increase of observations on Hopen. Hopen was officially discovered in 1613 by the Englishman Marmaduke, after whose ship, the *Hopewell*, the island is thought to be named. However, Dutch charts were already showing an island in this area before then, but under different names. There are remnants of a Dutch blubber station at Koefoedodden, date unknown, and hunters and trappers left their marks. In 1836 the schooner *Wettrenner* sank off the coast.

Regular overwintering on the island did not begin until 1908, when a party of six stayed. Three of their huts still remain, albeit in poor condition. There were four further such enterprises before the outbreak of World War II but generally scientists did not stay on the island throughout the year. There were several explorations of Hopen from 1871 to 1939, including those surveying and mapping in 1924, 1929, 1930 and 1939.

Hopen came into prominence in November 1942 when the Russian freighter *Dekabrist* was bombed while carrying supplies from New York via Iceland. There were 80 people on board. Four lifeboats put to sea but couldn't land on Hopen due to weather conditions and went off in search of shelter elsewhere. One boat, with the captain Belyaev, the ship's doctor Natalik, her boyfriend Borodin, the sailor Lobanov and 15 others, ended up back at Hopen after ten days of polar night and icy water. They saw huts and people through the midday twilight, but turned away and landed on an unknown, snow-covered beach. Initially, they lived off jetsam to begin with (the area had many wrecks), but half of them died. Survivors found a hut in a dreadful condition, but by 4 January only four people were left. In March, with the return of some daylight, they were able to explore. They found the huts they had seen from the sea, but there was no trace of any inhabitants. Eventually Belyaev, Natalik, Borodin and Lobanov were taken off by the U-boat *U-703*; first the captain, and then the three others. (Four at a time seemed a bit risky for the U-boat skipper.) Lobanov had been very ill and survived for only a few hours on board, but the other three survived, spending the rest of the war in a prisoner-of-war camp in Norway. Belyaev died in 1955. Natalik and Borodin married; Natalik lived in Grozny, Chechnya until the 1980s.

A weather station was put up by the Germans in 1943, using a specialised plane for ice landings. This was the AR232, which had 22 wheels on 11 axles for landing on soft ground. Its tracks can still be made out today. The station was manned, operators taking measurements from balloons floating at up to 28,000m. A newly developed ozone-measuring instrument was lost; it would have been interesting to have been able to compare measurements then and now. The last four operators were taken off the island as prisoners-of-war three months after the war's end.

The Norwegians took over the station and today it has a fuel supply for rescue helicopters. It is within the range of the Sysselmann's largest helicopter and is also served by the ship *Nordsyssel* and the coastguard. The base is also used for ice studies and for research into the aurora. It has a *brevhus* (post counter) with its own frank.

There was an earth tremor in August 1962, associated with nuclear testing that took place on Novaya Zemlya but was audible on Hopen. Fina bored two exploratory holes in 1971 and 1973, but found no oil. In August 1978, a heavily armed Tu-16 broke up while flying at only 100m above Werenskioldfjellet, killing all seven crew members. The wreckage was discovered accidentally two days later by operators from the station and later examined by the Sysselmann and representatives of the Soviet embassy in Oslo. It was seen as an invasion of Svalbard's airspace.

There are plans to build a radar installation to study ice in the Barents Sea.

In 2003, Hopen became a nature reserve. Knowing about this plan, a Norwegian company registered claim rights on alleged oil deposits on the island just the year before, and initially tried to sell these claims to the Norwegian state, claiming their economic interests were being harmed by the new protection. However, this was mooted when the Norwegian government forbade private searches for oil or gas in the Barents Sea region surrounding Svalbard. Hopen is rarely visited by tourists, apart from a few study cruises and the occasional yacht.

The future of the station on Hopen may be threatened by advances in remote control and automation in combination with improvements of weather satellites, which together with the considerable costs of such a distant manned station has triggered discussions about changing it into a remote-controlled weather station.

There are two relevant books in Norwegian: *Ishavsøya Hopen*, by Thor Iversen (with English summary); and *Hopen – Ishavsøy og meteorologisk stasjon*, by Oddmund Søreide.

4

Cruising

It's fair to say that the majority of tourists to Svalbard will spend some of their time on a cruise. A cruise combines the comfort of hotel accommodation, with unique views of foreign countries and their landscapes. As with land-based hotels, there are differences from ship to ship in the services offered and the quality of the accommodation. While being a comfortable way of travelling (except for possible storms, which are rare in summer), cruising is a more detached way of experiencing the country since one spends most of one's time on the ship. Even with programmes that emphasise excursions, you will be rarely on land more than six hours a day on average. For a list of companies offering cruises around Svalbard, see pages 96–8.

Cruises (and cruise ships) tend to break down neatly into two specific types: traditional cruises and expedition cruises.

TRADITIONAL CRUISES

Most of the cruise traffic comprises so-called 'overseas' cruises, usually bigger ships with a capacity of between 150 and 2,000 passengers (the record, so far), which include Svalbard as part of a bigger tour. These ships are not normally ice-strengthened and therefore travel only to the west and northwest of the main island, with typical landings in Longyearbyen and/or Ny-Ålesund, plus possibly a few classic landing sites such as Trinity Harbour in Magdalenefjord or Möllerhavn in Krossfjord. On these ships, the areas visited are just one component of the total experience, with on-board entertainment and the thrill of cruising majestically off the main island's coast just as important. At the same time, these cruises are also usually the easiest (and some of them even the cheapest) way of seeing at least something of Svalbard for those who cannot or dare not visit the archipelago in other ways, such as the infirm or elderly. This is particularly so for German, British, French, Dutch and Norwegian travellers, as some of these cruises start and end in their countries.

Be aware that these cruises also depend to some extent on the changing ice conditions in Svalbard. The events of both 2004 and 2011 are but the most recent examples of where extreme climatic conditions cause itineraries to change, with unusually dense drift ice blocking the mouth of Isfjord for ten days in the middle of July, preventing six cruise ships from visiting Longyearbyen.

In the *Cruise routes* section (page 138) later in this chapter, the parts of the coast of Svalbard that are most often visited by these cruises are described.

Cruise tourism to Svalbard has a tradition of more than 100 years (interrupted only by the world wars) and continues growing, both in terms of the number of ships and their size. Currently new regulations are under preparation for the cruise traffic, as the local authorities react to this growth and the possible problems that may result, from severe erosion at the most popular landing sites to the increased risk of accidents. The increasing use of heavy oil is also worrying, with disastrous environmental problems possible should there ever be a collision.

Already over the last several years, the regulations regarding cruise ships and their excursions have been tightened, with two armed polar-bear guards now compulsory for landings, and precautions introduced to prevent environmental damage, including the compulsory dissemination on board ship of information about caring for the environment, and guidance for passengers on land. As these ships' records for observing these rules are patchy at best, sanctions for the worst offenders are now under discussion.

Overseas cruises that include Svalbard are sold through regular travel agencies in most countries and, of course, online.

EXPEDITION CRUISES

So-called expedition cruises are voyages which in reality have little to do with real expeditions, except that they venture into less-visited, remoter areas where the programme has to be adapted constantly due to the conditions, especially the ice situation. In Svalbard, these cruises mostly try to reach the remoter parts in the northeast and east of Spitsbergen, where the chance of seeing polar bears and walrus are higher in summer than in the west. Routes taken and opportunities for going ashore are largely determined by the extent of ice, as well as by the wind and the state of the sea, particularly from June to the beginning of July. There are compensating charms, however: the beauty of this largely ignored part of Svalbard, for example, and the landscape forms, birds, seals, walrus and polar bears.

Despite this common ground, there are nevertheless huge differences between the ships themselves, which range from 20 to 200 passengers and from a simple two-star level of luxury to four+ star. The range of information and lecturing varies too. As a rule, the bigger ships offer the most comfort, while the smallest vessels have a more personal atmosphere. For landings, a smaller passenger number is preferable too: even though the big ships should have enough Zodiacs, it makes quite a difference both for nature and for the participants whether 50 or 150 passengers are brought ashore. Quite likely, a restriction on numbers will be introduced in the more remote parts of Svalbard within the next few years. For the quality of lecturing, the smallest vessels (under 40 passengers) may be too small to have more than one expert on board – but nor is this guaranteed on the biggest ships, either. Ships also have different 'typical' passengers: some cruises are known for being popular among people who consider it prestigious to be on such a cruise, while other cruises are preferred primarily because of their 'authentic' expedition style, with an emphasis placed on information and landings.

In view of all these differences, it is advisable to try to get a good overview of the market and book through a specialised agency, which can also organise a pre-programme in Longyearbyen for getting first impressions and for acclimatising. Spending a few days in Longyearbyen before joining an expedition cruise is a very good idea, especially if one can fit in a walking tour too, because then one is familiar with the conditions and the nature of the Arctic already, increasing one's enjoyment of the cruise itself.

Expedition cruises typically last seven to 14 days and use mostly ice-strengthened or even ice-breaking vessels, which can force themselves through drift or even solid ice up to a certain thickness. The difference between a small icebreaker and a good ice-strengthened vessel exists, but does not play the decisive role sometimes suggested by brochures as both try to minimise sailing in denser

above left   The change of season brings real metamorphosis to the landscape: in spring, the snow melt often causes flooding and creates glacial lakes throughout the valleys (WAP/S) page 13

above right   Summer transforms the Arctic land and flowers burst into bloom — despite its extreme northerly position, Svalbard and Franz Josef Land host an amazing variety of flora (AU) page 46

below   The capital shrouded in continual winter twilight — the polar night begins in Longyearbyen in late October and lasts until mid-February (I/KL/FLPA) page 65

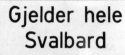

above Street smarts: road signs
left & right advise to park your
snowmobile and watch out
for polar bears! (both RN)

left Send a postcard from the
top of the globe at Ny-
Ålesund's post office, the
most northerly in the world
(SS) page 173

below A view of the coastal
settlement of Grumant
(DD/FLPA) page 144

above left   Trappers have been integral to Svalbard's history, and a handful of abandoned trapping settlements strewn about the archipelago recall a way of life all but extinct (m/S) page 187

above right   The traditional wooden Orthodox church is a feature of Russian Barentsburg (AJ/S) page 178

right   Living in such a remote capital has its advantages: a young boy gets a sled-lift to school in Longyearbyen (RN) page 164

below   The vibrant, Soviet-era murals on the walls of an office building depict life in the homeland (RN) page 178

above Unlike in other Arctic regions, reindeer (*Rangifer tarandus platyrhynchus*) in Svalbard are not domesticated (SS) page 48

left The most exciting of Svalbard's wildlife, the polar bear (*Ursus maritimus*) can rival Kodiak bears as today's largest land-based predators — males can weigh more than 800kg (PG) page 51

below A common sight throughout the archipelago, particularly in the summer, the arctic fox (*Vulpes lagopus*) is also the only indigenous land mammal on Franz Josef Land (JD/MP/FLPA) page 49

above Owing to Svalbard's ruthless whale-hunting past, the archipelago's whale population is today a fraction of what it used to be, but individuals such as this diving humpback (*Megaptera novaeangliae*) can still be spotted during the summer months (KS/MP/FLPA) page 53

right The bearded seal (*Erignathus barbatus*) is the second-largest pinniped in Svalbard after the walrus (AVZ) page 50

below Eco-tourists track a beluga whale (*Delphinapterus leucas*) (K/NGS/C) page 53

above left   Arctic tern (*Sterna paradisaea*) on Danskøya (AVZ) page 54

above right   Ivory gull (*Pagophila eburnean*) (j) page 54

left   Black and white common eider ducks (*Somateria mollissima*) nesting by the river at Kapp Linné, at the edge of the Isfjord (RN) page 54

below   Black-legged kittiwakes (*Rissa tridactyla*) fishing near the Monaco glacier — dozens of seabird species converge in the spring to breed on the cliffs (GJ/S) page 54

above **Brünnich's guillemot** (*Uria lomvia*) flying above the waters of the Isfjord in summer (RN) page 54

right **Barnacle geese** (*Branta leucopsis*) with goslings (AVZ) page 54

above Purple saxifrage (*Saxifraga oppositifolia*) is a species of edible plant very common throughout the High Arctic (WAP/S) page 46

left Though green floral cover is rare on Svalbard, the occasional mountainside of cotton grass (*Eriphorum virginicum*) can add real colour to the archipelago's Arctic topography (AU) page 46

below The volcanic island of Jan Mayen from the summit of Beerenberg, nearly all of which has been designated as a nature reserve (PF/S) page 228

ice because this costs not only more fuel but also more time. The icebreaker will be able to force its way through somewhat heavier ice, but will usually do this only if it is a limited zone of ice, otherwise the delay will be too big, especially on shorter programmes.

THE CRUISING SEASON

The cruising season lasts around 2½ months, from the beginning of June to the end of August. The start of the season is signalled by the thawing of snow and ice. The attractions of going early in the season lie in the Arctic spring, when there is still a great deal of snow in the mountains and much sea ice, the birds are returning to breed and the midnight sun climbs to its highest point. The chances of seeing the big mammals are greater during this period too, as they prefer to roam close to the ice border – if this border is more to the west coast, then there will also be some polar bears and walrus around in that area.

The high season is around mid-July. It is not uncommon to meet other ships, especially in the most popular places like Magdalenefjord or Ny-Ålesund – which may therefore be avoided by some of the expedition cruises because of the high density of sea traffic.

Late July and August are probably the best times on expedition cruises for circumnavigation attempts, which have a good chance of completing the trip then (and only then). I see a growing tendency in some catalogues for circumnavigation attempts to be advertised earlier and earlier, with some even setting off in the beginning of July, which in most years is bound to fail. Of course in the small print you'll find that programmes may be adapted to actual conditions, but nevertheless I find it misleading to offer circumnavigation attempts so early in spite of the low chance of success. My advice therefore, is not to book one of these early cruises if you can help it, or, if you do, be prepared for the fact that you may not get all the way round. That said, if taking one of these cruises is the only option, don't despair: there will still be plenty to see, experience and enjoy.

The cruise season ends, at least for the longer programmes, around late August or early September, as the period of midnight sun ends, many birds and flowers have gone, and the increasingly low light at night reduces the possibilities for nature photography (though this is partly compensated by a fantastic light with a low, hovering sun). Furthermore, the fierce autumnal storms sometimes begin by mid-September.

Important: early booking recommended! Requests for these expedition cruises have grown enormously, with many booked out rather early, in some cases more than half a year in advance. Owing to the short season, the big demand does not trigger an according expansion of capacity.

LIFE ON BOARD

The specific details will vary from cruise to cruise, but as a general rule you will end up with one or two excursions a day, interspersed with meals and lectures. Programmes will be issued each evening giving you the schedule for the following day, but you must be prepared for these to be altered – it's remarkable how quickly the weather can make a seemingly easy landing dangerous, and the primary function of the cruise staff is to keep you safe. Listen to them, and if they ask you to do something, there will almost always be a good reason for that request.

Your tour operator is best placed to tell you what clothing is required whilst on board, but generally speaking there will not be any particular dress code during the day. On some ships (generally speaking the bigger, more luxurious liners) there may be a dress code for the evening meal – sometimes going as far as requiring dinner jackets and ballgowns. Furthermore the last evening on most ships tends to be a little smarter, although quite what you wear is up to you – just don't expect the captain to speak to you if you insist on wearing that Hawaiian shirt you took along for a bet.

Clothing during landings is, in many ways, much more important – you aren't going to risk hypothermia in the ship's dining room (unless you have a particularly sniffy Maître d'), whereas you may be at risk during a landing if you are improperly dressed. Fortunately it's easily resolved with a little forethought. Clothing during landings needs to keep you dry and it needs to keep you warm. If it gets wet and the water penetrates then you will start to lose body heat – this is the precursor to hypothermia.

It's very common for those who work on these ships to adopt similar clothing to mountaineers – a system using three layers. The first layer, worn next to the skin, is intended to keep you dry. It does this by wicking – drawing your sweat away to the outer layers where it can safely be released without you losing heat. The second layer is what provides you with insulation – it traps the heat from your body, effectively cocooning you in warm air. The third layer is called the shell layer, and is in many ways the most critical. It needs to be waterproof from the outside, protecting you from rain or spray. It has to be windproof, preventing the loss of the heat trapped by the mid layer. It also should be strong enough to remain intact if subjected to bangs and scrapes. And it must be permeable from the inside, allowing the sweat to evaporate from the mid layer. Gore-Tex is the best known material for the outer layer, and it is expensive. It can be very tempting to skimp on this – to buy something a little cheaper. There is a very good chance that you will regret this saving in the long run. Furthermore it is very important that you cover your whole body – it's not unknown for passengers to turn up with nice new Gore-Tex jackets and an old pair of denim trousers. Ski-wear is also not suited to rides in small boats or landings in waves.

Landings using Zodiacs are often divided into 'dry' and 'wet', the idea being as a guide to suitable footwear. Frankly there is no such distinction – a 'dry' landing is just a 'wet' landing in benign conditions, and conditions can shift very, very quickly. The saying 'Prepare for the worst, and hope for the best' really sums it up. The most suitable footwear for a landing from a Zodiac or other small boat is a good-quality pair of knee-high rubber boots. Your Gore-Tex trousers should not be tucked into these – they should hang outside the boots, so that any water that splashes onto them will be directed down the outside of the boot, rather than into the boot and soaking into your socks. Some ships may advertise provision of boots for use by passengers, but you should be aware that these stashes are made up of boots left over by previous passengers – if you have particularly oddly shaped feet or a preference for one particular style you are strongly recommended to think about taking your own ones along with you. If you are landing for a hike, there is nothing to stop you taking a good stout pair of hiking shoes or boots along with you in a rucksack and changing them once you are safely on the beach.

Clearly, having both good outdoor clothing and some more elegant apparel for the social events of a more exclusive cruise can lead to problems with the weight of the total baggage. Either choose a different cruise which does not have these requirements or accept that you cannot be fully equipped for everything

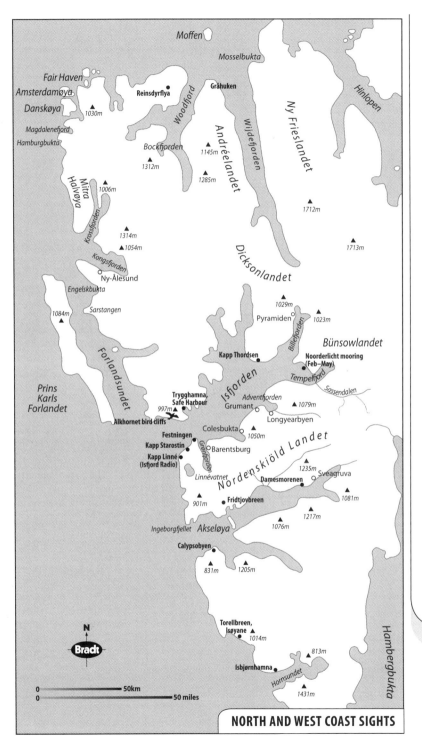

NORTH AND WEST COAST SIGHTS

137

(and therefore accept that you may not be able to take part in everything) or pay extra for excess baggage, which is probably a modest cost in relation to the total tour price anyway and will allow you to enjoy your tour fully.

Electronic cameras and video cameras are also OK on board as the ship will keep them warm and you can recharge batteries easily. But be careful of condensation when you get back to the ship; allow cameras to warm up slowly, and take care to protect your camera against splashwater and rain. Check, too, with your travel agent about electricity on board (voltage, socket types and so on).

CRUISE ROUTES

There are not really any established routes for cruises around Svalbard, predominantly because they are so heavily dependent on the ice, but it is worth giving a brief description of some of the destinations of cruise and coastal ships.

The following descriptions start at the north coast and work their way towards the south cape in a roughly anti-clockwise direction. This area is the most-visited part of the archipelago for cruises without special ice class due to the favourable ice conditions caused by the warmer waters of the Gulf Stream. The remoter parts are accessed only by expedition vessels utilising varying landing points.

While all the locations described below are in Svalbard, there may be the odd cruise that pushes out into Franz Josef Land as well. From the point of view of a passenger, the practicalities are identical, but descriptions of the potential landings can be found in the chapter about Franz Josef Land. Jan Mayen is unlikely to be visited on a Svalbard cruise as it lies halfway between Svalbard and Greenland.

WIJDEFJORDEN Next to Isfjorden, from which it is separated by a 21km isthmus, Wijdefjorden is Svalbard's largest closed fjord, about 110km long. To the east lies Ny Frieslandet, high country covered in ice for the most part which sends three notable glaciers into the fjord down 300–500m-high slopes. Andréelandet to the west is a sea of peaks with many small valleys. To the southwest lies the driest part of Svalbard, where the snowline starts as high as 800m. To the east of the fjord's southernmost arm, Austfjorden, the ice cover from Ny Frieslandet weakens to form wild alpine mountain scenery of very old and hard rock. Here are Svalbard's highest mountains, **Newtontoppen** (1,713m) and **Perriertoppen** (1,712m), rising from a glacier sea; a paradise for climbers, if only it were not so cut off. The end of Wijdefjorden is filled by the remarkable Mittag-Lefflerbreen glacier.

MOSSELBUKTA In 1872, during one of the first attempts to reach the North Pole, Nordenskiöld's expedition was surprised by pack ice and had to overwinter. A hut was built, named *Polhem* after their ship. The hut later served as shelter for Rüdiger and Rave, two members of the ill-fated German Schröder-Stranz expedition of 1912–13. The building is now a ruin but there is a **hunter's cabin** by the bay which in certain years has been used by overwintering trappers.

MOFFEN This ring-shaped pebble island is one of the most important resting places for walrus. It is flat and low (approximately 2m). It is protected as a **walrus sanctuary**, requiring that you keep a minimum distance of 300m.

GRÅHUKEN In 1872 six Norwegian hunting ships were forced to shore by the ice. Fifteen crew members worked to get to Isfjorden, only to die of scurvy on Kapp Thordsen. The promontory is named after the grey Devonian rocks.

In the German-speaking world, this is one of Svalbard's most well-known places. Here, just before World War II, Christiane Ritter overwintered with her husband and a friend and wrote *A Woman in the Polar Night* (as the English edition is called) – the undisputed international Svalbard bestseller with total international sales in several languages of almost 200,000 copies.

BOCKFJORDEN The southwesterly arm of Woodfjorden is a rarity on Svalbard: only here are the remains of volcanism with some remaining activity to be found – in the form of **thermal springs** (24°C) – near to an extinct Quaternary volcano. Unfortunately, visits have increased dramatically, especially by ships with 100 and more tourists, which evidently increases the risk of degrading the tundra here.

REINSDYRFLYA, LIEFDEFJORD AND MONACOBREEN Reinsdyrflya is a flat peninsula with an estimated 1,000 reindeer, which makes it the largest single population after Nordenskiöldlandet. The rocks and therefore also the beaches consist mostly of red sandstone. There are remains of a German World War II weather station. On its southern side, it is limited by the Liefdefjord – a major branch of Woodfjord, terminating in the impressive ice front of the Monacobreen (named after Albert I of Monaco, who was a major sponsor of Svalbard research).

FAIR HAVEN Fair Haven is a sheltered sound between the islets of Fugleøya, Fuglesangen, Klovningen and Norskøyane and was popular with 17th-century whaling fleets; there are around 100 whalers' graves. It had one of the largest blubber-processing stations (ten ovens) of the time. The island was used as a look-out post as it offered better views of whale activity than its neighbours.

AMSTERDAMØYA This island, in common with its neighbour, is more interesting for historical reasons than for its natural beauty. It was the most important Dutch whaling station of the 17th century. The only visible signs of the settlement of Smeerenburg, jointly founded in 1617 by the Dutch and the Danes, are what is left of the ovens. Originally there were nine or ten ovens but now there are the remains of only seven, the others having being pushed across the beach by ice movements. North of the former town lies a burial field from the period. A visit here would give a better insight into the life of a whaler of that time than any history book could do.

DANSKØYA Danskøya was also a whaling station and has the remains of three ovens (Frisians from Harling, c1636) at Virgohamna, as well as graves which are sometimes reopened by frost. The area is protected as an ancient monument. It seems that many graves were lost by sea erosion; some remaining 30 were dug by archaeologists and their contents (partly well conserved in the permafrost) preserved.

The island is also visited today for another reason: it was the site of several unsuccessful attempts to reach the North Pole by **balloon**. Well known are the attempts by Andrée (1896–97) and those by Wellman (1906–09), both of whom had balloon hangars in Virgohamna. These areas are all considered to be ancient monuments and must not be disturbed in any way. Most dominant are the remains of the Wellman activities, which were examined in detail in 1993 (P J Capelotti: *The Wellman Polar Airship Expeditions at Virgohamna, Danskøya, Svalbard*), but there are also a few traces of the installations of Andrée, the leisure cabin of Englishman Pike from the late 19th century and some old 17th-century whaling remnants at this interesting site. There are special regulations for landing here, an attempt to minimise further damage by visitors (following marked routes, required number of guides per group, etc – for details, contact the Sysselmann before a visit). With bigger cruise ships, it makes little sense to visit Virgohamna in view of these regulations and the risk of causing damage.

MAGDALENEFJORD Magdalenefjord is the most photographed landmark of Svalbard and its **postcard scenery** attracts more visitors every year than any other place apart from Longyearbyen – in spite of its relatively remote position in the far northwest. Magdalenefjord has an alpine feel, with steep sides and a glacier sliding into the sea. On the southern side there is the **Gravneset Peninsula** as the standard landing site with its beautiful beach and a nicely sheltered anchoring bay called Trinity Haven. The peninsula shows that this site has attracted men for centuries; in fact, even the discovery expedition of Willem Barents came here in 1596. On the high ground in the middle of the Gravneset, there is an extended graveyard with dozens of difficult-to-recognise whaler graves scattered over the hill and a memorial to the whalers on top; furthermore, there are three areas of remains of old blubber ovens from the 17th-century whaling period down at the beautiful beach. In the 17th century, this was mainly an English whaling base. In the steep mountain slope above Gravneset, little auks breed and on the beach and the lowlands of the peninsula, the chances are you'll meet arctic terns, skuas, barnacle geese and eider ducks.

Almost all passenger boats anchor in the shelter behind Gravneset, setting people ashore on the beautiful beach for a short walk, and the fjord is also popular for alpine expeditions due to its beauty and hard rocks.

About 20,000 visitors per year inevitably leave their traces, even with excellent environment-conscious behaviour. In fact, Gravneset is about the only place away from the settlements where tourism has left significant traces and often serves as an example of the problems of allowing tourism in Svalbard. Vegetation on Gravneset, especially in the graveyard area, has suffered severely during more than 100 years of cruise tourism and there has also been considerable damage to the historic remains from the whaling period – mostly due to sheer ignorance, as many of these traces are hardly recognisable to the layman without proper information.

Because of this situation, a number of measures have been taken by the Sysselmann since the 1990s to improve the situation:

- It is forbidden now to enter the actual graveyard area and the three small areas of the blubber-oven remains, all of which are clearly marked by chains.
- Furthermore, visitors are expected to move on vegetation-free ground only – the brilliant green low moss is regarded as vegetation, too.
- Because of the number of ships visiting, a police post is stationed here in the summer.
- The disturbance of birds has to be avoided.
- All rubbish, including cigarette stubs, and ash off grill fires, has to be taken back on the ship. This latter point has a long positive tradition on many ships anyway, and often, after passengers have returned to the boat, staff are sent out to clear up any litter.
- To guard against bears, ships must provide two properly armed guards when landing, preferably supported by some additional staff members as observers as well as ensuring the passengers stick to the environmental and safety standards while ashore.

In future, permission for ships to send passengers ashore here depends increasingly on the observation of these rules, and there's a police post with two men based here over the summer, who are in charge of a large area and not just Magdalenefjord. In my experience, 99% of all visitors are very willing to do their best to avoid environmental damage – though of course they need to be properly and well informed in advance. Not all ships are quite so successful at educating their guests, however, and I have observed some pretty thoughtless behaviour from some passengers. These ships may have reason to fear for their future permissions to go ashore here again.

HAMBURGBUKTA   A former station for Hamburg whalers from 1642 on, there are remains of a blubber oven here. The small, shallow bay has only a narrow and very shallow entrance, which is difficult to spot from a passing ship. A landing can be advised only under very calm and stable weather and sea conditions, as the ship has to anchor and drift on open sea outside the entrance.

KROSSFJORDEN   Together with its neighbour, Kongsfjorden, Krossfjorden is another of those destinations frequently visited by west-coast ships. The area is alpine in character, has very active glaciers (Tinayrebreen and Lilliehöökbreen) and forks into many smaller fjords and bays (Möllerfjorden, Möllerbukta, Kollerbukta, Mayerbukta and Tinayrebukta). Also of interest is Ebeltofthamna, where there are whalers' graves. A German telegraphy station opened there in 1912 but it was given up two years later when the building was moved to Kvadehuken, Brøggerhalvøya, west of the newly founded Ny-Ålesund, where it was used as a Norwegian weather station. Then there is 'Lloyd's Hotel', built in 1926 on the north shore of Möllerfjorden as an emergency shelter by the predecessors of today's German shipping line Hapag Lloyd. Near to Signehamna are the ruins of a German World War II weather station, one of the very few places in Svalbard where people died in combat. Like all pre-1946 relics, it is a protected historic monument.

KONGSFJORDEN   After Magdalenefjorden, this is the fjord most visited by cruisers and coastal ships. Here you'll find **Ny-Ålesund** (see *Chapter 6*, pages 173–6), once the most northerly permanent settlement in the world (a mining community until 1963, though now it's only a research base), and Blomstrandhalvøya, on the northern shore, named after the geologist Blomstrand. Since 1991, the name *halvøya* (literally 'half island', or 'peninsula') has been a misnomer; the glacier joining it to the mainland has been bisected and Blomstrandøya is now an island.

There are well-preserved remains of the attempts by Ernest Mansfield and his Northern Exploration Company Ltd (NEC) to make their fortune from quarrying marble. Unfortunately the marble was cracked through by frost, making it worthless. His settlement, Ny London, was founded in 1911 and sold to Norway in 1932. Although some of the houses were relocated to Ny-Ålesund, Ny London is still a striking place with lots of rusting machinery, etc, some of which are unique technical examples of their period.

Both sides of the fjord are attractive, particularly eastward toward the two glaciers, Kongsbreen and Kongsvegen, with the Tre Kroner, three peaks, named after three Scandinavian countries, rising behind: to the south, Dana, at 1,175m; then Nora, at 1,226m; and to the north, Svea, at 1,226m. Both glaciers, particularly the Kongsvegen, have retreated at least 10km in the last few years; this can be seen from the odd out-of-date postcard sold today, which shows the hill, Colletthøgda, enclosed in ice where now its western side is clear. The Tre Kroner are a symbolic landmark of the area.

ENGELSKBUKTA English whalers used to come here, their names for both the place ('Comfortless Cove') and the glacier at its end ('Comfortlessbreen') telling their own stories. The bay is visited only by smaller coastal boats.

SARSTANGEN, FORLANDSUNDET The flat promontory of Sarstangen protrudes into Forlandsundet and continues as shallows as far as Prins Karls Forlandet. This means that only smaller boats with a draft of less than 4m can pass the sound completely with particularly careful navigation off Sarstangen, and that the sound is often blocked with ice until July.

TRYGGHAMNA/SAFE HARBOUR AND YMERBUKTA This narrow bay is the first sheltered spot on the north side of Isfjorden and was the preferred anchorage for whale and walrus hunters. Occasionally, whales were also processed here. Today there are some remains of that time as well as an old trapper cabin in romantic decay. Alkhornet mountain on the west side of the entrance of the bay (and therefore also on the northern side of the entrance to Isfjord) is not only a characteristic landmark with its high rock wall, but also one of the major bird cliffs in Isfjord (housing mainly guillemots). Kjerulf glacier at the end of the bay has retreated a lot, but has still a nice bay surrounded by high ice walls on its western side. The eastern side of the bay is formed by Värmlandryggen, a geologically interesting structure with some strange castle-ruin-like rock formations: here, the folding has lifted the sediments almost upright – accordingly, a few steps will take you across millions of years. Geologically, this is the same structure as the famous Festningen on the southern shore of Isfjorden.

Owing to the variety of nature, Trygghamna and neighbouring Ymerbukta (with the larger Esmark glacier at its end) are used by some tour operators for summer wilderness tent camps and are visited by day cruises from Longyearbyen.

KAPP THORDSEN Here you will find the **Svenskehuset**, a large building originally erected in 1872 to serve the nearby exploitation of phosphate deposits, a Swedish endeavour that joined the long list of Svalbard failures. Sadly, the building was a temporary home to sailors from the Gråhuken incident (see page 138) and since then has also been known as the *Spøkelsehus* (Ghost House).

Thereafter, in 1882–83, it served the Swedish overwintering expedition as part of the first International Polar Year (the first, and successful, joint international attempt to co-ordinate polar research from several all-year stations all around the North Pole, collecting data continuously over a whole year) and is now a memorial to one of the first scientific explorations of Svalbard.

BILLEFJORDEN Billefjorden is the northernmost arm of Isfjorden. Of interest are the huge glacier **Nordenskiöldbreen**, breaking off into the fjord, and the Russian mining community of **Pyramiden** (see *Svalbard's Settlements and Stations*, pages 183–6), opposite on the western shore. South of Adolfbukta in front of the glacier are parts of the ruined huts of Brucebyen. In the northernmost bay, Petuniabukta, the Russian local mining company hit some oil and gas deposits here in 1994–95 while searching for coal. It seems likely that full-scale exploitation of these reserves will begin in the next few years. The recommencing of exploration is a highly political act, providing the Russians with an excuse to be a more prominent presence in the archipelago, as well as being a reason for environmental concern. Most geologists are fairly sure that the geological structures present do not indicate the existence of a very big oil or gas deposit here, so it is probably primarily geopolitics and the hunt for state subsidies by Russian companies that are the main motives.

Further on is the charming Skansbukta and its impressive mountain, Skansen. At the foot of Skansen is an unsuccessful gypsum mine from the 1920s, and on the face you can clearly see light and dark sedimentary strata, the white being gypsum/anhydrite. Opposite Skansbukta, the eastern side of Billefjord is formed by majestic rock walls and pillars, similar to Tempelfjord, with the typical horizontal sediment layers and plateau-type mountains (with fairly flat areas on top) of the area. Inner Billefjord is less visited by bigger ships, but a popular hiking area where some tour operators run summer wilderness camps and organise their own transport there and back from Longyearbyen.

TEMPELFJORD This fjord, with its 600m rock cliffs, is the impressive easternmost end of Isfjord. The Templet mountain, dominating the mouth, has marked horizontal strata and massive pillars looking like a giant fallen temple.

The back end of the fjord is filled with the ice masses of Tunabreen and Von Post Breen. The former still calves icebergs into the fjord, while the latter is retreating (melting). Tunabreen started a surge in late 2003, which continued in 2004 – unlike other glaciers with surge intervals of more than 50 to sometimes several hundred years, the last surge of Tunabreen before this was in the 1970s. The explorer Filchner crossed Von Post Breen on his way eastwards as part of his training for an expedition to Antarctica, hence the many German names found east of Tempelfjord. Halfway out again, on the southern side of Tempelfjord, lies Kapp Schoulz and an abandoned exploratory gypsum mine. In spring, Tempelfjord, with Tunabreen at its end, is a prime snowmobile day-excursion destination from Longyearbyen, though some attention and knowledge is needed on the fjord ice due to some instability.

SASSENDALEN AND SASSENFJORD The inner part of Isfjord, where it then divides into Billefjord and Tempelfjord, is called Sassenfjord, dominated by the impressive Templet mountain. Sassendalen is the largest river valley in Svalbard, with an extensive delta into the fjord. Sir Martin Conway followed the river inland on his first crossing of Svalbard. On the eastern side lies Fredheim ('home of peace'), the home of the 'King of Sassen', Hilmar Nois, the legendary 20th-century trapper who spent 39 winters and 50 summers in Svalbard, at times with his wife Helfried and his brother Edvin. Today the cabin is maintained by the Sysselmann and used for official guests and scientists.

Towards Longyearbyen, there is Diabasodden, a distinctive promontory with a rock wall consisting of igneous rock intrusions, which is one of the few pleasant bird cliffs that can be observed easily more closely from a ship. Arctic foxes sometimes patrol under the cliff for fallen-down chicks or eggs. Nearby, a local tour operator runs a summer wilderness tent camp that is also a popular base for nature photographers.

ADVENTFJORDEN Across from Longyearbyen (see *Svalbard's Settlements and Stations*, pages 159–72), on the north side of Adventfjorden, lie two former mining villages used in part as weekend cottages by Longyearbyen residents. Hjorthamn/Moskushamn were worked by the Norwegians from 1916 to 1921, but transport difficulties (among others) forced their closure. The remains of a conveyor track from the shaft entry high on the hillside down to the shore can still be seen. The village was used as a military headquarters during the war. Buildings by the mineshaft, known as the *Ørneredet* ('Eagle's Nest'), were renovated in 1991 by Longyearbyen residents, with the support of the Cultural Heritage department of the Sysselmann.

In 1929 musk oxen were introduced to the area from Greenland, followed by further introductions in Nordenskiöldlandet, though they died out. The last one is thought to have died in neighbouring Bjørndalen in 1986.

The second settlement, Advent City, nearer the entrance of Adventfjorden, was founded by the Spitzbergen Coal and Trading Company of Sheffield in 1904–05 but given up almost immediately. During the first winter the workers rebelled; they held the manager under house arrest and refused to work. The firm went bankrupt. Some of the buildings were moved to Hjorthamn in 1916–17 and today, some foundations, some coal and the old mine entrance are the only traces left of this English industrial adventure in Svalbard.

The place names *Advent*fjorden, *Advent*dalen, etc, are thought to be named after the English whaling ship *Adventure*.

GRUMANT The former Soviet mining community of Grumant is barely accessible, lying between cliffs at the mouth of the narrow Grumantdalen. Its origins date back to a pre-World War I British–Russian mining company, 'Anglogrumant'. In 1951–52, it was (together with its port, Colesbukta) the largest settlement in Svalbard, with 1,106 inhabitants, but it was deserted by 1962 due to the unavailability of its mines.

There are few buildings left, most of them crumbling, and one can only guess where most of the others stood. The former graveyard above the town is badly disturbed and the narrow-gauge railway to Colesbukta, which led through a now-destroyed tunnel, is impassable.

COLESBUKTA Colesbukta was originally a whaling station. The 19th century saw mining attempts in the bay itself and after World War II the establishment of the settlement of Colesbukta, a more suitable port for the nearby Russian mine of Grumant. A narrow-gauge railway line of about 6km connected the two settlements, easily Svalbard's longest surface railway, much of which was sheltered in a wooden construction against winter snowdrift, and parts of which are still visible above the coast. Together with Grumant, Colesbukta closed with the end of mining, but until 1988 did serve as a Russian base for exploratory coal drilling. Most of the old buildings have fallen in ruins and are beyond renovation.

A small amount of oil was discovered through a borehole at Kapp Laila on the western side of the bay. Relics of the Russian drilling station include deep and unwelcome Caterpillar tracks within a wide radius of Colesbukta.

North of the village is Rusanovodden, a cabin set up as a memorial to the Russian geologist W A Rusanov; it is from his Svalbard expedition of 1912 that the Russian claim to Grumant stems.

Based on exploratory drilling completed in the 1980s, the Russian mining company Trust Arcticugol has begun installing a new coal mine in Colesbukta, which is meant to replace the problematic current coal mine in Barentsburg sometime in the future.

GRØNFJORDEN Grønfjorden is a historical place: there were once whale-processing factories on both sides of the fjord, the last closing in 1912, and Svalbard's first telegraph station was here on Finneset until 1931. On the east side of the fjord's mouth is Kap Heer, with its Russian heliport. The World War II cannon that used to stand here has now been moved to Hotellneset, near Longyearbyen. Today, the most prominent feature of Grønfjorden is, of course, the Russian mining settlement of **Barentsburg**, dealt with in *Chapter 6*, pages 178–83.

FESTNINGEN Like a fortress wall, a vertical layer of Cretaceous sandstone projects into Isfjorden at Festningen. Nearby, footprints from an iguanodon have been found, a copy of which can be seen in Longyearbyen's **Svalbard Museum**. Owing to the upright sediment layers, such traces crumble away quickly, eventually revealing new ones. The same geological structure of 'up-risen' sediment layers continues in a north–south direction through much of western Spitsbergen, including Värmlandryggen on the northern side of Isfjorden (see *Trygghamna*, page 142).

KAPP STAROSTIN The cape is named after the last of the Russian trapper-monks, who died in 1826 after 39 winters in Svalbard. With his death came the end of the period of Russian fur-hunters. The nearby site of trapper dwellings was excavated in the 1980s.

KAPP LINNÉ Until the end of 2003, the radio station, Kapp Linné, on the southern side of the entrance of Isfjord, with its huge parabolic antennae, was the telecommunications lifeline for Longyearbyen, connecting the town with the rest of the world. Only here, where no mountains are in the way southwards, could the parabolic antennae of this ground station be directed at the geostationary telecommunication satellite just above the southern horizon as seen from here – due to the extreme northern position of the islands. In the 1990s, the station was automated and in 2004 it was replaced by the new twin glass-fibre sea cable, which stretches over the sea bottom between mainland Norway and Svalbard, providing a vastly expanded and less disturbed data-transfer capacity. Over the past few years, the station has been converted into an upmarket lodge run by adventure company Basecamp Spitsbergen (✆ 79 02 46 00; www.basecampspitsbergen.com). The several buildings that once housed satellite equipment and accommodations for the people that manned it have since been re-envisioned as a rustic-chic base for explorations into the surrounding wilderness and adjacent bird sanctuary, onto which the two-dozen rooms now look out.

LINNÉVATNET The second largest of Svalbard's few lakes, Linnévatnet is surrounded by jagged mountain ranges. The countryside has areas where underground springs keep the ground permafrost-free. Some stone objects found here have been considered as possible remains of the Stone Age, a theory which is dismissed today, even though a local Stone-Age population is conceivable as climatic conditions have in the past been much milder than today. By the mouth of the stream into the fjord (Russekeila), there used to be a Russian hunter's base, which has been excavated by archaeologists.

INGEBORGFJELLET The steep rock face on the north side of Bellsundet is an important guillemot colony. At its foot are the ruins of two unsuccessful pioneer mines.

FRIDTJOVBREEN The only glacier in Nordenskiöldlandet with an outlet to the sea is in retreat again, after it had an impressive surge as recently as 1995–96. The bay in front, Fridtjovhamna, can be reached only by a shallow, narrow entrance and is surrounded by a massive moraine, all that is left of the sudden surge of the glacier in 1860–61. Torell described the glacier in 1858 as still being inland, separated from the bay by a marsh, the bay being one of the best harbours of all Svalbard. The glacier moved forward about 10km during the winter of 1860–61, blocking the through-route north of Akseløya. In 1898, Nathorst described an ice front outside today's entry to the cove. Since then, the glacier has retreated nearly 10km, though never quite as far back as pre-1860 until a renewed surge in 1995–96, which was much smaller than that of 1860–61.

Anyone who goes to Fridtjovhamna and sees the giant moraine has a clear demonstration of the power of glaciation and its ability to change a landscape: this ice has, in only 130 years, completely filled a large bay, then freed it again, and then partly filled it up once more.

AKSELØYA Akseløya acts as a wall, separating Van Mijenfjorden from Bellsundet with two narrow sounds. Tidal currents are very strong here and in order to reduce the environmental risks of possible accidents, strict rules have been imposed for bigger ships that want to pass here: backup by a tug boat is required, aimed mainly at the huge coal vessels calling at Sveagruva in inner Van Mijenfjord. Akseløya is part of the Permian system, laid vertical by the folding of the west coast during the Tertiary period, also seen at Festningen and Värmlandryggen as previously mentioned. There are several breeding colonies of birds, among them eider. One of the few **trappers** has his isolated main cabin on the island.

DAMESMORENEN Damesmorenen is quite special, as it is one of the very few moraines which date from the long period between the end of the last ice age and the 'little ice age' which had its peak in the early 19th century. During this 'little ice age', most glaciers advanced further than ever before since the end of the last real ice age some 10,000 years ago – and this maximal advance occurring not 200 years ago scraped away all older glacial deposits in most places elsewhere in Svalbard. The giant Damesmorenen is one of the rare exceptions, where a glacier had a further advance prior to the 'little ice age': it comes from the furthest push of the Paulabreen and its side glaciers around six centuries ago. The front of the glacier today lies 30km further back in the fjord. Large mussel shells pushed up together with the moraine bear witness to an earlier presence of the sea and warmer climates. Possibly, Damesmorenen is the unlikely result of a coincidental joint surge of several of the tributary glaciers of Paulabreen, making it advance so far in a period of otherwise little glaciation.

CALYPSOBYEN AND RECHERCHEFJORDEN The Recherchefjorden is named after an ambitious scientific expedition by the French corvette *La Recherche* in 1839, which today is mostly known for the beautiful drawings and paintings by the expedition artist. The fjord was a favourite base for whalers. The buildings at Calypsobyen are relics of an attempt to mine coal in 1918–19.

TORELLBREEN AND ISØYANE The Torellbreen, divided into two halves by a low mountain range higher up, is the largest west-coast glacier. A close approach from the sea is impossible in larger boats as the water is too shallow. The islands in front of it, Isøyane ('ice island') among them, are bird sanctuaries and therefore out of bounds in summer.

ISBJØRNHAMNA The Polish research station, at the entrance to **Hornsundet**, has been here since 1957 (see *Svalbard's settlements and stations*, pages 186–7).

HORNSUNDET One of the most spectacular scenic corners of the west coast. Numerous glaciers terminate into the fjord's several side arms. The eastern end of the fjord, Brepollen, is almost surrounded by imposing glacier fronts. Between the glaciers, a number of mountains add to the spectacular scenery – first of all the mighty and wild **Hornsundtind**, which rises directly from the shore to its peak of 1,431m, much higher than any other mountain within 100km. Other remarkable elements of the scenery are the gigantic rock wall of Sophiakammen and the pointed needle of Bautaen.

It is only a few kilometres from here to Hamburgbukta on the east coast and it is a favourite journey of polar bears, the so-called 'Polar Bear Merry-go-round'; they are also frequent visitors to Hornsund, in the summer. There are many seabird colonies here, as well as remains from the heyday of whaling, walrus hunting and trapping and the important Swedish–Russian meridian expedition around the turn of the 20th century.

The name 'Hornsund', together with the low elevation of the glaciers that separate it from Hamburgbukta on the eastern side of the island, has given rise to speculation that it may be derived directly from the English name 'Horn Sound'. This indicates that it's a through-passage rather than just a bay, ie: that the area south of the fjord is connected to the north only by glacier ice, which closed the sound only after the discoverers visited in around 1600, as the ice cover of Svalbard has grown considerably with the climate getting colder over the centuries towards the peak of the 'little ice age' in the early 19th century. Radar measurements of the ice thickness could not solve the riddle satisfactorily as their margin for error was such that the land under the ice could be either just under or above sea level.

Despite its dramatic scenery and the chance of spotting polar bears, Hornsund has been little visited by bigger cruise ships because its entrance is often blocked by ice drifting around south Spitsbergen, pushed by the currents from the east. Only some bigger cruise ships with more flexible programmes (and who are capable of spotting that the area is clear of ice when passing by) and a number of longer expedition cruises (especially those circumnavigating Svalbard) include this fjord.

5

In Svalbard

GETTING AROUND

Detailed consideration of the pros and cons of various forms of travel within Svalbard is given on pages 93–8, but here is a brief look at the options. The following part of this chapter is mainly of interest for the very few who consider independent travel within the archipelago. For the vast majority of visitors, who come with a package tour, these aspects will be organised by their tour operator. However, it may be of interest nevertheless to have an overview of the possibilities as well as the restrictions.

GENERAL While it is very easy coming to Longyearbyen just by boarding a normal scheduled flight, it can be a major challenge to explore the remaining 99.9% of this vast Arctic wilderness. Outside the settlements, there is hardly any infrastructure that can be used by the traveller, with few easy-to-use connections between the settlements. Svalbard is truly the last big wilderness of Europe – in all senses: wilderness begins where the roads and paths finish, and this lack of paths is true for almost all of this remote archipelago. Even between the two main settlements, Longyearbyen and Barentsburg, there is no connection, and your only way to travel between the two is to embark on a tough two-day cross-country hike, take a snowmobile ride in winter, or join one of the day cruises between the two in summer. Except for the few accommodation options in the settlements, you will have to use your tent when exploring the outback as there are no cabins, etc, for tourists to use, with the exception of a few cabins for commercial dog-sledge programmes in winter.

For many potential visitors, it is difficult to imagine that major parts of Svalbard are extremely hard to reach, and often only at enormous cost, and are sometimes out of reach entirely for major parts of the year.

Tour operators offering arrangements in Svalbard, therefore, have to maintain their own special infrastructure for their customers – be it ships and boats or wilderness base camps. These are, of course, usually restricted to their clients only, and are not available to independent travellers.

Owing to the difficulties of independent travel, more than 90% of the visitors join an organised tour, while the remaining 10% seldom get further than Longyearbyen, unless they book organised excursions from there. Accordingly, organised tourism gets more attention in this book than in most others. However, each year there are also a few independent expeditions. For these groups, I have also included some information that I hope will prove useful.

BY AIR With the exception of Longyearbyen Airport, there are only two private landing strips in the archipelago (Sveagruva, used solely by the mining company, and Ny-Ålesund), plus a few additional landing sites for helicopters in the other settlements and bases. Both private landings and commercial sightseeing flights are forbidden, with special permission required for any landings off the official airstrips – and for purely tourist purposes, such permission will not normally be granted. Unfortunately, non-touristic helicopter use has risen over the years, even though the official stance is that helicopter use should be reduced – and has been forbidden for tourist purposes since 1992.

For non-touristic purposes, a helicopter charter can be arranged, provided permission is given by the Sysselmann. There is no sea- or ski-plane available.

BY BOAT For package tours on ships with a tour operator, see pages 96 and 98 and the offers by specialised travel agencies.

Within the archipelago, there is no scheduled ferry service. During the summer months, a few smaller boats (up to about 100 passengers) run sightseeing day cruises in Isfjord from Longyearbyen, mostly to Barentsburg but also to a few other destinations. All these tours run only if a minimum number of bookings (usually eight fully paying participants) is reached. These tours usually depart at the weekend, and can also be used as a one-way passage only, allowing you to stop at the destination (or somewhere along the way) for a night or more. Be warned, though, that not all companies will readily pick up embarking passengers along the way. An alternative, if you are part of a group, is one of the commercial passenger boats that can be chartered by the hour. So far, the season for these cruises lasts from early June (though often limited by ice at this time) into September. Schedules for these cruise offers are published one week in advance and can be found in the tourist information office and various hotel lobbies.

To areas outside of Isfjord, no such day cruises are offered. Nevertheless, passages may be possible by making a deal with one of the cruise ships operating around the archipelago. However, be aware that these ships are often booked and may be reluctant to pick up a passenger halfway. You will almost certainly have to pay for the whole tour, even if you are only sailing for a part of it and it's unlikely you'll get any guarantee that they will pick you up somewhere at a certain date. If you are very flexible, the best way for cheap transport may be waiting for eventual last-minute offers (published usually a week or so before departure). The season for these cruises lasts from mid-June to late August – outside this period, there are no transport possibilities for tourists to the remote parts of the archipelago.

☞ **Attention:** There is no local fishing fleet in Longyearbyen and the few private leisure boats of some locals are not allowed to sell passages. So do not imagine that you can, by persuasion and bribes, sail your way around the islands in small private craft, and don't plan any itinerary that involves using these methods of transport.

BY LAND Any motorised traffic is forbidden off the roads, and there are few roads here anyway, other than a few trunk roads around the settlements, with some exceptions for snowmobiles on snow-covered and frozen ground (which, of course, is limited to travel outside of the summer period). There are no connecting roads, not even paths or marked routes, between any of the settlements. Accordingly, it makes no real sense for visitors to bring their car or motorbike to Svalbard. For the limited road network of Longyearbyen (two trunk roads of 11km each leading out of the settlement), both bicycles and cars can be hired. Rental prices for cars start from NOK800 per day or NOK5,000 per week:

🚗 **Arctic Autorent AS** Postboks 184, NO-9171 Longyearbyen; 📞 91 70 22 58; 📧 info@autorent.no; www.autorent.no

🚗 **Longyearbyen Bilutleie** Postboks 63, NO-9171 Longyearbyen; 📞 79 02 11 88

🚗 **Svalbard Auto** Postboks 236, N-9171 Longyearbyen; 📞 79 02 49 30; 📧 post@svalbardauto.no; www.svalbardauto.no

Possibilities for bicycle rental vary from year to year – ask Longyearbyen Camping or the reception. Off-road biking is in many places severely damaging to the vulnerable vegetation, and in other areas (rough scree, mud, etc) highly unpleasant. However, within the limited road network of Longyearbyen, a bicycle is very welcome.

TOURIST INFORMATION

The **Norwegian tourist board** based in your own country can, among other things, provide information on accommodation, travel connections and getting to and from Svalbard.

The **Sysselmann's office** at Longyearbyen is responsible for all regulatory concerns in Svalbard and can provide information on permits, insurances, environmental regulations and so on.

There is a tourist information office in the Flerbruksbygg (multi-purpose building) in Longyearbyen. The Norsk Polarinstitutt in the Flerbruksbygg can also provide information (maps, scientific publications).

Svalbard Tourism (📞 79 02 55 50; *www.svalbard.net*), in the Forskningsparken building, which holds the Svalbard Museum, is part of the Svalbard Reiseliv AS (Spitsbergen Tourism Companies Association) – an association of tour operators and tourism-related companies in Longyearbyen. Among other things, a weekly list is published there which includes all current offers provided by the member tour operators, especially shorter arrangements like day excursions, which they report to Svalbard Tourism. Furthermore, a useful list with the opening hours of shops and other institutions can be picked up there.

Svalbard Tourism keeps a neutral position towards the member companies and will therefore not answer questions like 'Which is the best tour or the best company?'. Svalbard Tourism does not sell any tours, either; bookings have to be done directly through the member companies. Furthermore, the employees of Svalbard Tourism may not be able to give detailed advice to independent travellers about what routes they should take, and so on.

A neutral tourism information source that is independent of the Svalbard Reiselivsråd does not exist. But note that not all companies are or want to be members of Svalbard Reiseliv AS – whether on account of the cost of membership, or perhaps a disagreement with the environmental standards of the association, which of course are always a compromise between very different tour operators.

A training programme is offered under the leadership of Svalbard Tourism for local tour guides in an attempt to set a kind of minimum qualification standard. So far, only a minority of the tour guides working in Svalbard have participated and a number of companies prefer to train their guides themselves, partly setting even higher standards.

WEBSITES

Norsk Polarinstitutt www.npolar.no. Good for research questions related to Svalbard & Norwegian polar research in general, but not for tourist questions.

There are a few webcams with live (or virtually live) images:

www.snsk.no The SNSK website has a number of webcams: 1 based above the old quay in Longyearbyen, 1 in Svea & a third at Isfjord Radio.

www.svalbard.com/webcam The Svalbard. com website has a round-up of images from many of the webcams dotted around Svalbard.
www.unis.no The UNIS website displays an image of the Svalbard Research Park.

MONEY AND BANKING

The currency used is the Norwegian kroner (international abbreviation NOK, locally also nkr or kr), which is now also used in the Russian settlements when dealing with outsiders, although they still use roubles internally. The old local money of the various mining companies is no longer in use, but is an attractive collector's item.

Norwegian notes come in denominations of 50, 100, 200, 500 and 1,000 kroner, with 100 and 1,000 being the most common. Coins are of one, five, ten and 20 kroner, plus a 50øre coin (100øre=1kroner). New coins have been introduced in the last few years, but many of the old series are still to be found and may sometimes be used. The tiny 10øre coin was taken out of circulation at the beginning of the 1990s. Prices may sometimes state øre amounts that are not multiples of 50; in such cases, the price will be rounded up or down to the nearest 50øre for payment in cash.

Exchange rates in late 2012 were relatively easy to calculate approximately if you are coming from Britain, the USA or the euro zone. In round figures, these were NOK9 to £1, NOK6 to US$1 and NOK7 to €1.

Thanks to the arrival of tourism, paying with foreign currency is often possible in some shops, particularly if you have sterling, US dollars or euros. Don't expect a decent rate, though, if not paying with the official currency, NOK.

Changing cash in small quantities (as with all Norwegian banks) is not good business as high service charges are levied. Either change a lot at a time or club together with other travellers. Eurocheques are no longer accepted, but travellers' cheques (American Express) may get you a better rate.

The bank in Longyearbyen stands together with the post office, in a light-coloured building in the lower town next to the Lompensentret. There is a cashpoint here (one of only two in the archipelago – the other is at the airport arrivals terminal) in the bank entrance which accepts Visa and MasterCard and is accessible at any time.

Credit cards are widely accepted in most of the shops of Longyearbyen, mostly Visa and MasterCard, followed by American Express, Eurocard and occasionally also Diners Club. Tour operators do not necessarily accept credit cards in person (though they may well online) and they may be rejected on ships too, as well as in the other settlements of the archipelago. So be prepared to pay cash.

On average, a meal at a restaurant won't run to that much more than on the Norwegian mainland. A burger, for example, will cost you around NOK115, while a steak might well be double that, while a beer at a bar will cost you around NOK50. For accommodation, count on NOK1,000 in the off-season, and significantly higher than this in the peak summer months.

ACCOMMODATION

Nothing demonstrates better the massive changes in Svalbard than the rise in the number of available tourist beds: from nothing in the mid 1980s to nearly 800 by 2013.

There is nothing that could really be described as 'budget' – the sole campsite excepted, perhaps – and in addition there are distinct seasonal variations – very little will be open over the Christmas period, and many of the options close completely over the winter period. Price regimes can be complex, with significant increases around peak periods – Easter in particular. The overwhelming majority of accommodation is in Longyearbyen – the little that is available outside the town needs to be booked through the tour operators, with the exception of the hotel in Barentsburg. See pages 168–9.

Some other points to be aware of:

- It is customary to take off all shoes which have been used outside already in the entrances, continuing inside either simply in socks or using slippers (either brought along or sometimes also ready for guests in the entrance).
- Check-in time is usually from 14.00 onwards, check-out time is until 11.00. If arriving with a night flight, make sure that you booked your room for that night instead of having to wait until 14.00 the following day!
- For a surcharge, you can make yourself a packed lunch at the breakfast buffets to take with you on tour – doing this secretly without extra payment is regarded as unacceptable.
- There is no smoking in any public places in Norway and Longyearbyen.
- The top hotels charge even higher prices during the spring weekends.
- In the low season (between Christmas and New Year) most accommodation is closed.

EATING AND DRINKING

Places to eat are included under the relevant settlements in the following chapters. There is no authentic local Svalbard cuisine. Meals served in Longyearbyen are either traditional Norwegian food (Vinterhagen, Huset, Kroa) or international cuisine in the hotel restaurants. Huset often adds real local flair by offering various types of Arctic meat (reindeer, seal, whale, geese, ptarmigan) or polar fish species. In Barentsburg, typical Russian food is served (including very big breakfasts) – if you spend a night there, it is definitely worth giving the food a try.

ALCOHOL Alcoholic beverages are good value when compared with prices in shops elsewhere in Scandinavia. Sale of alcohol in the shops is restricted for residents who have ration cards. Visitors can get their rations by displaying their flight tickets (this system may change in the near future). Cruise passengers who stay in Longyearbyen for only a few hours are not sold alcohol in the shop (but can buy a drink, of course, in licensed places).

The only place to buy bottles of alcoholic beverages is a separate area of the supermarket **Svalbardbutikken** in Longyearbyen called Nordpolet; the choice is impressive. Amusingly, wine is not rationed as it was very rarely drunk in the days when the system was inaugurated. Should you want to head out drinking, there are a number of bars in Longyearbyen itself.

Standard Norwegian restrictions apply when bringing in alcohol in your luggage: people over 20 years of age may bring in either: one litre of spirits, one litre of wine plus one litre of beer; or two litres of wine or two litres of beer.

Drinking and driving is also forbidden (limit 0.2mg alcohol per ml of blood!) and is subject to penalties as stiff as those on the mainland – two to four weeks' imprisonment accompanied by fines of thousands of kroner, are not unheard of.

Please note that consumption of alcohol is allowed publicly only in licensed places. You should not sit or stand somewhere in public areas with a beer can or a wine bottle; even carrying bottles of alcohol uncovered is regarded as wrong.

DRINKING WATER Owing to the low temperatures and the nigh pure surroundings, surface water is drinkable just about everywhere. The eventual light brown, silty turbidity is due to finely ground rock materials from glaciers – that is, safe 'mineral water'. You should allow some time for the sediments to settle to the bottom. Only in some areas have there been any problems with water quality due to a possible sulphur content caused by local shale.

Drinking water in Longyearbyen comes filtered from the lake, Isdammen, and is of very good quality. In Barentsburg, the pipes are very rusty and it is recommended that, if you are going to drink it, you let the water run from the tap for a while before doing so.

☞ **Attention:** In the Fuglefjellet area between Bjørndalen and Isfjord just west of Longyearbyen, the lethal fox tapeworm *Echinococcus multilocularis* could establish itself due to the unique coexistence of both mice and foxes in this place – here, unboiled water should be avoided.

SHOPPING

A decent range of goods is available in Longyearbyen, whose shops have improved much as a result of the development of tourism as an important source of extra income, but also because local residents now use shops whereas in the past goods were provided for by the SNSK mining company. For standard day-to-day items the town has all you need.

For those wishing to undertake wilderness tours of several days, it may still be advisable to bring everything you may need instead of risk of waiting until Longyearbyen, where some items may not be available. Most organised tours have their own supplies and individual hikers are so few and far between that they have little influence on the market.

In Barentsburg there is only the souvenir shop in the culture house and the hotel. Locals in Barentsburg have their own supplies, which can be purchased only with the pay card issued by Trust Arcticugol to its employees.

OPENING TIMES The opening times of the smaller shops may be shorter than what most of us are used to. The best time to buy is 11.00–12.00 on a working day. Otherwise, a few of the kiosks are open longer; the opening hours of the airport cafeteria coincide with departure times for Norway.

PHOTOGRAPHY AND VIDEO

Photographers travelling to Svalbard must reckon on slightly lower light levels, even in summer, as the sun is not as high, even at midday, as it is in lower latitudes. That said, when the sun is out, the light bouncing off the snow, ice and water can be positively blinding. This can cause problems with automatic exposure systems (you may for instance find that all your beautiful white icebergs have turned a muddy blue, or that beautifully blue crevasse has got lost in the glare). It's well worth reading up on exposure compensation and bracketing techniques and experimenting with them before you leave.

5

SPECIALIST SHOPS

SOUVENIR SHOPS

Longyearbyen The town has souvenir shops in two locations, both right in the service building on the passenger pier Bykaia and in the centre.

Barentsburg There's a souvenir shop in the culture house, and some souvenirs on sale at the hotel bar. Look out for the excellent Russian picture book *Glacial Eldorado* about Svalbard. For collectors, the old Russian local money may be of interest, especially the old rouble and kopek banknotes. A more recent coin series from the 1990s has been in limited circulation, while coins minted after 2000 with pictures of famous recent catastrophes (World Trade Center attack, *Kursk*, Moscow theatre raid, flood, avalanche, etc) have never been introduced as local currency and are therefore a pure attempt at making a profit from collectors.

SOUVENIRS

Postcards There's a huge choice of pictures, including endless polar bear shots, which you can pick up in all settlements, price about NOK5.

Antlers and fossils These typical Svalbard souvenirs cost nothing, except the effort it takes to find them. As new ones appear all the time, there is (somewhat surprisingly) no problem in taking them, except in protected areas where collecting them is forbidden. For those in a hurry, they are also offered for sale in Longyearbyen.

Furs Many of us have our doubts about these, but you can be sure that fox (about NOK1,500), seal and polar bear (NOK25,000–35,000) have all been taken legally (the bear by Native Americans in Canada who have a quota), as have stuffed foxes and birds. You should be careful about obtaining these items in Russian areas, though, as there will be no official paperwork, which is essential for species on the CITES list, otherwise you may encounter problems at customs.

Maps Maps may be bought in the shop at the Norsk Polarinstitutt, at the Svalbard Museum, or in the Svalbardbutikken. The most detailed scale is 1:100,000, with a total of 63 different sheets covering the whole land area of the archipelago. For cruises, the 1:1,000,000 complete map or the four sheets in 1:500,000 are best. For many sheets, there is also a geological version already available. For finding maps at home, try specialised cartographic or geographic bookshops, or buy online from the Norsk Polarinstitutt (e *sales@ npolar.no; www.npolar.no*). Some service-minded tour operators provide their tour participants with good maps.

The huge technological advances in digital cameras over the last few years have resulted in a downturn in the film market, although those of you sticking with the tried and true should be able to find a limited selection of film on sale in Longyearbyen itself.

Batteries suffer in cold weather, and if your camera takes Ni-Cd or Ni-MH AAs it is well worth making sure that you charge them every evening and keep them warm while out in the field. Tuck your spares inside your fleece before you head out in the morning. Li-ion batteries (which are more common with dSLRs) don't suffer so much from the cold, but it's still not a bad idea to stash them somewhere warm. Some digital cameras (particularly the cheaper point 'n' shoot-style ones) may have trouble functioning in sub-zero temperatures.

Use of video cameras in Svalbard can be rewarding, especially with good digital cameras. Keep in mind that the cold can reduce battery capacities dramatically, so have a sufficient supply of spares and try to keep batteries warm. I also recommend packing photo equipment into water-resistant covers and robust cases.

Whatever you bring, make sure you have plenty of spare media and storage – there's nothing more frustrating than having to decide which of your lovingly taken photos you have to sacrifice because you decided that the extra memory card wasn't worth it. If you have the facility, it's worth having some sort of secondary backup system – either a hard drive or one of the portable photo storage devices made by a number of companies. This way you won't be cursing hitting the 'format' button accidentally and losing every photo you've taken.

MEDIA AND COMMUNICATIONS

POST Longyearbyen Post Office (*Postkontor;* ✆ 79 02 16 04; f 79 02 14 33; ⊕ 09.30–17.00 Mon–Fri, 10.00–16.00 Sat) is in the same building as the bank. Apart from the usual postal services, you can also get postcards and a special postmark.

Standard-sized postcards and letters under 20g cost NOK13 to send to the UK (NOK15 to the USA), and normally take three to five days to central Europe and Britain. All letter post is sent automatically by airmail, at least to the Norwegian mainland. If you are sending a post parcel, it usually makes sense to send 20kg, as lower weights are not that much cheaper.

There are postboxes dotted around built-up areas. The post offices in Barentsburg and Hornsundet are curiosities, in that they are part of the Norwegian system but are operated by Russians, Poles and Ukrainians.

Stamps may also be bought at many places selling postcards.

SEA FREIGHT Sea freight to Svalbard is mostly handled through Tromsø or Bodø in northern Norway. Even in summer it is irregular and you should allow at least four weeks for your gear to arrive. Also, your freight will be transferred from ship to ship and can suffer handling damage, so pack everything securely in europallet sizes. Freight charges rise dramatically the further north you go. It is worth remembering that the freighters are primarily intended for commercial concerns and that these take priority; delays of several weeks are possible! For prices, contact your local freight companies – but make sure that the offer you get really does include all extra costs to avoid unpleasant surprises when you pick it up in Longyearbyen!

Sea freight makes sense for bigger quantities or for items that cannot be sent by post (for instance kayaks). Otherwise, consider sending a post parcel. The addressee is either your tour operator if you have a booked package tour, or yourself at poste restante if travelling independently. The address: Your name, Poste restante, N-9170 Longyearbyen, Norway/Svalbard.

TELEPHONE Svalbard is fully integrated into the Norwegian telephone system, and Longyearbyen has been connected to the mainland since the beginning of 2004 by a glass-fibre sea cable, guaranteeing reliability and an enormous capacity of telecommunication services over the full spectrum, from analogue to ISDN

5

NORWEGIAN PUBLIC HOLIDAYS (2013)

1 January	New Year's day
28 March*	Maundy Thursday
29 March*	Good Friday
31 March*	Easter Monday
9 May*	Ascension Day
20 May*	Whit Monday
1 May	Labour Day. Still important for many connected to the Labour movement, but not celebrated as fully as it used to be.
17 May	National Day. Celebrations in the streets of Longyearbyen and even Ny-Ålesund.
23 June	Sankt Hansaften. Though this is a normal working day, it is characterised by a midsummer night's feast by the mouth of the Longyear stream, Isfjorden.
25 December	Christmas Day
26 December	Boxing Day

Should days fall close to each other in the week (eg: at Christmas), the days in between are also taken as holidays. In addition, Norwegians have other feast days which are not public holidays but which can be marked by the flags being hoisted (eg: royal birthdays). The starred holidays (*) indicate a moveable date.

LOCAL HOLIDAYS (NORMAL WORKING DAYS)

8 March	Solfesten: the return of the sun after the long winter months is celebrated. The first rays reached the steps of the former Skjæringa Hospital on this day, which was considered as the official return of the sun – the hospital is no longer there, but a reconstruction of its steps has been erected. This is celebrated on the following weekend by music, barbecues, races featuring weird sleds and so on. A major event in this context is the locally produced annual revue, which mocks events of the last year.
14 August	This is an unofficial feast day celebrated by the Svalbard Norwegians in honour of the day in 1925 when Norway's sovereignty was declared.

and ADSL. Its more than ample capacity also allows for the establishment of new companies who need excellent data connection and at the same time want to avail themselves of the low taxes and the relative legal safety of a western European country. There are also plans to connect other settlements and stations to the cable.

Owing to the ubiquity of mobile phones, the only publicly accessible telephone left on the island is located at the harbour and it accepts Visa cards. International calls follow the usual format – add 0044 for Great Britain, for example – and the international dialling code for Norway is +47.

Local land line numbers start with 790, followed by five more digits; mobiles tend to begin with 90 or 95. In all of Norway, normal telephone numbers are eight-figured, without any area codes.

Public telex, fax and video conferencing is available at the telephone office TeleNor (⏱ *08.00–16.00 Mon–Fri*). Svalbard Radio can help you get in touch with ships and there is a paging service available in Longyearbyen.

Cellular phones of the GSM system can be used in the area of Longyearbyen, Barentsburg and Sveagruva.

Internet is available at all hotels, generally for free to guests (though some even have unencrypted connections). You can also find several internet terminals at the town library. Owing to the NASA cable connection (see page 34), Svalbard's internet throughput speed tends to be blazing fast, rivalling if not exceeding anything you would find in any major European city.

RADIO A licence is necessary for the use of CB radio, but it is not worth the effort as the range is limited due to the mountainous terrain. The frequencies are not monitored by the rescue authorities.

SPORT

ANGLING The open North Atlantic and the Barents Sea are rich in fish, but the fjords of Svalbard are mostly too cold for bigger fish species. As for freshwater fish, arctic char can only be found in a very few streams and are protected now, with only limited quotas given to locals; you may as well leave your tackle at home. Fishing for Greenland shark has almost ceased as the liver is no longer commercially utilised. There are ideas of reviving Greenland shark fishing as a sport, but pulling up these fish from their typical depths of around 300–400m just for a photo usually kills them, which is definitely a reason to cease such practices. Schools of cod intruding into the fjords with occasional swells of slightly warmer water are sometimes followed by leisure craft – if they manage to spot them.

HORSERIDING A small riding stable was established in 1990 with five Icelandic horses. Originally it was intended as a tourist attraction, but it has become a magnet for local adolescents. Treks lasting more than one day are not currently offered and would damage the fragile tundra vegetation, as a look at the hoofmarks around the campsite might suggest.

HUNTING Regulations for hunting should be obtained in advance from the Sysselmann's office. Semi-automatic weapons with more than two shots are forbidden, as is hunting from motorised vehicles.

* Ringed and bearded seals may be hunted all year, except for periods in spring.
* Arctic fox may be hunted from 1 November to 15 March, but are fully protected on Bjørnøya.
* Reindeer populations have increased to the point where residents may hunt them, provided that they have passed a test and are authorised with an official quota in a specified area. This controlled hunting is also associated with scientific research. Each animal must be measured and its feet brought in for registration purposes.
* Only certain birds may be hunted, including ptarmigan, glaucous gull, fulmar, black guillemot, Brünnich's guillemot and pink-footed goose. A full list may be obtained from the Sysselmann's office. The season runs through September and October. Ptarmigan are fully protected on Bjørnøya.

In 2006 a tourist fee of NOK150 was introduced. The payments go into an environment fund for Svalbard, meant for publishing instructive information about proper use of the environment, monitoring and repairing damages, and other such projects.

While this fee for tourists is justified with the understandable argument that the user of the environment should pay, the same argument seems to be irrelevant for all the other users, many of whom do considerably more or comparable damage to the environment, than tourism: fishery, mining, local population, research, administration. In fact, it can be expected that the touristic payments to the environment fund will partly be used for purposes not related to prevention/repair of environmental damage by tourists.

Systematic interviews with tourists over the last few years have shown a high motivation among tourists to contribute financially to keeping environmental damage by tourism low and this willingness is part of the argument for the new tourist fee. However, in these interviews it was never asked what tourists think about being the only users to be charged such a contribution and probably even sponsoring measures against damage caused by other user groups who are not asked for any contribution to the fund. By this one-sidedness, the new fee fits into a tradition of highly different standards, just like the total ban on helicopter use in tourism (before the ban about 2–3% of all helicopter traffic), while much heavier types of helicopter use have grown. This one-sidedness, which can hardly be justified with environmental facts, gives all these initially good measures an unnecessary bitter taste – moral arguments like 'the user pays' seem hypocritical. Why not the same strict standards for all types of users?

SURFING There is a surf club in Longyearbyen. In principle, you can hire boards and suits for use on the Adventfjorden, but the activity of the club varies much from year to year – especially in the main holiday period from late June to mid-August.

SWIMMING There is a swimming hall in the sports complex next to Longyearbyen School which visitors may use; the opening hours are published at the entrance and in the tourist information office. It is sometimes closed for part of the summer for renovation. There is also a pool in Barentsburg, though it has been in a dire state over the past several years. The swimming hall in Pyramiden, once the world's most northerly, is closed, like all of the settlement, and damaged by frost.

Apart from these indoor pools, there are excellent beaches in many places in Svalbard, but only few dare to go for a swim with seawater temperatures around +5°C at best in summer.

Svalbard's Settlements and Stations

Longyearbyen is Svalbard's capital and the oldest existing settlement in the archipelago.

The aim of developing Longyearbyen into a modern Norwegian town, comparable with those on the mainland, has for all intents and purposes been met. There are good connections with the mainland through regular, year-round flights and communications technology has improved immensely. The town's infrastructure is similar to that found elsewhere in Norway in considerably larger places. While this range of facilities might surprise, it should be kept in mind that anything lacking in Longyearbyen is just an hour-and-a-half's flight away; on the mainland it is similarly no problem to organise supplies or assistance from a neighbouring community when needed. With Longyearbyen, there is no neighbouring settlement and in winter when ice hinders shipping, the community is still largely dependent on its local resources, which therefore have to be more extensive than in larger mainland settlements.

HISTORY

Foundation and development, 1900–45 Adventfjorden had been a base for whalers for centuries, with Russian hunters also operating there from time to time (a 19th-century map shows a Russian cabin on Hotellneset). The bay was visited from 1837 by explorers, using the peak of Nordenskiöldfjellet as a survey triangulation point. Hunters built a few cabins at the end of the century, using the fjord's shelter and navigability to ship out their pelts, down, etc, to Norway.

Growing interest in Svalbard travels led to the introduction of a summer steamship service to the mainland in 1895. The shipping company, Vesterålens Dampskibselskab, built a small hotel on the peninsula at the fjord's mouth, complete with the firm's own postal service, but this was given up the following year. The promontory is still called Hotellneset today and contains the airport and campsite. Thus, tourism joined hunting as one of the first commercial activities in Svalbard before coal.

It had been known for some time that coal was present around Adventfjorden. Five Norwegians came from Trondheim in 1900 to investigate, founding the Kulkompagniet Trondhjem-Spitsbergen. They could not finance the opening of seams, so tried to sell their coalfields two years later. Two businessmen from Boston, Frederick Ayer and John Munro Longyear, were on a family cruise in 1901 and entered Adventfjorden, where they had a look at the coalfields, in which they already had an interest in combination with an iron-mining and processing

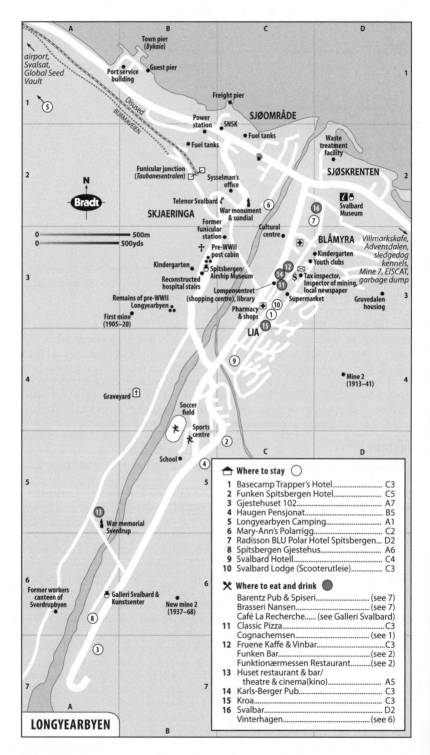

Where to stay ○

1 Basecamp Trapper's Hotel C3
2 Funken Spitsbergen Hotel C5
3 Gjestehuset 102 .... A7
4 Haugen Pensjonat B5
5 Longyearbyen Camping A1
6 Mary-Ann's Polarrigg C2
7 Radisson BLU Polar Hotel Spitsbergen ... D2
8 Spitsbergen Gjestehus A6
9 Svalbard Hotell C4
10 Svalbard Lodge (Scooterutleie) C3

✕ Where to eat and drink ●

Barentz Pub & Spiseri .... (see 7)
Brasseri Nansen .... (see 7)
Café La Recherche ...... (see Galleri Svalbard)
11 Classic Pizza C3
Cognachemsen .... (see 1)
12 Fruene Kaffe & Vinbar C3
Funken Bar .... (see 2)
Funktionærmessen Restaurant .... (see 2)
13 Huset restaurant & bar/
    theatre & cinema(kino) A5
14 Karls-Berger Pub C3
15 Kroa C3
16 Svalbar D2
Vinterhagen .... (see 6)

LONGYEARBYEN

project in mainland Norway. Even though the project in Norway was given up, an agreement was reached regarding Adventfjorden. In 1905, for a mere NOK18,000, the Americans purchased the coalfields together with a seventh of the Trondheimers' company. Further land on the south side of Isfjorden was annexed and the Arctic Coal Company (ACC) was founded in 1906, with Ayer, Longyear and 40 employees overwintering. The 'Amerikanergruva', Mine 1a, is still clearly visible above today's museum, though destroyed by the 1920 explosion and following decay. As in most of Spitsbergen's pits, the Tertiary coal lay in horizontal seams above sea level. This makes extraction relatively simple, except for limited thickness which makes for hard work. The permafrost keeps coalfaces relatively dry and access to the sea is good. The first of ACC's exports was in 1907.

To start with, production was limited at only a couple of thousand tonnes a year, but 'Longyear City' continued to grow, and 73 men and women lived there through the winter of 1910–11. Management staff comprised primarily Americans, while the hard labourers were Norwegians drawn into the difficult conditions by the more favourable pay than that available at home. The arrangement was subject to much criticism, not least because of cultural differences between management and labour, political ideology, and rising nationalism in a Norway only recently independent from Sweden. With justification or not, the Americans felt discriminated against by the administration on the Norwegian mainland. For example, the Norwegians refused permission for ACC to build a telegraph station connecting Longyear City with northern Norway, instead building their own at Grønfjorden (50km away) which could be reached from Longyear City only by boat in summer or skis in winter. And, although Svalbard belonged to no-one, Norway endeavoured (unsuccessfully) to bring ACC into its tax system.

Longyear City was Spitsbergen's largest settlement and where the majority of Norwegian workers were based. Other enterprises came and went but ACC continued to mine, with massive problems. There were criticisms of working conditions and regular workers' protests, normally answered by mass sackings; at one point even a wholesale replacement of Scandinavian with Chinese labour was considered. But by the winter of 1912–13 production had reached 30,000 tonnes. Mine 2 was opened up in Longyear Valley in 1913, by which time the population had risen to 385 (245 in winter).

From 1910 on there were international negotiations concerning the ownership, or sovereignty, of Svalbard. Perhaps with this in mind, the Americans had (it seems) considered divesting their interest, particularly in view of the constant friction with the Norwegian government on the mainland and worker unrest in Svalbard, and especially amid the difficulties experienced during World War I, which made operations in Svalbard very tough. At the same time, having experienced supply problems from England during the war, Norway gained interest in buying the well-organised American mining establishment. In 1916 ACC was sold to a Norwegian syndicate for NOK1.5 million, with an additional two million kroner's worth of shares in the newly founded Store Norske Spitsbergen Kullkompani A/S (SNSK). Other smaller companies were bought at the same time, and the Norwegian syndicate found itself in possession of 1,200km².

Under the new management, the business continued with (at first) reduced production. There were successes and there were problems. Mine 2 was completed in 1919; Mine 1 suffered an explosion, killing 26 men in 1920. The old Mine 2 carried on as the only working pit until 1937 (later set ablaze by a German grenade in 1943), when a new shaft was driven (New Mine 2), and New Mine 1 was opened in 1939.

A distinct class system operated before World War II. Workers had their own barracks with up to six in a room; functionaries had comfortable houses, sometimes with their families. Apart from the wives of management staff, there were few women apart from canteen waitresses. The workers' canteen received its first female staff in 1929 and the place began to tidy up a bit. Outnumbered, the women were besieged by charmers, and most of those not married already found their future partners here.

Alcohol was not a huge problem; banned by the Americans, it was rationed by the Norwegians. In any case, workers were aware of the dangers of mixing drinking with mining.

By 1925 there were 500 people during the winter. Improvements had been made and in the same year Longyearbyen saw its first priest, who also served as the schoolmaster. A church was built in 1921 and a proper school in 1938. There was already a hospital, built by the Americans in 1913 on Skjæringa, which was extended at various times. As the sun first reached the hospital steps after the long winter night (8 March), Solfesten was celebrated. This 'Celebration of the Sun' is a tradition maintained today.

Coal production reached 247,000 tonnes by 1940–41. The fjord was more heavily iced over in those days and exporting coal could be managed only in summer, while first supplies, even in early July, often had to be unloaded far out on the fjord ice and then brought to the settlement. Workers were primarily Norwegian (mostly from the poor north) and often made up of large groups from single villages: fathers and sons and brothers-in-law all working together. A Sysselmann had been introduced as the local state representative in 1925 after the formal acquisition of the archipelago by Norway through the 1920 Spitsbergen Treaty, and a Bergmester (Inspector of Mining) was appointed the following year. His was the highest position in Svalbard after the Sysselmann's.

World War II brought a sudden interruption to this development. Owing to the destruction wreaked, first on the technical mining-related surface facilities by the Allied evacuation force in 1941, and then especially by the attack of the *Scharnhorst* and the landing of troops on the exiled Norwegian garrison based in Longyearbyen which destroyed most of the settlement, only a few buildings were left intact in Longyearbyen from which to build a fresh start.

After the war A lively account of the post-war pioneering era is given in the book *Nord for Det Øde Hav* (English version: *North of the Desolate Sea*), written by Liv Balstad, wife of the first post-war Sysselmann.

Mines remained under the surface relatively unharmed by World War II and were able to restart production in 1945. Longyearbyen did not do so well, and a new development, Nybyen ('New Village'), was built below the New Mine 2. Building was also undertaken in Vannledningsdalen (the suburb of Haugen, meaning 'Hill') and on Skjæringa. The class system was maintained, with workers living near 'their' mines in Sverdrupbyen (the only settlement part that had survived the war) and Nybyen, while officials in Haugen and government staff lived in Skjæringa. The new hospital was built in Haugen in 1947, but was damaged by a mud flood in 1954; it was subsequently rebuilt and operated there until 1991.

New Mines 1 and 2 were exhausted by 1958 and 1967 respectively, but were replaced by Mine 5 in 1958 (the first time a mine had been established in one of the neighbouring side valleys) and Mine 4 in 1966 (established under the Longyear glacier, but which spent only a few years in operation). The last mines to be opened were Mine 6 (1969), Mine 7 (1972) and Mine 3 (also in 1972). Soon after the war it was realised that Svalbard's fields exceeded Norwegian demands for coal and foreign customers were sought. The market in Norway all but crashed, and other customers could hardly be found quickly enough.

The local domination by the SNSK continued after the war. Only the offices of the Sysselmann, the Bergmester, the telegraph office and the church were not owned or controlled by the company. Even the priest's duties as a teacher were paid for by SNSK. This was a company town.

Things started to change at the end of the 1960s. Firstly, the younger generation were not as bound by tradition as their forefathers and had no truck with the class system, and wanted the same living standards as on the mainland, where the new oil business in the North Sea brought unexpected wealth and higher general standards of living. And secondly, growing attempts by the Soviets to challenge and question Norwegian sovereignty led to the strengthening of the Sysselmann's office, which today has an all-year staff of about 20, plus extra summer workers. A central step was also the opening of the airport (against protests from the Soviet Union who suspected military intentions, though they were somewhat appeased once allowed to maintain a permanently manned Aeroflot office in Longyearbyen), which ended the winter isolation.

Slowly, SNSK, now state owned, ceded some of its functions to the state itself, beginning with the school in 1976, giving up its own currency system in 1980, and handing over the hospital in 1981. Later its streets were opened to the public. These developments were accelerated by the decline in the coal market. Today, out of a total population of around 2,080, only 220 work directly for SNSK.

Despite being relieved of the tasks of running several costly communal services, the deficits of coal mining increased due to sinking prices on the world market and a total production which was too low for using efficient modern technology. The thin coal seams also prevented the use of the most rational, economic technology. Higher production (and thus quicker depletion) was out of the question, as maintaining mining in Svalbard was regarded as a key element of the Norwegian presence.

This all changed with the end of the Cold War. By the late 1980s, the Norwegian government decided that it was time for a substantial reorientation and change in their policy towards Svalbard. For Longyearbyen, this meant diversification away from the previous coal monostructure and the company town to a modern, multi-faceted community with a variety of economic activities. Major newcomers were tourism (officially welcomed in controlled forms from 1989 onwards) and the massive development of research and higher education in Longyearbyen. Small private service companies (hairdressers, florist, shops, pay-TV and internet provider, etc) also grew in number. At the same time, clear signals were given to the state-owned mining company that the former high level of state subsidies would be unacceptable in future. This announcement caused a doomsday atmosphere in Longyearbyen during the 1990s – how could this place survive without mining as the core of the community, which seemed to be impossible without the comfortable state subsidies that had been taken for granted until then?

Mine 3, above the airport, the last mine with mostly manual work, closed in 1996, leaving only Mine 7 in the Longyearbyen area, leading to a sharp drop both in workforce and production.

Now, only some years later, the situation has changed dramatically. The SNSK is still the single biggest employer, but has retreated almost completely from dominating Longyearbyen, while tourism, the only industry that emerged with almost no direct state subsidies, has found its niche in the community and now employs more than 100 people. The establishment of UNIS, the Svalbard dependency of the Norwegian universities (Oslo, Bergen, Trondheim, Tromsø) with advanced studies and courses for international students, has brought a lot of young people to Longyearbyen, an age group which traditionally was underrepresented, as children usually left the island to take their higher education. An increase of big research facilities has broadened the mix of the society, too, and increased the multi-national flavour of the town. Maybe the biggest surprise, however, is the mining company itself. By the joint effort of a co-operative workforce and a creative management, the SNSK's new main mine near Sveagruva is now one of the most productive in the world. Being relieved of the Cold War limitations on supply, annual coal production has increased from about 300,000 tonnes in Mine 7 to about three million in Svea, facilitated by very favourable geological conditions including coal seams 5m thick, which allows for the very effective use of high mechanisation. Since 2002, the SNSK has even managed to make a profit – a quite unique achievement in European coal mining and a tremendous change compared to the doom and gloom mood of the early 1990s.

The threshold to the next major development step may have been passed in early 2004, when the new glass-fibre sea cable between the Norwegian mainland and Longyearbyen came into operation. It was financed largely by the ever-growing satellite ground station SVALSAT above Longyearbyen. Contrary to more southerly ground stations, SVALSAT profits from its extremely northerly position, which makes it possible to be in contact with any satellite on a polar orbit each time it passes over the North Pole about every 90 minutes, while stations further south may 'see' such a satellite on maybe only two or three of its daily 13–14 circles around the globe, the others being under the western or eastern horizon. Therefore, SVALSAT can empty the stored data of a satellite more frequently, which allows for a more efficient use of this storage for more data collection. The data is thus available more frequently and earlier, which is of major interest to people such as weather forecasters who want data as 'real-time' as possible. Understandably, this unique advantage gives SVALSAT more and more customers, but to satisfy them a glass-fibre cable (or rather two of them, dug into the sea bottom) had to be installed so the data can be transferred quickly and also without the temporal disturbances of the previous satellite link to the customers. As a positive side effect, this also meant that the rest of Longyearbyen suddenly had access to an enormous data transfer capacity too, and this, in combination with the archipelago's very low taxation and Norway's legal and political stability, makes Longyearbyen suddenly attractive for many new businesses. Some call centres have already opened, but there are potentially ample possibilities from graphic designers to the data centres of big companies, who could establish themselves here for tax reasons.

While Longyearbyen had about 1,100 inhabitants in the late 1980s, the figure is around 2,100 now and in view of more new establishments, an end to the growth is not yet in sight – even though the former economic benefits of living in Longyearbyen have decreased with sinking state subsidies and rising costs of living.

Longyearbyen today Many visitors are surprised to find a normal town where they expected a pioneer city. This is no rough, tough 'Man's World', but a place for families. There are two kindergartens, a school and a small church built in 1958 to replace its war-damaged predecessor. Svalbard's lone functioning church (there is one in Barentsburg but it is largely symbolic) belongs to the official Norwegian Lutheran Church and has a roomy hall and a vicarage. There is a priest, a catechist and one other member of staff. A service is held most Sundays in Norwegian, with other services sometimes taking place during the summer for visitors. The service is followed by communal tea (or coffee) and biscuits, which also takes place on two evenings a week, usually Tuesday and Friday. Anyone is welcome. The Svalbard priest probably has the largest parish in Europe, but also the most difficult to get around. He manages this by using the Sysselmann's helicopter. Being paid for by the Norwegian state, it is also part of the job of the Church in Longyearbyen to assist other denominations and religions present in the archipelago and provide somebody to conduct services for their communities. Therefore, occasionally Catholic and Orthodox priests are invited and brought to the Polish station in Hornsund or Barentsburg. Only the growing Thai population in Longyearbyen is currently left out, with a Buddhist priest yet to visit the archipelago in any official capacity.

As mentioned, telecommunication is state of the art, including a choice of TV programmes and very fast internet.

The small hospital has only eight beds and a dental surgery but is well equipped to deal with emergencies, staffed as it is with fully qualified surgeons. Extreme cases are flown to the mainland and also pregnant women are urged to give birth on the mainland in case of complications for which the 'Longyearbyen Sykehus' is not prepared. This widely spread town is hardly the most beautiful, but it offers a high standard of living. Houses are bright and comfortable. Amenities include a public swimming pool, a gym, a multi-purpose town hall (also used as a cinema and with a restaurant) and a library. Visitors returning to Svalbard after a long absence would hardly recognise the place. Originally the town stood on the hillside on the left (northwest) side of Longyear Valley (foundations of it are still recognisable above the museum); then it extended along the valley to Sverdrupbyen by the moraine. Next came Nybyen and Haugen, now on the right (southeast) side in the upper part of the valley. The building boom since the 1970s resulted in two new areas further down on the right side: Lia and Blåmyra, both with colourful, attractive and comfortable wooden houses. Because of this, Longyearbyen has historically grown in a circle around the valley.

Changes also happened in the old parts of course, like the Sysselmann's office on Skjæringa (1978, extended in 1988 and almost completely rebuilt and enlarged again after the disastrous fire in 1995) and the power station (1983) in the harbour area (Sjøområde) which supplies the whole town with heat and electricity and which will probably be renewed again in the near future. In Nybyen, the old buildings were tidied up and now house many of Longyearbyen's guests, while three hotels of higher standard in various parts of the town add to a total commercial accommodation capacity for visitors of about 800 beds.

The modern centre of town, developed in the new part of Longyearbyen, placed on the lower right-hand side of the valley since the early 1980s, includes the post office and bank building (1983) and the Lompen (1985), which originally housed the miners' changing rooms and bath, has been transformed with the disappearance of most mining from the Longyearbyen area to a shopping centre. After the supermarket, Svalbardbutikken, moved to the centre, Nybyen lost most of its commerce, and the heart of town is now the pedestrian zone of Lia in the centre. There are two youth clubs, a hospital and an office building, Næringsbygg, for local companies, as well as the Kulturhus, a new cultural building opened in 2011, which features a 3D movie theatre and a café. There is a range of shops including nearly half-a-dozen sports shops, as well as restaurants, a café, a pizzeria and several bars. Most roads are now blacktopped, removing the previous need for unpleasant slushy (or alternatively dusty) walks. Some feel that improvements to the town are overdone and that they risk leading to anonymity and a loss of Longyearbyen's special character.

New dwellings are being built all the time: on the slopes towards the shore road Blåmyra expanded northwards and up the slope, and a new mixed service and housing area is planned on the river side of the centre, though with some flood risks to be taken into account. The shore area (Sjøområde), formerly a chaotic jumble of workshops, warehouses, storage tents, boatsheds and material stores, is being 'sanitised'. One of the most important projects was the new pier Bykaia (Town Pier), started in 1994, which allows cruise ships to come into the town, rather than having to send passengers ashore in tenders. You will no longer need to clamber over four smaller boats moored together side by side because there was no space for them otherwise at the old pier.

Time is needed to appreciate this town and its treasures, and time is something that most visitors don't have. There are many clubs, for instance, including a museum club, a conservation club, and others covering sport, shooting, sailing, surfing and parachuting, dancing, music, a choir and the revue association, which annually prepares a very successful revue with a focus on local themes of the past year. There are film shows several times weekly; the disco isn't just for the young.

The local newspaper *Svalbardposten* comes out on Fridays and gives a good view of what's going on locally, focusing entirely on Svalbard issues. An alternative, the English-language *Ice People*, is published every Tuesday and covers similar topics. The most northerly newspaper in the world, it has a circulation of over 3,000, more than half going out of Svalbard. Newspapers from the mainland are hardly more than one or two days old, thanks to the regular flight connections of up to 16 times a week, and you'll find televisions, radios and high-speed internet connections in every home.

There are three kindergartens and the local school has 12 classes. Further education is available partly through distance learning, which is also well developed on the mainland due to the number of isolated communities there. Svalbard's university was established in 1993.

A favourite leisure activity is to cruise around on snowmobiles (see pages 78–9) as long as there is sufficient snow. Many inhabitants have weekend huts. In the summer holidays, many locals head south, to the mainland and further afield, so that the town is partially depopulated in July and August. A lot of the Norwegians you meet on the street in summer will be seasonal staff or visitors, not residents.

All in all, you can hardly tell Longyearbyen apart from any other Norwegian town, except perhaps for a greater range of leisure options and a more advanced infrastructure compared with a mainland community of similar size.

Still, there are differences:

- Crime in Longyearbyen is very low, and capital crime almost non-existent. An occasional problem in this wealthy society is youth boredom, which can lead to some vandalism.
- Unlike with its mainland communities, the Norwegian state does not want to develop Longyearbyen into a full life-circle community. The settlement is fully suitable for families, but a precondition for living in Longyearbyen is that one has the necessary resources and fitness for managing one's own life. There are no services available for elderly people who need assistance. A few pensioners do live in Longyearbyen, but once they can no longer take care of themselves, they have to leave. The same applies to other persons who need assistance once the family can no longer take care of them.
- The old class society has passed away, but a new one has emerged: while state institutions and state-owned companies (including the SNSK) provide their employees with fairly cheap accommodation, owning most of the buildings

from the company-town era, this is not possible for most private companies. Accordingly, employees of such companies have to rent accommodation at formidable prices which eats up a good portion of their wages. In many cases, a successful applicant has not been able to start a job due to lack of a place to stay and companies therefore may have difficulties with employing needed staff. With the rapid growth of the last few years there has been a severe lack of accommodation, while building is expensive in remote Longyearbyen and people are reluctant to commit themselves to building a house in a place where they know they have to leave once they are older and where future development depends on unpredictable national and international politics.

Scientific research Scientific research has grown considerably over the last couple of decades in Longyearbyen. Major players are the Norsk Polarinstitutt, research work connected to UNIS and the large facilities for atmospheric research, the biggest of them being the research radar station EISCAT. The opening of the Forskningspark quadrupled the area of UNIS and houses an extended local branch of the Norsk Polarinstitutt, an extension of UNIS, the Svalbard Museum, the tourist information office and additional science-related institutions and offices. This has provided the capacity to increase not only scientific activity, but also additionally contribute to a bigger and more varied local population and economy. With the wide range of scientific activity in Longyearbyen and Ny-Ålesund, fruitful contacts, exchanges and co-operation are made easier and increase, which in return makes Svalbard more attractive for further research projects.

Education The University Centre in Svalbard, UNIS, is a joint undertaking of the four Norwegian universities of Oslo, Bergen, Trondheim and Tromsø and was introduced not least as a means of balancing the loss of jobs caused by the closure of Mine 3. In August 1995 the king opened the new campus with its lecture theatre, laboratories, classrooms, study rooms and library – 3,200m² in all. Students and lecturers also have full internet access. The first 23 students were already studying Arctic geology and Arctic geophysics in temporary buildings as far back as 1993. The official language is English in order to attract foreign students, with a capacity so far of 100 places. As some courses last only a few weeks or months, the total number of students at UNIS per year is around 350, about half from outside Norway.

The expansion of UNIS roughly doubled its capacity, and also introduced new Arctic-related studies, especially in the previously lacking social sciences (history, archaeology, sociology). UNIS has a good website at www.uniss.no – it's aimed mainly at students but has much information of use to independent travellers as well.

Tourism Tourism is central to any plan for Longyearbyen and indeed Svalbard as a whole. Official studies carried out to date agree that the main attraction is that Svalbard is as yet unspoiled, and that it should remain so. Whether this is what happens remains to be seen. Certainly, tourism has the most elaborate set of regulations to control it and steer its development. A rapid growth in the first few years following the opening of the first proper accommodation for tourists, in Nybyen in 1989, was no real surprise. Today, Longyearbyen has about 800 tourist beds and the sum of annual overnight stays in Longyearbyen is above 86,000. The top season is April to early May, followed by the summer season with its peak between mid-July and mid-August, while the dark period remains a challenge. Still, the average annual occupancy of tourist accommodation is better than in most places in northern Norway, including North Cape.

WHERE TO STAY

WHERE TO STAY Accommodation in Longyearbyen breaks down essentially into three categories – hotels, guesthouses and apartments. Price schema tend to be rather more complex than is normal in other parts of the world, with almost all having considerable variations depending on the time of year. A couple of these have apartment accommodation available as well, so appear twice in the following listings. In addition to that listed below, a few of the tour operators may have accommodation available for those participating in their programmes.

Prices quoted for hotels are for a double room at high season. Prices during low/off-season can be as little as half these prices. On average, you'll pay below NOK1,000 for a room outside of the summer months, though this could reach as high as NOK2,000 in the peak season, and occasionally higher. Prices for apartments and guesthouses are quoted at high season unless otherwise stated. For locations and listings, see map, page 160.

Hotels

⌂ **Basecamp Trapper's Hotel** (16 rooms) Postboks 316, NO-9171 Longyearbyen; ✆79 02 46 00; e svalbard@basecampspitsbergen.no; www.basecampspitsbergen.no. A small hotel in the centre, built in the 1990s, extended, rebuilt & redecorated by the current owner into a kind of rough 'n' romantic trapper style – a style which ends, however, at the doors to the modern bathrooms. Some like the design, some call it kitsch, though it does have a personal, cosy atmosphere, & a location just above the centre of Longyearbyen. *NOK1,050.*

⌂ **Funken Spitsbergen Hotel** (88 rooms) Postboks 500, NO-9171 Longyearbyen; ✆79 02 62 00; e hotel@spitsbergentravel.no; www. spitsbergentravel.com. Originally built in 1947 (when Longyearbyen was still a company town) as an accommodation block for the company's workers, the Spitsbergen Hotel has been extensively modernised & refurbished but retains its charming traditional maritime atmosphere (ie: gorgeous exposed wood everywhere) while offering some top-notch rooms. It has its own restaurant (with an excellent view overlooking the settlement), conference wing, bar, library, sauna, billiards room & elevator to all floors, & internet access for guests. It's situated in the valley above the centre of Longyearbyen & is closed during Nov, Dec & Jan. *NOK2,350, inc b/fast.*

⌂ **Radisson BLU Polar Hotel Spitsbergen** (67 rooms) Postboks 554, NO-9171 Longyearbyen; ✆79 02 34 50; e sales. longyearbyen@radissonblu.com; www. radissonblu.com. Advertises itself as the world's 'northernmost full service hotel', & that's a pretty accurate description. The accommodation part was used for functionaries during the

Lillehammer Winter Olympic Games in 1994 & was afterwards removed to Longyearbyen & supplemented with a spacious reception/ restaurant/bar/conference building with an excellent view of Adventfjord. Offering a high standard of accommodation & service, the Radisson also boasts its own sauna, internet access for guests, the Barents Pub (a licensed lounge & coffee bar), & the Restaurant Nansen with a view of Isfjorden & Hiorthfjell mountain. Situated between the centre & the harbour area, it is open throughout the year. *NOK1,960 (sgl NOK1,650), inc b/fast.*

⌂ **Svalbard Hotell** (17 rooms) Postboks 538, NO-9171 Longyearbyen; ✆79 02 46 00, e post@ svalbardbooking.com; www.svalbardbooking.com. The archipelago's newest property is this chirpily decorated hotel which opened in 2011. Done up in plush carpets & bright colours & featuring some modern design touches such as massive photographs of polar bears on the walls above the beds, it's located at the end of the main shopping street. *NOK1,190.*

Guesthouses

⌂ **Gjestehuset 102** (31 rooms) Svalbard Wildlife Service, Næringsbygget, Postboks 164, NO-9171 Longyearbyen; ✆79 02 57 16; e info@ gjestehuset102.no; www.gjestehuset102.no. This was formerly known as the Millionærheimen, the residence where the wealthiest miners ('the millionaires') stayed. These days it is a simple guesthouse in a renovated former miners' accommodation block. Clean rooms with simple furniture, toilets/showers shared by several rooms on the same corridor, self-service kitchen, self-service laundry facilities, Wi-Fi, living rooms &

b/fast room. Bicycles for rent. Run by a friendly couple. *Dbl NOK950, dorm bed NOK340; rates inc b/fast.*

🏠 **Haugen Pensjonat** (9 rooms) AS Poli Arctici A/S, Postboks 648, NO-9171 Longyearbyen; ✆79 02 17 05; m 91 38 34 67; e post@haugenpensjonat. no; www.haugenpensjonat.no. Located in Haugen, this guesthouse has double rooms with shared bathroom/kitchen. Internet available. *Dbl NOK1,200.*

🏠 **Mary-Ann's Polarrigg** (42 rooms) Postboks 17, NO-9171 Longyearbyen; ✆79 02 37 02; e info@polarriggen.com; www.polarriggen. com. Simple accommodation in industrial area close to the harbour, hidden away between the technical areas of construction companies. Small & very simple rooms but pleasant public spaces including winter garden, self-service kitchen, restaurant, bar, sauna; personal atmosphere. Toilets/showers shared by several rooms on same corridor. *Dbl NOK855, 4-person room NOK2,800; b/fast NOK135.*

🏠 **Spitsbergen Gjestehus** (75 rooms) Postboks 500, NO-9171 Longyearbyen; ✆79 02 63 00; e guesthouse@spitsbergentravel.no; www.spitsbergentravel.no. Originally miners' accommodation blocks & a former canteen, these buildings were renovated & opened as the first true tourist accommodation in Longyearbyen in 1989. Also known as the Nyben Guesthouse (after the part of town it's in), it has light rooms with simple furniture, & toilets/showers shared by several rooms on the same corridor, all very clean & nice. Other facilities include a self-service kitchen, self-service laundry facilities & living rooms. The former canteen became the reception & b/fast buffet hall. Very friendly, personal & informal with a very helpful reception, the Nyben is also a good place to meet other global nomads. It lies about 1.5km inside the valley, close to the glaciers above Longyearbyen centre. Closed usually from Sep to Feb. *Dbl NOK915, rates inc b/fast.*

Apartments

🏠 **Radisson BLU Polar Hotel Spitsbergen** (27 4-bed apts) Located in an annexe to the hotel, the apartments include a small kitchenette, a bedroom with bunk beds, double sofa bed in the living room, bathroom with shower/WC, & also a TV & telephone. *4-person apt NOK2,560 (NOK1,650 for 1 person); rates inc b/fast.*

🏠 **Spitsbergen Gjestehus** The small apartments have beds for 4 persons: 2 beds in a bedroom, & a double sofa bed in the living room. The rate covers up to 4 people staying in the apartment. *NOK1,960, inc b/fast.*

🏠 **Svalbard Lodge (Scooterutleie)** Postboks 538, NO-9171 Longyearbyen; ✆79 02 46 60; e post@svalbardbooking.com; www. scooterutleie.net. Fully equipped 2- & 3-room apartments holding up to 4 & 6 persons respectively. *2-room apt NOK2,850, 3-room apt NOK2,850; not inc b/fast.*

Camping

⛺ **Longyearbyen Camping** Postboks 6, NO-9171 Longyearbyen; ✆79 02 14 44 or 79 02 10 68; e info@longyearbyen-camping.com; www. longyearbyen-camping.com. Until 1988 this was the only official tourist accommodation in Longyearbyen, & is still the world's northernmost campsite with its own facilities. Nicely situated on the tundra of a flat coastal plain by the bird lagoon & under the airport, with a fantastic view across much of Isfjord including spectacular glaciers & mountains, the campsite is excellent for travellers who want to be as close as possible to nature. The service building is usable only during the summer months (late Jun to early Sep) & includes a cooking & eating room with panoramic view, showers & toilets. Tents & other equipment can be rented. Camping is not allowed elsewhere in a wide area around Longyearbyen, & there is no rental of cabins or places for mobile homes on the campsite itself. No reservations in advance are needed, except for bigger groups or equipment. Your tent should be fairly stable in the wind in case of possible rough weather (though you can rent one for NOK100), & frost is quite rare during the summer season. *Rates: spring (late Apr) NOK150 pp per night, summer (Jun–Sep) NOK100 – outside of these dates you may camp for free but the service buildings will not be open; warm showers (token-operated) NOK10.*

✖ **WHERE TO EAT AND DRINK** Generally, it must be said that Svalbard has no cuisine of its own, nor much locally produced food either, except for a few kinds of game meat and arctic char. Even locally caught fish are absent, because of the lack of a local fishing fleet, and as with the reindeer, seal and whalemeat, the fish on your dish is probably brought over from the mainland. So in general expect mostly good continental food, with a few traditional Norwegian meals. Many of the eating places are based in hotels or guesthouses, and their full details can be found under *Where to stay*. For other locations, see map, page 160.

In addition to the restaurants, there are a number of bars where you can go and hang out. Some of them do food to help you soak up the alcohol.

Restaurants

✗ **Barentz Pub & Spiseri** At the Radisson BLU Polar Hotel (see page 168); ☏ 79 02 34 66; ⊕ noon–02.00 daily. A busy place throughout the week with entertainment & music every so often. The menu includes Italian pizza, steaks, pasta & tapas.

✗ **Brasseri Nansen** At the Radisson BLU Polar Hotel (see page 168); ☏ 79 02 34 57; ⊕ noon–22.30 daily. A modern brasserie with international & Arctic cuisine. Stupendous view of Isfjorden & Hiorthfjell mountain.

✗ **Classic Pizza** Small kiosk at the entrance to Lompensentret that sells cheap pizzas & the world's most northerly kebabs (NOK99).

✗ **Fruene Kaffe & Vinbar** Postboks 454, NO-9171 Longyearbyen; ☏ 79 02 76 40. In the centre of town at the Lompensentret, a coffee shop & deli which serves lunch, Italian coffees, freshly baked & home-made breads, cookies & much-talked-about cakes.

✗ **Funktionærmessen Restaurant** At the Funken Spitsbergen Hotel (see page 168); ⊕ 18.00–22.00 daily. This is in Longyearbyen's historic dining place where the mining company's blue-collar workers used to eat. The menu has been inspired by French cuisine & an interesting collection of wines. Solid views of Longyeardalen valley, glaciers & Hiorthfjell mountain.

✗ **Huset** Postboks 434, NO-9171 Longyearbyen; ☏ 79 02 25 00; e booking@huset.com; www. huset.com; café ⊕ 16.00–midnight Sun–Fri, 14.00–midnight Sat; restaurant ⊕ 19.00–22.00 daily; nightclub ⊕ 23.00–02.00 Fri & Sat, NOK60 entrance fee after midnight. Set a little bit up the valley from the centre of town, this top-notch, white-tablecloth Arctic spot easily serves the best meals in town thanks to its newly installed Swedish chef & manager, & features a fully licensed café, à-la-carte restaurant, nightclub/bar & even a cinema & performance stage. They have an exceptionally well-stocked wine cellar & can arrange tours with wine tasting.

✗ **Kroa** Postboks 150, NO-9171 Longyearbyen; ☏ 79 02 13 00; e post@ kroa-svalbard.no; www. kroa-svalbard.no. Situated in the town centre, this restaurant & bar built out of wood from the old coal mines comes a close second to Huset for both its charm & for the taste & selection of its meals. In addition to the à-la-carte restaurant, they also serve kebabs & pizzas & – hang on to your political correctness here – whale & seal.

✗ **Vinterhagen** At Mary-Ann's Polarriggen (see page 169). The décor is based on the lives of the coal miners & trappers of the old Svalbard, & they have an outdoor bar based around a large wooden hot tub holding up to 8 people. Great menu with some real Arctic delicacies.

Cafés and bars

♀ **Café La Recherche** Galleri Svalbard, Postboks 350, NO-9171 Longyearbyen; ☏ 79 02 23 40; e galleri.svalbard@lokalstyre.no. Up in the Nyben district & set in Svalbard's art gallery, this serves wine, mineral water, beer & various warm drinks.

♀ **Cognachemsen** An attic cognac bar set into Basecamp Spitsbergen's Trapper's Hotel.

♀ **Funken Bar** At the Funken Spitsbergen Hotel (see page 168); ⊕ 18.00–02.00 daily; from 16.00 Fri. More a cosy lounge than a bar, with an open fire, comfy armchairs & a library of books.

♀ **Karls-Berger Pub** ☏ 79 02 25 11; m 90 76 29 33; e mail@karlsbergerpub.no; www. karlsbergerpub.no; ⊕ until 02.00 daily. Set just within the Lompensentret, this cosy & cramped spot has ample charm, though some come for the collection of some 1,000 different whiskies & other spirits.

♀ **Svalbar** ☏ 79 02 50 00; e post@svalbar.no; www.svalbar.no. This spacious bar is packed with a lively atmosphere of vinyl couches, pool tables, a dartboard & football shown round the clock on the TV. They serve very good burgers, & offer probably the cheapest Carlsberg in town (NOK44).

ENTERTAINMENT Entertainment in Longyearbyen is limited, of course, but given its small population can be surprisingly lively.

There is typically something of a **disco** on Friday and Saturday nights in Huset, accompanied by much alcohol, with a second one often taking place in the **Barents Pub**, which tends to serve as a last-ditch pickup joint – in as much as one can exist up here. Major events often also use Huset. The **church hall** [160 B3] has meetings two evenings a week and on Sundays after service. Tea and biscuits are provided. There are one or two film shows a week in the Kulturhuset [160 C3], and occasionally in the multi-purpose hall in Huset. Films are usually months behind release in Europe and are normally shown in their original language with Norwegian subtitles.

The Longyearbyen **Folkebibliotek** [160 C3] (*Public library;* ⊕ *hours are somewhat erratic: 11.00–18.00 Mon, Wed & Thu, 11.00–16.00 Tue & Fri, 11.00–14.00 Sat*) is on the upper floor of the Lompensentret and carries mainly Norwegian titles. Apart from books, it also offers a free-of-charge internet terminal.

SHOPPING AND OTHER PRACTICALITIES Most of these are in the town centre (see map, page 160), many in the Lompensentret [160 C3] – the shopping centre in the middle of Longyearbyen. A couple of the hotels and bars have associated souvenir shops selling, well, souvenirs.

Bydrift Longyearbyen Postboks 475, NO-9171 Longyearbyen; ☎79 02 23 00; e bydrift@lokalstyre.no; www.lokalstyre.no. To all intents & purposes the local administration of Longyearbyen, responsible for supply of power, water & sanitation, road works, the fire brigade & property management.

Gullgruva [160 C3] Postboks 522, NO-9171 Longyearbyen; ☎79 02 18 16; e troldmyr@online. no. Selling gold & silver necklaces, silverware, souvenirs, gifts, jumpers, T-shirts, fleeces & so on.

Ing G Paulsen Postboks 490, NO-9171 Longyearbyen; ☎79 02 32 00; e igp@spitsbergentravel.no; www.spitsbergentravel.no/igp/. Linked to Spitsbergen Travel, they supply snowmobiles (& associated bits & bobs), rifles, computers & other large items.

Isbjørnbutikken (Polar Bear Store) Postboks 437, NO-9170 Longyearbyen; ☎79 02 11 10. A central kiosk & souvenir shop with long opening hours.

Marina van Dijk Postboks 72, NO-9171 Longyearbyen; ☎79 02 11 96. This long-standing resident of Svalbard creates jewellery inspired by Arctic nature, silver- & goldware & jewellery from local materials. Many of her works can be purchased at Galleri Svalbard (see page 172).

Norsk Polarinstitutt [160 D2] www.npolar.no. Based at the Forskningsparken (the same building as the Sysselmann & museum), they sell a great collection of hiking maps & guidebooks as well as various scientific paraphernalia.

Pole Position Spitsbergen [160 B1] Postboks 514, NO-9171 Longyearbyen; ☎79 02 49 90; e mail@pole-position.no; www.pole-position.no. A logistical company offering support & agency services to ships, aircraft & expeditions. They're found down in the port area.

RaBi's Bua Postboks 385, NO-9171 Longyearbyen; ☎79 02 10 48; m 48 27 62 04; e lrkb@start.no. Knitwear, embroidery, womenswear, childrenswear, curtains & accessories. They also repair clothing, should you need it.

Radisson BLU Polar Hotel Radisson BLU Polar Hotel (see page 168). Souvenir shop.

Skinnboden [160 C3] NO-9170 Longyearbyen; ☎79 02 10 88; www.skinnboden.no. This excellent clothing shop on the main drag across from Basecamp Spitsbergen specialises in seal- & reindeer-hide shoes & bags. They sell pairs of elf-like seal-skin boots (NOK2,100) that have effectively become the UGGs of Norway & are all the rage in Oslo these days. You can also finally pick up that polar bear hide (& head) for the living room – for a cool NOK80,000 – as well as knives, postcards & a few touristic books.

SpareBank 1 Nord-Norge [160 C3] Postboks 518, NO-9171 Longyearbyen; ☎91 50 22 44; www. snn.no; ⊕ 10.00–15.30 daily (cash desk 10.00–13.00). Offers a full range of banking services, including cashpoint, foreign currency, insurance, cash withdrawals, cheques & foreign exchange service to & from accounts abroad.

Sportscenteret [160 B5] Elvesletta, NO-9170 Longyearbyen; ☎79 02 15 35; e post@ sportscenteret.no; www.sportscenteret.no. Sports & outdoor gear.

Svalbardbutikken [160 C3] NO-9170 Longyearbyen; ☎79 02 25 20; www. svalbardbutikken.no. The Svalbard branch of the Norwegian Co-op network, the shop stocks a variety of articles including groceries, fresh bakery products, clothing, electrical items, photo products, cosmetics, pharmaceutical products, gift items, souvenirs, toys & alcohol – the only place in town where you can buy a tipple, in fact. You need to make it there early to get fresh milk or bread.

Svalbardhalle [160 B5] NO-9171 Longyearbyen; ☎79 02 23 05 or 79 02 18 18. Sports centre, swimming pool, sauna, squash, indoor climbing wall, indoor target range & a workout room. *A swim costs NOK65.*

WHAT TO SEE AND DO

Svalbard Museum [160 D2] (*Postboks 521, NO-9171 Longyearbyen;* ☎ *79 02 64 92 or 79 02 64 90;* e *kontor@svalbardmuseum.no; www.svalbardmuseum.no;* ⊕ *high season 10.00–17.00 daily, low season 12.00–17.00; entry fee NOK75)* The museum is Longyearbyen's biggest attraction and is visited by 15,000 people a year. The museum was founded in 1981 and is located in an old stable, one of the oldest buildings still standing. It is well organised according to themes, with topics covered including geography, climate, geology, flora, fauna, old whaling and trapping activities, mining, World War II and Svalbard's role in polar exploration. The realistic exhibition of mining in the roof space, complete with sound effects, was put together in 1991 in recognition of the 75th anniversary of the SNSK concern.

Spitsbergen Airship Museum [160 B3] (*Postboks 644, NO-9171 Longyearbyen;* m *91 38 34 67 or* m *95 73 57 42;* e *ingunn@spitsbergenairshipmuseum.com; spitsbergenairshipmuseum.com;* ⊕ *12.00–17.00 Wed–Sun; entry fee NOK75)* The most recent addition to Longyearbyen's coterie of museums, the Spitsbergen Airship Museum retells the story of the role that airships have played in the exploration of the Svalbard archipelago. It houses an impressive collection of artefacts and memorabilia from the various expeditions, with more promised for the future. Across the street from the church.

Galleri Svalbard [160 A6] (*Postboks 475, NO-9171 Longyearbyen;* ☎*79 02 23 40;* e *galleri.svalbard@lokalstyre.no; www.gallerisvalbard.no; admission NOK70)* Sited up near Nyben, the gallery has an exhibition of historical maps, a slide show about Svalbard and works by well-known Norwegian artists such as Kåre Tveters. Next to it is **Longyearbyen Kunstsenter**, where artists and craftsmen can rent rooms as studios, workshops and sales rooms.

Global Seed Vault [160 A1] This 'doomsday' seed bank was constructed in 2008 to hold the seeds representing several hundred thousand crop varieties from every part of the globe. Though only professional researchers can visit the vault (for obvious reasons), the sleek cement structure, built 120m into the mountain, is interesting to gaze at from the outside.

Atelier Aino [160 A6] (*Postboks 372, NO-9171 Longyearbyen;* ☎ *79 02 10 02;* m *48 12 02 27;* e *ag@ainogrib.com; www.ainogrib.com; admission free)* The artist Aino Grib exhibits paintings, drawings and prints inspired by and painted in Svalbard. The gallery is now located in Galleri Svalbard.

HISTORY The presence of coal on Brøggerhalvøya had been known for centuries. Christian Anker's Green Harbour Coal Company annexed the area in 1909, but did little with it before selling it to a group from Ålesund, western Norway, in 1916. That coal could be extracted commercially must have been realised earlier, as the former German weather station was moved to Kvadehuken in 1914 to be nearer the coalfield. This was the forerunner of the Norwegian geophysics station of 1920–24.

By then the world's most northerly permanent settlement, Ny-Ålesund was founded in 1916 by the Kings Bay Kull Compani A/S as a coal mine. Unlike other Svalbard fields, coal seams here lay near the coast, well below sea level and the permafrost, conditions which led to many explosions and deaths. Early production was in any case not significant, and experiments with a fishery and a hotel (Nordpolhotellet) had already been made before World War II.

In 1945 coal mining began again in earnest. By the end of the 1950s there were 200 people in these parts, with a full-time school, hospital and newspaper. From 1948 to 1963 there were more explosions, resulting in 80 casualties. The final explosion, on 5 November 1962, could be heard as far away as Longyearbyen, and the Norwegian administration duly closed the mine officially the following year.

After several years of no activity, Ny-Ålesund re-emerged as a research base, with the former mining company now transformed into a management company which runs the settlement, and finances itself mostly through selling services and renting out facilities to its customers – mainly research institutions. Its former long name – Kings Bay Kull Compani (KBKC) has been shortened to Kings Bay AS.

As reminders of the mining period, there are old buildings and a lovingly restored locomotive (once again, the most northerly) which had been used for transporting coal to the loading station. In the 1990s, investment was made in an attempt to retain historic features, recalling polar exploration and mining activities. A small museum has since been opened for this purpose.

Historically, Ny-Ålesund is best known for its role in 20th-century polar exploration and for its aviation pioneers. Graf Zeppelin was here in 1910. Roald Amundsen and Lincoln Ellsworth were here in 1925 on their way to the North Pole in two Dorniers, though they reached only 88°N before having to turn back. Byrd started from Ny-Ålesund in 1926 in his attempt to become the first to fly over the Pole, an attempt that he claimed was successful (though one which has since been disputed), and in the same year Amundsen and Nobile set off over the Pole to Alaska in their airship *Norge*. Their anchor pylon is still here, just outside Ny-Ålesund, but the hangar has long since gone. Nobile was also back in 1928 as part of the ill-fated *Italia* expedition.

There are many memorials in and around the place: Amundsen's bust near the Norsk Polarinstitutt, the *Italia* memorial, the Amundsen–Ellsworth memorial, and the memorial to those who lost their lives in the mine.

Furthermore, the place can boast a host of 'most northerly' records, among them the post office (in the well-known, tiny old green hut in summer only; otherwise, it's handled by the reception in the community centre), the art gallery, the steam train and the greenhouse.

NY-ÅLESUND TODAY Ny-Ålesund is above all a research base, with a remarkable history that you can see evidence of in its buildings and design. Its former landmark, the ESRO satellite antenna domes of the 1970s, have disappeared in favour of the huge geodetic telescope and the survey station for atmospheric studies on Zeppelinfjellet which has its own cable car (though, alas, it's reserved for staff and

6

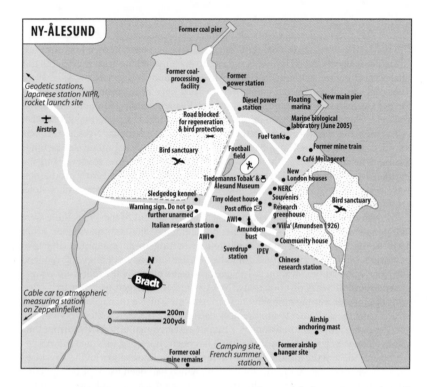

NY-ÅLESUND

Former coal pier

Former coal-processing facility

Former power station

Geodetic stations, Japanese station NIPR, rocket launch site

Diesel power station

Floating marina

New main pier

Airstrip

Road blocked for regeneration & bird protection

Marine biological laboratory (June 2005)

Fuel tanks

Bird sanctuary

Football field

Former mine train

Café Mellageret

New London houses

Tiedemanns Tobak' & Ålesund Museum

NERC

Sledgedog kennel

Tiny oldest house

Souvenirs

Bird sanctuary

Warning sign. Do not go further unarmed

Post office

Research greenhouse

AWI

Italian research station

Amundsen bust

'Villa' (Amundsen 1926)

AWI

Sverdrup station

IPEV

Community house

N

Chinese research station

Bradt

0 — 200m
0 — 200yds

Cable car to atmospheric measuring station on Zeppelinfjellet

Airship anchoring mast

Former coal mine remains

Camping site, French summer station

Former airship hangar site

scientists only). The main focus here is on atmospheric and climatic research, and geophysics. The Arctic Marine Laboratory opened at the beginning of June 2005, and has increased the importance of both ongoing and new biological programmes. It is also the northernmost lab of its kind in the world. Smaller fields of research include glaciology, geology, geomorphology, zoology and botany.

To provide optimal conditions for research into such subjects as atmospheric studies, which depend on minimal local emissions, high environmental standards are a key issue to the settlement. This is visible for instance in the elaborate sorting system for rubbish for eventual recycling, the modern, top-notch diesel power plant, and the internal attempts at reducing exhausts, for instance by successfully promoting non-motorised transport for the employees and the scientists living here. This emphasis on research as the main industry has led also to a cool-ish attitude towards tourism. To a limited extent, tourism is welcome because of the extra income it brings in – especially from cruise ships, which pay high landing fees. But at the same time the potential conflict between tourism and research is universally acknowledged. Therefore, no active steps are taken to promote tourism in Ny-Ålesund. Furthermore, seats on the flights between Longyearbyen and Ny-Ålesund, and accommodation, are reserved first of all for scientists and official visitors, while tourists can book these services only at short notice (about a week in advance), and only then if there is any free capacity left.

Kings Bay AS, the owner of both the settlement and all the land around it, is working hard to mend earlier damage done to the vegetation, which is a long-lasting project under Arctic conditions. Both locals and visitors are expected to stay strictly on the roads, taking no shortcuts or strolls on the tundra, in order to give its recovery a chance.

Fishing is another activity which brings humans into contact with Ny-Ålesund; trawlers stop here for replenishment, post and a land excursion in between days out on the sea.

Today the scientific community of Ny-Ålesund is very international. Nations with their own stations are China (since 2003–04, and the biggest station of all), France, Germany (AWI – the second-oldest permanent station since 1988), Great Britain (NERC), Italy, Japan, Norway (Norsk Polarinstitutt, the oldest permanent station, having come into being in the late 1960s), South Korea and the USA. Together with the technical and administrative staff of the Kings Bay AS, there are about 50 winterers, while summer sees some roughly 200 inhabitants.

Ny-Ålesund's importance as an international scientific community has risen over the years, starting with the German Koldewey Station of 1988, which is located all year round in the 'Blue House'. The station is supported by the Alfred Wegener Institute (AWI) in Bremerhaven and is used for extended studies (especially in meteorology) and as a base for other undertakings. There is a French summer research camp near Ny-Ålesund and the new French base in the settlement. Cambridge University has a material base in the village, as well as camps inland. Britain's biologists can come to the Harland Station of the National Environmental Research Council (NERC); the Japanese have an all-year National Institute for Polar Research (NIPR) base at the airfield; and the Italian Instituto sull'Inquinamento Atmosferico has been operative since 1996 after a setback during building in 1995. Of primary importance is the **Norsk Polarinstitutt**, which arrived here in 1968 and moved into a modern designed building in 1998.

A high-tech geodetic measuring station with a huge parabolic precision telescope replaced the former ESRO station for measurements of the Earth's movements (changes of shape) and sea-level changes. In its vicinity is the launch site for research rockets.

With the increase of research activity in Ny-Ålesund, the growing potential for conflict and competition, together with a negative influence on the state of the local environment (which at the same time is of utmost importance for many of the projects) became apparent. To counter this, a co-ordinating committee (NySMAC) has been established, which tries to arrange compromises and joint solutions between the various interests. This complements the efforts of Kings Bay AS itself, which is also interested in a good balance between more research activity (and thereby a better economy for itself) and conditions that are attractive for existing and new projects (including environmental issues).

OTHER PRACTICALITIES If you are interested in visiting Ny-Ålesund, please remember that the place is a scientific settlement and only receives tourists on day trips arriving with cruise ships. All of Brøgger Peninsula is the private property of the Kings Bay AS which gives it the right to impose restrictive regulations. If you intend to visit Ny-Ålesund by plane, you are requested to contact Kings Bay AS (NO-9173 Ny-Ålesund; ✆ 79 02 72 00; e booking@kingsbay.no; www.kingsbay.no (inc webcam)) to learn in further detail what might be possible and arrange something. Kings Bay AS owns the airport and harbour and the only ways to get here, beside a cruise, are by a small boat or skidoo (and this would only be permitted for permanent residents of Svalbard). There are no facilities geared towards tourists – this includes accommodation and places to buy food.

WHAT TO SEE AND DO As a service to visitors and at the same time a measure of reducing possible conflicts, Kings Bay AS has developed an excellent multi-lingual system of information boards spread all over Ny-Ålesund, which mark a circular tour of about 1.5km on the roads around the small settlement. Starting from the pier, there is to the left the picturesque old steam train of the mine near Mellageret ('Flour Storage', today a café run by and for the locals). Next, you pass the tiny London Houses, which were relocated here from their original place across the bay in the English pioneer mine of Ny London. This is followed by the British NERC station while on the other side of the street is the local museum and then, on the left-hand side again, the tiny, light-green post office building next to the small, oldest-surviving house of the settlement from 1907.

By now, you will have reached the central square with the Nordpolhotellet (one of the accommodation buildings for guests), the Amundsen bust, the modern building of the Norsk Polarinstitutt and, towards the inner part of the fjord, the community-centre house (canteen and social rooms for people living in Ny-Ålesund and the King's Bay administration – there is no access for visitors). If you pass the community centre (known as the 'Service Building'), you will have an open view of the metal anchoring mast of the airships of Amundsen and Nobile (1926–28) against a panorama of the inner fjord with its big glaciers – please stop here without walking out onto the tundra. Next to you you'll find the Chinese, French and Korean stations. Turn round and follow the road on the upper side of the central square westwards, passing the Norsk Polarinstitutt to your left and the German AWI Koldewey Station (the blue house) on the right, then to the left again the Italian station (in the second row) with the German laboratory building in the third row behind it. The road leads to a junction, where signs ask non-armed visitors not to follow the various gravel roads leading from there out of the settlement. Here one comes across the local sledge-dog kennel, usually with some dried seals hanging there as dog food. Nowadays, the dogs are kept purely for pleasure and as tour comrades and attentive polar bear guards when out on camping tours. Turning to your right, you begin to wander in the direction of the fjord again, and towards the modern diesel power plant, with some concrete towers further in the distance (an old power station and coal-processing plant). Turning right again, you will soon be back to the old steam train. Set in the same building as a small visitor's centre is a small museum which offers an exhibition on Ny-Ålseund's history from the establishment of the coal mining facility up to today's international research community; it consists largely of various pieces of equipment and photographs.

☞ **Attention:** The tundra immediately off the roads is partially protected as bird sanctuaries – please stay on the road, as by doing so you will also minimise your impact on the tundra. From the road, you will have a good chance in summer of observing barnacle geese, eider and long-tailed ducks – and, of course, the arctic terns, some of whom breed on the roadside and attack anybody who comes close to their well-camouflaged eggs or young on the bare ground. If you are attacked, circle with an arm raised and a finger above your head and keep on moving instead of stopping and watching – the attacks will end after a few metres, saving the bird and the unprotected offspring valuable energy. Remember, all birds are protected – damaging one of them by hitting it with a stick, rucksack or umbrella means starvation for that bird and its offspring and is forbidden. People have more brain than the bird, so move on a few metres instead. Do not go near or touch scientific instruments and (as always) respect the cultural landmarks in the area. The risk of polar bear encounters outside the settlement has to be highlighted and appropriate precautions should be taken.

HISTORY Sveagruva is situated at the end of Van Mijenfjorden. Shipping is made difficult by the Akseløya, which blocks off the fjord almost completely at its mouth, causing strong tidal currents in the narrow sounds and keeping the winter ice in the fjord for much longer.

Swede Bertil Högbom arrived here in 1910, an event which, along with subsequent expeditions, led to the founding of a coal mine by Aktiebolaget Spetsbergens Svenska Kolfält in 1917. It was subsequently sold to Svenska Stenkolaktiebolaget Spetsbergen in 1921, but given up after a fire in 1925. The company formed to build up operations again, Nya Svenska Stenkolaktiebolgaet Spetsbergen, had no success and sold on to the SNSK in 1934. The Swedish era had mined 400,000 tonnes.

From 1934 to 1937 there were approximately 30 workers busying themselves in Sveagruva, but no real commercial work was carried out as SNSK concentrated their efforts on Longyearbyen. The mine was destroyed by U-boat attack in 1944, rebuilt in 1946 and produced 200,000 tonnes of coal up until 1949, when it was again closed. (Longyearbyen's productivity was sufficient for SNSK's needs.)

In the following decades, coal reserves were investigated and a plan drawn up at the end of the 1970s provided for an annual production of a million tonnes a year, with a population of 700. In reality, the plan was only partly met, due to difficulties in extraction and shipping. Still, there were 80 to 100 workers employed from 1980 onwards and the settlement's infrastructure was greatly improved by 1987, by which time the world market had led to a fall in prices so the mine was forced to close yet again.

Eleven men maintained the mine to production standards and occasional exploratory work was carried out. Remaining coal stocks and the few tonnes produced here and there were shipped out now and again.

From the mid 1990s onward, Svea again experienced a quick expansion of activity, leading to its present status as one of the most modern and productive coal mines in the world, replacing Longyearbyen as the main Norwegian mining place in the archipelago. It has an annual production of about three million tonnes of high-quality coal which is sold to a number of European customers and operates – quite uniquely in Europe – profitably. As the shipping season is very short – Akseløya, which blocks the entrance of Van Mijenfjord almost entirely, is the reason fjord ice forms earlier and lasts longer here – a new and efficient coal port needed to be constructed, too. This is busy in summer to load one big coal ship (PANMAX class, up to 70,000 tonnes) after the other, which have to pass the narrow sound at Akseløya on the way out and in. In view of this critical passage, pilot service is compulsory here, plus a standby tug boat, to avoid a possible accident which could harm the environment.

Svea is run basically like an oil platform – workers are flown in and out for weekly shifts from and to Longyearbyen. In Svea, there is a focus on hard work, while private life takes place in Longyearbyen. Only very few of the employees live in Svea continuously for longer periods and due to political guidelines of the state as the owner, the SNSK is not interested in developing Svea into a normal settlement with a wide range of facilities, which would be at the expense of Longyearbyen. Svea is deliberately run like a remote extension of Longyearbyen.

In addition, some research activity is done in Svea occasionally, using existing buildings as a base. SINTEF, a technology-oriented research organisation in Norway, has often been active with various projects.

OTHER PRACTICALITIES The SNSK, as the owner of Svea, runs a very clear policy of restricting activity in Svea primarily to coal mining. Tourism is not encouraged and there have been a number of episodes where unannounced hikers were shown very clearly that they were not welcome. It can appear that Svea intentionally tries to avoid any reputation as a place that could serve independent travellers as a stopover. The company website www.snsk.no does, however, have some photos and a very brief description of the town.

Facilities and services Put simply, there is no infrastructure available in Svea to visitors other than official guests of the mining company and specifically, no access to their canteen, accommodation or supplies. The flights between Longyearbyen and Svea are run under the management of the SNSK and are not offered to others, as the SNSK requires practically all of the capacity for its own purposes.

There is no passenger ship service between Svea and the other settlements or the mainland, except for the occasional and irregular calls of supply and coal ships.

BARENTSBURG

HISTORY Grønfjorden was for centuries a resting place for whalers and a camp for hunters. Industrial activity started after 1900, with a whale-processing base by the company A/S Spitsbergen of Tønsberg (1905–12) on Finneset, supplemented by a seasonal post office at Green Harbour (1908) that opened for summer tourists (until 1932) and the Norwegian all-year telegraph station from 1911 until 1930, when it moved to Longyearbyen.

Simultaneously, interest in coal extraction also began at the turn of the century with the arrival of the Kulkompaniet Isefjord Spitsbergen in 1900. ACC, founder company of Longyearbyen, annexed a large field on Grønfjorden's east side in 1905 and three Norwegian companies arrived in 1908 and 1909. The first organised exploratory extraction started in 1912 and in 1916 a new concern, Store Norske Spitsbergen Kulkompani A/S (SNSK), together with ACC, bought out most of the smaller businesses. Others went, via a Russian firm, to the Dutch NV Nederlandsche Spitsbergen Compagnie (Nespico) by 1920. They were the first to officially operate in Grønfjord and effectively founded Barentsburg. In 1932, the settlement and its surrounding lands passed to the Soviet state-owned Trust Arcticugol, having ended up in economic trouble during the aftermath of the global economic depression of the late 1920s. Since then, the mining settlement has remained the private property of this Russian state company, just like the land of Longyearbyen, and many of its buildings are owned by the SNSK. Accordingly, the Russian company can deny access to the settlement for visitors on the legal basis of being the landowner, but the settlement nevertheless remains under Norwegian sovereignty.

Barentsburg was largely destroyed in the course of the Allied evacuation of 1941 and finally by the battleship *Tirpitz* in 1943 during its attack on the garrison of exiled Norwegian troops based there. The Soviets began rebuilding in 1948 and by 1962, with the closure of Grumant, Barentsburg had become the most important Soviet settlement in Svalbard. Up until now, Barentsburg has been the site of the Svalbard headquarters of the Russian mining company Trust Arcticugol (head office in Moscow) and also of Svalbard's Russian consulate, which moved into a then-impressive new building in 1983. Before 1990, Barentsburg's population was similar to that of Longyearbyen, home to between 1,100 and 1,450 inhabitants. A new power station was built in 1975 and a large research centre in 1984.

Social provisions in Barentsburg were impressive and extensive and included a kindergarten, a school, a large hospital, a library and a 50m swimming pool.

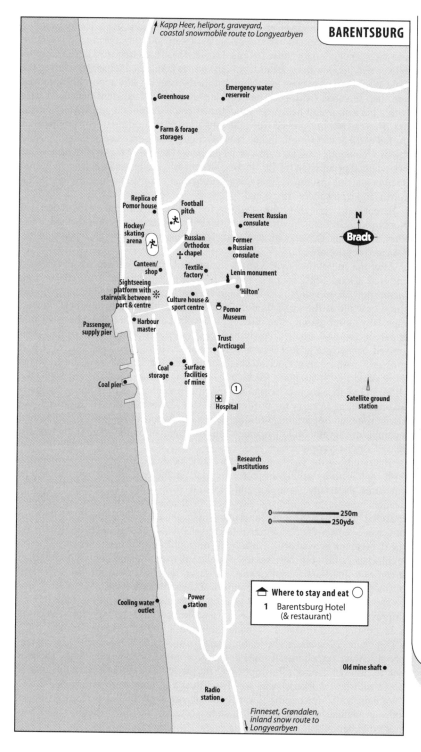

Kapp Heer, heliport, graveyard,
coastal snowmobile route to Longyearbyen

BARENTSBURG

Greenhouse

Emergency water
reservoir

Farm & forage
storages

Replica of
Pomor house

Football
pitch

Present Russian
consulate

N

Hockey/
skating
arena

Russian
Orthodox
chapel

Former
Russian
consulate

Bradt

Canteen/
shop

Textile
factory

Lenin monument

Sightseeing
platform with
stairwalk between
port & centre

Culture house &
sport centre

'Hilton'

Pomor
Museum

Passenger,
supply pier

Harbour
master

Trust
Arcticugol

Coal
storage

Surface
facilities
of mine

Coal pier

①

Satellite ground
station

✚
Hospital

Research
institutions

0 ────── 250m
0 ────── 250yds

Cooling water
outlet

Power
station

⌂ **Where to stay and eat** ◯

1 Barentsburg Hotel
(& restaurant)

Old mine shaft ●

Radio
station

Finneset, Grøndalen,
inland snow route to
Longyearbyen

The heliport is at Kapp Heer, north of the town. Opened in 1960, it was extended in 1976–78 and contains hangars, workshops, a warehouse, a large radar installation and accommodation for those stationed there. There used to be five large transport helicopters, but now there are only two, the others being used for spares. During the Cold War, there were open suspicions on the Norwegian side about this oversized and then secretive (with even its own canteen and kindergarten) helicopter base with a huge crew and helicopter models that could be refitted quickly for combat use. These suspicions proved true following the declassification of documents after the fall of the Soviet Union. Today, Trust Arcticugol have expressed interest in using the two remaining craft for commercial purposes (ie: tourist flights) but have so far been denied permission by the Norwegians, on account of the lack of the required documents and insurance. There is a geophysical observatory nearby, where the aurora and atmosphere are studied.

Barentsburg is also the centre for Russian mineral exploration in Nordenskiöldlandet. Previous expeditions have caused friction between the Russians and the Sysselmann due to the heavy use of tracked vehicles which has damaged vegetation.

After the end of the Soviet Union, the remote Russian settlements in Svalbard endured a hard time: supplies suddenly became irregular and unreliable and, increasingly, hard *valuta* (stable foreign currencies) was expected in payment for supplies while at the same time the customers for the coal in northern Russia, especially power plants, often did not pay at all. Shortages in Barentsburg became apparent: food became extremely basic and often went out of date or had even arrived partly rotten, fuel was lacking for boats and helicopters, the mine had problems with getting much-needed spare parts and at one time the Russians even asked the Norwegians for help – regarding clothes for children. Soon, the children had to leave the Russian settlements in Svalbard as the mining company was not willing to carry the burden of the extra costs they caused. Research – in Soviet times an important additional activity in Barentsburg – which maintained a complex of several buildings including accommodation for some 100 scientists, ceased almost completely.

Thankfully, at the right time, the inventive local director began experimenting with capitalism by selling an increasing part of the coal production to Western countries, especially Denmark and Holland, from whom he received urgently needed supplies in return. As elsewhere in Russia today, this kind of business included high margins for the Russian top management involved, enabling the local director to send both of his children to English private schools and to boast of being the richest man in Svalbard – while being untroubled by the taxation system for the archipelago, which officially has to be applied all over Svalbard but is ignored when it comes to the Russian settlements. However, to some extent this self-organised business saved the Russian settlements over these difficult years.

The lack of sufficient supplies of proper materials for the mines took its toll: improvisation, including the use of a cheaper but less safe type of explosives, caused a devastating coal dust and methane explosion in the Barentsburg mine in 1997, killing some 20 workers and setting parts of the mine ablaze, while the violent pressure wave ruined installations in the mine tunnels over a wide range. The year before, an even greater catastrophe had hit the Russian settlements: a full charter plane with new workers on its way from Russia to Longyearbyen crashed into a mountain while descending towards the airport, with all 143 persons on board killed immediately. In memory of these two catastrophes, an Orthodox chapel was erected in Barentsburg.

BARENTSBURG TODAY Since 2000, Russia has begun to remember its remote outposts in Svalbard and their strategic value. Subsidies for Trust Arcticugol increased (though efficiency didn't), and sadly the standard of living in Barentsburg still remains lower than in Soviet times, despite considerable donations of clothes, old computers, and so on by the Norwegians. At least the kindergarten and the primary school have been reopened, though in a very improvised way. A clear sign for renewed interest is the increase of Russian research and the first steps taken towards establishing a new mine at Colesbukta, where Russia used much of its political muscle against Norway, not only to get permission but also to minimise all claims by environmental and other laws which require detailed documentation on minimising the effects on the environment. The new mine is intended to be connected by road to Barentsburg and to replace the current Barentsburg mine, which is limited in its reserves and geologically difficult. (The **Rusanov Memorial Hut** on Rusanovodden, Colesbukta, is also worthy of mention. Rusanov's Svalbard travels, before World War I, were the precursors to Russian settlement and mining in the area. Unfortunately, written information is in Russian only.)

Changes in the restructuring of the Russian presence in Svalbard take time – not least because there are strong rivalries behind the scenes competing for funds granted by the Russian state, with many influential players on various levels wanting to have their share. In the meantime, Barentsburg and especially Pyramiden deteriorate, thus increasing the future costs. With investment in the infrastructure and an effective management, Barentsburg could have the most attractive port of Svalbard as an additional source of income, due to its proximity to the open sea and the fewest ice problems in winter of all Svalbard's settlements, making it a suitable place for a service port for fishing and other marine activities in the area. With the coming road to Colesbukta, a road connection also to Longyearbyen and thus to the island's main airport would become plausible, removing yet another advantage of Longyearbyen. However, such a concept seems far away when one looks at Barentsburg today. The hotel is standing mostly empty and tourism is accepted only as long as it brings easy, quick money, relying on the Norwegian day cruises and snowmobile groups who come here on a speedy visit and pay for the use of harbour and guidance. This requires no investment and no marketing, using the existing infrastructure and staff on the payroll of the mining company. Income achieved by this minimal strategy is estimated at somewhere under NOK1 million per year, which goes only a small way towards improving the economy of Barentsburg. Considerable potential is ignored here as it seems to be more attractive for top management and possibly also some of its allies in the Russian ministries to focus on acquisition of high state subsidies rather than trigger developments that could reduce the current overwhelming need for state funding.

Nowadays, the population of Barentsburg is around 350 (including about 30 children) after several tranches of reductions. Curtailing of wages, deteriorating food supplies and poor hospital equipment have led to unrest and even hunger strikes and increasing pressure by the top management on the workforce to keep information about the situation under wraps. The dissatisfaction of the population leads also to more aggression, which erupts in occasional violence, especially in connection with drinking. In a sensational case of 2005, a Norwegian court passed a sentence of just four years on a man convicted of committing murder in Barentsburg the previous year; the court accepted that social unrest and oppression in Barentsburg to some extent offered mitigating circumstances in favour of the convict.

GETTING THERE AND AROUND The Russian small tug boats and their helicopters have no certificates for commercial passenger transport, and therefore the only means of transport between Longyearbyen and Barentsburg is, in summer, the almost daily return **boat excursions** from Longyearbyen to Barentsburg (which offer a detour to one of the glaciers in Trygghamna or Ymerbukta on the north side of Isfjord). These include a stop of about 1½–two hours in Barentsburg – just enough for a quick look around the town and museum. A local Barentsburg guide of varying English-language competence is generally included in the excursion price.

In addition to these day cruises, some of the longer expedition cruises (three to 14 days) offered by ships based in Svalbard over the summer include a stop in Barentsburg.

In winter, if there is enough snow and acceptable weather, Barentsburg is one of the two standard day excursions for **snowmobile** groups, who also stay there for about two hours.

Between these seasons, Barentsburg may be just about inaccessible for tourists.

On foot, with good terrain conditions, it takes about two or three days through 50km of wilderness to walk from Longyearbyen to Barentsburg.

Direct access to Barentsburg from outside Svalbard is close to impossible. There are two or three calls by supply ships and some coal ships. Furthermore, very few bigger cruise ships include Barentsburg on their Nordic round tour.

WHERE TO STAY AND EAT

⌂ **Barentsburg Hotel** NO-9178 Barentsburg; ☏ 79 02 18 14; m 95 30 68 86. Built in the 1980s & renovated in 2012, with a number of double rooms that are also available for single use. Spacious rooms (mini apartments) with simple furniture & their own bathroom with shower/toilet/washing basin, all of a very simple standard, comparable with Western standards of the 1960s. There is a restaurant with carefully carved wooden wall covers that serves also as an eating & drinking room for the rare hotel guests served by the small hotel kitchen. Small staff with limited command of English, but friendly. Owing to very low use, the staff may be difficult to find; making contact in advance can turn out to be difficult too, but if you keep trying you should be able to get through. The hotel bar serves warm meals to tourists for around NOK100 per meal. They don't get many guests, so try to give some advance warning before turning up. *Dbl cNOK600 per room per night, without b/fast.*

OTHER PRACTICALITIES Only the souvenir shops in the culture house and in the hotel are accessible to tourists – there are no other shops except the post office in the hotel. Also, there are no tourist activities offered except for guidance for groups and the folklore show on special order for bigger groups.

WHAT TO SEE AND DO From a tourist's point of view, apart from the unusual experience of seeing a Russian settlement within a Norwegian archipelago, the **Pomor Museum** is clearly worth a visit – with a remarkable geological collection of rock types, minerals and fossils and an at least equally interesting, rich collection of excavated artefacts from the early Russian hunting settlements (excavated by the co-founder of the museum, Professor Vadim Starkov). These two collections are unparalleled anywhere else in the archipelago. Though the exhibits are mostly in Russian, it's well worth a look.

Another surprising aspect is the local **farm** with cows and pigs (though their stocks were massively reduced in winter 2003–04) and the local **greenhouse** – all this an answer to the problems caused by the months of isolation over the winter, where no fresh supplies can be expected without an airport. Lenin still has an attentive eye on the settlement with a statue in his honour, and there's plenty of typically Soviet (and typically dilapidated) architecture, with big concrete and brick buildings standing in contrast to the small, individual wooden houses in Longyearbyen. In the hotel, there is also the Barentsburg post office of the Norwegian post, run by Russian staff when needed. If the sports hall is open, have a look into the impressive swimming hall (shoes off, please, and don't even think of going swimming in the rarely clean water) with large green plants inside standing in stark contrast to Arctic scenery outside the windows. For some cruises, the excellent local amateur groups perform their lively and enthusiastic folklore show, which is worth visiting even by visitors who normally try to avoid such things.

The souvenir trade has been confined to a central souvenir shop, controlled by the top management, which at the same time stopped the former souvenir market, which was not only more picturesque but also gave locals the chance of earning some extra money. Accordingly, it is doubtful how much of the income from souvenir sales actually helps the normal population. On sale are mainly painted, traditional wooden items, many of them made locally, plus some paintings by Russian amateur artists. Certainly, these are true made-in-Svalbard souvenirs in contrast to a lot of imported mass production in shops in Longyearbyen. A special souvenir is the local paper money, now worthless as currency, though the newer coins from the 1990s and especially after 2000 lack authenticity, having been minted with sale to tourists in mind. There is also a cinema and a library (full of Russian literature).

PYRAMIDEN

HISTORY The second Russian settlement, Pyramiden, named after the impressive pyramid-shaped mountain above it, has lain abandoned since its evacuation in late 1998. Located on Billefjord, at the inner end of Isfjorden, its history starts with the founding of a small Swedish mining enterprise.

An expedition led by Bertil Högbom came here in 1910 and in 1921 the area was controlled by Svenska Stenkolsaktiebolaget Spitsbergen, who also had interests in Sveagruva. Following economic difficulties, the company sold out to Russky Grumant in 1926, who in turn sold to Trust Arcticugol in 1931. Commercial extraction did not really start until 1940 and was immediately halted by the evacuation of 1941. Undamaged by World War II, production was able to restart in 1948. Initially, the Soviet consulate was based here.

Throughout its active decades, Pyramiden focused more wholly on coal extraction than Barentsburg, where research also played a certain role. The coal deposits, here Carboniferous, are inside the Pyramid mountain at several levels. Coalfields are extensive, with reserves for many years, but the geology is difficult, with seams falling and rising at changing angles and interrupting thrusts. In the 1990s, the mine had a total length of about 60km of tunnels in the mountain and 32 openings. A new level was opened only in 1994 and a modern German preparation plant installed in 1993–95 for improving coal quality for export to western Europe. Extensively modernised from 1975 to 1985, Pyramiden had accommodation for up to 900 inhabitants, a swimming pool (the world's most northerly), kindergarten, primary school, greenhouse and a farm with dairy herd, pigs, hens and until the early 1990s even a horse. Similar in architecture to Barentsburg, partly even using the same construction plans for some houses, Pyramiden profited from its location in the wide Mimerdalen, which allowed for more generous planning in contrast to Barentsburg and its steep slope. The centre of the settlement is arranged around the huge central square, gently rising, with the culture house at its top and the

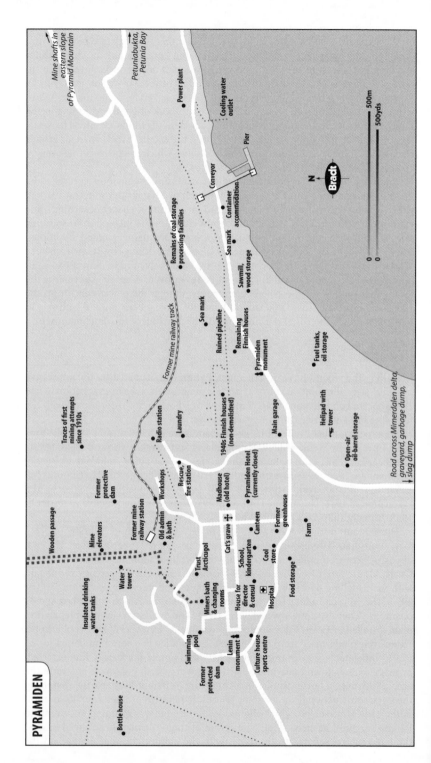

PYRAMIDEN

Mine shafts in eastern slope of Pyramid Mountain

Petuniabukta, Petunia Bay

Power plant

Cooling water outlet

Pier

Conveyor

Sea mark

Container accommodation

Remains of coal storage processing facilities

Sawmill, wood storage

Former mine railway track

Sea mark

Ruined pipeline

Remaining Finnish houses

Pyramiden monument

Fuel tanks, oil storage

Traces of first mining attempts since 1910s

Former protective dam

Radio station

Laundry

1940s Finnish houses (non-demolished)

Helipad with tower

Main garage

Open-air oil-barrel storage

Road across Mimerdalen delta, graveyard, garbage dump, slag dump

Wooden passage

Mine elevators

Former mine railway station

Workshops

Rescue, fire station

Madhouse (old hotel)

Pyramiden Hotel (currently closed)

Former greenhouse

Farm

Insulated drinking water tanks

Water tower

Old admin & bath

Trust Arcticugol

Cat's grave

School, kindergarten

Canteen

Cool store

Food storage

Miners bath & changing rooms

House for director & consul

Hospital

Swimming pool

Lenin monument

Culture house sports centre

Former protected dam

Bottle house

N

Bradt

0   500m
0   500yds

Lenin monument still in front of it, looking down the square with an impressive scenic view of the settlement against the huge white Nordenskiöld glacier across the bay. Of all the settlements in Svalbard, Pyramiden has probably the most attractive setting after Ny-Ålesund.

At the same time, Pyramiden is most hindered by long-lasting winter fjord ice, which may cover the inner fjord up to six months per year unless icebreakers are used. This, together with the more difficult geology in the mine, led to the closure of Pyramiden in 1998, when the Russian mining company could no longer maintain the two settlements due to unreliable supplies and reduced subsidies.

PYRAMIDEN TODAY Before this, in the 1990s, a modest tourist industry had started to develop mostly day excursions from Longyearbyen, while my company also had regular programmes using the Pyramiden Hotel. A further development of tourism into a substantial economic activity in Pyramiden failed due to lack of interest by the Russian management. The hotel was reopened for the summer seasons of 1999 and 2000 on an improvised basis (by then, the water- and heating-pipe systems had already been destroyed by winter frost), but without a long-term perspective and therefore without the necessary marketing efforts, this proved to be ineffective for the Russian mining company.

In winter, Pyramiden has been completely abandoned since 1998, while in summer, a small team of Trust Arcticugol staff is based here – originally initiated and funded by the Russian state for cleaning up the area, but in reality mainly used for removing re-usable equipment for Barentsburg and for extracting valuable materials (scrap metal), which has been sold by the Trust management to Western buyers. Little maintenance has been done by Trust Arcticugol and damage has been speeded up by the extraction of valuable materials, for instance by using explosives for dismantling metal masts quickly, which at the same time shattered nearby windows. Maybe even more worrying is the neglect of the protective gravel walls, which guided floods around Pyramiden, as the settlement was built on the delta fans of several streams, which in the melting season can become violent. Today, these walls have been all but washed away and floods have already started their destructive work.

In principle, Russia has rediscovered the value of its strategic outposts, but the Trust Arcticugol management has no immediate interest in conserving the settlement until a new reason for Pyramiden is found, inclusive of attractive subsidies. Instead, continuing to extract sellable materials seems to be the most profitable solution – all the while hoping for access to further state funds for a later revitalisation (which in fact could be even bigger, the more the settlement is demolished until then).

Possibilities exist for renewed activity in the area, starting with the Russian oil industry's plan to explore and maybe later exploit the oil and gas deposits found some 10km away from Pyramiden on the other side of the fjord. In the end this would not help Pyramiden very much, while also bearing considerable ecological risks. Another possibility is the ambitious concept of transforming Pyramiden into a base for international research and ecotourism.

Meanwhile, decay continues – including the risk of a huge mess of materials – some of which, like old oil barrels, etc, are harmful – being scattered by floods and storms over a huge area.

OTHER PRACTICALITIES While the Pyramiden Hotel was closed in 2000 and was undergoing renovation in 2011, it has not yet reopened as of this book's publication date. However, there are currently three containers which are being used as basic accommodation for visitors who come with tour operators. Still, there are no facilities and services to speak of and accordingly, there is only limited transport available for getting there (occasional day cruises from Longyearbyen in summer, in spring a few longer snowmobile excursions into the area). Excursions to Pyramiden are often combined with visits to the Nordenskiöld glacier.

For the visitor who strolls along the ghost town on his own – a very special experience – I have included a lot of details on the map to aid with orientation.

☞ **Attention:** Apart from neglect and even intentional demolition by Trust Arcticugol (as well as the forces of Nature), tourism of both Longyearbyen inhabitants and others has also become a serious threat to Pyramiden. During the last few years, a number of locked doors have been broken open with force, souvenirs stolen from the buildings, and doors and windows left open to wind, snow and rain, leading to speedy decay. Subsequent visitors take the open doors as a sign of neglect by the owner and some seemingly feel free to plunder and even vandalise the buildings.

As stated by the Sysselmann, breaking into buildings in Pyramiden (like everywhere) is illegal, as is stealing souvenirs. Visitors should follow basic rules of proper conduct, even though the impression can easily arise that Trust Arcticugol itself does not pay much attention to its property.

HORNSUND

HISTORY In contrast to the Norwegian and Russian settlements, relatively little is known of the Polish research station in Isbjørnhamna ('Polar Bear Harbour'), on the north shore of Hornsundet. It is known affectionately as 'Little Poland' to its nine inhabitants who stay there through the year and 15 or more summer residents. The station's official website can be found at http://hornsund.igf.edu.pl.

Polish exploration of the Arctic has a long tradition, going back to those educated people who were unlucky enough to be transported to Siberia under the tsarist regime. These Polish prisoners were among the first to write scientific reports of Arctic Siberia.

A number of Polish expeditions to Svalbard had already taken place in the 1930s, concentrating on the heavily glaciated parts of the south. There are still many place names from this time: Polakkbreen, Pilsudski, etc. World War II and the Stalinist era stopped these activities for 20 years.

The Polish station was founded in 1957–58 as part of the Third Geophysical Year (an ambitious project whereby a number of nations contributed to measuring programmes, experiments and stations for the whole year), allowing research to be carried out without political interference. It has been maintained ever since, making Poland one of the few countries to keep a permanent presence in the archipelago. For Polish scientists of many disciplines (geology, biology, meteorology and so on), 'Little Poland, under the protection of the Sysselmann' (as written at the entrance to the station as a little side dig to the Soviet Union, which tried to keep Poland under control during the Cold War) had incalculable worth. Anxiously, the Polish scientists tried to protect this base against abuse by refusing to be secretive towards the Norwegians – for instance when the Soviet Union asked for the secret installation of a marine sonar system 'for scientific purposes' (which in practice would have been very useful for tracking submarines in the Greenland Sea) and when they informed the Norwegians about Soviet helicopter crashes in the area (which the Soviets tried to keep secret). For Poland, this station was one of the few possibilities for international co-operation outside of the narrow boundaries set by the Eastern Bloc. There were other advantages, too, for example the unpolluted waters contrasted strongly with those of the Baltic and made marine biologists' work so much easier.

HORNSUND TODAY Political restrictions have now been removed, but economic ones remain. Polish scientists continue to be pleased to have the chance to study here and hope that they may continue to do so. For this and scientific reasons, they work closely with the Sysselmann's office and the Norsk Polarinstitutt. The relationship between the Norwegians and Poles is excellent, despite the distance between Hornsund and Longyearbyen.

Long-term projects are studying geophysics, seismics, meteorology and the ionosphere (those northern lights!). Other individual projects include geology, glaciology, geomorphology, marine biology, ecology and oceanography. Scientists from other countries are welcome guests.

NORWEGIAN STATIONS

Apart from the settlements already discussed, Norway has two all-year stations in Svalbard, both with their own postmark! Officers are stationed for short contracts, normally of six months.

BJØRNØYA RADIO The meteorological station and Bjørnøya Radio is manned by a crew of around a dozen.

Despite its remoteness, a surprising number of visitors come here every year in small expedition-cruise ships or yachts. A few souvenirs may be bought. Nearby is the Hammerfesthuset, Svalbard's oldest building. Since 1972 there has been a small museum and 1993 saw a major renovation of the station. Here, too, automation is on its way, which may one day lead to remote operation of this station, like others. See also the section on *Bjørnøya*, pages 128–30.

HOPEN RADIO The more remote of the stations, Hopen is a meteorological base. Originally established as a German weather station during World War II, Norway took it over after the war and rebuilt it. There are four operators stationed here. In late 2004, there were discussions about automating the station, thus saving the high expenses of a manned station that hit the tight budgets of the Norwegian meteorological service. However, this idea seems to have been buried again for the moment, as Norway considers some outposts in its Arctic territories as important both for underlining sovereignty and for practical reasons (bases for rescue operations and research, additional observations which cannot be done by a remote-controlled station). See also the section on *Hopen*, pages 131–2.

TRAPPER STATIONS

Trapper presence has a long tradition in Svalbard, interrupted only by World War II. Nowadays there are only a couple of trappers who overwinter each year.

In 1991 a Dane took over an unused trapping area by the mouth of Isfjorden. In line with the principles of the Spitsbergen Treaty, there have been a few non-Norwegian trappers in the last few years: there was a Pole, for instance, and a German with his Norwegian girlfriend, whom he married during their stay.

Trapper stations still remaining on the main island can be found at Akseløya, Austfjordneset, Farmhamna, Kapp Wijk, Mosselbukta and Mushamna. Of these stations, only Kapp Wijk and Akseløya have been in the hands of the same

6

trappers for many years, while the other stations are taken over by new people almost every year.

Owing to the ban on hunting polar bear, life has become economically more difficult for trappers. Income from skins and down can be as low as NOK15,000–30,000 a year. Nevertheless, the sacrifice is, for some, worth making for the unfettered, independent lifestyle.

Despite the difficulties, the number of people overwintering in this way is stable. Trappers are not inherently against the, er, trappings of civilisation: cabins may have washing machines, skidoos and CD players, even internet via satellite or radio links.

Nevertheless, be aware that these people have on their own chosen this lonesome lifestyle – and almost certainly not so they can be bothered by tourists hoping to bring something a bit more exotic into their holiday slide shows.

The Sysselmann is responsible for all licensing and the organisation of trapping areas. In national parks and reserves, all hunting is forbidden.

In spite of the isolation, a modern trapper is fundamentally different in one aspect from his colleagues some 50 or more years ago: at that time, being a trapper was a profession chosen for economic survival in the face of widespread poverty in northern Norway. Most trappers today are in their trade primarily because of the lifestyle, and could, if they wanted to, earn their living elsewhere (most of them in fact having normal jobs and live as trappers just for a year or two for the experience).

DRILLING STATIONS

Drilling stations searching for mineral resources are amongst the most extreme outposts of civilisation.

Since the mid 1990s, there has been a pause in drilling for oil, but the search for oil and gas in and around Svalbard will continue. Recent borings, which have found little with economic potential, have been at Reindalpasset, inner Nordenskiöldlandet, 1990–91 and Kapp Laila/Colesbukta, winter 1993–94, where a small amount of crude oil was found. There are vague plans for future drilling at Kvalvågen (Heer Land, on the east coast). With oil and gas exploration and exploitation gradually moving north into the Barents Sea, drilling in Svalbard has become an attractive proposition again, even if nothing is found there, because drilling on land is cheaper than marine drilling and does allow scientists to draw some conclusions about the geology under the neighbouring seas (see page 4).

Independent of the oil exploration, there is also drilling by mining companies, especially by the Norwegian SNSK. It keeps its drilling stations busy in a large area around Sveagruva, exploring promising coal seams for the time when the current mine will be exploited in some 20 years' time, and in other places prospecting other minerals like gold in the St Jonsfjord area.

Part Three

FRANZ JOSEF LAND

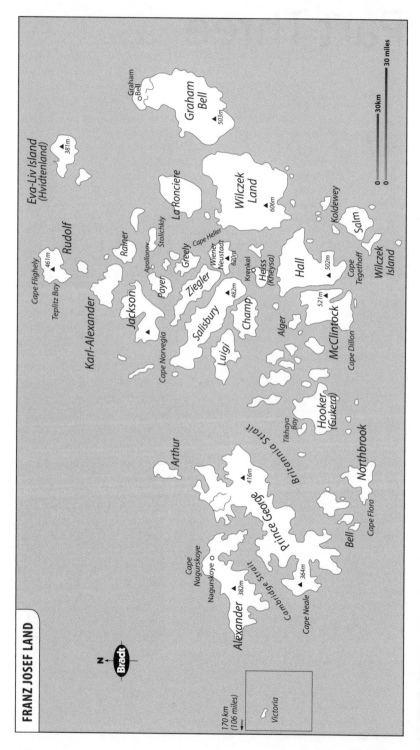

FRANZ JOSEF LAND

Eva-Liv Island
(Hvidtenland)

▲ 381m

Graham
o Bell

Graham
Bell
▲ 503m

Rudolf

Cape Flighely
▲ 461m
Teplitz Bay

Rainer

La Ronciere

Wilczek
Land
▲ 606m

Karl-Alexander

Apollonov
Payer
Stolichkiy

Greely

Cape Hellet

Wiener
Neustadt
▲ 620m

Koldewey

Salm

Jackson

Cape Norvegia
▲

Ziegler
▲ 482m

Salisbury

Krenkel

Heiss
(Kheysa)

Cape
Tegethoff

Wilczek
Island

Luigi

Champ

Hall
▲ 502m

Alger

McClintock
▲ 521m

Cape Dillon

Arthur

Tikhaya
Bay

Hooker
(Gukera)

Britannia Strait

Cape
Nagurskoye o

Nagurskoye

Alexander
▲ 382m

Cambridge Strait

Prince George

▲ 416m

Northbrook

Bell

Cape Flora

▲ 364m
Cape Neale

N

Bradt

170 km
(106 miles)
↓

Victoria

0   30km

0   30 miles

7

Franz Josef Land

Since the enormous changes brought about in the former Soviet Union, Franz Josef Land is no longer a shrouded, secretive group of islands east of Svalbard between the Russian mainland and the North Pole. From 1930 to 1990, the archipelago was almost completely off-limits to Western visitors and little information leaked out about it from inside the Soviet Union. Accordingly, much of the geographic information available today still dates back to before the 1930s and both the history of the archipelago during the Soviet period and the fairly intensive Soviet research work done there during this period are hard to assemble together.

GEOLOGY AND GEOGRAPHY

Just like Svalbard, Franz Josef Land rises out of the European continental shelf. The group is more northerly than Svalbard, the southernmost island being roughly level with the north coast of Spitsbergen, and the northernmost island (Rudolf) being 120km nearer to the North Pole than Rossøya. The archipelago's surface area is roughly 16,135km² and varies greatly with the effects of glaciers reaching and retreating from the sea. The two largest islands, Alexander and Prince George, are both about the same size as Edgeøya in eastern Spitsbergen.

The land is composed of two dominant rock types. Late Triassic and Jurassic sedimentation lie in near-horizontal strata, reaching 200m high in the south at Cape Flora, on Northbrook Island, but gradually sloping down to sea level at the north coast. Fossilised tree trunks found in these layers are evidence of previously warmer conditions. Over the Jurassic sedimentary rocks is a basalt layer, up to 500m thick, with dolerite intrusions, formed in the Cretaceous period by huge volcanic lava eruptions. The geology in the area of Franz Josef Land is characterised by a high density of tectonic fault lines, which served as weak zones for later erosion, thus explaining the unusually strong division of the archipelago into many relatively small islands. Following the faults, the volcanic top layer has been broken, pushed, split and eroded over time, leading to insular plateau tops with vertical rock walls characterised by the typical, usually upright and column-like structures of these igneous rocks.

Flat-topped hills and solitary mountains or plateaux with vertical faces of hard igneous rocks rise above the coastal lowlands, from the gentler slopes of the underlying sediments or directly from the sea. These are found mainly in the west but also in the south, where the topography would call to mind the USA's Monument Valley were it not for the ice. Further east, where the lava top layer was either non-existent or has been eroded away, the landscape is softer, with lower elevations.

Here in Franz Josef Land, too, are signs that the old shoreline was higher than today's; the islands look to be rising out of the ice sea at a rate of two to three millimetres a year.

Elevations above sea level reach 300m in the north, to 600m in the south of the archipelago. The highest hilltop is 670m, on Wilczek Land.

Ice is clearly the most dominant feature of the landscape, covering about 85% of the archipelago as glaciers and ice domes, in most cases breaking off into the sea without leaving any ice-free areas on land. Resulting icebergs are not the biggest (there is no room on the land for the build-up of the necessary ice thicknesses due to the limited size of the islands), but they can still be single flat-topped bergs up to 400m long and many of them sail all the way down to the southeast of Spitsbergen. Airborne radar measurements in 1994 recorded the thickest ice layers in the ice caps of Graham Bell and Hall islands with more than 400m thicknesses. Contrary to Svalbard, no glaciers of the 'surging type' could be found in Franz Josef Land.

Comparisons with observations of 1872 show that the glaciers are in retreat, which ties in with the observation that most parts of the glaciated areas are below the snowline in late summer today, which means that all the snow of the winter melts away over the summer on most of the glacier surfaces and therefore cannot contribute to the formation of new glacier ice there. An interesting detail are fossil ice caps at low level and without ice supply from higher above. Owing to the general climate of the area these should have disappeared, but they extend their lifespan by reflecting much of the summer sun energy and by cooling down the air above them, which delays the melting process.

As in Svalbard, there are strong indications that the ice cover of the islands has in the past been far less than in comparison to today. The ice cover seems to have reached its post ice-age maximum only around 1,000 years ago, with the most recent peak in the 19th century – the 'little ice age' we also find in Svalbard. Between 5,000 and 9,000 years ago, the archipelago may even have been almost free of ice, though still with tundra, but with a much milder climate. Evidence of this include the antlers of reindeer found in the islands, 26 of which have been dated to being between 6,400 and 1,300 years old. A colder climate and an increase in ice coverage has thwarted the existence of a reindeer population in Franz Josef Land for about the past 1,000 years. The pioneer explorers, who came to the archipelago in the late 19th century, suffered from the peak of that glaciation regarding both land and sea ice, both of which have retreated since then, though they're still far greater than they were in the first millennium AD.

The few ice-free zones of today provide a stark, colourful contrast to the mostly whitish landscape, offering grand rock scenery and surprising demonstrations of the adaptability of life to the harshest conditions.

The flat coastal plains are full of lakes and ponds (the archipelago has over 1,000), which, as with the many streams, are fed mainly by the summer's meltwater. Mostly, the ice-free areas are too limited in size for the development of true rivers and clear riverbeds. The longest river is on Prince George Island and is only 19km long.

All in all, it is a bizarre, laconic landscape, with its nearest equivalent in Svalbard being Kong Karls Landet, though there it exists without the glaciation.

Sea ice is also an important factor of the archipelago, both as a part of the scenery and as an important practical factor for travelling, often lasting unbroken in the channels between the islands long into the summers, preventing safe landings on many shores; at these times, access is normally only by helicopter.

CLIMATE

There is no branch of the Gulf Stream that reaches the 75 islands. The ocean's temperature range even in summer is ±1°C. The islands are mostly joined together by fast ice from winter to early summer and it is rare at any time of the year that all the islands can be reached by sea. This is High Arctic indeed. The level and range of the ice cover is very variable from year to year; although one ship may get through one year, the next year, much further south, another would be held prisoner by ice. In early September 1995, a tourist vessel managed to reach Rudolf Island hardly meeting any dense drift ice at all, while in 2003, even a strong icebreaker had to give up at 80°50'N in late July, retarded too much by a solid sea ice sheet in the channels, 1.8m (6ft) thick.

Wind and sea currents cause a phenomenon called *polynia* – a Russian word that has entered international scientific language, which is used to describe the fairly large ice-free zones in the sea that occur even in deepest winter, where developing ice is transported away and access of sea ice from other regions is prevented by the force of wind and currents. In Franz Josef Land, polynias form both in the north and in the south.

Winds from the east and north dominate and bring very cold air. In the south of the archipelago and in winter, southerly winds are not uncommon.

Precipitation is slightly higher than in Svalbard, at 100–330mm, but the islands can still be considered dry. Almost all precipitation is snow.

Temperatures are, on average, lower than those in Svalbard. This difference is noticeable to visitors. The warmest areas are in the south and centre, where mean temperatures in July can reach just over +1°C. The annual mean is –12°C, with known daily records of +12°C and, at the other extreme, –46.2°C. On Rudolf Island, the northernmost, an average of only 41 days a year over 0°C was recorded during the mid 1960s, while the statistics for Tikhaya on Hooker Island show an average of 60 such days per year in the same period – one of the many figures which shows the differences within this fairly limited archipelago, where Tikhaya is in the mildest zone.

WILDLIFE AND CONSERVATION

FLORA The extreme Arctic conditions mean that higher vegetation is limited. Land plants are restricted mostly to a few flatlands and southerly slopes. There are just under 60 flowering plants and over 50 kinds of moss. Many of the plant species are rare and limited to a few sites. Most prevalent are some of the 16 grass species and terrestrial algae.

The most fertile stretches of land like Cape Flora and Cape Tegetthoff are to be found in the southwesterly and central areas, where there are a few small, flat patches covered in vegetation, spread around and separated from each other. There are also guano-rich areas under and near breeding colonies such as Rubini Rock on Hooker Island. Most of the 57 plants also occur elsewhere in the Arctic and include: arctic chickweed (*Cerastium arcticum*), scurvy grass (*Cochlearia groenlandica*), draba (*Draba macrocarpa*), poppy (*Papaver radicarum* or *dahlianum*), arctic buttercup (*Ranunculus sulphureus*) and at least half-a-dozen saxifrages.

There is one tree, a tiny creeping willow (*Salix polaris*).

FAUNA The only indigenous land **mammal** is the arctic fox. Reindeer occasionally come across the ice, as newer antler finds have shown, but due to the colder climate and extensive glaciation of the last 1,000 years there is insufficient vegetation to support a stable population.

Polar bears are mostly linked to the sea ice of the archipelago, but come onshore, too, and walrus are plentiful in the seas. It is thought that walrus were hunted until 1953, with perhaps 10,000 being killed in the area. The population is recovering and about 2,000 live here now, occasionally moving between here, Svalbard and Novaya Zemlya. It could be that regeneration of Svalbard's walrus population depends on animals from Franz Josef Land. Satellite observations of tagged animals have shown a female majority in Franz Josef Land, with mostly male animals on Spitsbergen.

Apart from walrus, there are three other pinnipeds: bearded seal form the majority, with ringed seals and harp seals also found.

Off the coast, white whale, killer whale and narwhals can often be seen. Cruises in the 1990s repeatedly spotted Greenland right whales, in schools of up to 30 individuals, while single individuals of this extremely decimated species are a rare sight elsewhere in Arctic waters. For Belugas (white whales), the coast off Franz Josef Land seems to be one of the prime summer habitats in the Barents Sea.

There are 14 species of typical and more numerous breeding **birds** (for the High Arctic, 'numerous' means 'over 300 individuals'). The most common are the little auk, kittiwake and fulmar, with perhaps 10,000–15,000 of each. Black guillemots seem to be more frequent than in Svalbard and ivory gulls are not a particularly rare sight either. The most important breeding colony of the archipelago is Rubini Rock, Hooker Island, near Tikhaya, with mainly kittiwakes, Brünnich's guillemots, fulmars and little auks. If one includes visitors, the number of bird species rises to about 40. Of special note are the autumn migrations of Brünnich's guillemot; the young crash into the sea before they can fly and whole families swim for weeks before reaching the east coast of Greenland.

Ptarmigan are the only overwintering land-based birds.

ENVIRONMENTAL PROTECTION Even more so than in Svalbard, the condition of the environment in Franz Josef Land is characterised by extreme contrasts. Most of the island group is unaffected by local human activity; even the walrus population has regenerated to the point where it can help that of Svalbard, and the salvation of the Atlantic Greenland right whale lies in this area. As with Svalbard, the major pollutants are not the few explorers, scientists and others but global pollution of both the atmosphere and the food chain.

Most of the archipelago consists of truly pristine wilderness, dotted by tiny but often extreme zones littered with the careless remnants of human activity. The current evacuation of practically all stations is not necessarily a benefit for the local environment, because the old systems continue rotting and eventually leak out all kinds of substances.

Almost all Western visitors are shocked by the lack of consideration shown to the fragile Arctic environment. Rubbish, rotten hulks, seeping oil and petrol cans and all sorts of detritus are to be found right where they were discarded. Deep ruts, some still fresh after 50 years, score the ground. Seventy years of carelessness is not going to disappear easily. It is to be hoped that pressure from tourists may have a part to play. The Russians need the money and may listen to criticism as a result.

With a wider perspective, these easily visible eyesores are as nothing compared with the problems of nuclear waste, chemical warfare dumps, etc, in other parts of the Russian Arctic. Luckily, Franz Josef Land has been spared these problems. There are no such dumps in or close to the archipelago and the sea currents, which move south to southwest, away from the islands, ensure that there is little danger. On the other hand, there is no point in blaming only the Russians: radioactivity in the northern Barents Sea is in fact only a fraction of what is measured in many places in the Baltic Sea and much of the low radioactivity measured around Svalbard and even in parts of the Barents Sea can in fact be traced back to Sellafield!

Damage by tourists is, thus far (and for the foreseeable future), very limited. Care must be taken that seabird and walrus colonies are not disturbed, and it is very important that what little vegetation there is should remain untouched. Keeping damage by tourists down to a minimum level should not pose much of a problem, with no more than some 100 to 1,000 visitors a year likely for the time being, most of them being no more than cruisers who set foot on land for only a few hours at a time. (A much greater risk is that the political climate may swing back to its secretive ways, and the islands will be shut off again with no outside witnesses to examine what is going on.)

Russia declared Franz Josef Land and the surrounding seas (total 42,000km²) a nature reserve in 1994. They have graded it as *sakasnik* (limited use possible), as opposed to the much more stringent *sapovednik* (protected; any use prohibited). The future will tell if this is a cheap public relations exercise, but at least it shows that pressure has some effect. However the new status has led to quarrelling in Russia; formally, Franz Josef Land belonged to Archangel Oblast, but Murmansk, Moscow and Krasnoyarsk have all put in claims – with reasons ranging from hopes for an income from tourism (especially the easily earned access fees) to the riches that could be accrued from the seabed. Oil and gas exploration have already started in the southern Barents Sea where, among others, the biggest natural gas deposit of the whole European north has been found.

HISTORY

The human history of Franz Josef Land is extremely short, beginning only in the late 19th century, and was dominated from pioneer times until 1930 by explorers and hunting expeditions. The exploratory expeditions were led by men from Austria, Great Britain, the USA, Holland, Norway, Italy and Russia, whereas hunting expeditions were primarily Norwegian. For the traveller, the charm of these islands lies in the many well-preserved traces of past explorers. Apart from some special natural features, the historic sites, often linked to certain expeditions, are a central aspect of visits to the archipelago. For this reason, we present the history here in the order of these expeditions.

DISCOVERY Nothing is known (and no traces are found) of human activity in the archipelago prior to the 19th century.

Until 1860 Norwegian hunters did not venture much further than Spitsbergen's west and north coast, as the ice prevented them from travelling with any facility. As previously mentioned, ice conditions around 1800 were among the heaviest since the end of the last ice age. Gradually, in the second half of the 19th century, individual ships were able to travel further and further east, and explorers discovered that the ice wasn't always as bad as had been imagined – though this was most likely due to gradually favourable climatic conditions.

In 1863 Elling Carlsen of Tromsø completed the first known circumnavigation of Svalbard, for which he was decorated.

In 1865 Nils Frederick Rønnbeck from Hammerfest and his harpooner Aidijærvi took their schooner *Spitsbergen* eastward from Nordaustlandet and came across a previously unknown country, presumably Franz Josef Land. However, there is no firm record of this because in those days it was common for sailors to keep their discoveries to themselves for fear of competition. There had been rumours of land existing between Svalbard and Novaya Zemlya for 300 years – in fact, the Soviet Union claimed the real discovery of Franz Josef Land because a Russian scientist had predicted the existence of land in that area from observations of the drift ice in the Barents Sea, which indicated an obstacle in the north.

1872–74: *ADMIRAL TEGETTHOFF* (PAYER/WEYPRECHT) The official discovery of the land falls to the Austro-Hungarian expedition of Julius Payer and Carl Weyprecht (with the famous Elling Carlsen as ice pilot). Having left Bremerhaven with their purpose-built and well-equipped *Admiral Tegetthoff* in June 1872 to explore the Northeast Passage, they got trapped in the ice on 1 October 1872, already west of Novaya Zemlya, which pushed them northwards. On 30 August 1873, unknown land came into sight, which they named 'Kaiser Franz Josef Land'. Two months later, the insecure ice froze solid off the coast of Wilczek Island, allowing the first landing before the second involuntary wintering. Next spring, still trapped, Payer took the chance of exploring the unknown territory in a tough wintry expedition all the way up to Rudolf Island, reversing at Cape Fligely, today known as the northernmost point of Eurasia. He produced the first map of the mid part of the archipelago, but mistook sea ice further north as land stretching towards the North Pole – a misconception that created frustrations for later explorers. As the ice continued holding the *Tegetthoff* in its grip, they gave up the ship, dragging the boats over the rough ice, finally reaching open water and being rescued by Russian ships at Novaya Zemlya, having lost only one man in the space of twice as many years.

1879: DE BRUYNE In the years that followed more adventurers headed toward this new land. The Dutchman de Bruyne set off in 1879, but within sight of the coast, he was stopped by dense drift ice – after an even less successful attempt the year before.

1880 AND 1881–82: LEIGH SMITH The expeditions of Benjamin Leigh Smith in 1880 and 1881 were the next to set foot on land, this time in the southwest, first exploring the formerly unknown south side of the archipelago from Wilczek Island to Alexander Island around 1880. Smith returned to the same area in 1881, after ice prevented him from advances into other regions, and set up a cabin, 'Eira Lodge', on Bell Island. (The oldest building of the archipelago, the cabin is still in good shape.) Just afterwards, Smith's ship *Eira* was crushed by ice at neighbouring Cape Flora, forcing the expedition to winter there – cut off by drift ice from their nice, new cabin on Bell Island just 20km away. With some dark (but necessary) humour, they therefore called their primitive and improvised shelter 'Eira Cottage'. Luckily, there were ample polar bears and walruses as sources of food, and before *Eira* sank, most provisions and materials were saved. The winter was used for scientific observations – the third wintering, albeit as involuntary as the prior two, in the area of the newly discovered archipelago. The following summer, they rowed the rescued boats of the *Eira* for 43 days until they reached northern Novaya Zemlya, where they came upon several Western expedition ships who rescued them.

1894–97: JACKSON–HARMSWORTH AND NANSEN

Briton Frederick Jackson, sponsored by newspaper magnate Harmsworth, set out on a carefully planned large-scale expedition to Franz Josef Land in 1894, having been rejected by the admired Nansen when applying to be a member of the FRAM expedition (Nansen wanted exclusively Norwegians with him), which had set off one year before on its famous ice-drift experiment. Jackson established a big and well-equipped wintering base 'Elmwood', made of prefabricated elements on Cape Flora, in addition to the expedition vessel *Windward* frozen in just off the shore. From there, the intention was to explore both the archipelago in detail and try to reach the North Pole on the land bridge that was expected to lead northwards – not least as a result of wrong sightings from the northernmost land point (Rudolf Island) of the *Tegetthoff* expedition. During their three years, they mapped and explored in detail the complete western part of the archipelago, up to Cape Mill on Jackson Island, and realised that the former general belief in a huge unknown landmass stretching towards the Pole was a myth. Finding out that there was no land to the north to travel easily on and that Franz Josef Land was, in reality, a highly scattered archipelago of many comparably small islands, forced Jackson to give up on the idea of travelling to the Pole.

As happens often in history, the expedition did not become famous because of their great scientific achievements, but because of an element of the human touch: on 17 June 1896, two persons were discovered out on the pack ice off Cape Flora, struggling towards the expedition base. Jackson, approaching the two men, who in every way bore the marks of people who had spent a long time away from civilisation, suddenly burst out in surprise: 'Aren't you Nansen?' – 'Yes, I am Nansen'. It was a minimal dialogue, conducted in the deserted middle of nowhere, yet it soon became almost as famous as Stanley's 'Doctor Livingstone, I presume?'. Nansen and Johansen had left the FRAM expedition in summer 1895 when it became apparent that the drift would not lead across the Pole. Having forgotten to wind up their clock, the two had no possibility of calculating their longitudinal position. So they had no idea exactly where they were when they finally saw some unknown islands (Eva-Liv Island) on 24 July, which by no means matched the descriptions Nansen had received about the north of Franz Josef Land with the vast areas of Petermann and King Oscar Land extending northwards of Rudolf Island as observed by Payer. Nevertheless, the two Norwegians roughly charted the unknown areas along their way. As the season advanced, they decided to winter at what is now known as Cape Norvegia on Jackson Island in a primitive shelter made of low stone walls, a driftwood log, and with walrus hides as a roof. The next spring, they slowly fought their way over the rapidly breaking-up ice between the islands southwards, finally hitting on Jackson. Insufficiently equipped for crossing longer distances of open Arctic ocean between drift ice, the two Norwegians would probably have perished soon after on Franz Josef Land were it not for this meeting with Jackson, the man whom Nansen had earlier rejected as an expedition member on the FRAM.

Nansen's idea of using their fragile kayaks to get to Svalbard, using Giles Land in between as a stepping stone, would have failed as Giles Land turned out merely to be one of many myths. Using Jackson's maps, Nansen could integrate his own observations from the north of the archipelago into the already-known geography of Franz Josef Land. By this, practically the whole of Franz Josef Land was at least roughly explored, with the exception of a few parts in the east; furthermore, it could now be said with a final certainty that there could not be any extensive land areas further north. *Windward* sailed back to Europe with Nansen, Johansen and much of the scientific results, while Jackson completed his exploration of western Franz Josef Land with a third wintering, returning home in 1897. He left Elmwood as a well-equipped base with lots of provisions for later expeditions, thinking in particular of Andrée's planned balloon project. Later, bitterness arose in Jackson in view of all the fame Nansen collected with his publications and speeches about his expedition, where he also made use of all the cartographic work of Jackson, giving him little credit for his cartography abilities and for his rescue, while the Jackson expedition went largely ignored.

1898–99: WELLMAN The US journalist Walter Wellman, whose name has already appeared in this book thanks to his previous (1894) and later (1906–09) attempts to reach the North Pole from Svalbard, sponsored by *National Geographic* magazine, made a similar attempt from Franz Josef Land, in this case by means of sledge, as the first in a series of attempts to use the archipelago as a springboard for the Pole.

Wellman reached Franz Josef Land in 1898, collecting a building and many provisions from Jackson's Elmwood in order to set up his own wintering base at Cape Tegetthoff. A small party, led by Baldwin, was sent out to Cape Heller to set up a supply dump and build a small stone shelter covered with walrus skin as an advanced cache (euphemistically called 'Fort McKinley') for the planned dash to the Pole in 1899. The dump was manned by two volunteers, Bjørvik and Bentsen, to look after the 27 dogs placed there – possibly the most extreme intentional wintering in the history of Arctic exploration. On the orders of Baldwin, and in spite of the filled cache just next to them, they were allowed to use only one outworn sleeping bag together, tea and coffee in free quantities, a few cans of meat, free quantities of the meat of any walrus they shot, a total of four candles and fuel only for cooking. From the start, on 22 October, they lived on polar bear and walrus, cooked on a single stove, with the temperature inside the shelter never rising above –20°C, and with both of them shivering in the cramped and insufficient sleeping bag. Bentsen fell ill in the first few weeks and died on 1 January; Bjørvik had sworn to protect his colleague's body from polar bears and spent the rest of the winter with the deep-frozen body in the shelter. Wellman arrived on 27 February, shocked by the conditions of this wintering of which he had only now become aware, and took Bjørvik with him on the polar expedition. They didn't make it, turning back instead. On 5 April they got back to Cape Tegetthoff, and Bjørvik experienced a warm room for the first time in nine months.

Like his predecessors, Wellman did not reach the Pole, but added a number of details to the map, especially the east of Wilczek Land and Graham Bell Island – previously uncharted areas. The diary of Baldwin, the second-in-command, gives interesting insights into attitudes and thoughts, including an amazing arrogance towards the Norwegian expedition members – despite a simultaneous admission that the expedition depended heavily upon their skills and experience. See *The Franz Josef Land Archipelago – E B Baldwin's Journal of the Wellman Polar Expedition, 1898–1899*, edited by P J Capelotti.

1899–1900: DUKE OF ABRUZZI AND 1901: STØKKEN The next attempt to reach the Pole was financed and led personally by the Duke of Abruzzi. At the beginning, luck was with them, allowing them to navigate their expedition vessel *Stella Polare* through mostly open water all the way up to the northernmost point, Teplitz Bay on Rudolf Island. Here, they set up a wintering base on land above the frozen-in vessel, which by then was damaged by ice pressure. In spring, under the leadership of Cagni, a team of 12 set off northwards with sledges, with most of the personnel forming part of several support groups who would return to the base once they'd given their assistance. Three of these men – Ollier, Querini and Støkken – never returned. Cagni got as far north as 86°34'N, closer to the Pole than anybody else before, but had to give up and struggle back through very difficult and partly broken moving ice, covering a total of 1,200km in 104 days. In the meantime, the group in the base was busy with repairing and freeing the vessel from the grip of the ice, being able to leave only in mid-August and then having a very difficult tour back with heavy ice in the British Channel – quite different from the year before.

In 1901, Captain Støkken, the father of the missing Norwegian expedition member, organised a private search expedition, but did not get much further than Cape Flora, where they erected a memorial column for the three missing expedition members.

1901: MAKAROV Except for a Russian carpenter on the Jackson–Harmsworth expedition, it took until 1901 for a Russian expedition to land in Franz Josef Land – under the leadership of Admiral Makarov in 1901. This was primarily a hydrographic expedition, which visited only the south of the archipelago, including a stop at Cape Flora. At the time, Makarov was testing a new type of ship he helped build, one that had enormous influence both on future traffic in ice-covered waters and for the Russian dominance in them: the icebreaker. The *Yermak*, the ship which made its trial run on this expedition, was the world's first true icebreaker.

1901–02: BALDWIN–ZIEGLER The US millionaire Ziegler hoped to stake his place in the history books by financing expeditions that would lead to breakthroughs in polar exploration. For his first North Pole expedition from Franz Josef Land, he chose Baldwin as his leader. The expedition, including 42 men, 15 ponies and 400 dogs, set up its main base on Alger Island with two prefabricated cabins; the expedition vessel *America* was frozen in near the shore, connected to the camp with a telephone and electricity line. Equipment included the gas apparatus for producing hydrogen for balloons, of which 15 were sent out to the outside world with all kinds of messages, from running commentaries on their progress to requests for more coal. Even a painter, Porter, accompanied the expedition (and the next one), leaving behind a valuable collection of paintings. The winter was spent in meteorological measuring, preparing and placing several caches to support the actual advance to the Pole, and for documenting Nansen's shelter on Jackson Island. Apart from this, no results were achieved and a generally miserable atmosphere owing to Baldwin's poor leadership seems to have prevailed – no real surprise in view of Baldwin's dubious performance already on the Wellman expedition.

1903–05: FIALA–ZIEGLER In spite of the massive public criticism for the minimal results of the first expedition, Ziegler immediately outfitted a second one, under the leadership of Anthony Fiala, who displayed solid personal qualities when serving as a member of the first expedition. This time, Rudolf Island was reached and the main base was set up there. Alas, the *America* was gradually crushed by the ice during the winter, which deflated the spirits and created severe logistical problems regarding their return journey from this remote northern land to the south of the archipelago. Part of the expedition moved by sledge to Cape Flora the following spring to look out for a relief vessel, while the attack on the Pole was postponed by Fiala to the next spring due to various weather and equipment problems. The group at Cape Flora luckily found a coal seam above the camp, which solved their energy problem during the expected second wintering. With the expedition spread over such a long distance from Rudolf Island to Cape Flora, transport and communication became a constant problem, leading to the establishment of yet another wintering party – the third – in between the first two in the base camp of the Baldwin–Ziegler expedition (which is now known as Camp Ziegler on Alger Island). In view of the obstacles in heading northwards from Rudolf Island the following spring (such as the ice pressure and the large cracks in the ice), Fiala gave up all attempts of reaching the Pole and retreated from the north of the archipelago to the south, where they were picked up by the *Terra Nova* (later Scott's ship to Antarctica) in summer 1905.

1886–1930: NORWEGIAN HUNTERS In parallel with these expeditions, there were others: the hunters. There were at least 116 visits by Norwegians to Franz Josef Land between 1886 and 1930, all but five of them summer hunting trips that were based on small vessels. The primary goal, of course, was to fell polar bear and walrus. With this utilisation of the archipelago's natural resources and their continuing presence in the archipelago, the Norwegians were now in a uniquely strong position. It is not unlikely that there had been some earlier Norwegian hunting expeditions to Franz Josef Land as early as the 1860s – journeys that were kept secret out of fear of competition.

1912–15: EARLY RUSSIAN EXPEDITIONS In 1912, a privately financed Russian expedition under the leadership of Georgiy Sedov set sail with the *St Foka* for Franz Josef Land, again with the aim of reaching the Pole. Difficult ice forced them to spend a first winter on Novaya Zemlya; and again in the summer of 1913 they got no further than Hooker Island, where they wintered in a bay which Sedov called Tikhaya Bukta – 'Calm Bay' – on account of its flat, undisturbed ice. Weakened by scurvy, regular observations were carried out all through the winter, which many years later convinced the Russians to establish a permanent station at the site. In spite of the sickness, Sedov began his Pole expedition in spring 1914, only to die of exhaustion on Rudolf Island, where he is buried. *St Foka* made it – just about, being down to the last piece of coal – to Cape Flora, where most of the buildings and even parts of the ship itself were chopped up and used as fuel for the kettles, in order to make the home voyage possible.

At Cape Flora, the members met the two last survivors of the Russian *St Anna* expedition, which set out under Brussilov at the same time as Sedov in 1912, with the aim of checking the Northeast Passage and the hunting possibilities thereabouts. They were caught in the ice, drifting helplessly for two winters, until 11 of the crew left the ship on a march southwards. Only two of them finally arrived at Cape Flora, and nothing was ever heard of those who had stayed on board the *St Anna*, nor indeed the nine others who had left the ship at the same time as the two survivors. One of the survivors published the dramatic account of their Arctic odyssey (in English: Albanov, V I, *In the Land of White Death*).

On their way home, they passed unnoticed the *Hertha*, sent out to search for the two missing vessels – without success. But the captain of the *Hertha* hoisted the Russian flag on Cape Flora, thereby staking the first official Russian claim to the islands.

Including the *Hercules* of Rusanov, which disappeared east of Novaya Zemlya in 1912, in total three Russian polar expeditions of that year ended in disaster. World War I, the Revolution and the ensuing civil war put a stop to Russian polar expeditions for a decade in Franz Josef Land. After that, the islands were visited again from the Soviet side by the expedition vessels *Persej* (1923), *Elding* (1926) and *Sarnitsa* (1927).

1926 AND 1928: SOVIET AND ITALIAN CLAIMS Until at least 1926, Franz Josef Land was regarded as a 'terra nullius' (no-man's-land), where all could operate on an equal footing. In view of an official discovery by Austria-Hungary, international (and mainly non-Russian) scientific activity and an overwhelming Norwegian dominance in economic exploitation, the Soviet Union had no plausible claim over the archipelago according to the standards of international law. Nevertheless, the Russians were excluded from the negotiations of the Spitsbergen Treaty of 1920 in spite of very substantial Russian interests there, both historic and economic (ie: the Russian mine in Grumant on Spitsbergen), which made the islands a Norwegian territory in 1925. This probably added to Russian awareness of its interests in the north after years of revolutionary internal trouble and increased domestic focus. On 15 April 1926, therefore, the USSR issued a decree, claiming all areas north of the Russian mainland to the North Pole to be Soviet territory. This decree had little practical impact immediately, and even on the official Soviet maps issued in 1926 and 1928, Franz Josef Land was marked as being outside of the Soviet Union. But in 1928, plans were made for the establishment of permanent Russian stations both on Novaya Zemlya and in Franz Josef Land. This forced the Norwegian government to protest officially in Moscow against this unilateral decree of annexation.

As a little footnote, it can be mentioned here that the government of fascist Italy also forwarded a claim on sovereignty over the archipelago in 1928 after the disaster of the Nobile expedition – arguing that the *Tegetthoff* was equipped with an engine from the now-Italian city of Trieste (and that several expedition members were from that area too).

1928: SEARCH FOR *ITALIA* AND AMUNDSEN'S *LATHAM* PLANE The crash of Nobile's airship *Italia* and the subsequent search for survivors, followed by the search for the *Latham* plane in which Amundsen and his pilot had disappeared while searching for Nobile, drew international attention to both the European Arctic and to Franz Josef Land, which might well have encouraged the Soviet government to underline its claims. US polar enthusiast Louise Boyd sent her *Hobby* under Norwegian Riiser-Larsen to Victoria Island, Alexander Island and Cape Flora, where she unloaded material for building a replacement for the mostly ruined cabins – though she then had to retreat to Eira Haven. *Vesleskari* also took part in a search of the area, visiting Cape Harmsworth and Victoria Island as well as hunting walrus. But the strongest presence was that provided by two new Soviet icebreakers: the *Krassin*, under the command of the Russian polar pioneer Samoilovich, and the *Sedov*, which at the same time also hunted polar bears. Having found items of the Nobile expedition east of Svalbard, the *Krassin* headed east to Prince George Island, where it dropped an expedition group of 15, as well as building material for a cabin and provisions for six months. They annexed the land in the name of the Soviet Union, using the somewhat far-fetched argument that Franz Josef Land was discovered, at least in theory, by the Russian Krapotkin in 1870, who postulated the existence of land in this region due to observations of the drift ice situation in the Barents Sea (this hypothesis, incidentally, had already been presented in 1865 by the German Baron von Schilling; Krapotkin used almost his exact words when presenting his theory five years later).

1929: METEOROLOGICAL STATION The upgrading of Russian activity led to a reaction from the Scandinavian side. In 1929, Norway tried to send two scientific expeditions and Sweden one to Franz Josef Land, but difficult ice conditions prevented all of them from going ashore, causing the abandonment of the Norwegian plan to set up a meteorological radio station.

Thanks to their new icebreakers, the ice conditions of 1929 were not a problem for the Soviet side. Under the leadership of the famous Russian polar experts Samoilovich, Schmidt and Vize (a member of the 1912–14 *St Foka* expedition to the same wintering site), the *Georgiy Sedov* broke through the ice belt and reached Hooker Island. Here they set up a meteorological research station in Tikhaya Bay at exactly the same place where Sedov wintered 15 years earlier, leaving a wintering crew of seven there, including another Russian polar hero, Krenkel. This station was in use without interruption until 1963. On the same voyage, the *Sedov* also determined the site for the planned station on Rudolf Island.

1930: ISOLATION OF THE ARCHIPELAGO To underline the claim to Franz Josef Land, the Soviet Union positioned a patrol vessel at the archipelago which chased and captured Norwegian hunter boats until they signed a declaration that they would never again enter such waters for hunting.

At the same time, an expedition of Norges Svalbard-og Ishavsundersøkelser (NSIU) visited the archipelago on *Bratvåg*, led by the geologist Dr Gunnar Horn plus a zoologist and a botanist. On the way they discovered the remains of Andrée's last camp on Kvitøya in the northeast of Spitsbergen, before unloading building material for cabins on Victoria Island and Cape Forbes (Prince George Island). Certainly, the background for this expedition was not just purely scientific – until 1929, Norway had shown practically no interest in the scientific exploration of Franz Josef Land. Rather, this expedition was an attempt to balance the Soviet expansion in the archipelago. It turned out to be the final attempt. For the next 60 years, the Soviet Union sealed off the islands almost completely against Western visitors. In the beginning, with only limited resources on the Soviet side, Franz Josef Land and especially Victoria Island (claimed specifically by the Soviet Union in 1932, on the occasion of the first ever Russian visit to the island) were still visited occasionally by a few boats on hunting expeditions, which sneaked themselves in, with the latest to my knowledge in August 1939. But Norway gave up offering real political resistance against the annexation of the archipelago by the Soviet Union after 1930. A key reason for this Soviet success was the young Soviet icebreaker fleet, which was unique and provided for access to the islands, while Norway was severely hindered with its weak hunting vessels by the massive ice of these crucial years.

1931–41: SOVIET BUILD-UP, ARCTIC AVIATION One of Nansen's last ambitions was the systematic use of aircraft for research in polar regions, which led to the foundation of the International Aeroarctic Association under his leadership. A result of this, though after his death, was the flight of the airship LZ 127 *Graf Zeppelin* with an international crew (including Russians) and a flight over the European Arctic, including a landing at Tikhaya Bay and aerial photography of large parts of the archipelago. This was the start of intensive use of aircraft in the Russian Arctic, with the Russians from now on using their own constructions.

On the ground, the Soviet Union quickly expanded its presence. A major impulse was 1932–33, the Second Geophysical Year. Tikhaya Station was extended and a weather balloon facility set up. A station was also set up on Rudolf Island, becoming the most northerly inhabited point of the Soviet Union. Victoria Island was claimed for Russia.

In 1934–37, the Tikhaya Station became a more permanent settlement, with two-dozen people based there including three babies born by 1936. Aircraft were seen more regularly, including the location of a seaplane in Tikhaya in 1935 that specialised in cartographic surveys. A temporary airfield was built on Rudolf Island on the ice cap, the starting point for the successful flights of four heavy four-engined Antonov ANT-6 transporters to the North Pole in 1937, which established the first manned drifting station there under the leadership of the Russian polar hero Krenkel.

1941–45: WAR IN THE ARCTIC Most Russians were evacuated from Franz Josef Land after the German attack on the Soviet Union, with the exception of the seven men at the Tikhaya weather station. These men continued their work throughout World War II, noticing nothing of their temporary neighbours, the Germans, who had set up a weather station of their own only 100km away in 1943–44 in the north of Alexander Island, but had to be evacuated after becoming sick from trichinosis after eating polar bear meat.

THE COLD WAR PERIOD Soon after World War II, Franz Josef Land gained strategic importance for the Soviet Union as a base for bombers, especially after the development of the Soviet nuclear bomb. In 1952, a big military airbase was constructed on Alexander Island, very close to the site of the German war weather station, and named Nagurskoe, after the Polish-born pioneer of Russian military aviation, Jan Nagórski. Though this base lost much of its strategic importance after 1956 with the introduction of Soviet intercontinental missiles, the military kept it in regular use and nowadays it is the only permanently manned place in the entire archipelago – as well as being, not coincidentally, the only forbidden zone for visitors.

Research was also intensified in the archipelago from the 1950s onwards, though often in a military context: glaciology was used to provide information about the possibilities of using glaciers for military runways or even as shelters for planes in ice caves.

The next push in the field of Arctic research came with the Soviets' participation in the International Geographical and Geophysical Years 1957–59. The new Krenkel base was built on Heiss (Kheysa) Island, which was in permanent use until 2000, with sometimes up to 70 people overwintering. Tikhaya base was closed in the following year (1959) in favour of the new installations at Krenkel, largely because Tikhaya was in many ways untypical for the archipelago, with its special mild local climate, etc. But the military and secret service maintained the veil of secrecy over the archipelago. Apart from a French group at Krenkel who studied the ionosphere in 1967, the decades until 1990 saw Franz Josef Land completely cut off to the West. By 1990, the Soviet Union had five permanently manned bases in the archipelago: Krenkel as the main scientific station; the small radio and research station on Rudolf Island; the secret military airbase Nagurskoe; the less-secret military heliport on Graham Bell Island; and the military weather station and outpost on Victoria Island. In addition, Tikhaya was still used occasionally for minor summer activities. Generally, activity was very much confined to the station areas, while most of the other regions of the islands have hardly been visited.

1990 TO TODAY The beginning of the 1990s saw a thaw in relations. Following in the footsteps of a group of Norwegian historians, including Susan Barr, who visited the archipelago in 1990 on a Russian–Norwegian expedition, more and more Western visitors have been going to Franz Josef Land, beginning with scientists, in co-operation with Russian institutions. The Norwegian polar institute co-operated with Russian partners in summer research projects from 1990 to 1994, even making use of a small joint summer base in Tikhaya. US and British institutes co-operated with Russian partners in glaciology, oceanography and geophysics. Austria installed a small research base in connection with the *Tegetthoff* film project on Ziegler Island in 1993 and a Russian–French–German co-operation equipped Krenkel with a testing device for a new 'heat pump' for use in polar areas.

In tourism, the pioneer was German adventurer Arved Fuchs, who managed to get permission to visit Franz Josef Land in 1991 as part of his circumnavigation of the polar ocean aboard his traditional ice-strengthened sailing vessel *Dagmar Aaen*. Several specialised tourism companies soon followed. Once Russia was no longer able to fund its large fleet of polar research and duty vessels, the various institutions had to develop survival strategies – for instance chartering out a section of their ships to Western tour operators. Since 1992, tourist voyages to Franz Josef Land on modern Russian ships have been offered internationally, and helicopter arrangements from/to the islands from the mainland have also been organised.

However, all these new international activities were largely based on the old structures. For some years, this old system continued working: the research bases were kept open, fuel was still cheap, and corruption had not yet taken full control. Then the collapse reached Franz Josef Land. In 1994, the military bases on Graham Bell and Victoria islands were given up, followed by the station on Rudolf Island in 1995. As the last blow, even Krenkel was evacuated in 2000.

Until 2004, Nagurskoe was the only manned base in the whole archipelago, a largely symbolic presence with a guard of only about 20 men conscripted to preside over the dilapidation. At the same time, a dramatic evacuation process began in the once highly subsidised Arctic north of mainland Siberia. Many airports and ports have now fallen into disuse, many settlements are completely or partly evacuated, supply lines have collapsed and fuel is nowadays more expensive in many parts of northern Russia than in Western countries. This large-scale disappearance of infrastructure both on the Siberian mainland and in Franz Josef Land itself has been one of the reasons why the once-blooming international co-operation of the early 1990s has again ceased. A second is corruption and blackmail, which has made projects increasingly expensive and financially impracticable. Finally, there is the military and the secret service, who have zero interest in allowing foreigners into these remote regions. From 1999 to 2002, Franz Josef Land once again disappeared almost completely from the list of possible travel destinations, both for tourists and for scientists – including Russians – as the archipelago was sealed off. The rare occasions for short tourist visits during these years comprised a few passages on Russian icebreakers along the Northeast Passage or to the North Pole. Only since 2003 has it become possible once again to book longer cruises specifically to Franz Josef Land, initially only on the powerful diesel-electric Russian icebreaker *Kapitan Dranitsyn*, and now on an increasing number of cruise ships operating in the archipelago. This reopening is one sign of the return of Russian interest in the far north; another is the installation of a small modern Russian scientific station at the Krenkel base on Heiss Island in September 2005, personally supported by the deputy chairman of the Russian state *duma* (parliament) and Russian polar hero Artur N Chilingarov.

In June 2009, the archipelago became part of the newly established Russkaya Arktika National Park which, at 14,260km², is the third largest national park in Russia and the largest marine protected area in the Arctic. Russia says it has plans to develop the area, which includes the Northern part of Novaya Zemlya, by introducing well-managed ecotourism and by cleaning up former military sites. The park is of high importance for Arctic marine mammal populations and hosts one of the largest bird colonies in the Northern Hemisphere.

On 3 August 2011, the *National Geographic Explorer* became the first non-Russian expedition vessel to call at the archipelago since 1928, landing at Cape Flora on Northbrook Island.

PRACTICAL INFORMATION

Franz Josef Land is visited today almost exclusively by organised tourist expeditions. Having been closed to visitors for roughly 60 years and with fairly few visits before that, a voyage to the archipelago has a touch of the pioneer spirit about it – especially in view of the conditions. There are places in the archipelago which have never been stepped on by people even to this day.

WHEN TO VISIT In practice, **summer** is currently the only possible season for visits to Franz Josef Land. Ice conditions here are generally more difficult than in Svalbard, so in general August to early September should be the period when the ice creates fewest problems and where the snowmelt on land has reached its maximum (though with a certain risk of thin fresh snow on some days). Accordingly, the late season is especially good for getting around in the archipelago as far and as unhindered as possible and for having historic sites with as little snow cover as there can be. With a particularly strong icebreaker, earlier visits can be done, though an icebreaker will be considerably slowed down and can even stopped by thicker ice. Given the low speeds when breaking heavy ice, much time can be lost – and much fuel consumed. Therefore, even an icebreaker tour cannot necessarily guarantee that all advertised places can be reached, and you may need to be prepared to be slapped with a hefty fuel surcharge. While ice can be more of a problem in July, this is usually the better part of the season for both birdwatchers and those interested in the flora – as well as for those who hope to see the midnight sun high above the horizon. In addition, the easiest and safest opportunities for close observation of big mammals – polar bear and walrus – are normally right from the ship looking onto the ice. The chances are of course higher when there is much ice, usually early in the season.

HIGHLIGHTS In the European Arctic, Franz Josef Land is probably one of the best places for seeing **big mammals** – polar bear, walrus and also some whale species. You also have a chance of spotting the extremely rare **Greenland whale**. For **Belugas**, the archipelago is one of the most popular regions of the Barents Sea in summer. Ornithologists keen on rare High-Arctic species such as **Sabine's gull** (*Xema/Larus sabini*) and **Ross's gull** (*Rhodostethia rosea*) may find them up here. As for the landscape, this is a place for minimalists, being mostly dominated by ice on land and sea. **Icebergs** are bigger here on average than in Svalbard. Where land is free of ice, it often forms stark contrasts – with some spectacular rock faces and **natural rock sculptures**, and with surprising demonstrations of how life can adapt to these harsh conditions, including some amazingly strong colours displayed by some of the flowers and lichens.

For the enthusiasts of **polar history**, Franz Josef Land is a must due to the touching and well-preserved remains from the pioneer days of Jackson, Nansen, Wellman, the Duke of Abruzzi, Ziegler, Sedov, and so on. And then there is the challenge of possibly getting to the northernmost land point of Eurasia at 81°52'N – assuming the ice permits, of course.

RED TAPE Franz Josef Land (Zemlya Franca Josifa) was annexed by the Soviet Union between 1926 and 1932 (Victoria Island) and now belongs to Russia, where it forms part of the Archangel Oblast. In 1994, Russia declared Franz Josef Land and the surrounding seas (a total of 42,000km^2) a *sakasnik* nature reserve, which permits limited utilisation and puts the usual limitations on travel. The area of 50km around the military airbase of Nagurskoe on Alexander Island is a closed zone.

All visits to Franz Josef Land require special permission from the Russian authorities. In practice, permission has seldom been forthcoming since 1999 and today permission to visit the archipelago for tourist purposes is granted to only a few Russian tourism companies, and not normally to independent travellers. During the last few years a number of scientific research projects, both Russian and foreign, have tried in vain to get permission to enter.

On organised cruises just to Franz Josef Land, beginning and ending in Svalbard or northern Norway, a Russian visa was not demanded in 2003 and 2004, but the cruise *was* accompanied by customs officers the whole time. Since 2005, Russian visas are required and the tours will start and end in Murmansk, with a plane from Helsinki/Finland. The Russian Visa Service is notably poor at responding to enquiries, something you may want to factor into your plans. That said, if you are travelling with a cruise company they should be able to sort out the formalities and required invitation for you.

GETTING THERE The only realistic way of getting to Franz Josef Land is to join a cruise. While it may theoretically be possible to travel there by private yacht, it's highly unlikely that the Russians will grant you a visa – unless you have a definite in with one ministry or other.

Some of the companies which advertise cruises to Franz Josef Land are listed below. Note that not all of these leave from or return to Longyearbyen. Life on board these cruises will be the same as for those operating around Svalbard, so do see the chapter on *Cruising* for an idea of what to expect.

Nordic Travel 13 Kluchevskoe Shosse, Petrozavodsk, Russian Federation 185005; +7 8142 56 02 01 or +7 905 212 7846 (Russia); e info@nordictravel.ru; www.nordictravel.ru
Polar Cruises 20525 Dorchester West, Bend, OR 97702, USA; +1 541 330 2454 (USA); e info@polarcruises.com; www.polarcruises.com
Quark Expeditions 93 Pilgrim Park, Suite 1, Waterbury, VT 05676, USA; +1 888 892 0334 (USA); e info@quarkexpeditions.com; www.quarkexpeditions.com
The Great Canadian Travel Company 158 Fort St, Winnipeg, MB, R3C 1C9, Canada; +1 866 949 0131 (CAN); www.greatcanadiantravel.com
Victory Adventure Expeditions Malaga 114, Punta Arenas, Chile; +56 61 22 70 98 (Chile); +54 911 5562 9404 (Argentina); e sailing@victory-cruises.com; www.victory-cruises.com/

Organised trips The first years of expedition cruises to Franz Josef Land came to an unpleasant end in 1999, when the Russian military denied an expedition cruise vessel access to the archipelago in spite of written permission from the Russian prime minister. After a pause of four years, tourist cruises heading specifically to Franz Josef Land made it through successfully aboard several icebreakers. Even for these powerful vessels, ice conditions can be a challenge and itineraries are always subject to changes.

Franz Josef Land is also included in other voyages, too, such as the Russian nuclear icebreakers that venture to the North Pole, where a slight deviation to Franz Josef Land is the only possibility of getting a short glimpse of some High-Arctic land. With good reason most Arctic territories outside of Russia (Greenland, Canada and Svalbard) deny access to nuclear-powered vessels in view of the risks in case of a stranding or collision. There is also the yet-unsolved problem of Russia's nuclear waste, which is a good reason for many to abstain from supporting use of these ships by booking tours on them – not least of all because the money earned is certainly not used for solving the waste problem.

Independent travel Independent travel to Franz Josef Land is near to impossible: currently, there is no regular transport to the archipelago except for the occasional rare military-supply tour to Nagurskoe or the cruises arranged for organised groups and scientific projects. Using the cruises just for transport is not only expensive but also highly unlikely – tourism companies are reluctant to accept responsibility for picking a passenger up after having dropped them off in light of the immense uncertainties created by weather and ice.

OTHER PRACTICALITIES As the whole archipelago is currently abandoned except for the tiny guard force at the military airbase of Nagurskoe and the equally small research base at Krenkel, there are hardly any local facilities available.

What to take Regarding equipment, travelling in Franz Josef Land is comparable with similar ways of travelling in Svalbard (see pages 105–18). Be aware of the fact that there is nothing whatsoever on sale in the islands and no medical service. Rescue operations have to be organised from Svalbard or the Russian mainland and will accordingly be absurdly expensive.

Maps Currently, no detailed maps are yet available for Franz Josef Land. Aviation maps (ICAO) are an alternative, though offer no detailed scale. There are very good Russian navigation maps, but these are not exactly readily available.

THE ISLANDS

For easier orientation with Russian maps of the archipelago, we have included the Russian names of the islands in Cyrillic. Остров/Острови means 'Island'/'Islands', Земля means 'Land'.

ALEXANDER ISLAND (ОСТРОВ КАРЛА-АЛЕКСАНДРА) The south was first visited by the Leigh Smith expedition in 1880 and explored in detail by Jackson in 1897. The remains of the wartime German weather station (1943–44) are at Cambridge Bay, with an outer depot at Cape Nimrod. The station was mostly removed in the 1950s. The Soviet strategic airbase Nagurskoe was built in 1952 and has effectively been left to fall into decay – something that cannot be prevented by the current small guard of about 20 men. However, a part of the base is still in use, and scientists from the Moscow Institute for Geography occasionally come for research work. For visitors, the area is a forbidden zone with a perimeter of about 50km around the base.

ALGER ISLAND (ОСТРОВ АЛДЖЕР) Only partly glaciated, this island has a fairly low wide area along its southern coast. On Alger, the Baldwin–Ziegler expedition established its main base for the wintering of 1901–02, which was also used by a group from the Fiala–Ziegler expedition of 1903–05 for wintering in 1904–05. The base consisted of a main station with two octagonal prefabricated huts and a connective building as the main structure, surrounded by minor constructions including facilities for producing hydrogen for balloons, 15 ponies and hundreds of dogs. The main station was – unfathomably, it would seem – connected to the frozen-in ship by an electric line and telephone. Today, the station is in ruins, but still one of the best-preserved bases of the pioneer period. There is also an additional outpost of the Ziegler expeditions some kilometres away from the main station.

APOLLONOV/STOLICHKIY ISLANDS (ОСТРОВ АПОЛЛОНОВА/ОСТРОВ СТОЛИЧКИ) Situated in the northernmost part of the Austria Sound, these tiny islands are one of the common haul-out sites where walrus can often be watched on the beach.

BELL ISLAND (ОСТРОВ БЕЛЛ) A flat, smaller island, almost free of ice, with a big lagoon and a bell-shaped, single mountain. Benjamin Leigh Smith built a cabin here in 1881, which he was unable to use afterwards and the *Hobby* found shelter here in 1928 for repairs during a search for the Nobile expedition. The cabin remains intact – it is the oldest house in Franz Josef Land – but it is completely empty.

CHAMP ISLAND (ОСТРОВ ЧАМП) Mostly glaciated, the main attraction is the geodes at the ice-free part of the south coast – naturally grown spheres of rock, many almost perfectly round like medieval cannonballs, though some are more irregular, and ranging in size from a few centimetres to 2m. They developed originally in the sediment layers as harder concretions, thus remaining on the surface while the softer sediments around eroded away, before rolling down the slope towards the beach. Near the landing site is a bird cliff (populated mainly by kittiwakes) – with its characteristic dark igneous rock columns.

HEISS (KHEYSA) ISLAND (ОСТРОВ ХЕЙСА) As a successor for the station in Tikhaya Bay (Hooker (Gukera) Island), a new station was erected for the Geophysical Year 1957–58 around a small crater lake in the ice-free eastern part of Heiss (Kheysa) Island. Named after the Russian polar hero, Krenkel, it became the biggest of the research stations in the archipelago. Closed in 2000, it is today a big group of decaying buildings, leaking fuel tanks and wreckages, including the remains of an Ilyushin plane. In summer 2005 a small Russian hydrometeorological research station was reinstalled at Krenkel on the initiative of Artur Chilingarov (deputy chairman of the Russian state *duma*). The island itself was named after veteran Arctic explorer Isaac Hayes, but the name was Germanised by German cartographers from a transliteration of the Russian name, since which the misnomer 'Heiss' (which means 'hot' in German) has become the accepted nomination.

EVA-LIV ISLAND/HVIDTENLAND (ОСТРОВ ЕВА-ЛИВ/ОСТРОВ БЕЛАЯ ЗЕМЛЯ) Hvidtenland (Norwegian for 'White Land') comprises the three small northeasternmost islands. This was the first piece of land which Nansen and Johansen discovered on 24 July 1895 after two years in the ice, when they approached the archipelago from the north. Nansen mistook Eva-Liv as two separate islands, naming them after his wife and daughter. It was revisited in spring 1905 by three men of the Fiala–Ziegler expedition during their search for the three lost expedition members. Since then, the islands have had few further visitors, if any.

GRAHAM BELL ISLAND (ОСТРОВ ГРЕЭМ-БЕЛЛ) One of the largest islands of the archipelago, with a wide, flat, ice-free tundra zone in the north. This was the site of a Russian Air Force depot (one airbase boasted a 7,000ft year-round compacted-ice runway) and helicopter supply base, which was shut down in 1994. The bigger southern part is completely covered with a huge ice dome called Kupol Vyetreniy ('Windy Dome'), probably the thickest in the archipelago with a maximum 500–550m of ice and a maximum height above sea level of 580m. Here, a joint ice-core drilling project was carried out in 1997 by researchers from Moscow and Ohio, which managed to drill 315m down into the ice. The hope is to eventually find ice layers in the frozen depths with an age of 8,000–10,000 years, which could increase our knowledge about the development of the climate after the end of the last ice age.

GREELY ISLAND (ОСТРОВ ГРИЛИ) An almost completely ice-covered smaller island in the northern centre, Greely plays host to 'Kane Lodge', used by the Ziegler expeditions initially as a cache and, on the second expedition, it was also used as a transitory camp.

HALL ISLAND (ОСТРОВ ГАЛЛЯ) Cape Tegetthoff is the most common place visited here, with its amazing range of pinnacles that resemble the back of a monstrous stegosaurus, and handsome flora including brilliantly coloured poppies and some breeding birds (black guillemots, kittiwakes, etc). One of Jackson's octagonal 'Elmwood' cabins was moved from Cape Flora (on Northbrook) to Cape Tegetthoff by Wellman in 1898 and used as a winter base for the attempt on the North Pole the following year; much is still left of the ruin. On the rocks to the east, a Russian memorial plate commemorating the discovery expedition of the *Tegetthoff* has been mounted, with Wilczek Island as the place of their first contact with land.

HOOKER (GUKERA) ISLAND (ОСТРОВ ГУКЕРА) Sedov was trapped by ice in Hooker's Tikhaya Bay in 1913 and wintered here, commemorated by Russia with a cross. The first long-standing base was built here in 1929. Tikhaya Station was in continuous operation until 1959, by which time Krenkel Station was fully operational. Twenty iced-up buildings remain, as well as a hangar, scientific equipment, rubbish and the wreckages of tracked vehicles and planes. In the early 1990s, a small Russian–Norwegian summer research station reactivated some of the buildings.

The other attraction of the island is Rubini Rock, easily the most important bird colony of the whole archipelago. In the breeding period, it may be populated by up to 7,000 pairs of Brünnich's guillemots, 5,000 pairs of kittiwakes and – in the lateral scree slopes – about 2,000 pairs of little auks. Other species present in smaller numbers include fulmars, glaucous gulls and black guillemots. The bent, dark columns of igneous rock decorated with orange lichen add further aesthetic qualities to the picture. Don't venture onto the slopes on both sides of the rock, however – not strictly because of the birds, but because of the brilliantly green moss carpets that are extremely delicate.

JACKSON ISLAND (ОСТРОВ ДЖЕКСОНА) The island in the northern centre of the archipelago was first reached by the Jackson expedition, who landed at Cape Mill, the northernmost point of their travels, on 2 May 1895. Nansen and Johansen arrived at what then became Cape Norvegia on 28 August, where they decided to spend the winter, building for this purpose a low shelter with a roof made of a driftwood log and walrus hides. The site was again visited by the Baldwin–Ziegler expedition in 1902, followed by many others, including the occasional tourist expedition from the 1990s onwards. The shelter's walls, the driftwood log and some bones and skulls of walrus and polar bear are still there. A memorial plate was set up in 1990 by the Russian–Norwegian historical expedition, which documented the site again.

MCCLINTOCK ISLAND (ОСТРОВ МАК-КЛИНТОКА) One of the bigger southern islands and almost completely glaciated, McClintock is where you'll find Cape Dillon, on the island's southwest corner, which served as a base and a temporary look-out camp for the Fiala–Ziegler expedition of 1905 while they waited for relief.

NORTHBROOK ISLAND WITH CAPE FLORA (ОСТРОВ НОРТБРУК) Cape Barents, in the southeast of Northbrook, has been visited by several expeditions, but the most important site, visited by most expeditions of the pioneer time, was Cape Flora. It is still possible to assign many of the artefacts visible on the site to the various expeditions.

- The south of the island, including the cape, was first visited briefly by the Leigh Smith expedition of 1880.
- In 1881, the yacht *Eira* was crushed by ice off Cape Flora. The 25 crew saved themselves and much of the material, then built a shelter (Flora Cottage) and overwintered on Cape Flora. As the shelter was built right on the low cliff, which is exposed to strong erosion, most of it had disappeared by the time of documentation in 1996.
- The Jackson–Harmsworth expedition of 1894–97 built its solid winter quarters 'Elmwood' on Cape Flora as their central base for three years with four octagonal prefabricated houses and some log cabins. Above the base, right under the slope of the mountain, expedition member Mouatt was buried in spring 1895. Off the cape on the sea ice, the famous meeting of Jackson and Nansen took place on 17 June 1896. A plate commemorating this event was installed in 1996.
- Much of Elmwood was removed in 1898 by Wellman for re-use at Cape Tegetthoff.
- The Duke of Abruzzi expedition left some provisions for emergencies in 1899 and paid a short visit in 1900.
- An obelisk to commemorate those lost on Cagni's 1900 North Pole attempt was erected in 1901 by Støkken senior, which is still standing.
- In 1904–05, the remaining structures served the Fiala–Ziegler expedition as an additional, improvised and overcrowded wintering base, contributing much to its deterioration. This expedition also mined 20 tonnes of coal from the coal seam high above the cape.
- The Sedov expedition spent a few days here in summer 1913, before continuing to Tikhaya, from where an expedition member made an additional visit to Cape Flora with messages in March 1914. At that time, the station was already in quite a sorry state.
- In 1914, the Russian *St Foka* of the Sedov expedition reached Cape Flora almost out of fuel, finding here the last two survivors of the lost *St Anna* expedition. At that time, there were still two large buildings (a log cabin and one of the octagonal prefabricated houses from Jackson) and a smaller cabin (constructed by the Fiala–Ziegler wintering team from found materials) standing, though both were in a desperate condition. To be able to travel home, they had to tear

down the two buildings from Jackson in order to fire the kettle of their steam engine, leaving behind only the small cabin. Later in the same year, the Russian *Hertha* hoisted the Russian flag here to occupy the island.

- The *Hobby*, while on a search in 1929 for remains of the *Italia* and *Latham* expeditions, unloaded a cabin at Cape Flora as a replacement for the mostly older constructions.

Since then, the site has been visited by numerous Soviet and, most recently, tourism expeditions too, which led to changes and, sadly, some pilfering. Today, there is one almost-intact small cabin left, the memorials, and some foundations and items scattered on the ground. Owing to the typical polynia (see page 193) off the south coast, which usually allows easy access, Cape Flora is probably the most visited place of the archipelago.

(PRINCE) GEORGE ISLAND (ЗЕМЛЯ ГЕОРГА) Second-largest island of the archipelago, glaciated except for some promontories and a bigger area in the north. The south was first visited by the Leigh Smith expedition in 1880, with the first complete mapping by Jackson in 1897. The Russian icebreaker *Krassin* landed at Cape Neale in 1928 to set up a big cabin, and in 1930 a Norwegian cabin was built at Cape Forbes.

RUDOLF ISLAND (ОСТРОВ РУДОЛЬФА) This is the northernmost island of the archipelago and Cape Fligely at 81°52'N is also the northernmost land point of Eurasia. Payer got to Cape Fligely in 1874 and erected a primitive shelter. The Duke of Abruzzi got to Teplitz Bay in 1899, wintering in Camp Abruzzi, and the Baldwin–Ziegler expedition got here in 1902, setting up a depot, while the Fiala–Ziegler expedition established their main camp here for two winters. One member, Sigurd Myhre, was buried here, his cross restored by the last Russian station crew in 1995. The second person buried on the island was Georgiy Sedov in 1914; a memorial to him was erected in 1970. The meteorological station was put up in 1932 in connection with the International Polar Year 1932–33 and served until evacuation in 1941. It also served as an advanced airbase for Soviet aviation activities in the High Arctic. A smaller station was erected after World War II, but was closed in 1995 – a year with exceptionally good shipping conditions, in which the *Professor Molchanov* managed to sail to Rudolf Island with a group of tourists encountering virtually no ice on the way.

On my visit to the station in July 2004 as expedition leader on the *Kapitan Dranitsyn*, the buildings were clearly decaying, and filled with ice and snow. Of the pre-World War II stations in Teplitz Bay, seemingly very little has survived later Soviet activities.

VICTORIA ISLAND (ОСТРОВ ВИКТОРИЯ) Victoria Island lies between Franz Josef Land and Svalbard, and was annexed by the USSR in 1932. This tiny, low island is almost completely covered by an ice dome, reaching a maximum height of about 60m in the middle. Only to the west and to the north do two, almost vegetation-free, flat gravel capes stick out of the ice. On the northern one there was a small military weather installation until 1994, but a decade later the empty station was in clear decay, with fuel very slowly seeping out of huge rusting tanks.

WILCZEK ISLAND (ОСТРОВ ВИЛЬЧЕКА) The *Admiral Tegetthoff*, caught in the ice off Novaya Zemlya in 1872, came to a halt here for the winter of 1873–74 as its ice field froze to the coastal ice off this tiny bleak island with its basalt cliffs. From here, its crew did all the exploration of the newly discovered archipelago up to Rudolf Island. On one of the cliffs, there is still the grave with its cross for Otto Krisch, the only participant of the expedition that died. The grave was wrongly reported as missing in 2003 (despite having previously been rediscovered by visitors in 1991–93), but was seen there in 2004.

WILCZEK LAND (ЗЕМЛЯ ВИЛЬЧЕКА) One of the largest in the archipelago and holding one of the major ice caps, this island was partly mapped by Payer in 1874, followed by Wellman in 1898–99. During his expedition, the incredible wintering of Bentsen and Bjørvik took place (see page 198). Bentsen's grave and cabin walls are still well preserved at Cape Heller, in addition to a Soviet memorial column. If you visit, please avoid the cabin's interior in order to prevent damage to the artefacts inside.

ZIEGLER ISLAND (ОСТРОВ ЦИГЛЕРА) As part of the Austrian 1,000-year celebrations, the television company ORF filmed the story of the Payer–Weyprecht expedition. Huge quantities of materials were brought here by a Russian icebreaker in 1993 and a replica of the *Admiral Tegetthoff* was built, albeit 100km from the actual historic site. At the same time, a small scientific Austrian station was installed in containers, which has been out of use since 1996 due to a more restrictive Russian attitude and a lack of transport. The ship replica and the film base were finally collected in 1996, but frost and snow prevented a complete removal of materials, thus leaving more waste on this site than the total of that generated by tourism so far on the archipelago. The scientific container station is still there, waiting for future research activities.

Part Four

JAN MAYEN

Greenland
Sea

Jan Mayen

Norwegian
Sea

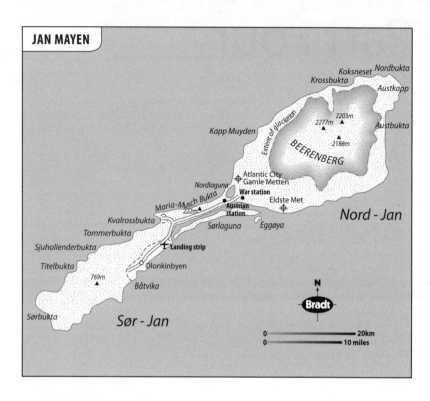

8

Jan Mayen

GEOLOGY AND GEOGRAPHY

Not everybody knows that Norway has one other Arctic outpost apart from Svalbard: the tiny, lonely volcanic island of Jan Mayen, 450km from Greenland's east coast and 550km north of Iceland. Lying at 71°N, Jan Mayen is no further north than the tourist-friendly Nordkapp (North Cape) in northern Norway, but the cold east Greenland current puts this island firmly into the Arctic zone.

Geologically, Jan Mayen is very different from other Norwegian northern hemisphere territories. It is relatively young and contains Norway's only active volcano. It has many geological similarities to Iceland, both islands sitting on an active extension of the Mid-Atlantic Ridge. In fact, both of them originate from the same geological processes: as a deep-sea ocean, the Atlantic started developing only about 200 million years ago, when the supercontinent Pangaea of the Permian period broke up into several plates, which, swimming on the liquid mantle of the Earth, drifted apart.

In this way, the Atlantic started developing in the growing gap between Eurasia and Africa to the east and the two Americas to the west. The bottom of this gap was filled by magma seeping through cracks, creating a long submarine mountain range all along the middle of the new ocean. The submarine volcanoes along the centre line of this mountain range deep under the surface are the youngest, while to the sides, the material becomes increasingly older, forming the basis of the deep-sea floor, which has then been gradually covered by sediments.

In the case of the Atlantic, this submarine chain of volcanoes is called the Mid-Atlantic Ridge, mostly hidden hundreds or thousands of metres under the ocean surface. Down there in the eternal darkness, the volcanic activity is the basis for fascinating structures and amazing, strange forms of life. Above the ocean surface, this volcanism is visible directly or indirectly only in a few places, where the activity was strong enough to build up volcanic islands from a depth of 3,000–6,000m under sea level to sometimes more than 2,000m up in the air – we see therefore only the smallest part of these huge volcanoes and can follow them all along the Mid-Atlantic Ridge from Antarctica right up to the Arctic, including Bouvetøya, Tristan da Cunha, Saint Helena, Ascension, Saint Paul, the Azores, Iceland and finally – and furthest north – Jan Mayen.

Jan Mayen is part of the newer history of the Atlantic, which began in the north much later. The spreading and movement of the plates which led to the beginning of volcanism under the Jan Mayen of today started about 30 million years ago, in the Tertiary period. Greenland, which broke off the continental plate, forming a kind of mini continent between the North American and the Eurasian plates, did not only move away from Scandinavia, but also advanced faster to the north than Europe, causing with this movement intensive volcanic activity in the fracture zone to its east, which finally broke through the ocean surface as the island of Jan Mayen. Hidden in the water, there are more such volcanic cones to the north and south of the island.

Today, about 380km² of the volcanic island is above the waterline, reaching the impressive height of 2,277m above sea level on the rim of the central crater of the elegant volcanic cone called Beerenberg. This is the dominating element of the north of the island which has a total length of 56.3km in a southwest–northeast direction, and a maximum width of 15.8km. The island is shaped a bit like a cudgel or truncheon with two distinct regions, Nord-Jan and Sør-Jan, of roughly equal size.

NORD-JAN Nord-Jan is the head of the cudgel and is centred on the Beerenberg cone. There are lava flows down all sides spilling from its central crater, most of them covered in glaciers. Five glaciers reach the sea, breaking off into floes. Most of the volcanic activity is outside of the crater towards the steep northern coast – but you can also see steam rising from the flat shore and shallows linking Nord-Jan's south coast with Eggøya ('Egg Island'). Owing to very rare visits after the Dutch whaling period, little information is available regarding older eruptions except for two coincidental minor observations from 1732 and 1818. The latest eruptions were in 1970 (creating an additional 4km² of new land as lava flowed from a crack in northern Beerenberg into Krossbukta, causing a temporary evacuation of the station as a precaution) and in 1985.

Nord-Jan rose out of the sea some two million years ago and was probably high enough 12,000 years ago to start glaciation. The upper parts of Beerenberg, including the crater, are some 4,000–7,000 years old and the movement north of much of the volcanic activity has occurred since then. The island is being built upon by this activity and appears to be moving northwards, as is the entire Mid-Atlantic Ridge. The highest part of the wall of the now-inactive central crater is 2,277m above sea level – and about 5,000m above the ocean floor out of which the island rose.

SØR-JAN Sør-Jan is of volcanic origin – something evident from the small craters and lava fields here and there – but it is not as active as the north. The landscape is hilly (there are 20 to 30 peaks of 100m to 700m) and the south coast drops steeply into the sea. A coastal plain stretches along the northwest coast of Sør-Jan.

A narrow isthmus (up to 222m high) connects north and south. A sand spit on the south side of this chain of hills has been built by ocean currents, leaving a lagoon walled off from the sea. There are two similar constructions to the north, one without a lagoon. The best landfalls are on either side of the isthmus, along with the most important human settlements.

Signs of earlier shorelines are to be found: those at 5m above today's sea level are approximately 1,500–2,000 years old, and those at 10m some 3,500–4,000 years old. Under the sea are signs that Jan Mayen has at some point in its history (most likely several million years ago) sunk. Deep under the water there are also signs of erosion that show an area which must have been above sea level at some stage.

The tidal range is minimal, about half a metre. There are no rivers (the only streams there are formed by meltwater) and nor are there any lakes, apart from the two lagoons. The landscape is typical of the Arctic.

CLIMATE

Jan Mayen's climate is also Arctic. The highest monthly mean temperature is in August: +5.4°C, with October to April lying below freezing. March is the coldest month, at –5.1°C mean, so the extremes of cold felt elsewhere don't apply here. The annual average is –3.6°C.

Precipitation averages 648mm, much higher than in Svalbard but no more than the drier parts of central Europe. However, cloud cover, drizzle and fog make this feel like a damp place, statistics be damned. There are probably only three absolutely clear days a year and around 88 foggy days; to see Beerenberg completely clear of cloud is considered a sensation. Storms are common and can be violent, with wind speeds up to 150km/h.

WILDLIFE AND CONSERVATION

FLORA The approaching visitor sees Jan Mayen as a desert of dark rocks and sand, with white glaciation on Beerenberg (insofar as you can see it at all through the mist!). But in sheltered areas plant life can be interesting. Apart from the heavy wind erosion, conditions for flora are not too terribly bad: there are not the extremes of temperature found elsewhere in the Arctic and there is a constant supply of water, even though the porous volcanic rock lets most of it drain away.

Mosses are common because of the damp environment. Higher plants are found in sheltered areas. So far, 72 species are known on Jan Mayen, including a fern, a horse-tail, two clubmosses and a 10cm creeping willow (*Salix herbacea*). As parts of the island is almost inaccessible and the area in general is little-frequented, new findings of species should not surprise one too much, like the water aven (*Geum rivale*) as the latest entry in 1993, discovered by station member Dag Kvammen.

More than half of the species grow all around the Pole (circumpolar) and almost all are found also in Norway, Iceland and/or Greenland. It is thought that seeds made their way to Jan Mayen by the wind, driftwood, or by birds – either in their feathers or in their stomachs. An interesting exception is five kinds of dandelion (*Taraxacum*), four of them endemic, and the other found elsewhere only on Iceland from which the four endemic species have seemingly developed.

The amount of groundcover is minimal, too little to support any grazing mammals. Nearly all plants (except the mosses) grow in sheltered hollows or between rocks. On exposed sites, especially beach areas where storms and sand permanently threaten to damage or bury the plants, only a few species can withstand the conditions, like the oysterplant (*Mertensia maritima*) – often standing 100m apart.

Particularly hostile to plant growth are the coastal zones which are hit by the breakers, where the material is constantly moved around. Additionally, in the wintertime pieces of drift ice are pushed up several metres onto the beaches by waves and wind pressure, scraping the coast several metres above and under the waterline. But under a water depth of two to three metres, out of the reach of the destructive ice, there is an amazingly abundant and varied marine flora and fauna. This also partially supports the sparse life on land by providing food to seabirds, which in return fertilise the land with their droppings, rich in nutrients from the sea.

FAUNA There is scarcity, too, in the animal world. Among the land mammals, only the polar fox belongs to the local fauna – with the peculiarity that 90% of the foxes are of the much rarer dark variety, the so-called blue fox. This has a clear advantage over the white variety in the mostly dark landscape of Jan Mayen, where in winter many stretches are blown free of snow. Although they have been protected for several decades after centuries of merciless trapping, recent sightings are non-existent. It is possible that they are extinct or that their numbers have fallen below a critical level so that regeneration is unlikely on genetic grounds. Even before the

Plants listed below are in alphabetical order of scientific Latin names, with English and Norwegian names alongside. Note that although some species may have several popular names, only one is given here while a couple of species have no common name, in which case none is given. In a few cases, there are also competing Latin names – again, only one is stated here. The list is based on the Jan Mayen website (*www.jan-mayen.no*).

PTERIDOPHYTA

Cystopteris fragilis	bladderfern	Skjørlok
Diphasiastrum alpinum	alpine clubmoss	Fjellamne
Equisetum arvense	polar horse-tail	Polarsnelle
Huperzia arctica	fir clubmoss	Polarlusegras

DICOTYLEDONES

Alchemilla glomerulans	lady's mantle	Kildemarikåpe
Arabis alpina	alpine rock-cress	Fjellskrinneblom
Beckwithia glacialis		Issoleie
Bistortia vivipara		Harerug
Cardamine bellidifolia	high alpine cress	Høgfjellskarse
Cardamine pratensis angustifolia	cuckoo flower	Polarkarse
Cassiope hypnoides	mossy mountain-heather	Moselyng
Cerastium alpinum	alpine mouse-ear	Fjellarve
Cerastium arcticum	arctic mouse-ear	Snøarve
Cerastium cerastioides	starwort mouse-ear	Brearve
Cochlearia groenlandica	polar scurvygrass	Polarskjørbuksurt
Draba alpina	golden whitlow-grass	Gullrublom
Draba nivalis	snow whitlow-grass	Snørublom
Draba nivalis x norvegica	(natural crossbreed)	Snø- x Bergrublom
Draba norvegica	rock whitlow-grass	Bergrublom
Draba oxycarpa	pale whitlow-grass	Bleikrublom
Empetrum nigrum hermaphroditum	crowberry	Fjellkrekling
Epilobium anagallidifolium	alpine willowherb	Dvergmjølke
Euphrasia wettsteinii	mountain eyebright	Fjelløyentrøst
Geum rivale	water aven	Enghumleblom
Harrimanella hypnoides	moss bell heather	Moselyng
Honkenya peploides	sea sandwort	Strandarve
Koenigia islandica	Iceland-purslane	Dvergsyre
Loiseleuria procumbens	alpine azalea	Greplyng
Mertensia maritima	oysterplant	Østersurt
Minuartia biflora	tufted sandwort	Tuearve
Minuartia rubella	mountain sandwort	Nålarve
Omalotheca supina	alpine cudweed	Dverggråurt
Oxyria digyna	mountain sorrel	Fjellsyre
Potentilla crantzii	alpine cinquefoil	Flekkmure
Ranunculus acris acris	meadow buttercup	Engsoleie

Ranunculus hyperboreus amellii	tundra buttercup	Tundrasoleie
Ranunculus pygmaeus	pygmy buttercup	Dvergsoleie
Rumex acetosa acetosa	common sorrel	Engsyre
Rumex longifolius	northern dock	Høymole
Sagina caespitosa	tufted pearlwort	Stuttsmåarve
Sagina nivalis	snow pearlwort	Jøkelsmåarve
Salix arctica		Tundravier
Salix herbacea	dwarf willow	Musøre
Saxifraga cernua	drooping saxifrage	Knoppsildre
Saxifraga cespitosa	tufted saxifrage	Tuesildre
Saxifraga nivalis	alpine saxifrage	Snøsildre
Saxifraga oppositifolia	purple saxifrage	Rødsildre
Saxifraga rivularis	highland saxifrage	Bekkesildre
Saxifraga tenuis	dwarf saxifrage	Grannsildre
Sibbaldia procumbens	sibbaldia	Trefingerurt
Silene acaulis	moss campion	Fjellsmelle
Taraxacum acromaurum	dandelion var.	Taggløvetann
Taraxacum brachyrhunchum	endemic dandelion var.	Løvetann var.
Taraxacum croceum	dandelion var.	Fjell-løvetann
Taraxacum recedens	endemic dandelion var.	Løvetann var.
Taraxacum torvum	endemic dandelion var.	Løvetann var.
Tripleurospermum inodorum	scentless mayweed	Ugrasalderbrå
Veronica alpine alpina	alpine speedwell	Fjellveronika

MONOCOTYLEDONES

Calamagrostis neglecta groenlandica		Polarrørkvein
Carex bigelowii	stiff sedge	Stivstarr
Carex lachenalii	hare's-foot sedge	Rypestarr
Carex maritima	curved sedge	Buestarr
Deschampsia cespitosa cespitosa	tufted hair-grass	Vanlig sølvbunke
Festuca rubra richardsonii	red fescue	Polarrødsvingel
Festuca vivipara	viviparous fescue	Geitsvingel
Luzula arcuata	curved wood-rush	Buefrytle
Luzula confusa	curved wood-rush	Vardefrytle
Luzula nivalis	arctic wood-rush	Snøfrytle
Luzula spicata	spiked wood-rush	Aksfrytle
Phippsia algida	snowgrass	Snøgras
Poa alpine vivipara	alpine meadow-grass	Fjellrapp
Poa arctica arctica		Vanlig jervrapp
Poa glauca	glaucous meadow-grass	Blårapp
Poa pratensis alpigena	smooth meadow-grass	Seterrapp
Puccinellia capillaris	northern salt-marsh grass	Vrangsaltgras
Trisetum spicatum	northern oat-grass	Svartaks

8

Large parts of the island are almost inaccessible, especially the cliffs and steep slopes and glaciers coming down from Beerenberg, which makes a full overview of the avifauna difficult. Birds are listed alphabetically by scientific Latin name, followed by English and Norwegian names. Not included are rare visitors – more than half of the observed species. The regularly updated Svalbard Birds website (*www.svalbardbirds.com*) has a list of observed birds organised by date going back to 2005.

Alca torda	razorbill	Alke
Alle alle	little auk	Alkekonge
Anser brachyrhynchus	pink-footed goose	Kortnebbgås
Anthus pratensis	meadow pipit	Heipiplerke
Arenaria interpres	turnstone	Steinvender
Calidris alba	sanderling	Sandløper
Calidris alpina	dunlin	Myrsnipe
Calidris canutus	red knot	Polarsnipe
Calidris maritima	purple sandpiper	Fjæreplytt
Cepphus grylle	black guillemot	Teist
Charadrius hiaticula	common ringed plover	Sandlo
Clangula hyemalis	long-tailed duck	Havelle
Cygnus cygnus	whooper swan	Sangsvane
Fratercula arctica	puffin	Lunde
Fulmarus glacialis	fulmar	Havhest
Gavia immer	common loon	Islom
Gavia stellata	red-throated diver	Smålom
Haematopus ostralegus	oystercatcher	Tjeld
Larus canus	common gull	Fiskemåke
Larus fuscus	lesser black-backed gull	Sildemåke
Larus hyperboreus	glaucous gull	Polarmåke
Larus marinus	great black-backed gull	Svartbak
Larus ridibundus	black-headed gull	Hettemåke
Motacilla alba	pied wagtail	Linerle
Numenius phaeopus	whimbrel	Småspove
Nyctea scandiaca	snowy owl	Snøugle
Oenanthe oenanthe	northern wheatear	Steinskvett
Plectrophenax nivalis	snow bunting	Snøspurv
Pluvialis apricaria	golden plover	Heilo
Rissa tridactyla	kittiwake	Krykkje
Somateria molissima	common eider	Ærfugl
Stercorarius parasiticus	arctic skua	Tyvjo
Stercorarius skua	great skua	Storjo
Sterna paradisaea	arctic tern	Rødnebbterne
Sturnus vulgaris	starling	Stær
Turdus iliacus	redwing	Rødvingetrost
Turdus pilaris	fieldfare	Gråtrost
Uria aalge	common guillemot	Lomvi
Uria lomvia	Brünnich's guillemot	Polarlomvi

arrival of man, a large population could not be supported on this barren island as the foxes' staple diet is made up of seabirds and their eggs.

There are sporadic visits by small numbers of bearded seals and ringed seals, and polar bears, too, reach the island every couple of years or so.

Around 100 species of birds have been observed on Jan Mayen, though the majority of them have to be regarded as errants, brought here by mis-navigation or storm. Only 17 of the species can be regarded as common local breeders; these include an amazing number of fulmar, little auk, puffin, black guillemot, Brünnich's guillemot, common guillemot, razorbill, kittiwake, arctic skua, glaucous gull, great black-backed gull, eider and long-tailed duck, purple sandpiper, arctic tern, meadow pipit and snow bunting. Another six breed here only occasionally or in numbers of fewer than ten pairs. In addition, there are about 15 species that do not breed here normally, but are common visitors. Note that there are no ptarmigan on Jan Mayen.

SEA AND WATER LIFE As there is virtually no fresh water, there are few freshwater fish. There is a population of mostly small, underdeveloped arctic char in the north lagoon (38m deep but with no connection to the ocean above sea level), with a few big individuals which have turned to cannibalism. The small arctic char of the lagoon serve as food for the common loons, which breed here in some years.

For all typical birds of Jan Mayen, with the exception of the snow bunting, the sea is directly or indirectly the main source of food. The same goes for the arctic fox.

The waters immediately surrounding Jan Mayen are full of plankton. The cold east Greenland current meets the Gulf Stream and – apart from being the root cause of the ubiquitous mist – stirs up the water from the deep, making it rich in nutrients. This, together with the long days of the polar summer, provides the ingredients for a rich food chain and encourages the migrating birds to spend their summers in this area. The same applies to huge numbers of seals, especially on and around drift ice. This serves not only as a resting place but also as a good area for the seals to find food due to the special ecosystem under the ice floes, starting with algae which grow under and in the ice. A typically large region of drift ice in the vicinity of Jan Mayen is the so-called Vestisen (Western Ice) which has a large stock of seals. It is therefore a popular traditional hunting area for Norwegian sealers, who come here in February and March to shoot or club (with the *hakapik*) their prey. In earlier centuries, the Greenland right whale appeared here in huge numbers, too, to feed on the masses of plankton, leading to the short era in the 17th century when Jan Mayen was a Dutch whale-processing base. Almost driven to extinction, the few Greenland right whales of today are a rare sight.

ARTHROPODS There are some 200 species of tiny arthropods, mostly living on discarded organic material, a few larger insects, including a couple of butterflies, and a couple of species of spiders.

THE ENVIRONMENT Jan Mayen has not been affected by man as much as Svalbard or Franz Josef Land, although, of course, there are small amounts of damage to the environment around the settlements, and man has all but eradicated the arctic fox.

The Norwegian Ministry of the Environment has set out some directives to be followed in order to limit damage. The most important rules can be summarised as:

- All wildlife is fully protected unless a special exception is given. Even animals for which such an exception has been granted may not be hunted from 24 to 31 December or from Good Friday to Easter Monday.

- Automatic weapons, poisons, explosions, traps and seal nets are forbidden.
- Hunting with motorised transport is forbidden.
- Fishing may be carried out only with rods or with nets of 40mm minimum mesh size. No boat may have more than three nets and nets must be no longer than 25m and be buoyed with boat identification marked upon them. No watercourse may be altered and no barriers put up against schools of fish. Freshwater fishing, including in the lagoons, is forbidden from 26 July to 10 August.
- Landing animals is banned.
- The Environment Ministry may be subject to paying compensation for damage caused by any protected species.
- Use of firearms and horns is forbidden within 1km of a bird colony; planes flying over bird colonies must remain at least 500m above them.
- The Bodø police chief is responsible for enforcing these regulations.

HISTORY

DISCOVERY The first discovery of Jan Mayen is unknown. Irish monks under the abbot St Brendan (circa AD489–580) were known to travel north and west, probably reaching Jan Mayen, Greenland and possibly America. The Vikings were active some 400–600 years later, but their chronicles are lacking in detail and there is much room for speculation. In view of archaeological finds pointing to Viking presence on Greenland and North America, it seems likely that they also reached Jan Mayen. In any event, Jan Mayen itself has no archaeological proof that either ever made it there.

The Venetian, Nicolo Zeno, undertook many voyages of exploration from 1390 to 1405, sometimes with his brother Antonio. Sketches from his log and charts he prepared have many errors, but he clearly showed a volcano east of Greenland and north of Iceland (where Jan Mayen is), and directly next to it the cloister of St Thomas. His diary tells of monks using warm springs for heating and kayaks for hunting, which could have meant Inuit, although neighbouring parts of Greenland have no active volcano.

In the Ekroldalen, on the south side of Beerenberg, there are remains of what seem to be the foundations and ruins of walls and artificial irrigation systems which may have supported such a settlement, although natural formation cannot yet be ruled out. A skull has been found, believed to be female.

It is possible that Henry Hudson came to Jan Mayen in 1607, and Thomas Marmaduke in 1612. The Englishman John Clarke saw the island three times in 1614, naming it 'Isabella' and landing to collect 11 walrus. Three Dutch ships came to the area in the same year, one of them captained by Jan Jacobs May, after whom the island was finally named. As with the case of America, names do not always honour the 'true' discoverers.

THE WHALERS The discovery of Jan Mayen and its rich hunting grounds was welcomed by Dutch whalers, who were tired of constantly arguing with other countries, especially Britain, in Svalbard. Commercial interests from various Dutch towns aligned in order to assemble a whaling fleet from 1614 onwards, the Noordsche Compagnie. In its first year, it moved its main activities from Svalbard to Jan Mayen. On average there were ten whaling vessels at sea and catches were large. By 1634 the company was losing strength and by 1642 the land-based stations on Jan Mayen were beginning to close down. As with Svalbard, the decimated whale population had to be hunted further and further from the island, which made the use of land stations for processing ineffective due to the lengthy transport time involved in bringing the catch back to shore.

During the period of Dutch whale processing on Jan Mayen, there were five whaling stations, all of them visible in some form or other today: Kvalrossbukta (formerly Noorderbaai), Titelbukta (formerly Suydbaai), Sjuhollendarbukta, Maria-Muschbukta and the bay near Kapp Muyden. There were ten processing ovens, showing a presence equivalent to that in Svalbard. The clearest remains are at Kvalrossbukta, even though the sea has claimed its share, which the surf gives up piece by piece. The cannons now standing in front of the military post were found in 1964 and are evidence of defences against competition. There were archaeological digs here in 1983 and 1988.

There was only one wintering attempt by seven Dutchmen in 1633–34, all of whom died of scurvy, leading to the name Sjuhollendarbukta (Seven Hollanders' Bay) for the place where they perished.

As with Svalbard, all of the remaining artefacts from this period are automatically protected by law as historical monuments.

SCIENTIFIC EXPLORATION In the footsteps of the whalers came the scientists. Zorgdrager landed on the island in 1699, charting it with accuracy. The following years saw only passers-by, two of whom recorded volcanic activity.

The first real scientific expeditions came in August 1861, under the leadership of Carl Vogt and Georg Berna. The Englishman Leigh Smith visited here in 1872, and again in 1880 (when he brought a photographer), and the Norwegian Northern Sea expedition mapped the place at a scale of 1:200,000 in the summer of 1877.

The First International Polar Year (1882–83) was the first attempt to intensify polar research through international co-operation between exploring nations, which all contributed to simultaneous research projects all over the polar areas for an entire year. This concept was developed by Carl Weyprecht, leader of the former Austrian expedition which discovered Franz Josef Land in 1873. The Austrian contribution to this unprecedented international endeavour was a scientific wintering on Jan Mayen – again, like the expedition to Franz Josef Land, sponsored by the generous and science-oriented Count Hanns von Wilczek. This first overwintering took place in an outstandingly well-constructed, roomy, prefabricated station. Life was organised to counter the depressive effects caused by the lack of sun and the physical effects of a lack of vitamins. With meteorological measurement, weather reports, tidal observation and a study of the magnetic field, there was plenty to do, leading in the end to a huge amount of data depicting, for the first time, a whole year on the island. In addition, Jan Mayen was mapped to a scale of 1:100,000; as late as in 1958 this was still the most accurate map.

Von Wilczek allowed his station buildings to be used by subsequent researchers and hunters, all of whom had to apply to him for permission. He presented the station to Denmark in 1918, who never used it. Though repaired in 1919 and 1928, the buildings experienced considerable decay and were therefore not used by the next Austrian expedition, which wintered on Jan Mayen in a new station during the Second International Polar Year (1932–33). The old station in Maria-Muschbukta was plundered for materials during World War II and only the foundations remain today.

HUNTERS Jan Mayen was never a particularly profitable place for hunters, the blue fox being the sole exception due to its rare and therefore exclusive and expensive dark fur. Fox trapping required wintering because only during the colder months do the foxes have their valuable thick winter fur. The wintering of trappers on Jan Mayen started in 1906–07, when a team of Norwegian hunters – who at the same time also collected data for the Norwegian weather service – managed a sensational catch of 100 pelts, only to then lose them in a shipwreck on the way back home. Nevertheless, this success drew some serious attention to the place.

Most expeditions were organised by Norwegian businessmen, who equipped and financed the expeditions and received half of the income from them. In view of the limited fox population, a quick decline in their number was inevitable, especially because the foxes on Jan Mayen had no natural enemies and were accordingly tame.

From 1923 onwards, trapping results dwindled. The introduction of a quota could not save the fox population but instead led to a new systematised process. Instead of killing the foxes in traps, they were first caught alive and fed; the choicest were killed for their furs while the others were set free, thus maximising the income from the limited quota. This system led to a growing number of the white variety in the fox population – with white pelts less valuable and thus the first to be set free. The final disaster for the fox population came with the installation of the permanent Norwegian weather station. While the exploitation of the fox population by hunters would have ceased as soon as the results became too poor, fox hunting was a popular leisure-time activity and earned extra income for the station members. As a result, the foxes became, for all intents and purposes, extinct and it is now uncertain whether there are any foxes left at all on the island. The blanket protection enacted in 1965 was too little, too late.

Other animals played only a minor role. Eiders on Jan Mayen are few in number, and therefore there is little to be made in collecting their down. Eggs and birds added variety to the trappers' menu, but for the commercial collection of eggs the terrain has proved too difficult an obstacle.

Hunting polar bears was not commercially viable, either: these animals appeared only rarely on Jan Mayen and the mass hunting around Svalbard had killed the prices – a good blue fox reached up to four times the price of a polar bear skin. This was somewhat different during the period of Dutch whaling, when the strong smell of the boiling blubber attracted polar bears from far away. In 1628 the whalers killed a record 70 bears near their stations.

ANNEXATION, OCCUPATION, CLAIMS AND SOVEREIGNTY ... AND THE START OF THE WEATHER SERVICE The steps towards Norwegian sovereignty over the island occupy one of those fantastic stories that are typical of pioneer areas, full of queer characters and absurd quarrels.

In 1916 Christoffer Ruud claimed the central section of the island as his own, and a year later the whole of the island. He registered his claim with the Norwegian government, which considered Jan Mayen to be no-man's-land but reluctantly passed on his claim to other countries. Only Denmark protested, on the grounds that Ruud was also claiming the formerly Austrian station given to the Danish state. Ruud could not finance his fanciful plans of a modern whaling base and tried to exert pressure on the Norwegian government by threatening to sell his rights to others, even though, as a patriot, he would have preferred a Norwegian solution (ie: state assistance).

Two other parties made claims to the same administration in 1917 and 1918. The first, comprising Hagerup, Gudmunsen and Tolløfsen, had a hunting party stationed on Jan Mayen and claimed their territory on this basis. The hunters included Artur Oxaas, well known in Svalbard as a trapper. The territory was virtually the same as Ruud's. Oxaas himself was the second claimant, registering as his the entire northwest coast, the central portion and Sør-Jan. The Norwegian government duly recorded all claims without comment as to their justification.

In 1921 another player came on to the scene: one Hagbard Ekerold, who was planning to set up a weather and telegraph station on Jan Mayen. Norway's Foreign Ministry saw Ekerold's plans as more in line with their ideas of what constitutes an acceptable claim (ie: permanent settlement and use) and gave him rights to a part of the island on behalf of the Norwegian weather service. By 1922 Ruud was bankrupt and the state bought him out in 1926 for NOK10,000. Ruud carried on with his claims and court cases until 1936. Despite losing, he received a lifelong pension of NOK100 a month from the state. Norway's action in initially ignoring the claim by Ruud, and subsequently supporting Ekerold's claim on practically the same area and finally even annexing the island, could be considered unfair treatment of Ruud. The Norwegian state, though not officially accepting Ruud's rights, nevertheless decided to give him the aforementioned pension as a kind of unofficial compensation.

Back in 1921, Ekerold's position was still not as simple as he had hoped. Birger Jacobsen, a geologist known to Ekerold from his Svalbard days, sailed to Jan Mayen just before Ekerold and became the first to stake a claim, in his case for rights to set up a mine on the island. In 1921, supported by two businessmen, Jacobsen went to Jan Mayen, built a camp by the north lagoon and waited for his opponent. But Ekerold landed unnoticed on the south coast and built his station where it would provide better radio contact with the outside world. Not only that, when they did finally meet, Ekerold's control of the radio station meant that it was his version of the story that first reached the rest of the world. Jacobsen's only advantage was that he had control of the driftwood, which normally found its way to the northern shores. This proved to be insufficient when his supplies failed and he finally had to ask Ekerold for help. In the end, Jacobsen retreated.

Full of confidence, Ekerold now asked for the whole island, a request that the administration found potentially too explosive regarding possible international protests, and chose instead to annex the central portion in the name of the Norwegian Meteorological Institute, and only as a later second step, in 1926, the whole of Jan Mayen.

Having run a weather station on the island continuously since 1921, Norway took sovereignty in 1930, with no substantial protest from any other nation. Denmark handed over rights to their old station in 1933. Curiously, the settlement of claims and counter-claims within Norway itself took far longer, ending with Norway's 1952 purchase of any further claim from Jacobsen's heirs (he had died in 1942), for NOK170,000.

The weather data from Jan Mayen was, and still is, of high value, as the weather systems on their way eastwards can be studied here, 1,000km before they reach northern Norway and the Barents Sea. Jan Mayen therefore improves weather predictions considerably for the fishing fleets and other seafarers in these areas and on land.

WORLD WAR II TO THE PRESENT Jan Mayen turned out to be the only part of Norway which remained completely under Norwegian control throughout World War II.

In 1940 Ekerold's station (Eldste Metten) was deliberately damaged to prevent its use by the Germans and the island was evacuated. During the course of the war, the Luftwaffe flew over the island regularly with reconnaissance and weather-service planes. There were a few reconnaissance landings and an automatic German weather station was secretly installed by a German submarine in September 1944, which remained undetected by the Allied forces until briefly before the end of the war. Two German planes crashed into Jan Mayen in 1942, one of them undetected until 1950. But there was never any German occupation. The Allies sent a 50-strong contingent of Norwegian troops to the island in 1941, which built a weather station of their own, in Jøssingdalen. In 1943 an American unit came to set up a radio station that specialised in locating enemy radio stations in the Arctic. They contributed to the discovery of German military weather stations both in east Greenland and Svalbard, while the German automatic station on Jan Mayen itself remained, from late 1944 onwards, undetected for a long time. In 1944, the Norwegians moved into the American base, which had become known as 'Atlantic City'. They soon moved out again, the comfortable lifestyle and its associated culture shock proving too much.

After the war, a new civil meteorological station was erected in 1949 above the north lagoon, which today is known as Gamle Metten. It was operational until 1962. A hurricane in 1950 took a man's life, blowing him 140m away. As a result, ropewalks were built between all station buildings.

The Cold War brought Jan Mayen even greater prominence. In 1959 a military station was installed on the southeast side for the operation of NATO's new LORAN-A radio navigation aid system. The civil weather service also moved to the new base, called 'Olonkinbyen' after a Jan Mayen veteran. A post office was introduced, with its own postmark, and in 1960 a 1,200m-long landing strip, capable of taking Hercules transporters, was installed. LORAN-A was soon supplemented with LORAN-C, a much more precise system that was also useful for directing US submarines. A veil of secrecy was lowered over the station, which in its strongest days had a crew of up to 40 men, including, until 1964, two US officers. The presence of these American officers was regarded as especially tricky because Norway, when joining NATO, had declared that in order to avoid tensions with its neighbour Russia, it would not accept the stationing of foreign troops on its territory. With the advance of radio and telecommunication and navigation technology, especially by satellite, LORAN lost importance. In 1977, LORAN-A was switched off and in 1994 the US Coast Guard, then in charge of LORAN, stopped financing LORAN-C on Jan Mayen. Today, the station is still run by the Norwegian military, but the secrecy is mostly gone and the total crew, including the weather service, has been reduced now to just 17–18 members at any one time, including both men and women. The station master, a military officer, is at the same time the local police chief, whereas the rest of the team is mostly made up of civilians – weather-service employees, technicians, electronics experts, kitchen staff and a doctor. The station also includes the coastal radio service of Jan Mayen Radio, used mainly for the fishing around the island, but also for emergency cases in the North Atlantic. In 2004 discussions were underway about withdrawing all crews from the island together and switching over to an automated weather station, controlled remotely. Leaving the island altogether seems to be too drastic a solution for Norway when also taking into account claims on the economic zone around Jan Mayen, and considering the station is still occupied and maintained.

Being based on Jan Mayen is one of the most remote positions of employment in the world and even the runway is of little use in bad weather, which frequently causes trouble for the supply flights in this rough region of the North Atlantic. To keep up spirits, the crew is well equipped with spare-time facilities. It boasts a shooting club, an amateur radio club (a popular radio contact for radio amateurs all over the world), six renovated cabins spread over the island as accommodation for private tours, and the famous 'Jan Mayen Nude-Bathing-Club' with its exclusive membership certificate – handed out only after a nude swim in the chilly sea under the critical eyes of the club leadership. The website www.jan-mayen.no gives some impression of life in this Arctic base.

POLITICS AROUND JAN MAYEN Apart from the dwindling military importance of this small station, the main interest of Norway in Jan Mayen is the sea around the island – so far mainly with its rich fishing resources, though in the distant future possibly also its mineral resources on the sea bottom.

Since the 1950s there has been talk of building a proper harbour on Jan Mayen, but nothing has yet come of it due to the enormous costs involved. Traditionally, fishing has a very strong political lobby in Norway. Therefore, it was natural that Norway followed the Icelandic example and declared its own economic 200-mile zone around Jan Mayen in 1978. This led to conflict with Iceland and Denmark, as the claimed Jan Mayen zone cut into both Iceland's own zone and Denmark's (who have a zone around Greenland). Iceland declared that Jan Mayen was just a rock and therefore not allowed to have its own economic zone at all under international law. But the permanence of settlements and stations means that Jan Mayen can be considered an island. Finally, Norway and Iceland came to an arrangement over their overlapping claims: Iceland accepted that Norway can claim an economic zone around Jan Mayen, while Norway in return gave up its claims on the relatively small overlapping zone to the benefit of Iceland. The overlap with Greenland proved to be more of a sticking point as it covers 80,000km². Here, Norway demanded the use of the so-called mid-line principle, which Denmark rejected in view of the extreme difference in size between Greenland and Jan Mayen, where using the mid-line principle would have given Jan Mayen a huge area in the disputed zone in comparison to its size. In 1988, Denmark took Norway to the International Court of Justice in The Hague, where Norway had lost already once before, in the 1930s, when making an exaggerated claim on sovereignty over a part of east Greenland. This time, the court decision again supported the Greenland position, allocating most of the disputed zone to Greenland.

PRACTICAL INFORMATION

In 2010, nearly all of Jan Mayen was declared by the Norwegian government to be a nationally protected nature reserve. The stated intention of the regulation is to preserve the island, the marine life and the ocean floor, though curiously, in the same year, the Norwegian government ponied up NOK10 million for environmental studies linked to the exploration of petroleum reserves in the seas surrounding Jan Mayen. The effect of these new regulations is that tourist boats are neither allowed to land nor to set up camp anywhere in the nature reserve area. Visiting boats are allowed to moor in two locations on the southern half of the island that are not part of the reserve, and technically groups can camp there as well (though this is hardly popular with the base personnel present). Yet both of these locations are too far from Beerenberg to allow for a hike and climb up to the mountain in one day. So even if the 'spririt' of the new regulations does not intend to restrict tourism on Jan Mayen, this effectively makes it impossible to safely and efficiently visit the impressive glaciated volcanic cone of Beerenberg and the north side of the island. While the government decision has been appealed by a few small operators, these new regulations seem to allow for zero special dispensation and thus far there appears to be little interest in helping facilitate tourism to the island. As a result, a number of outfitters who once operated journeys to Jan Mayen no longer do so. In the past, Jan Mayen has seldom been visited by many tourists anyway, however, and there is also no commercially viable way for independent travellers to get there; any transport there is primarily military. Apart from the few companies that still operate to and from the island, the only option for visiting is by sailing there privately, a feat performed by several yachts every year. Even then, permission for landing is required and one should not count on any supplies being available at the station. In the past, Jan Mayen has been visited annually by 200–500 persons, plus some 1,000–2,000 more who pass close to the island, getting, if they're lucky, a glimpse of Beerenberg.

WHEN TO VISIT **Summer** – late June to late August is clearly the best season for visits to Jan Mayen. In the other parts of the year, storms are more frequent and in winter and spring drift ice can be an additional problem for smaller boats. In winter, visibility is poor due to short days, with the polar night in December/early January.

HIGHLIGHTS The **landscape** is perhaps the island's main highlight, with the dark lava and the white of ice and snow both contrasting with the few colourful patches of luscious green vegetation and colourful flowers. Then of course there's the clear shape of the impressive conical **Beerenberg** and the island's dramatic **cloud formations** and **light shows**. Ornithologists and botanists will find plenty of interest. Visitors with historic interest should visit the old 17th-century **whaling places** (Kvalrossbukta, Sjuhollendarbukta, Krossbukta, Titeltbukta, Sørbukta, Nordbukta, etc), where some remains are still visible on land and more are occasionally washed out of the beach cliff. Other sites of historic interest are the remains of early **scientific activities** (Austrian station in Maria-Muschbukta), some old **trapper cabins** and the various former **meteorological stations**. Little of military history is left at the respective sites (Atlantic City, Jøssingdalen, Jacobsendalen, Jamesonbukta, Eggøya, Flykollen near Kapp Wien and the Danielssen crater with some remains of crashed German planes, etc). And then there is, of course, the present station **Olonkinbyen**, with two impressive old cannons from the whaling period from Kvalrossbukta and a collection of historic finds in a small station **museum**.

RED TAPE Jan Mayen is part of the Kingdom of Norway – and, in contrast to Svalbard, has no special international treaty status. However, the island has a special legal status within Norway, based on the Norwegian Jan Mayen Law. Therefore, not all laws of the mainland apply to Jan Mayen as well, and similarly, there are Norwegian laws that apply specifically to Jan Mayen alone. The most important rules for visitors are the following:

- There are strict regulations for protecting the environment and cultural heritage (see *The environment*, pages 221–2) – inform yourself about these regulations before travelling to the island.
- Permission for visiting the island has to be acquired in advance. The Norwegian authorities stress that visitors without official duty on the island cannot rely on finding any usable infrastructure or supplies. It is not the station's duty to take care of tourists. When applying for permission, be prepared for lengthy delays of possibly a few months' duration due to the very irregular postal deliveries to and from the island. There are cases where permission for a short visit could be obtained at short notice when appearing by boat off the island, but this attempt can also fail.

- For stays of less than 24 hours, permission is granted in advance by the local police authorities on the island, represented by the Jan Mayen Station Commander (*FLO/IKT stasjon Jan Mayen, Stasjonssjefen, N-8099 Jan Mayen, Norway;* ☏ *+47 32 17 79 02 (commander office), +47 32 17 79 00 (station);* e *post@www.jan-mayen.no; www.jan-mayen.no*). Office hours are nominally 09.00–16.00 (CET) but they do stress that poor communications may mean a delay of up to four months, so it might be worth contacting them some time before you intend to arrive.
- For stays of more than 24 hours, permission needs to be granted in advance by the Norwegian police authorities in the police district of Salten, Bodø, on the Norwegian mainland (*Salten politidistrikt, Postboks 1023, N-8001 Bodø, Norway;* ☏ *+47 75 54 58 00;* e *post.salten@politiet.no; www.politiet.no*).

There is no commercially viable way of getting to Jan Mayen except for cruises or on your own/chartered boat – there are no ferries, no supply ships accepting paying passengers, and no scheduled or charter flights that could be booked. All supplies and people transports to and from the island are managed by the Norwegian authorities using vessels and aircraft of the air force or coastguard, which do not accept tourists as passengers.

GETTING THERE Jan Mayen can be reached by **ship/boat** or by **plane** (private planes are normally not accepted). As the island has no port or sheltered bays, landings are possible only on beaches where wind and surf are favourable. Suitable landing sites are the beaches southwest (Båtvika, small bay) and northeast of the station or Kvalrossbukta on the northwest side of the island. A road across the thin and low isthmus connects Kvalrossbukta with the station. Other beaches suitable for landings, depending on wind and surf direction, are located on either side of Eggøya, Krossbukta in the north, and at the northwest coast also Maria-Muschbukta, plus several small bays in the southwest (Sjuhollandarbukta, Titeltbukta). For more sailing details see *Den Norske Los – Arctic Pilot, Svalbard – Jan Mayen* in the *Appendix*, page 234.

By aircraft: the gravel runway near the station has a length of 2,400m and is limited to official use by the supply and duty aircraft of the Norwegian Air Force and coastguard (*kystvakt*), effectively meaning that tourist arrival by air is non-existent.

Organised trips Only a handful of companies run trips specifically to Jan Mayen. Life on board these cruises will be the same as for those operating around Svalbard, so see the chapter on *Cruising* for an idea of what to expect.

Borea Adventures Hlidarvegur 38, 400 Isafjörður, Iceland; ☏ +354 869 7557 or 899 3817; e info@boreaadventures.com; www. boreaadventures.com. This top-notch Icelandic-run expedition company runs 11-day expeditions to Jan Mayen that include glacial summits to Mt Beerenberg & a range of smaller hikes. Departures from Iceland. *Price: €2,650pp.*

EcoExpeditions Box 2028 Hillevåg, 4095 Stavanger, Norway; ☏ +47 90 04 13 30; e info@ ecoexpeditions.no; www.ecoexpeditions.no. They run climbing-orientated expeditions globally, 1 of which is a trip to Jan Mayen geared around a climb of Beerenberg. They also run adventure sailing trips to Svalbard & Bjørnøya (Bear Island). *Price: €3,150 pp.*

Explore! Nelson Hse, 55 Victoria Rd, Farnborough, Hants GU14 7PA, UK; ☏ +44 845 291 4542; e res@ explore.co.uk; www.explore.co.uk. Departing from Aberdeen & arriving in Svalbard, these 10-day journeys take in the Shetland Islands & Jan Mayen, with hikes to Kvalrossbukta for birdwatching & to visit the remains of the Dutch whaling station there. *Price: £1,260pp.*

The Polar Front Park Rd North, Chester le Street, Co Durham DH3 3SU; m +44 7703 323 086; e info@thepolarfront.com; www.thepolarfront. com. The Polar Front is a family-operated adventure travel company, specialising in sailing expeditions to Arctic waters. Their fleet has just undergone an extensive renovation. *Prices available on request.*

Some big cruise ships pass the island without landing, typically on the traditional Nordic round cruise: central European ports – Iceland – Jan Mayen (passage) – Svalbard – Norway – central Europe. There are also a few study or expedition cruises on smaller vessels (50–200 passengers), which try to include a landing on the island, depending on the weather and permission. These offers vary considerably from year to year; check at specialised agencies. Finally, there is the possibility of going there by yacht – either by joining a trip heading for Jan Mayen, or by using your own/chartered boat.

Independent travel Independent visits to Jan Mayen are normally either by private boats or else scientists, experts on duty missions, journalists, or very limited visits by relatives and friends of the station crew members who have managed to secure permission from the Norwegian authorities.

OTHER PRACTICALITIES There is a post office in Olonkinbyen with a limited range of souvenirs, but this is intended for use by the station staff rather than by tourists. There is no accommodation, and no meals, provisions or fuel for sale. Transportation on the island is not for tourist use either, and there is not a single helicopter based on Jan Mayen. There are a few cabins dotted around the island but again these are only intended for use by station staff. There is a doctor among the station crew, with a small medical station, who may be consulted for assistance in case of urgent medical problems.

For an official visitor (scientists and other experts, journalists, etc) working on a project in co-operation with the meteorological station or the military, the station may assist with services if agreed in advance.

The official Jan Mayen website (*www.jan-mayen.no*) is somewhat primitive in its layout and design, but has some solid information and is worth a visit even if you aren't planning a trip to the island.

Maps Maps of Jan Mayen are published by the Norsk Polarinstitutt (NPI) in Tromsø. As topographic maps, there is one sheet in scale 1:100,000 and two sheets in scale 1:50,000 (named Blad 1 Sør-Jan and Blad 2 Nord-Jan), which can be ordered through specialised bookshops. Geologically, Jan Mayen is included in the Bedrock map of Svalbard and Jan Mayen, 1:1,000,000.

Appendix

FURTHER INFORMATION

This literature index includes the texts in English that this book is based upon. The selection of literature in other languages, namely Norwegian and German, that served as a background for this book, is considerably larger. This index is sorted here first by region and within each region alphabetically by the name of the authors or publisher. The section *Arctic and polar publications* lists titles about both the Arctic and Antarctic that also include interesting and relevant information pertaining to the areas dealt with in this book. Many of the titles are no longer in print but may be found in libraries and on the secondhand book market.

ARCTIC AND POLAR PUBLICATIONS – INCLUDING AREAS DESCRIBED IN THIS BOOK

Arctic Pilot Vol II – Comprising Iceland, Jan Mayen, Svalbard and the East Coast of Greenland together with the Greenland and Barents Seas 6th edition, 1961, Hydrographic Department under the authority of the Lords Commissioners of the Admiralty, London, 1961. Attachment: *Supplement No 8-1973 to Arctic Pilot Vol II (6th Edition, 1961)*, Hydrographer of the Navy, London, 1973.

Barr, Susan *Norway: A Consistent Polar Nation? Analysis of an image seen through the history of the Norwegian Polar Institute* KOLOFON AS, Oslo, 2003.

Barr, Susan *Norway's Polar Territories* Aschehoug, Oslo, 1987. Booklet on the territories of Norway both in the Arctic and Antarctic.

Barr, William *The Expeditions of the first International Polar Year, 1882–83* Technical Paper No 29, The Arctic Institute of North America, The University of Calgary, 1985.

Barrington, D *The Possibility of Approaching the North Pole Asserted* T and J Allman, London, 1818. One of the many educated publications from before the late 19th century, which advocate that the North Pole is ice-free.

Basberg, Bjørn L, Ringstad, Jan Erik and Wexelsen, Einar *Whaling & History – Perspectives on the Evolution of the Industry* Publikasjon Nr 29 Kommandør Chr Christensens Hvalfangstmuseum, Sandefjord.

Brown, R N Rudmose *A Naturalist at the Poles – The Life, Work & Voyages of Dr W S Bruce the Polar Explorer* Seeley, Service & Co Ltd, London, 1923. Antarctic, Franz Josef Land, Novaya Zemlya, Spitsbergen.

Brown, R N Rudmose *The Polar Regions – A Physical and Economic Geography of the Arctic and Antarctic* Methuen & Co Ltd, London, 1927.

Capelotti, P J *The Svalbard Archipelago – American Military and Political Geographies of Spitsbergen and Other Norwegian Polar Territories, 1941–1950* McFarland & Company, Inc, Publishers, Jefferson (NC) and London, 2000. CIA reports on these areas with partly amazingly poor or wrong information (provoking comparisons with recent CIA intelligence on Iraq), a document from the start of the Cold War in the Arctic.

Cherry-Garrard, Apsley *The Worst Journey In The World* Vintage, 2010. Long out of print and now revived by Vintage, this classic first-hand account of Scott's harrowing expedition to the South Pole is largely considered the best piece of writing on polar exploration ever. Cherry-Garrard was the youngest member of Scott's team and a member of the rescue party which later located Scott's frozen body. Loaded with specifics about scientific discovery.

Clarke, Basil *Polar Flight* Ian Allan, London, 1964. History of polar aviation.

Day, David *Antarctica: A Biography* Oxford University Press, 2013. The newest title out there on the other pole, this is a stellar overview of how the continent was won, and why its discovery was seen as such a conquest. Well researched and footnoted, the text is dense writing at times, but wade through and you'll come away something of an expert.

Doyle, Sir Arthur Conan *Dangerous Work: Diary of an Arctic Adventure* British Library, 2012. This gorgeous travelogue was penned by the creator of Sherlock Holmes when he was just 20 years old. Doyle spent half a year as a ship's surgeon on an Arctic whaler, and his adventurous journal – which has been uniquely reproduced here as a facsimile photographed from the original parchments – documents the exciting Golden Age of seafaring with humour and daring.

Dufferin, The Marquess of *Letters from High Altitudes* John Murray, London, 1857. Available in full online.

Earth Science. Way North – Our Natural and Cultural Heritage University of Tromsø, Tromsø Museum, 1992. Booklet with variety of articles on the northern lights, climate, climate history, volcanism on Jan Mayen.

Francis, Gavin *Empire Antarctica: Ice, Silence and Emperor Penguins* Chatto and Windus, 2012. This lyrical, very personal account of life at the end of the world was written by a doctor who spent over a year at Antarctica's isolated Halley research station. Most evocative is the camaraderie Francis experienced living among communities of the continent's emperor penguins. The writing is a superb amalgam of old-fashioned suck-it-up adventure tale with insightful modern travel writing.

Haas, Robert *Through the Eyes of the Vikings: An Aerial Vision of Arctic Lands* National Geographic, 2010. This ungodly photographic book, shot over three years, showcases the beguiling work of aerial photographer Haas, whose panoramas of the North give the reader pause. His stunning landscapes span colour palettes and ranges of patterns that you'd never even dreamt existed somewhere so brutally inhospitable to humans. Horses, caribou and polar bears make some spectacular cameos.

Hagen, Asbjørn *Notes on Arctic Fungi – I Fungi from Jan Mayen. II Fungi collected by Dr P F Scholander on the Swedish–Norwegian Arctic Expedition 1931.* Det Kongelige Departementet for Handel, Sjøfart, Industri, Håndverk og Fiskeri/Norsk Polarinstitutt, Oslo, 1950.

Hansen, John Richard, Hansson, Rasmus and Norris, Stefan *The State of the European Arctic Environment* EEA Environmental Monograph No 3, European Environmental Agency Copenhagen/Meddelelser No 141 Norsk Polarinstitutt, 1996.

Hansson, Rasmus *Norway and the Polar Regions* Norsk Utenriksdepartement, Oslo, 1998. Booklet on Norwegian polar history, territories, research.

Hartwig, G *The Polar World: A Popular Description of Man and Nature in the Arctic and Antarctic Regions of the Globe* Longmans, Green, and Co, London, 1874 (2nd edition). Detailed polar history until the mid 19th century.

Heide-Jørgensen, Mads Peter and Lydersen, Christian (editors) *Ringed Seals in the North Atlantic* NAMMCO Scientific Publications Volume 1, The North Atlantic Marine Mammal Commission, Tromsø, 1998.

Herbert, Wally *Across the Top of the World – The British Trans-Arctic Expedition* Longmans, London, 1969.

Huebert, Rob and Shadian, Jessica M *The Arctic in Global Affairs: A Region in Transformation* Continuum, 2012. This not-all-academic title looks specifically at what is transforming the Arctic, dipping into areas of trade, environmental policy, international relationships and global governance. A good part of the book tries to answer the question: who owns (or who should own) the Arctic? Should appeal to anyone with some interest in the geopolitics of the North.

Lamont, James *Yachting in the Arctic Seas or Notes of Five Voyages of Sport and Discovery in the Neighbourhood of Spitzbergen and Novaya Zemlya* Chatto and Windus, London, 1876.

Larsen, Thor and Norderhaug, Magnus *The Arctic* North Sea Press/Grøndahl Production, 1979.

Leslie, Alexander *The Arctic Voyages of Adolf Erik Nordenskiöld 1858–1879* Macmillan and Co, London, 1879.

Liljequist, Gösta H *High Latitudes – A History of Swedish Polar Travels and Research* Swedish Polar Research Secretariat/Streiffert Förlag AB, 1993.

Lønø, Odd *I Transplantation of the Muskox in Europe and North-America. II Transplantation of Hares to Svalbard* Meddelelser Nr 84, Norsk Polarinstitutt, Oslo, 1960.

Lopez, Barry *Arctic Dreams – Imagination and Desire in a Northern Landscape* Vintage, 1999. This classic, prosaic work won the National Book Award in 1986, and it still wows with its descriptions of the mythologised landscapes of the Arctic.

Ludecke, Cornelia and Summerhayes, Colin *The Third Reich in Antarctica: The German Antarctic Expedition 1938–39* Erskine, 2012. Though many of the fieldnotes from this unique expedition were lost in the war, this exhaustively researched book is a fascinating tale of exploration that might well have changed history. Delves into some very interesting detail about the Nazi party's ideology of self-sufficiency.

Magnusson, A H *The Lichen-genus acarospora in Greenland and Spitsbergen* Meddelelse Nr 27, Det Kongelige Departementet for Handel, Sjøfart, Industri, Håndverk og Fiskeri/ Norges Svalbard-og Ishavs-Undersøkelser, Oslo, 1935.

Maxtone-Graham, John *Safe Return Doubtful – The Heroic Age of Polar Exploration* Constable and Company Ltd, London, 2000. An approach to the polar heroes from a psychological and sociological perspective.

McClintock, James *Lost Antarctica: Adventures in a Disappearing Land* Palgrave Macmillan, 2012. Expertly written by a professor of Polar and Marine Biology with over a dozen Antarctic expeditions under his belt, this book gives an interesting and personal glimpse into some of the environmental research currently being carried out at the end of the world. It's one of the more readable accounts of the realities of climate change experienced up close.

Meurs, Rinie van *Polar Odyssey* GMB uitgeverij/Oceanwide Expeditions/Pica Press, 2000. Pictorial book by a highly experienced and travelled guide on expedition cruises in the Arctic and Antarctic.

Ministry of Environment (Hrsg) *Environmental Regulations for Svalbard and Jan Mayen – T-516.*

Mirsky, Jeannette *To the Arctic! The Story of Polar Exploration from earliest Times to the Present* Allan Wingate, London & New York, 1949 (previous edition *To the North!* from 1934).

Nansen Arctic Drilling Program NAD Science Committee *The Arctic Ocean Record: Key to Global Change (Initial Science Plan)* In: Polarforschung 61/1-102, 1991.

Nicklin, Charles *Among Giants: A Life with Whales* University Of Chicago Press, 2011. Extraordinarily photographed book by National Geographic's top marine mammal specialist, this large-format title tells the story of humpbacks, narwhals, sperm whales, orcas and many others through stunning imagery.

Nobile, General Umberto *My Polar Flights – An Account of the Voyages of the Airships ITALIA and NORGE* Frederick Muller Limited, London, 1961.

Norsk Polarinstitutt (The Norwegian Polar Research Institute) and Norges Sjøkartverk *Den Norske Los – Arctic Pilot – Farvannsbeskrivelse Sailing Directions, Svalbard – Jan Mayen* Bind 7/Volume 7, 2nd Edition 1998. Norges sjøkartverk/Norsk Polarinstitutt, 1998. Detailed description of all coasts, supplemented with information on nature and history.

Orleans, The Duke of *Hunters and Hunting in the Arctic* David Nutt, London, 1911. Translation from French, about travelling in Franz Josef Land, Jan Mayen and Spitsbergen.

Report on the Activities of Norges Svalbard og Ishavsundersøkelser 1927–1936 Skrifter om Svalbard og Ishavet Nr 73, Det Kongelige Departementet for Handel, Sjøfart, Industri, Håndverk og Fiskeri/Norges Svalbard-og Ishavs-Undersøkelser, Oslo, 1937.

Report on the Activities of Norges Svalbard og Ishavsundersøkelser 1936–1944 Skrifter om Svalbard og Ishavet Nr 88, Det Kongelige Departementet for Handel, Sjøfart, Industri, Håndverk og Fiskeri/Norges Svalbard-og Ishavs-Undersøkelser, Oslo, 1937. Aktivitäten in Spitzbergen, Ostgrönland, Südgrönland, Jan Mayen.

Roberts, Peder *The European Antarctic: Science and Strategy in Scandinavia and the British Empire* Palgrave Macmillan, 2011. Academic tome written in an elegant and accessible manner, this study looks at how the unknown southern polar regions were imagined by the Scandinavian nations and the Brits as projections of European dreams, apprehensions and mores. It engages in fascinating ways about how commercial and scientific interests aligned and diverged while these countries studied and explored the Antarctic throughout the 20th century.

Rudels, Bert *On the Mass Balance of the Polar Ocean, with special emphasis on the Fram Strait* Skrifter Nr 188, Norsk Polarinstitutt, Oslo, 1987.

Sage, Bryan *The Arctic & its Wildlife* Croom Helm Ltd, London, 1986.

Sandler, Martin W *The Impossible Rescue: The True Story of an Amazing Arctic Adventure* Candlewick, 2012. This Pulitzer Prize nominated author has woven together missives, expedition reports and images to recreate the details of this whaling adventure – and the rescue mission that followed it. A heartbreaking tale of staggering bravery and perseverance.

Schofield, Ernest Conyers and Nebit, Roy *Arctic Airmen – The RAF in Spitsbergen and North Russia 1942* William Kimber & Co Ltd, London, 1987.

Schulz, Florian *To the Arctic* Mountaineers Books, 2012. Possibly the most stunningly photographed book on the Arctic, Schultz's large-format photo essay opus spanning an entire year brings the North to life. The wildlife photography in this tome – which covers stunning shots of muskoxen, caribou and polar bear – may well bring you to tears. Accompanied by the photographer's personal tales of working in the field.

Scoresby, William *An Account of the Arctic Regions with a History and Description of the Northern Whale-Fishery* David & Charles, Newton Abbot, 1969. Reprint of the 1820 original. Whaler captain Scoresby provides very detailed early observations also of Jan Mayen and Svalbard.

Smith, Laurence *The New North: The World in 2050* Profile, 2012. Penned by a UCLA professor, this thought-provoking title analyses trends in population growth, migration, natural resources, climate change and globalisation to forecast a shift in political and economic focus to the Arctic. Smith's strong yet disconcerting arguments suggest that the northern countries of Russia, Alaska, Canada and Scandinavia will thrive while more southerly nations will encounter coastal flooding, water shortages, crowded conurbations and aging populations. Accessible, insightful and informative.

Soot-Ryen, T *Some Pelecypods from Franz Josef Land, Victoriaøya and Hopen – Collected on the Norwegian Scientific Expedition 1930* Meddelelse Nr 47, Det Kongelige Departement for Handel, Sjøfart, Industri, Håndverk og Fiskeri/Norges Svalbard og Ishavs-Undersøkelser, Oslo, 1939.

Soper, Tony *The Arctic – A Guide to Coastal Wildlife* Bradt Travel Guides Ltd, UK/The Globe Pequot Press Inc, USA, 2005.

Staaland, Hans *On the Salt Excretion in the Little Auk, Plotus alle (L)* Reprint aus Norsk Polarinstitutt Årbok 1974, Oslo, 1976, S 119-127.

Stonehouse, Bernard *North Pole – South Pole – A Guide to the Ecology and Resources of the Arctic and Antarctic* Prion, London, 1990. Pictorial book with informative text.

Størmer, Per *Bryophytes from Franz Josef Land and Eastern Svalbard – Collected by M Olaf Hanssen on the Norwegian Expedition in 1930* Meddelelse Nr 47, Det Kongelige Departement for Handel, Sjøfart, Industri, Håndverk og Fiskeri/Norges Svalbard og Ishavs-Undersøkelser, Oslo, 1940.

Talcott, Dudley Vaill *North of North Cape – The Arctic Voyages of the 'Norkap II'* John Lane the Bodley Head, London, 1936. Voyages to Franz Josef Land, Spitsbergen, Jan Mayen, northeast Greenland and Iceland around 1925.

Thorén, Ragnar *Picture Atlas of the Arctic* Elsevier Publishing Company, Amsterdam, 1969. Selected aerial and surface photos plus texts for all Arctic regions including Svalbard, Jan Mayen, Franz Josef Land.

Thorshaug, K and Rosted, A Fr *Researches into the Prevalence of Trichinosis in Animals in Arctic and Antarctic Waters* Meddelelser Nr 80, Norsk Polarinstitutt, Oslo, 1956.

Tønnessen, J N and Johnsen, A O *The History of Modern Whaling* University of California Press, 1982, translated (partly shortened) from Norwegian (Original: Den Moderne Hvalfangsts Historie; Opprinnelse og Utvikling, 4 Bände, published 1959–1970, Norges Hvalfangstforbund).

UNIS *Glacial and Oceanic History of the Nordic Seas, the Polar Ocean and the Barents Sea – Margins, Fjords and Deep Oceans.*

Walker, Gabrielle *Antarctica: An Intimate Portrait of the World's Most Mysterious Continent* Bloomsbury, 2012. A BBC broadcaster and writer for New Scientist brings us this evocative cover-it-all book on the science, history, exploration, landscape, wildlife and beauty of the Antarctic. A touching, informed and informative work.

Wallace, Joseph *The Arctic* Gallery Books, New York, 1988. Pictorial book.

Wilkins, Sir Hubert *Under the North Pole – The Wilkins–Ellsworth Submarine Expedition* Brewer, Warren and Putnam, 1931. On the preparations for the ill-fated plan of a submarine expedition.

JAN MAYEN Observe that a number of publications dealing with Jan Mayen may also be listed under *Arctic and polar publications* in the first part of this literature index.

Maps for Jan Mayen are published by the Norsk Polarinstitutt in Tromsø and can also be purchased through specialised geographic bookshops in other countries. As topographic maps, there is one sheet in 1:100,000 and a set of two sheets in 1:50,000.

Anda, E, Orheim, O and Mangerud, J *Late Holocene Glacier Variations and Climate at Jan Mayen* In: Polar Research, 1985, 3 ns, 129–140. Kopie.

Barr, Susan *Kulturminner på Jan Mayen – Historical remains on Jan Mayen* Meddelelser Nr 108, Norsk Polarinstitutt, Oslo 1985. Bilingual Norwegian–English. Details including pictures of almost all known historic sites on Jan Mayen.

Jan Mayen – Vulcanic Island in the North Atlantic Ocean Heft 2/1998, Circumpolar Journal, Volume 13, Arctisch Centrum, Groningen, 1998.

Johnson, G L and Campsie, J *Morphology and Structure of the Western Jan Mayen* Fracture Zone Reprint aus Norsk Polarinstitutt Årbok 1974, Oslo, 1976.

Lid, Johannes *Bryophytes of Jan Mayen* Meddelelser Nr 48, Det Kongelige Departement for Handel, Sjøfart, Industri, Håndverk og Fiskeri/Norges Svalbard og Ishavs-Undersøkelser, Oslo, 1941.

Lid, Johannes *The Flora of Jan Mayen* Skrifter Nr 130, Norsk Polarinstitutt, Oslo, 1964.

Myhre, Annik M, Eldholm, Olav and Sundvor, Eirik *The Jan Mayen Ridge: Present Status* In: Polar Research, 1984, 2 ns, 47–59. Unvollständige Kopie (pages 48–53 missing).

Orvin, Anders *The Place-Names of Jan Mayen* Skrifter Nr 120, Det kongelige Departement for Industri of Håndverk – Norsk Polarinstitutt, Oslo, 1960.

The Norwegian North-Atlantic Expedition 1876–1878 (den Norske Nordhavs-Expedition) Christiania, Grondahl, 1880–87.

Websites
Among a number of websites which are listed in search engines but offer only very limited information about Jan Mayen, there are some to which I would like to draw your attention:

www.jan-mayen.no The official website for the island, developed mainly by some station crew members and well worth a visit.

home.online.no/~vteigen A collation of other websites of interest.

FRANZ JOSEF LAND
Observe that a number of publications dealing with the archipelago may also be listed under *Arctic and polar publications* in the first part of this literature index.

Albanov, Valerian I *In the Land of White Death – An Epic Story of Survival in the Russian Arctic* Modern Library, USA, 2000. Translated diary of one of only two survivors of the 1912–14 *St Anna* expedition.

Baldwin, E B (edited by P J Capelotti) *The Franz Josef Land Archipelago – E B Baldwin's Journal of the Wellman Polar Expedition, 1898–99* McFarland Publishers, USA, 2004. The diary of the second-in-command of the Wellman 1898–99 Franz Josef Land expedition, supplemented by editor Capelotti with comments and additional pictures; it is also an interesting insight into the way of thinking of Baldwin and his contemporaries.

Barr, Susan (editor) *Franz Josef Land* Polarhåndbok Nr 8, Norsk Polarinstitutt, Oslo, 1995 (English). Fairly detailed hardback book about the archipelago, with an emphasis on history but also covering natural history; many photographs.

Barr, Susan (editor) *The FRAM anniversary cruise to Zemlja Franca-Iosifa 23 August – 5 September 1996* Norsk Polarinstitutt Meddelelser Nr 149, Oslo, 1997. Study reports on Cape Norvegia and Cape Flora, history, zoology, glaciology and ozone.

Brontman, L *On Top of the World – The Soviet Expedition to the North Pole 1937* Victor Gollancz Ltd, London, 1938. On the installation of the first drifting North Pole station by planes from Franz Josef Land.

Chernov, Yu I *The Living Tundra* Cambridge University Press, 1985, translated from Russian (Original: 1980). Detailed introduction to tundra nature in the north of the Soviet Union.

Decker/Gavrilo/Mehlum/Bakken *Distribution and Abundance of Birds and Marine Mammals in the Eastern Barents Sea and the Kara Sea, late Summer 1995* Norsk Polarinstitutt, Meddelelser No 155, Oslo, 1998.

Dibner, V D (editor) *Geology of Franz Josef Land* Meddelelser No 146, Norsk Polarinstitutt, Oslo, 1998. Dibner is editor of the standard Russian book on the geology of the archipelago, and offers a collection of relevant contributions to this issue in English.

Fiala, Anthony *Fighting the Polar Ice* Doubleday Page & Company, New York, 1907. Narrative description of the Fiala–Ziegler Franz Josef Land expedition.

Gjertz, Ian and Mørkved, Berit *Environmental Studies from Franz Josef Land, with Emphasis on Tikhaia Bay, Hooker Island* Norsk Polarinstitutt, Meddelelser Nr 120, Oslo, 1992.

Gjertz, Ian and Mørkved, Berit *Results from Scientific Cruises to Franz Josef Land* Norsk Polarinstitutt, Meddelelser Nr 126, Oslo, 1993. Walrus, ornithology, snailfishes.

Golovkin, Alexander N and Bakken, Vidar *Seabird Bibliography 1773-1994 – Northwest region of Russia* Norsk Polarinstitutt, Meddelelser No 152, Oslo, 1997. English bibliography of Russian publications on the subject.

Grieg, J A *Some Echinoderms from Franz Josef Land, Victoriaøya and Hopen, collected on the Norwegian Scientific Expedition 1930* 1935. Booklet.

Hanssen, Olaf and Lid, Johannes *Flowering Plants of Franz Josef Land – Collected on the Norwegian Scientific Expedition 1930* Skrifter om Svalbard og Ishavet Nr 39, Det Kongelige Departementet for Handel, Sjøfart, Industri, Håndverk og Fiskeri/Norges Svalbard-og Ishavs-Undersøkelser, Oslo, 1932.

Jackson, Frederick G *A Thousand Days in the Arctic* Harper & Brothers, 1899. The detailed description of Jackson's 1894–97 wintering expedition in Franz Josef Land.

Jackson, Frederick G *The Lure of Unknown Land* G Bell and Sons Ltd, London, 1935. Shortened narrative expedition report by Jackson on his 1894–97 wintering expedition in Franz Josef Land.

Kostka, Robert (editor) *The Franz Josef Land Archipelago – Remote Sensing and Cartography* Petermanns Geographische Mitteilungen, Ergänzungsheft 293, Justus Perthes Verlag Gotha, 1997.

Lynge, B *Lichens – Collected on the Norwegian Scientific Expedition to Franz Josef Land 1930* Skrifter om Svalbard og Ishavet N 38, Det Kongelige Departementet for Handel, Sjøfart, Industri, Håndverk og Fiskeri/Norges Svalbard-og Ishavs-Undersøkelser, Oslo, 1931.

Nansen, Fridtjof *Farthest North*. Originally three volumes, various reprints and also shortened versions on the market. Description of the 1893–96 FRAM voyage and the attempt of Nansen and Johansen to reach the North Pole, leading to their rescue by Jackson in Franz Josef Land.

Northern Sea Route Dynamic Environmental Atlas Norsk Polarinstitutt, Meddelelser Nr 147, Oslo, 1998.

Papanin, Ivan *Life on an Icefloe* Hutchinson & Co, London, 1947. On the first North Pole drifting station, established in 1937 from Franz Josef Land.

Payer, Julius *New Lands within the Arctic Circle: Narrative of the discoveries of the Austrian ship 'Tegetthoff' in the years 1872–1874* 2 Vols, Macmillan, 1876. Narrative detailed expedition report on the discovery of Franz Josef Land.

Ransmayr, Christoph *The Terrors of Ice and Darkness* Paladin, London, 1992 (translated from German). Novel about a young Austro-Italian dreamer to follow the tracks of the Payer–Weyprecht discovery expedition of Franz Josef Land.

Rowe, Elana Wilson *Russia and the North* University of Ottawa Press, 2009. This engaging volume discusses the volatile and often disorganised economic and political aims of Russia, whose vast range of policies span concerns from domestic migration politics to oil and gas development.

Smolka, H P *Forty Thousand against the Arctic* Hutchinson London, 1938. Narrative history of the exploration and opening of the Soviet Arctic.

Solheim, A, Musatov, E and Heintz, N (editors) *Geological Aspects of Franz Josef Land and the Northernmost Barents Sea*, Norsk Polarinstitutt, Meddelelser No 151, Oslo, 1998.

Websites There is no official website for the archipelago, though I maintain a website (*www.franz-josef-land.info*), which has extensive information about the island. Through search engines, you will find a changing variety of sites, especially about recent scientific activities and possibly also some tourist offers. Be aware of the many ways of spelling Franz Josef Land (with or without hyphens): Franz-Joseph-Land, Franz-Josef-Land, Franz-Josephs-Land, Franz-Josefs-Land, Frants-Josef-Land, Zemlya Franca Iosifa (English transcription of the Russian name) or Russian in Cyrillic letters: Земля Франца-Иосифа.

SVALBARD Observe that a number of publications dealing with the archipelago may also be listed under *Arctic and polar publications* in the first part of this literature index.

Maps for Svalbard are published by the Norsk Polarinstitutt in Tromsø and can also be purchased through specialised geographic bookshops in other countries. As topographic maps, there is one sheet in 1:2,000,000, one sheet in 1:1,000,000, a set of four sheets in 1:500,000, a set of three huge sheets in 1:250,000 and a set of 62 sheets in 1:100,000 – the last series in colour only for the more frequently sold sheets, otherwise in black-and-white. Furthermore, a wide range of thematic maps has been published, including geological maps in 1:1,000,000 and 1:500,000 for all parts of the archipelago and in 1:100,000 for most of the main island. Be aware of rapid changes in the landscape, especially around glaciers – maps may therefore be quite outdated in details, in spite of repeated updating.

Exploration

Ahlmann, Hans Wilhelmson (editor) *Scientific Results of the Swedish–Norwegian Arctic Expedition in the Summer of 1931*, parts XI–XIV, in: Geografiska Annaler, Centraltrykkeriet Esselte ab, Stockholm, 1936. Expedition to Hinlopen Strait area.

Beattie, Owen *Frozen in Time: The Fate of the Franklin Expedition* Greystone, 2004. An excellent account of the devastating tragedy that befell these early British explorers, including new research on the mysterious illness that ran throughout the ship. Includes newly published photographs (and an introduction by Margaret Atwood).

Beechey, Frederick William *A Voyage of Discovery Towards the North Pole, Performed in His Majesty's Ships* Dorothea *and* Trent, *under the Command of Captain David Buchan, R N, to which is Added a Summary of all the Early Attempts to Reach the Pacific by Way of the Pole* Richard Bentley, London, 1843. The ships sailed from the Shetland Islands into western and northern waters above 80° north and returned along the edge of the Greenland pack ice. The objective was to discover a passage to the Pacific via Arctic waters.

Binney, George *With Seaplane and Sledge in the Arctic* George H Doran Company, New York, 1926. Account by leader of major Oxford University expedition in 1924.

Brázdil, R and others *Results of Investigations of the Geographical Research Expedition Spitsbergen 1985* Univerzita J E Purkyně v Brně, 1988. Results of geographical Polish–Czech Hornsund expedition.

Brown, R N Rudmose *Spitsbergen: An Account of Exploration, Hunting, The Mineral Riches & Future Potentialities of an Arctic Archipelago* Seeley, Service & Co Ltd, London, 1920.

Bull, Colin *Innocents in the Arctic: The 1951 Spitsbergen Expedition* University of Alaska Press, 2007. Very interesting and personal chronicle of a Birmingham University expedition compiled from journals, scientific diaries, field notes and expedition members' tales. Great reading.

Capelotti, Peter J *By Airship to the North Pole: An archaeology of human exploration* Rutgers University Press, New Jersey, 1999. History of the Wellman balloon expedition and the registration of its relics in Virgohamna.

Conway, Sir William Martin *Early Dutch and English Voyages to Spitsbergen in the Seventeenth Century* Kraus Reprint, Millwood, NY, 1967. Facsimile-reprint of the 1904 original, includes the first translations of the Dutch pioneers Hessel Gerritsz (1613) and Jacob Segersz (1634) into English.

Conway, Sir William Martin, *No Man's Land – A History of Spitsbergen from its Discovery in 1596 to the Beginning of the Scientific Exploration of the Country.* Facsimile-reprint by Antikvariat A/S, Oslo, 1995 (Original: 1906, England). The first detailed history book on the archipelago and still very recommendable.

Conway, Sir William Martin *The First Crossing of Spitsbergen – Being an Account of an Inland Journey of Exploration and Survey, with Descriptions of several Mountain Ascents, of Boat Expeditions in Ice Fjord, of a Voyage to North-East-Land, the Seven Islands, down Hinlopen Strait, nearly to Wiches Land, and into most of the Fjords of Spitsbergen, and of an almost complete circumnavigation of the main Island* J M Dent & Co, London, 1897. Detailed classic among the expedition publications of the pioneer period.

De Geer, Gerard *Excursion guide for the Spitsbergen excursion of the 11th International Geologist Congresses* P A Norstedt & Söner, Stockholm, 1910. Interesting pictures and maps of most glaciers in Isfjord 1882–1905.

Furse, Chris (editor) *Arctic Expedition Handbook and BSES Svalbard Scrapbook* Hegg Hill Farm Trust, Smarden, Kent, 1997. Reports on the BSES Spitsbergen expedition 1996.

Glen, A R *Under the Pole Star – The Oxford University Arctic Expedition 1935–6* Methuen Publishers, London, 1937. British wintering research expedition on the inland ice of Nordaustlandet.

Haartsen, Tialda and Louwrens Hacquebord *400th Anniversary of the Discovery of Spitsbergen by the Dutch Explorer Willem Barentsz* 1996. A5 brochure for this exhibition at UNIS with background information on discovery, nature, Smeerenburg, whaling.

Harland, W B *The Cambridge Spitzbergen Expedition, 1949* Royal Geographical Society, 1952. First edition.

Hoel, Adolf *The Norwegian Svalbard Expeditions 1906–1926* Resultater av de norske statsunderstøttede Spitsbergenekspeditioner (Skrifter om Svalbard og Ishavet) Bind 1 Nr 1, Det Norske Videnskaps-Akademi i Oslo, Oslo, 1929. Reports on the expeditions of Monaco/Isachsen 1906 and 1907, then of Hoel, Staxrud, Koller, Luncke, and others.

Martens, F *Observations Made in Greenland, and other Northern Countries* London, 1711. A translation of the German original of 1675. The nature observations of this doctor on a whaling ship in 1671 are regarded as the beginning of scientific examination of Svalbard.

Mittelholzer, Walter *By Airplane towards the North Pole – An Account of an Expedition to Spitsbergen in the Summer of 1923* George Allen & Unwin Ltd, London, 1925, translated from the German original. Account of the pilot of a support plane for Amundsen – as Amundsen's expedition failed, the plane did reconnaissance flights and proved the usefulness of aerial photography for mapping the interior.

Nathorst, A G, Hulth, J M and De Geer, G *Swedish Explorations in Spitzbergen 1758–1908.* Reprint from YMER, H 1, Stockholm, 1909. Exploration history, detailed bibliography and maps register.

Nordenskiöld, Adolf E and Otter, Fr W von *Swedish North-Polar Expedition, 1868* Article in Proceedings of the Royal Geographical Society, Vol XIII, Session 1868–69, London, 1869, pages 151–170. Expedition report and discussion.

Nünlist, Hugo *Spitsbergen – The Story of the 1962 Swiss-Spitsbergen Expedition* Nicolas Kaye, London, 1966. Alpine expedition between Blomstrandbreen and Monacobreen.

Parry, Capt William Edward *Narrative of an Attempt to Reach the North Pole in Boats Fitted for the Purpose, and Attached to HMS Hecla in the Year 1827* John Murray, 1828. Attempt to reach the Pole by ship from the north coast of Spitsbergen.

Phipps, Constantine John *A Voyage towards the North Pole undertaken by His Majesty's Command 1773* London 1774. Attempt to reach the Pole by ship from the north coast of Spitsbergen.

Polish IGY Spitsbergen Expeditions in 1957, 1958, and 1959 Nauka O Ziemi I, Universytet Wroclawski, in Boleslawa Bieruta Zeszyty Naukowe Serie B Nauki Przyrodnicze Nr 4, Warszawa/Wroclaw 1960, Panstwowe Wydawnictwo Naukowe. Glaciological and meteorological research in Hornsund.

Troubetzkoy, Alexis S *Arctic Obsession: The Lure of the Far North* Thomas Dunne Books, 2011. There's plenty of historical and political background in this book, but the real allure is the intrigue and romance with which the author describes the undying need for early explorers to the Arctic to discover the ends of the earth for themselves.

Watkins, H G *The Cambridge Expedition To Edge Island* Royal Geographical Society, 1928.

Geology/Wildlife/Nature

Blyth, J D M *German meteorological activities in the Arctic, 1940-45* Polar Record, Vol 6, Cambridge 1951, pages 185–226.

Brekke, Bente and Hansson, Rasmus (Hrsg) *Environmental Atlas Gipsdalen, Svalbard – Reports on the Quarternary Geology, Vegetation, Flora and Fauna of Gipsdalen, and the Marine Ecology of Gipsvika* Norwegian Polar Research Institute, Rapport nr 61, Oslo, 1990. Report set up in connection with the plans of a British company to start coal mining in Gipsdalen.

Brückner, Helmut and Halfar, Ralf H *Evolution and Age of Shorelines along Woodfjord, Northern Spitsbergen* Article in: Z Geomorph N F, Suppl-Bd 97, pages 75–91, Berlin, September 1994.

Camphuysen, Kees *Birds and (marine) mammals in Svalbard, 1985–91* SULA 1993 vol 7 – special issue, Zeitschrift der Neederlandse Zeevogelgroep, Zeist, 1993.

De Geer, Gerard *A Geological Excursion to Central Spitsbergen* Kungl Boktryckeriet, 1910.

De Geer, Gerard *On the Physiographical Evolution of Spitsbergen – explaining the present attitude of the coal horizons* Geografiska Annaler, 1919, H 2, Svenska Sällskapet för Antropologi och Geografi, Stockholm, Centraltryckeriet, 1919.

Derocher, Andrew E *Polar Bears: A Complete Guide to Their Biology and Behavior* The Johns Hopkins University Press, 2012. Informative, captivating account (with excellent photography) of the ecosystems of polar bears and how they have survived such adverse conditions for millennia.

Dowdeswell, Julian and Hambrey, Michael *Islands of the Arctic* Cambridge University Press, 2002. Gorgeously photographed book on Arctic landscapes, flora, fauna and climates, with accompanying text that goes into detail about the science of glaciers and other landscape phenomena. Written by two authors clearly passionate about this part of the world, the book will appeal to anyone with an iota of interest in the environmental issues currently threatening the Arctic.

Dowson, Nick *North: The Amazing Story of Arctic Migration* Candlewick, 2011. Unique look at the land, sea and air animals who every year venture south from the North in order to breed, feed and survive.

Fenton, James and Sue *Svalbard – Portrait of an Arctic Summer – An Introduction to the Environment of Spitsbergen* Footprints of Abernyte and Inverasdale, 1997. Thin softcover pictorial book about tours with various tour operators in the 1970s–1990s and the nature.

Gjærevoll, Olav and Rønning, Olav I *Flowers of Svalbard* Tapir Forlag, 1989. Depicts and describes the 30 most common flower species, useful also to the visitor without botanic knowledge. Colour photos.

Gordon, Seton *Amid Snowy Wastes – Wild Life on the Spitsbergen Archipelago* Cassell and Company, London, 1922. Impressions of the photographer of Oxford Expedition 1921 – Bjørnøya, west coast and parts of Isfjord.

Gulden, Gro and Kolbjørn Mohn Jenssen *Arctic and Alpine Fungi – 1* Soppkonsulenten, Oslo, 1985 (1st volume, about Arctic/polar fungi in general).

Gulden, Gro and Kolbjørn Mohn Jenssen *Arctic and Alpine Fungi – 2* Soppkonsulenten, Oslo, 1988 (2nd volume, focusing specially on Svalbard).

Harland, W B, Anderson, Lester, Monasrah, Daoud and Butterfield, Nicholas J *The Geology of Svalbard* Geological Society, 1997.

Hisdal, Vidar *Svalbard Nature and History* Polarhåndbok nr 12, Norsk Polarinstitutt, Oslo, 1998. Good concise introduction, updated and rewritten successor of the author's *Geography of Svalbard from 1985*, available also in Norwegian.

Hoel, Adolf *The Coal Deposits and Coal Mining of Svalbard (Spitsbergen and Bear Island)* Resultater av de norske statsunderstøttede Spitsbergenekspeditioner (Skrifter om Svalbard og Ishavet) Bind 1 Nr 6, Det Norske Videnskaps-Akademi i Oslo, Oslo, 1925.

Hop, Haakon, Kjetil, Sagerup, Martin, Schlabach and Geir, Wing Gabrielsen *Persistent Organic Pollutants in Marine Macro-bentos near Urban settlements in Svalbard; Longyearbyen, Pyramiden, Barentsburg and Ny-Ålesund* Norsk Polarinstitutt Internrapport Nr 8, Tromsø, 2001.

Isachsen, Gunnar *The Hydrographic Observations of the Isachsen Spitsbergen Expedition 1909-1910*. Kristiania, 1912. Videnskapsselskapets Skrifter I Mat-Naturv Klasse 1912.

Kaltenborn, Bjørn P and Reidar Hindrum *Opportunities and Problems Associated with the Development of Arctic Tourism – a Case Study from Svalbard in the Norwegian Arctic – A report prepared for the Arctic Environmental Protection Strategy (AEPS) Task Force on Sustainable Development and Utilisation* 1997. Ecological problems, development and management challenges of Svalbard tourism.

Karlkvist, Anders, and others (editors) *Swedish Research in Svalbard – A Cruise Report* Swedish Polar Research Secretariat, Stockholm, 1994. Booklet on Swedish research and mining activities on Spitsbergen 1758-1992.

Klekowski, Romuald E and Weslawski, Jan Marcin (editors) *Atlas of the Marine Fauna of Southern Spitsbergen – Vol 1 Vertebrates* Polish Academy of Sciences Institute of Ecology Institute of Oceanology, Gdansk, 1990. Trilingual (Polish, English, Russian), for each animal text, drawing, distribution map.

Klekowski, Romuald E and Weslawski, Jan Marcin (editors) *Atlas of the Marine Fauna of Southern Spitsbergen – Vol 2 Invertebrates Part 1* Polish Academy of Sciences Institute of Ecology Institute of Oceanology, Gdansk, 1991. Trilingual (Polish, English, Russian), for each animal text, drawing, distribution map.

Kobalenko, Jerry *Arctic Eden: Journeys Through the Changing High Arctic* Greystone, 2010. A comprehensive photographic survey of Arctic travel, with heavy focus on wildlife and plant life.

Korte, J de *Birds, Observed and Collected by 'De Nederlandske Spitsbergen Expeditie' in West and East Spitsbergen, 1967 and 1968-69; Second Part* Beaufortia No 257, Volume 19, 30 May, 1972, Institute of Taxonomic Zoology (Zoological Museum) University of Amsterdam. Mainly Edgeøya, some Hornsund, Kvalpynten, Hopen.

Korte, J de *Birds, Observed and Collected by 'De Nederlandske Spitsbergen Expeditie' in West and East Spitsbergen, 1967 and 1968-69; Third Part* Beaufortia No 261, Volume 20, 28 September 1972, Institute of Taxonomic Zoology (Zoological Museum) University of Amsterdam. Mainly Edgeøya, some Hornsund, Kvalpynten, Hopen.

Kovacs, Kit and Nicklin, Flip (Fotograf) *Bearded Seals – Going with the Floe* In: National Geographic, Vol 191, No 3, March 1997, Washington, DC. About seal research in Svalbard.

Krawczyk, Adam and Weslawski, Jan Marcin *Remarks on the Past and Recent Records of Walrus, Odobaenus rosmarus rosmarus Linnaeus, 1758, from South Spitsbergen Coasts* Polish Polar Research 8/2/S135-143, 1987.

Krüll, Franz, Demmelmeyer, Helmut and Remmert, Hermann *On the Circadian Rhythm of Animals in High Polar Latitudes* In: Naturwissenschaften 72, Springer-Verlag, 1985, pages 197-203. Research on seasonal activities of snow buntings in Svalbard in relation to the changing spectral composition of the sunlight.

Laing, John *A Voyage to Spitzbergen; containing an account of that country, of the zoology of the north, of the Shetland Islands; and of the whale fishery* Edinburgh, 1818.

A

Lowen, James *Antarctic Wildlife* Princeton University Press, 2011. This comprehensive field guide will be of interest to any aficionado of polar wildlife and water fauna, and should enable you to easily identify the creatures you encounter while out on expedition. Features extensive in situ photography of the various species and not merely illustrations.

Lynge, B, *A Small Contribution to the Lichen Flora of the Eastern Svalbard Islands – Lichens collected by Mr Olaf Hanssen in 1930* Meddelelser Nr 44, Det Kongelige Departementet for Handel, Sjøfart, Industri, Håndverk og Fiskeri/Norges Svalbard- og Ishavs-Undersøkelser, Oslo, 1939.

Mehlum, Fridtjof *Birds and Mammals of Svalbard* Polarhåndbok Nr 5 Norsk Polarinstitutt, Oslo, 1990. Excellent concise introduction to the most common breeders, with photographs and names in several languages. Though primarily for Svalbard, this book is also very useful for Franz Josef Land and Jan Mayen, which have quite similar – though more limited – fauna.

Piepjohn, Karsten *The Svalbardian–Ellesmerian deformation of the Old Red Sandstone and the pre-Devonian basement in NW Spitsbergen (Svalbard)* In: Friend, P F & Williams, B P J: *New Perspectives on the Old Red Sandstone.* Geological Society, London, Special Publications, 180, pages 585–601, London, 2000.

Piepjohn, Karsten, Brinkmann, Lars, Grewing, Anke and Kerp, Hans *New data on the age of the uppermost ORS and the lowermost post-ORS strata in Dickson Land (Spitsbergen) and implications for the age of the Svalbardian deformation* In: Friend, P F & Williams, B P J: *New Perspectives on the Old Red Sandstone.* Geological Society, London, Special Publications, 180, pages 603–609, London, 2000.

Prokosch, Peter *Breeding Sites and Distribution of Geese in the Northwest Isfjord Area, Svalbard, 1982* In: Skrifter Nr 181, pages 135–139, Norsk Polarinstitutt, Oslo, 1984.

Prokosch, Peter *The Wintering Sites of Svalbard Pink-footed Geese Anser brachyrhynchus in Germany – Present Situation* In: Skrifter Nr 181, pages 25–28, Norsk Polarinstitutt, Oslo, 1984.

Pye, Norman *Some Geographical Observations during an Expedition to Billefjorden, Spitsbergen, 1938* Manchester Geographical Society Journal, 1938–39, 1939, Vol 49, pages 26–47.

Rosing, Norbert *The World of the Polar Bear* Firefly, 2010. Put together after two decades of research and observation, this gloriously photographed account is easily in the top three of polar bear-related image books out there today.

Rønning, Olaf I *The Flora of Svalbard* Polarhåndbok Nr 10. Norsk Polarinstitutt, Oslo, 1996. Detailed, systematic presentation and identification of the complete vascular flora of Svalbard, with all higher plant species. Very useful for Franz Josef Land and Jan Mayen too, with many similar species. Update of first edition (1979).

Skakuj, Michal and Weslawski, Jan Marcin *Supplement to the Atlas of the Marine Fauna of Southern Spitsbergen – Field guide to seabirds and sea mammals of Spitsbergen and Barents Sea* Arctic Ecology Group, Institute of Oceanology, Polish Academy of Sciences, Sopot, 1990s (no date). Waterproof booklet with drawings and short texts about the species.

Stensiö, Erik Andersson *Triassic Fishes fromt Spitzbergen* Diss Vienna (Uppsala), 1921.

Stirling, Ian *Polar Bears: A Natural History of a Threatened Species* Fitzhenry & Whiteside. 2011. Stirling, the world's foremost polar bear scientist, brilliantly details what we know today about these mytholgised animals, showing how they have evolved in the face of real adversity and the effect that global warming will have on the species.

Trevor-Battye, A *The Birds of Spitsbergen* The Ibis, 1897.

Weitschat, Wolfgang and Lehmann, Ulrich *Biostratigraphy of the Uppermost Part of the Smithian Stage (Lower Triassic) at the Botneheia, W-Spitsbergen* Mitteilungen aus dem Geologisch-Paläontologischen Institut der Universität Hamburg, Heft 48, pages 85–100, Hamburg, 1978. Stratigraphy and descriptions of the fossils including photos.

Tveit, Bjørn Olav *A Birdwatcher's Guide to Norway – Where, When and How to find the Birds of Norway including Svalbard* Ørn Forlag, 2011. Self-explanatory title, this is a must for anyone with a pair of binoculars heading to the North.

Werenskiold, W and Oftedal, Ivar *A Burning Coal Seam at Mt Pyramide Spitsbergen* Resultater av de Norske statsunderstøttede Spitsbergenekspedisjoner, Bind I, Videnskapsselskapet i Kristiania, Kristiania, 1922. Includes also geology of Pyramiden mountain and history of its exploration.

Worsley, David *The Geological History of Svalbard – Evolution of an Arctic Archipelago* Statoil, Stavanger, 1986. Excellent pictorial book about the geological development of Svalbard.

Wüthrich, Christoph *Die biologische Aktivität arktischer Böden mit spezieller Berücksichtigung ornithogen eutrophierter Gebiete (Spitzbergen und Finnmark) – The biological activity of arctic soils with special consideration of ornithogenic soils (Spitsbergen and Finnmark)* Physiographica, Band 17, Basler Beiträge zur Physiogeographie, Basel, 1994. Dissertation at the Geographisches Institut der Universität Basel.

History/Ethnography/Travelogue

Anderson, Alun *After the Ice: Life, Death, and Geopolitics in the New Arctic* Smithsonian, 2009. Thoroughly researched book by the former editor-in-chief of *New Scientist* magazine on the multiple reasons behind the tenuous future of the world's Arctic regions.

Arlov, Thor B *A Short History of Svalbard* Polarhåndbok Nr 4, Norsk Polarinstitutt, Oslo, 1989.

Banerjee, Subhankar *Arctic Voices: Resistance at the Tipping Point* Seven Stories Press, 2012. This edited volume profiled narratives from several-dozen researchers, activists and authors across a range of topics, including war, human rights and global warming.

Bay, Arne J *Postal History of Svalbard from 1896* Self-published Oslo, 2003.

Bjerck, Hein B and Johannessen, Leif Johnny *Virgohamna – In the Air toward the North Pole* Sysselmannen på Svalbard, Miljøvernavdelingen, Longyearbyen, 1999. A5 brochure on history and protection of cultural heritage in Virgohamna (whaling, Pike, Andrée, Wellman) and Northwest Spitsbergen National Park.

Byers, Michael *Who Owns The Arctic?* Douglas & Mcintyre, 2010. Accessibly written account of the complex geopolitical relationships involved in managing the lands and waters of the Arctic, and what lies in store for the region given the current age of unprecedented climate change.

Carpenter, Edmund et al *Upside Down: Arctic Realities* Yale University Press, 2011. Interesting, engaging book by a series of anthropologists that looks at the changing traditions of native arts and artefacts by the peoples of Arctic societies.

Cone, Marla *Silent Snow: The Slow Poisoning of the Arctic* Grove Press, 2006. *LA Times* investigative reporter travels across the entire Arctic to look at the looming destruction of the Arctic's environment.

Davidson, Peter *The Idea of North* Reaktion, 2005. Something of an anthropological-meets-philosophical take on how the topography of the North has been imagined, explored and represented in pictures and words over the past several centuries.

Davies, Pete *The Devil's Flu* (paperback) New York, 2000. On the Spanish flu epidemic around World War I, graves of which were excavated in Longyearbyen in 1998.

di Robilant, Andrea *Venetian Navigators: The Voyages of the Zen Brothers to the Far North* Faber and Faber, 2011. Charming, brilliantly written account of two brothers' journey from the Mediterranean to the Arctic in the 14th century.

Dole, Nathan Haskell *America in Spitsbergen – The Romance of an Arctic Coal-mine* Boston, 1922. On the history of Longyear City under the Americans.

Duncan, Kirsty *Hunting the 1918 Flu – One Scientist's Search for a Killer Virus* University of Toronto Press, 2003. The story of the excavation of the epidemic victims on Longyearbyen graveyard – from the perspective of the expedition leader, also a story of many oversized egos in research.

Emmerson, Charles *The Future History of the Arctic* The Bodley Head, 2010. This hulking tome holds a broad survey of the international importance of the Arctic's landscapes and resources presented in an engaging, accessible and enjoyable manner by a brilliant global risk analyst.

Fairhall, David *Cold Front: Conflict Ahead in Arctic Waters* Counterpoint, 2012. Penetrating look into the role the Arctic plays in global geopolitics and international relations, with some striking predictions on the future of the region.

Fife, Dale *North of Danger* E P Dutton, New York, 1978. Fiction adventure story for the youth about a youngster staying back on purpose during the 1941 evacuation.

Francis, Gavin *True North: Travels in Arctic Europe* Polygonn, 2010. Travelogue that blends history and first-person narrative, with some striking observations of some of the people Francis gets to know along the way.

Grant, Shelagh D *Polar Imperative: A History of Arctic Sovereignty in North America* Douglas & McIntyre, 2011. Comprehensive look by a leading Canadian author and professor at how Canada has managed to secure its hold over much of the world's Arctic lands.

Harrison. John *Forgotten Footprints: Lost Stories in the Discovery of Antarctica* Parthian, 2013. This amalgam of geography, history and personal narrative looks towards Antarctica's most visited landmasses for anecdotes of the whalers, pilots, tradesmen, scientists and adventurers who first ventured off to explore the great unknown continent.

Holm, Kari *General Information about Longyearbyen and the Surroundings May 30 1991* Self-published, 1991. Detailed dictionary-like guide to Longyearbyen today and in the past.

Kavenna, Joanna *The Ice Museum: In Search of the Lost Land of Thule* Penguin, 2006. Stellarly penned by brilliant observer Kavenna, winner of the Orange Broadband Award for New Writers, this great book is half travelogue/reportage, half history essay and follows the great Arctic explorers who never tired in chasing their idea of the North.

Kjærnet, Thorfinn and Ian, Gjertz *Svalbard* Aune Forlag AS, Trondheim, c1995. A5 softcover pictorial, texts in Norwegian, English, German, and French.

Kolbert, Elizabeth *The Arctic: An Anthology* Granta Books, 2008. An excellent collection of first-person accounts of exploration, fiction and history, with appearances made by Nansen, Rasmussen, London and Verne.

Kraska, James *Arctic Security in an Age of Climate Change* Cambridge University Press, 2011. A survey of global Arctic military security and defence policies that help explain the importance of the region to an increasingly trans-national world.

Lainema, Matti and Nurminen, Juha *A History of Arctic Exploration: Discovery, Adventure and Endurance at the Top of the World* Conway, 2009. A titanically sized coffee-table tome, this extremely descriptive new history of northern exploration covers the likes of Barents, Bering and Franklin, as well as lesser-known figures such as Chelyuskin. The text is complemented by a hundreds of stunning illustrations, charts and the kinds of ornate old maps of discovery that will inspire you to quit your job and hit the road.

Lynch, Wayne *Planet Arctic: Life at the Top of the World* A&C Black, 2010. Beautiful coffee-table book with large-format images of Arctic flora and fauna by one of Canada's leading outdoor photographers.

Mathisen, Trygve *Svalbard in the Changing Arctic* Gyldendal Norsk Forlag, Oslo, 1954. Legal status, history and politics.

Norsk Polarinstitutt *The Place-Names of Svalbard* Skrifter Nr 80 og 112, Ny-Trykk, Norsk Polarinstitutt, Oslo, 1991. Detailed information source regarding origin of place names.

Parry, Bruce *Arctic* Conway, 2010. This tie-in to the BBC documentary has 150 outstanding photographs alongside Parry's stellar text, which is heavily based on the human experiences that currently characterise the Arctic.

Prestvold, Kristin *Smeerenburg Gravneset – Europe's First Oil Adventure* 2001.

Reilly, John T *Greetings from Spitsbergen: Tourists at the Eternal Ice 1827–1914* Tapir Forlag, Oslo, 2010. This handsome collection of photographs and postcards from the golden age of Arctic tourism (before 1914).

Roberts, David *Four Against the Arctic: Shipwrecked for Six Years at the Top of the World* Simon & Schuster, 2005. Engaging recounting of an 18th-century Russian shipwreck in Svalbard that takes great pains to show the failings of previous historians' accounts.

Sale, Richard and Potapov, Eugene *The Scramble for the Arctic: Ownership, Exploitation and Conflict in the Far North* Frances Lincoln, 2010. This is a compelling, insightful and intelligent work into the geopolitical issues currently surrounding heated discussions on the Arctic region.

Ulfstein, Geir *The Svalbard Treaty – From Terra Nullius to Norwegian Sovereignty* Scandinavian University Press, Oslo, 1995. Extensive study on the legal status created by the Spitsbergen Treaty.

Wheeler, Sara *The Magnetic North: Travels in the Arctic* Vintage, 2010. Classic travel writer Wheeler's observations on her multiple journeys up in the Arctic deftly weave in geology, history, humour, myth, controversy and keen commentary.

Wilkins, George H *Flying the Arctic* Grosset & Dunlap, 1929.

Wilkinson, Alec *The Ice Balloon: S. A. Andree and the Heroic Age of Arctic Exploration* Knopf, 2012. Swedish born Andrée – the only person to try to venture to the North Pole by balloon – set off for the North in 1897; his body was found 33 years later. This is the story of what happened. This remarkable, insightful history of heroism, dreams and discovery is written by one of America's foremost writers.

Academic/Governmental

Barents. Spitsbergen. Arktika. Conference Proceedings, Barentsburg, 1996. Moscow, 1997. Contributions to historic research round Barents, archaeology, environment, glaciology, tourism, etc.

Justisdepartementet *Regulations relating to tourism and other travel in Svalbard* Publication G-1067, 1998. Brochure by the Norwegian Ministry of Justice.

Justisdepartementet *Treaty of 9 February 1920 relating to Spitsbergen (Svalbard) – Act of 17 July 1925 relating to Svalbard – The Mining Code for Spitsbergen (Svalbard)* Royal Ministry of Justice – Det kongelige justis- og politidepartementet, Oslo, 1988. English texts of the two fundamental legal documents for Svalbard.

Kings Bay AS *Opportunities for Arctic Environmental Research – at the Ny-Ålesund International Research and Monitoring Facility in Ny-Ålesund, Svalbard, Norway* Leaflet, c2000. Introduction to institutions and facilities.

Miljøverndepartementet *Guidelines – Management Plan for Tourism and Outdoor Recreation in Svalbard T-1097* Oslo, c1995. Plan for governmental tourism management in Svalbard 1995–99.

Norsk Polarinstitutt and Kings Bay AS *Ny-Ålesund – International Research at 79° N* Norsk Polarinstitutt/Kings Bay AS, 1998 (3rd edition). A4 brochure.

Starkov, Prof Dr Vadim *On Location: Recherche Bay* Article in: Science in Russia No 4, July–August 1997, pages 44–49. Archaeological research in Recherchefjord (early Russian hunters, Dutch blubber oven, base of Russian Chichagov expedition).

Trust Arcticcoal *Coal of the Arctic* Moscow, 1992. Russian–English brochure of the Russian mining company Trust Arcticugol in Svalbard.

Biography/Memoir

Adams, Paul *Arctic Island Hunter* Georg Ronald, London, 1961. 'Apprentice' of the most famous Norwegian trapper Hilmar Nois in 1958, spent altogether three years in Svalbard.

Balstad, Liv *North of the Desolate Sea* Souvenir Press, London, 1958. Lively written memories of the wife of the first post-World War II Sysselmann about the reconstruction period of Longyearbyen.

Bjertnes, Thorleif *The Diaries of Thorleif Bjertnes – Nordaustlandet 1933–1934* Svalbard Museum 1st edition, Longyearbyen, 2000. Translated from Norwegian. Diary of a wintering in the area Brennevinsfjord – Lady Franklinfjord – Lågøya.

Farnes, Olav *War in the Arctic* DARF Publishers, London, 1991, translated from Norwegian (Original: Lege på mange fronter). War memories of the Norwegian military doctor, including also Spitsbergen (1944).

Gilson, Martha Phillips *A Woman's Winter on Spitsbergen* In: The National Geographic Magazine, volume LIV, number two, August 1928, National Geographic Society, Washington, DC, pages 227–246. The author was the wife of the local American mining engineer Gilson.

Kempf, Christian *A Journey to Svalbard Polar Territory* Editions Messene Jean de Cousance Editeur, 1999. Translated from French, pictorial book.

Kennedy, Ludovic *Sub-Lieutenant – A Personal Record of the War at Sea* B T Batsford Ltd, London, 1942. Experiences in a British Home Fleet destroyer flotilla 1940 and 1941, including Spitsbergen 1941. War publication, partly censored.

Moore, Tim *Frost on my Moustache – The Arctic Exploits of a Lord and a Loafer* Abacus, London, paperback edition, 2000. Humorous Svalbard travel story, mixing quotations from Lord Dufferin's own experiences.

Ritter, Christiane *A Woman in the Polar Night* University of Alaska Press, 2010. This translation from the best-selling German memoir is an intensive description of a wintering as a trapper wife at Gråhuken at the north coast in the 1930s, penned with insight and some real humour.

Rothery, Agnes *Norway – Changing and Changeless* Faber and Faber Ltd, London, c1939–40. Norway travel narration, including a cruise to Svalbard on the *Stella Polaris*.

Scott, Jack Denton *Passport to Adventure* Random House, Inc, New York/Toronto, 1966. Travel of the author and his wife in Asia and Europe including Svalbard (trip on chartered boat to Nordaustlandet c1965), not too adventurous, really.

Simpson, Myrtle *Home is a Tent – Family Travels in the Arctic and Equatorial America* Victor Gollancz Ltd, London, 1964. Worldwide experiences of Doctor Simpson's family, also in Svalbard 1959.

Stannard, Martin *Evelyn Waugh – The Early Years 1903–1939* Flamingo, 1993. Biography of the American author, who also participated in a Spitsbergen expedition.

Sutton, Richard L *An Arctic Safari with Camera and Rifle in the Land of the Midnight Sun* C V Mosby, 1932.

Language

Danbolt-Simons, Margaretha *Complete Norwegian: A Teach Yourself Guide* McGraw-Hill, 2011. Already in its 5th edition, this is one of the best language courses for learning colloquial Norwegian.

Haugen, Einar *Norwegian English Dictionary* University of Wisconsin Press, 1974. Still the best dictionary around is this classic written by a Norwegian-American professor of linguistics at Harvard.

Janus, Louis *Norwegian Verbs and Essentials of Grammar* McGraw-Hill, 1999. A concise book for language learners aiming to get the basics of verb usage in an easy-to-breeze-through volume.

Langenscheidt *Universal Dictionary Norwegian* Langenscheidt, 2011. This fairly comprehensive (400-page) dictionary is up to date and comes in a more compact size than the Haugen tome.

Strandskogen, Åse-Berit and Strandskogen, Rolf *Norwegian: An Essential Grammar* Routledge, 1994. Excellent overview of all aspects of Norwegian grammar, lucidly explained with plenty of examples.

Ziukaite-Hansen, Laura *Beginner's Norwegian* Hippocrene Books, 2012. Comes with two CDs that have native speaker recordings of many of the dialogue examples presented in the book.

Ziukaite-Hansen, Laura *Norwegian Practical Dictionary* Hippocrene Books, 2011. Containing some 18,000 entries, this comprehensive bilingual dictionary features common expressions, phrases and sentences that rely heavily on modern proper usage, with a particular emphasis on technical vocabulary.

Websites Google 'Svalbard' or 'Spitsbergen' and you'll get back a multitude of websites, most of which will try to sell you some type of tour. While there can be substantive information on these sites, you're much better off beginning at one of the following:

www.svalbard.net The official website for a conglomeration of the major tourism operators in Svalbard, but also has useful lists of accommodation, restaurants and other shops that might be of interest to visitors. It's also good for independent travel advice.

www.svalbard.com An online forum which, if not exactly bustling, is at least active and moderately up to date.

www.visitnorway.com The official site of the Norwegian Tourist Board, which offers advice and information for things to do in Svalbard, as well as some excellent photography.

Index

Entries in **bold** indicate main entries; those in *italics* indicate maps